All about New NVivo Windows

The 2020 Edition of the Global Success in Qualitative Analysis

By Bengt M. Edhlund & Allan G. McDougall

FORM & KUNSKAP AB • P.O.BOX 4 • SE-645 06 STALLARHOLMEN • SWEDEN • +46 704611226
SALES@FORMKUNSKAP.COM • WWW.FORMKUNSKAP.COM

NVIVO

NVivo is a registered trademark of QSR International Pte Ltd.

WORD, EXCEL, ONENOTE

Word, Excel, and OneNote are registered trademarks of Microsoft Corporation.

ENDNOTE

EndNote is a registered trademark of Thomson Reuters.

EVERNOTE

Evernote is a registered trademark of Evernote Corporation.

LIMITED LIABILITY

This document describes the functions and features valid for NVivo in combination with Word 2003, 2007 or 2010. Form & Kunskap is unable to predict or anticipate changes in service performance or functionality of later versions or changes of respective software that might influence or change the described features.

ISBN 978-1-71674-757-1

FOREWARD

The **All about New NVivo Windows** is here. The 2020 release of NVivo qualitative data analysis software is here! Coined as “the New NVivo”, this latest version of the software includes many new options and a cleaner user interface. As with all of NVivo’s major releases, we have written a new book. We hope you enjoy.

You may be asking, shouldn’t the follow up to 2018’s NVivo 12 be called NVivo 13? Why the New NVivo? It could be because 13 is an unlucky number. More likely the new name denotes the integration of myNVivo, an new online portal for NVivo users.

This book has two authors who share distinct yet com plementary views on NVivo. Bengt Edhlund is a software trainer with decades of experience teaching and writing about research software. Dr. Allan McDougall is a qualitative researcher who has worked with NVivo 8 through 12 in health, non-profit, academic and commercial contexts.

We have co-authored this book to provide instruction to NVivo users of all skill levels and experience with both qualitative data analysis and qualitative research methods. We break down the functional components of this intricate software while striving to provide practical, anecdotal advice for using NVivo for every stage of your qualitative data analysis project. Further, we strive to provide advice on using NVivo in a collaborative environment, a topic on which we are aware many of our colleagues are interested.

Research is like woodworking: a quality product will always be the result of combining several tools and techniques. Form & Kunskap AB was founded by Bengt in 1993. We are a training company focused on researchers. We believe that software alone cannot solve the needs of researchers and their teams. We pride ourselves on providing our clients with well-written material and professional support. Our many years of teaching experience helps our clients productively tackle their data analysis needs. Whie we believe it is important to always select market leading software products, we also believe in helping our clients identify solutions that go beyond a single software solution.

Please enjoy our book and feel free to contact us at any time at: info@formkunskap.com

TABLE OF CONTENTS

1. INTRODUCING THE NEW NVIVO

Welcome to All about New NVivo Windows

Welcome to All about New NVivo Windows, your guide to the world's most powerful qualitative data analysis software. The purpose of this book is to provide a comprehensive guide to every feature of NVivo. For beginners, you will find explanations of key concepts and recommendations for starting your first NVivo project, importing your data, analyzing your data, and sharing your findings with collaborators.

Some people find it hard to wrap their heads around NVivo, and you might be one of those people. Perhaps you have been playing around with the software already and you don't really 'get it'. This book offers that one simple description of what to do with NVivo and how you can make it work for you. There is no one right way to use NVivo, but we have enough collective experience to offer some best practices that will help you along your journey.

For experienced users, you will find a comprehensive introduction to NVivo's advanced features, including social network analysis, sentiment coding, and crosstabs. You may wish to skip to page 19 for our summary, What's New in the New NVivo?

Whatever your skill level using NVivo, this book has been written by two authors who combine theory and practice to offer readers a helpful guide to improve technical capability and practical application.

Bengt M. Edhlund

Bengt Edhlund is the author of several books, including *NVivo 7, 8, 9, 10, 11, and 12 Essentials*. He is Scandinavia's leading research software trainer. As a former telecommunications engineer, Bengt has published 22 books on academic informatics tools such as NVivo, EndNote, PubMed, and Excel. All of Bengt's books are available in English and Swedish. He has trained researchers from every corner of the globe, including Canada, Sweden, Norway, China, Egypt, Uganda, and Vietnam. A trainer who takes pride in his students' success, Bengt provides all of his clients with customized NVivo support solutions via Skype or email.

Allan G. McDougall, PhD

A former student of Bengt's, Allan is a qualitative researcher with extensive NVivo experience. He has used NVivo in collaborative corporate and academic environments on diverse projects related to his area of qualitative health research and health professional education. While Bengt knows every facet of NVivo's various functions, Allan is an NVivo user who provides practical tips based on years of personal experiences applying NVivo to create dozens of qualitative research solutions.

What is the New NVivo?

Whether you work with grounded theory, phenomenology, ethnography, document analysis, attitude surveys, or mixed-methods approaches, you will at some point need to bring order and structure to your data. The New NVivo allows researchers to organize and analyze a wide variety of data, including but not limited to documents, images, audio, video, questionnaires and web / social media content.

We have worked with researchers tasked with analyzing hundreds of interviews and focus group discussions. Other analysts we know have been tasked with analyzing thousands of surveys blending quantitative and text-based data. Time and again, we enjoy helping both individuals and multi-user teams use NVivo to quickly and eaily analyze datasets large and small.

Key Components of an NVivo Project

The purpose of this section is familiarizing you with NVivo's distinct terminology. The terms **Sources**, **Codes**, **Cases**, **Coding**, and **Queries** are the building blocks of an NVivo project. We will provide in-depth explanations of these terms whether you decide to read chapter by chapter or pick and choose topics of interest.

Below is a simplified diagram of an NVivo project's key components:

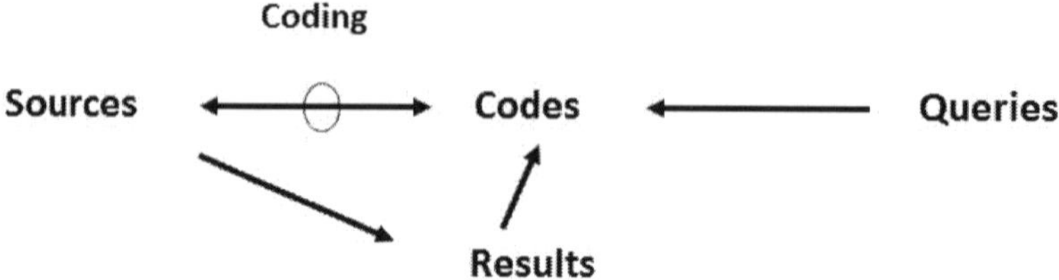

Sources are your data. Sources can be documents, audio, video and image files, memos, websites, research articles, or entire surveys. Sources can be imported into NVivo, or they can be linked from other locations like the web. Some Sources, like documents, can also be created directly inside NVivo using its built in word processor.

A key feature of NVivo is that discrete units of data can be organized into highly flexible containers, or **Codes**. Codes can be actual parts of your data, like a snippet of audio or a passage of text. Codes can also be concepts or organizational structures based on your own ideas to designate properties, phenomena, or keywords that characterize aspects of your data. Importantly, Codes allow for the addition of meta-data that can apply tangible information about your dataset, such as demographic or geographic information, to support organization and analysis. Later in the book, we will explain the important distinction between two types of such containers: **Codes** and **Cases**—suffice it to say for now that Cases use meta-data to organize the practical components of your research, while Codes use conceptual information to relay analytic findings.

Coding is the activity of building codes. Coding means that words, sentences, paragraphs, audio snippets, video segments, or survey comments organized with Codes. We'll discuss how you can code data yourself or use the power of auto-coding to automatically organize large portions of your dataset.

Queries are the backbone of qualitative data analysis with NVivo. Queries are basically special searches and filters that can be saved and reused as your project develops. Results of queries can also be saved, used to generate Codes, Coding Natrices, and data visualizations like charts and word clouds.

A Crucial Note on NVivo Projects

When working with NVivo, it is important to understand that the word project has two meanings. The first, more conventional meaning is simply your research project. But in this book, we will use another meaning for the term: when we say **Project**, we mean an NVivo **Project file**. As we discuss below, NVivo creates a single file that will serve as an amalgamation of your Project Items, which include Sources, Coding, Queries, and a host of other analytic units like Diagrams and Sets. NVivo allows you to organize your data into both **Project Items** and then to arrange them into folders.

Importantly, items and folders in NVivo are 'virtual' in relation to a Windows-based or Mac-based environment. In an NVivo Project, folders are similar to Windows or Mac OSX folders, but NVivo has special rules for how folders are handled—for example only certain types of folders are allowed to be organized hierarchically, and certain types of folders can only accommodate certain types of items. Like a computer operating system, Project Items and folders can be edited, copied, cut, pasted, deleted, moved, etc. But whatever changes you make, they are all localized to the Project file.

Visualizing your Project

An overall picture of how a project can be developed is:

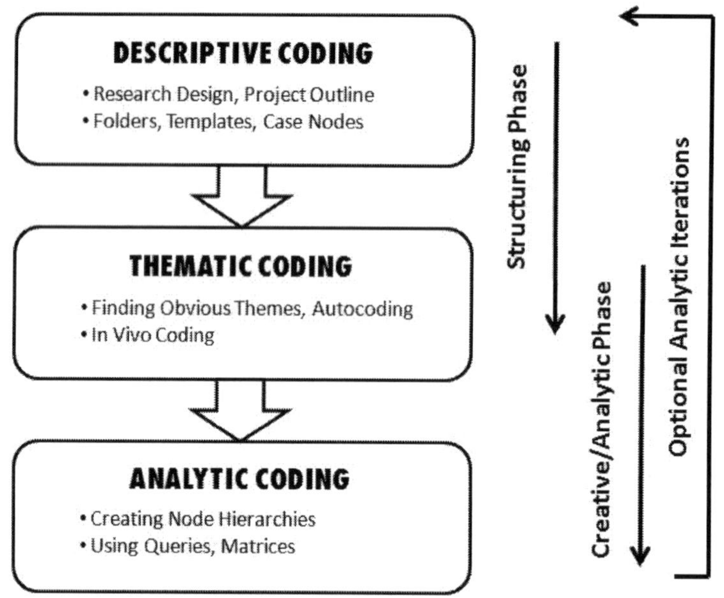

NVivo helps to organize data so that analysis and conclusions will be safer and easier. The ultimate goal may be described as follows:

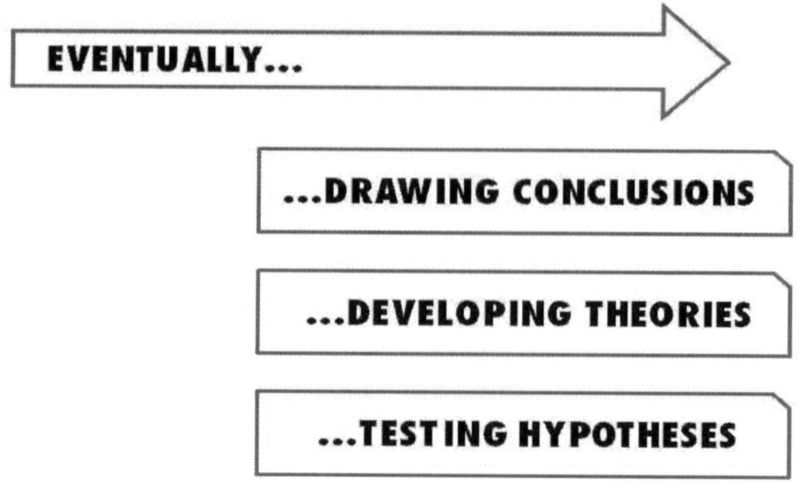

- ♦ -

Exploring this Book

This book begins by describing the system requirements for the New NVivo. Chapter 2 describes how NVivo's user interface is designed and basic settings for optimizing your software. Chapter 3 explains how to create, save and backup your NVivo Project file.

Chapters 4 - 8 cover how to import, create and edit text, audio, video, and picture data. Chapter 9 outlines how to create Memos and Links. Chapters 10 - 13 explain Codes, Cases, Classifications and Coding—the lifeblood of qualitative data analysis with NVivo. Chapters 14 and 15 discuss creating Queries, saving them and creating Codes from Query results.

Chapter 16 deals with NVivo's powerful functionality to support literature reviews and bibliographic data, with Chapter 17 describing the Framework Method of conveniently viewing and summarizing your data in Framework Matrices. Chapter 18 moves into managing surveys and questionnaires, called Datasets in NVivo.

Chapter 19 describes capturing data from the web and social media and Chapter 20 describes how to handle Social Network Analysis and Sociograms. Chapter 21 and 22 highlight NVivo's functionality for working with Evernote and OneNote 2010. Chapter 23 talks about finding and sorting various items within an NVivo project. While Chapter 24 deals with important aspects of collaboration using NVivo when you are a part of a research team. Chapters 25 - 27 describe how to graphically illustrate a project using Maps, Charts and Diagrams. And Chapter 28 describes building reports and extracts from your NVivo Projects.

Finally, Chapter 29 reviews the help functions available in NVivo, and Chapter 30 contains our glossary.

Graphic Conventions

In this book we have applied some simple graphic conventions with the intention of improving readability:

Convention	Example	Comment
Commands	Go to **Concept Map | Item | Add Project Items → Options**	Ribbon menu **Concept Map** and menu group **Item** and Menu option **Add Project Items,** if available select an option
Menus	Go to **File → Options**	Main menu and options with **Bold**
Mouse functions	Right-click and select **New Query → Compound...**	Right-click with the mouse and select menu and sub-menu with **Bold**
Tabs	Select the **Layout** tab	Optional tabs with **Bold**
Functions	Select *Advanced Find* from **Options** drop-down list	Variable with **Bold,** the value with *Italic;* Heading with **Bold,** options with *Italic*
Buttons	Confirm with [**OK**]	Graphical buttons within brackets
Keyboard commands	Use the [**Del**] key to delete	Key is written within brackets
Typing	Type `Bibliography` in the textbox	`Courier` for text to be typed
Text	.. `[1-3]` is shown in the textbox	`Courier` for shown text
Keyboard shortcuts	.. key command **[Ctrl]** + **[Shift]** + **[N]**	Hold the first (and second) key while touching the last

Before you Install New NVivo

The New NVivo requires users to register with myNVivo, an online portal for managing subscriptions to NVivo products, including the Collaboration Cloud and NVivo Transcription. The first time you run NVivo, you will be prompted to log into myNVivo. Your software will automatically be activated if you have registered a valid license. In some cases, your institution or employer may install and activate NVivo licenses.

From there, installation is made in two steps: the 'installation' which requires an active license and then the 'activation' which requires logging into myNVivo. The activation registers the user data in a customer database at QSR and is a license control function. A typical single-user license will allow you to install NVivo on two computers. If you are the license owner, you can re-assign your seat to another user through the myNVivo portal.

System Requirements - Minimum

- 2 GHz dual-core processor or faster
- 4 GB RAM or more
- 1680 x 1050 screen resolution or higher
- Microsoft Windows 8 or later
- Approximately 5 GB of available hard-disk space or more depending on data storage need
- Internet Explorer 11 or later (for NCapture)
- Google Chrome 44 or later (for NCapture)
- Internet Connection

System Requirements - Recommended

- 3 GHz quad-core processor or faster
- 8 GB RAM or more
- 1920 x 1080 screen resolution or higher
- Microsoft Windows 8 or later
- Approximately 8 GB of available hard-disk space or more depending on data storage need
- Internet Explorer 11 or later (for NCapture)
- Google Chrome 44 or later (for NCapture)
- Internet Connection

We recommend that your machine complies with those recommendations even if you are working with smaller projects.

Some Notes on NVivo and Macintosh Computers

There are crucial differences between installing NVivo on your Mac and using the software called NVivo for Mac. These tools are not the same. The commercial release of NVivo for Mac took place in 2014. The software was released as a stripped-down version of NVivo 10 that was missing many of the software's core features such as the ability to handle surveys and questionnaires—called Datasets in NVivo parlance. Since then, a number of important updates have allowed NVivo for Mac to come closer to the functionality offered by NVivo. However, the drawbacks of NVivo for Mac's feature list were made plainly clear on the release of NVivo.

The purpose of this book is to describe NVivo and its functions. While many of the functions are available in NVivo for Mac, many more are not. At the present time, it goes beyond the purposes of this book to compare and contrast the features of NVivo for Mac and NVivo for Windows—these comparisons are available on the developer's website.

Handling Other File Types

NVivo can convert certain other file types to its native type. This takes place when such file is selected for opening with NVivo or when NVivo intends to import such file into its project.

In some cases NVivo will ask for certain software for the conversion and may suggest direct download with a link.

File types presently possible to convert are:

- Earlier versions of NVivo
- NVivo for Mac
- Atlas.ti
- MAXQDA
- REFI-QDA

Atlas.ti, MAXQDA, and REFI-QDA are subject to restrictions depending on software versions and releases. When you are considering such conversions, you are welcome to contact support@formkunskap.com

Final Comment on Graphic Management

Of interest to researchers who also dabble in graphic design software, such as Adobe InDesign or Microsoft Visio, NVivo allows most charts to be exported as a Scalable Vector Graphic file type (.SVG). These image files are optimized for web viewing and are suitable for importing into graphic design software. After a small amount of tweaking, your NVivo chart could be optimized for your next conference poster presentation. Feel free to follow up with us if you want more information on working with your .SVG files outside of NVivo.

What's New in New NVivo?

You'll learn all about what's new in NVivo throughout this book, but we thought it would be important for our more advanced readers to have a guide to find out the ins and outs of NVivo's new features:

- Updated user interface and a new, more comprehensive Navigation View
- Expanded use of smart context dependent Ribbon menus
- Simplified terminology for various functions and tools
- Highly automated multi-language transcription service allows transcribing of audio and video files from NVivo
- New Crosstab Query for detailed demographic analysis
- Export to SPSS file type, .SAV, for Classification sheets, Coding matrices, and the result of Crosstab Queries

2. THE NVIVO INTERFACE

This chapter is about the architecture of the NVivo screen, which resembles the interface of Microsoft Outlook. Appendix A, The NVivo Screen (see page 395), shows an overview of the main NVivo window.

A work session usually starts in with the selection of a folder in the Navigation View by selecting a folder relevant to your analysis, which leads to the List View where you can select a certain Project Item. The Detail View appears when you open a Project Item where you can study that item's content.

Project work is done through the Ribbon menus, keyboard commands or via the menu options brought up by right-clicking your mouse. For more information about these commands, Appendix B (see page 397) is a summary of NVivo's keyboard commands.

> **Tip:** We suggest simply opening your NVivo software and experimenting with the interface. Challenging yourself to play around in NVivo is a great way to learn!

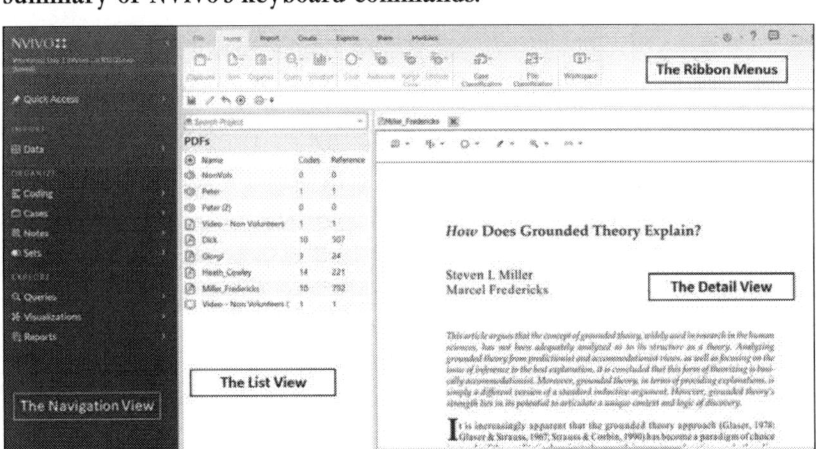

You will also find a Status Bar below the four areas comprising the main NVivo screen.

The Status Bar displays contextual information that depends on the cursor position of your mouse. It can display the current user, number of items in a folder, number of Codes and references associated with a Project Item, or the row number and column number in a Dataset.

The Navigation View

The Navigation View accommodates the main folders. Each main folder has a given set of default subfolders. The subfolders can be collapsed or expanded with the small leftmost triangle. Here you can also create your own custom subfolders.

The new Quick Access main folder allows you to assign any subfolder to be added under Quick Access (see below).

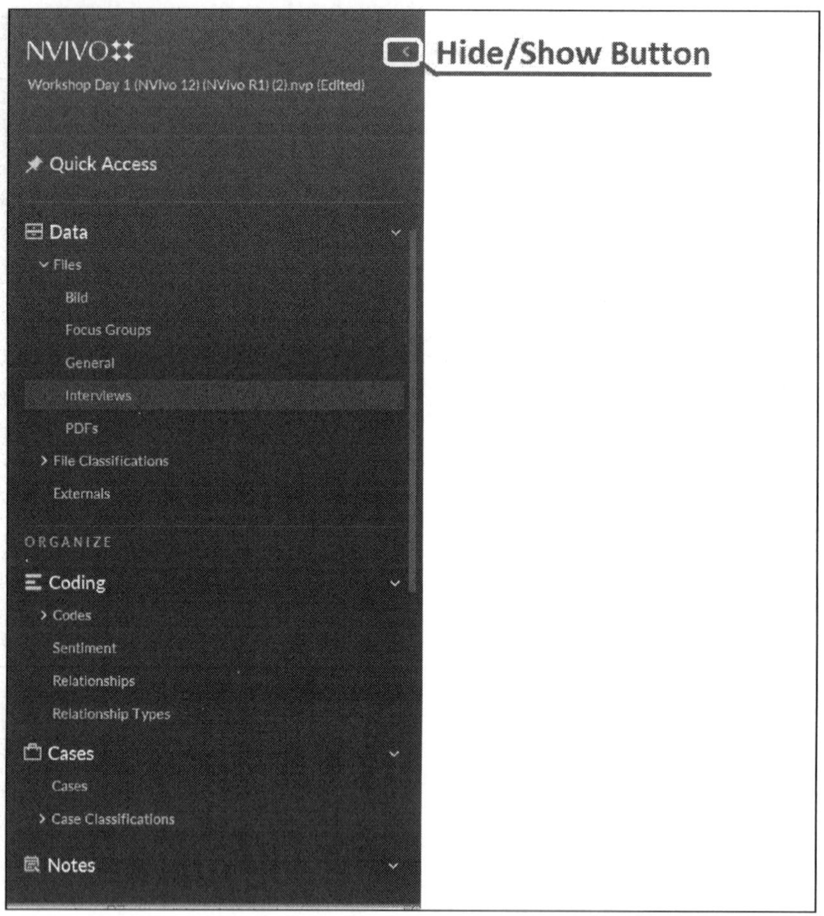

The Virtual Explorer

Each Navigation button contains a number of folders where relevant Project Items are stored. The folders associated with each Navigation Button are displayed in the Navigation View.

Virtual file paths are called Hierarchical Names. Only folders and Codes have hierarchical names in NVivo. In the NVivo environment, hierarchical names are written with a double backslash between folders and a single backslash between a Code and its child Code.

For example:

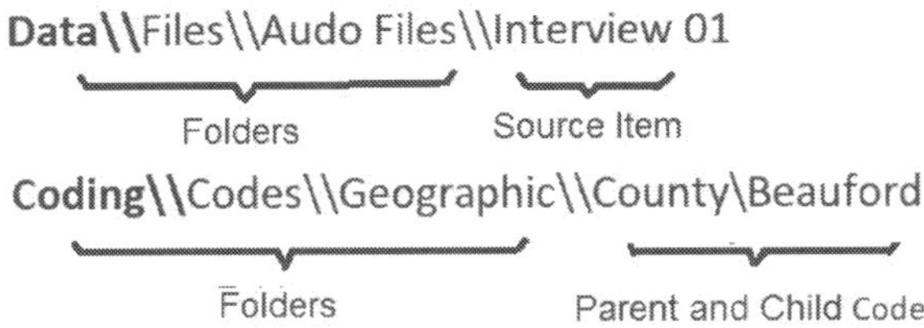

Did you know? NVivo folders are called ***virtual folders*** as opposed to folders in a Windows environment. NVivo folders are ***virtual*** because they exist only in the NVivo project file. In most cases, ***Virtual folders*** perform like any Windows folder - you can create sub-folders, drag and drop project items into allowable folders, copy and paste folders. Certain folders are predefined in the NVivo project template and cannot be changed or deleted whereas other folders can be created by the user.

Creating a New Folder

NVivo contains a core set of template folders that cannot be deleted or moved. Users can create new subfolders under some of these template folders, including Files, Externals, Codes, and Cases.

1. Select one of the folders in the Navigation Window under which a new subfolder will be created.
2. Go to **Create | Folder**
   or right-click and select **New Folder...**

For each new folder, the **New Folder** dialog box appears:

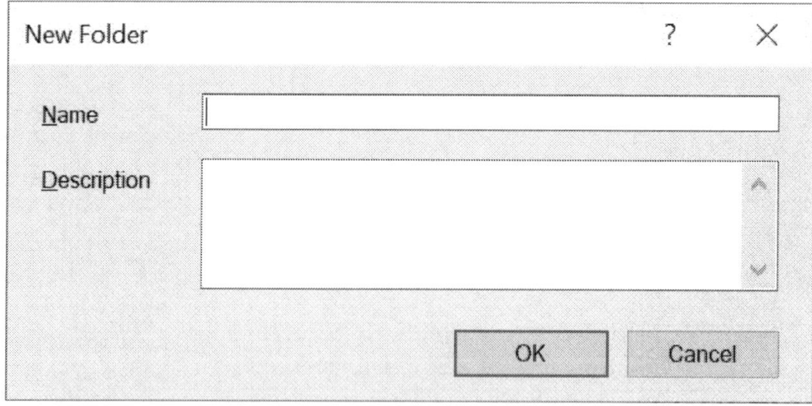

3 Type a name (compulsory) and a description (optional), then **[OK]**.

Deleting a Folder

Deleting a folder also deletes its subfolders and all contents therein.

1 Select the folder or folders that you want to delete.
2 Right-click and select **Delete**
 or **[Del]**.
3 Confirm with **[Yes]**.

The Quick Access Main Folder

Any folder except the Main Folders on top level can be added to the Quick Access folder.

1 Select the folder that you want to add to the Quick Access.
2 Right-click and select **Add to Quick Access**.

To remove a folder from the Quick Access folder:

1 Select the folder that you want to remove from the Quick Access.
2 Right-click and select **Remove from Quick Access**.

The List View

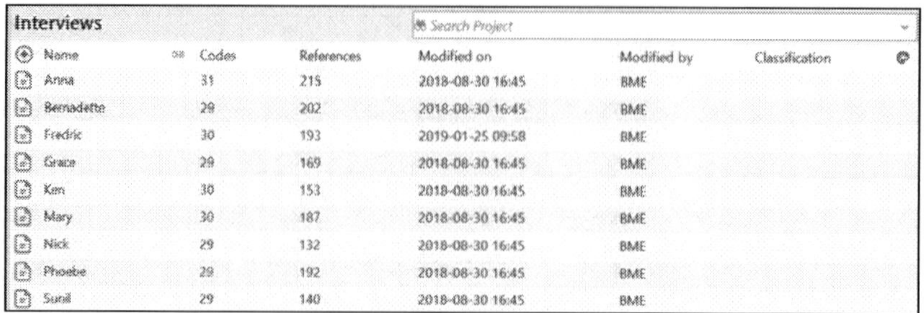

Name	Codes	References	Modified on	Modified by	Classification
Anna	31	215	2018-08-30 16:45	BME	
Bernadette	29	202	2018-08-30 16:45	BME	
Fredric	30	193	2019-01-25 09:58	BME	
Grace	29	169	2018-08-30 16:45	BME	
Ken	30	153	2018-08-30 16:45	BME	
Mary	30	187	2018-08-30 16:45	BME	
Nick	29	132	2018-08-30 16:45	BME	
Phoebe	29	192	2018-08-30 16:45	BME	
Sunil	29	140	2018-08-30 16:45	BME	

The List View appears similar to a list of files in Windows, but NVivo calls these Project Items within an Item List. All folders are

Project Items. All Project Items in the Internals, Externals and Memos folders - and their subfolders - are *Source Items.*

During the course of a project, you may need to revise the item lists when items are created, deleted or moved. At times it may be necessary to refresh the item list:

1 Point at the List View, right-click and select **Refresh** or **[F5]**.

Item Properties

All items have certain characteristics that can be changed or updated through the item's properties menu:

1 Select the item in the List View that you want to change or update.
2 Go to **Home | Item → 'Properties' → Document Properties...** or **[Ctrl] + [Shift] + [P]** or right-click and select **Document Properties...**

An item properties dialog box (in this case, **Document Properties**) may look like this:

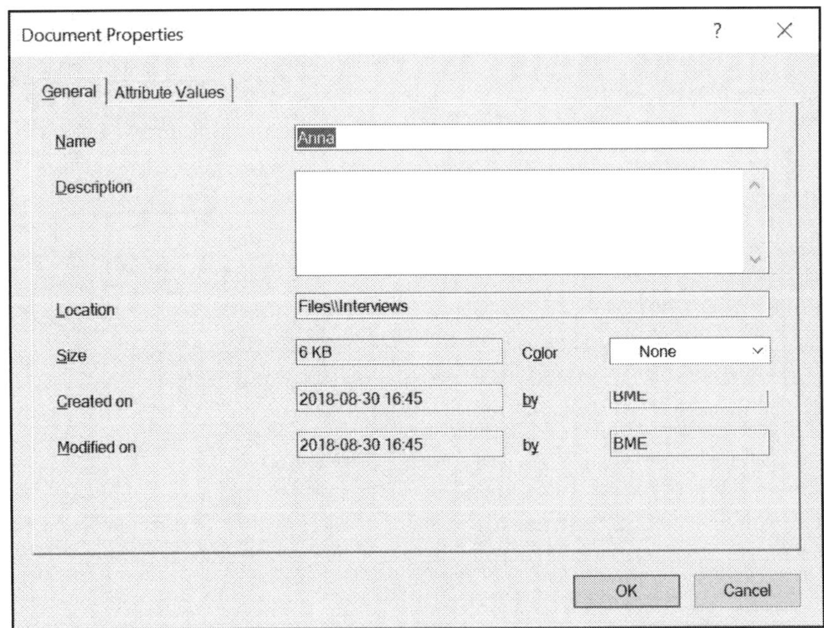

All information in this dialog box is editable and the text in the text boxes **Name** and **Description** is also searchable with the **Find** function, see Chapter 23, Finding and Sorting Project Items. Most experienced NVivo users know the project properties shortcut off by heart because this is fastest way to reach an item's Descriptions, a profoundly useful function in NVivo we'll spend more time on in Chapter 24, Collaborating with NVivo.

Setting Colors

Source items, Codes, Cases, relationships, attribute values or users can be color marked individually. NVivo has 15 pre-defined colors. Colors serve as visual cues for project researchers and as a result they can be used for a number of reasons. Most importantly, a color assigned to a Code will be visually represented in coding stripes (see page 195). The color marking is shown in the List View.

1. Select the item or items (without opening) that you want to color mark.
2. Go to **Home | Item → 'Properties' → Color → <select>** or right-click and select **Color → <select>**.

Classifying an Item

All Source Items (except Framework Matrices) and Cases can be classified and thus associated with meta-data. We'll discuss this further in Chapter 12, Classifications, but for now this is a reminder that working with items takes place in the List View.

1. Select the item or items that you want to classify.
2. Go to **Home | Item → 'Properties' → Classification → <select>** or right-click and select **Classification → <select>**.

Viewing Options

The default List View for Files (*Details*) is shown above in the first figure of this section. But there are three more options for viewing items in the List View: *Small, Medium and Large Thumbnails.*

1. Click on any empty space in the List View.
2. Go to **Home | Workspace → 'List View' →<select>**.

alternatively

2. Right-click and select **List View → <select>**.

The result of choosing *Large Thumbnails* may look like this:

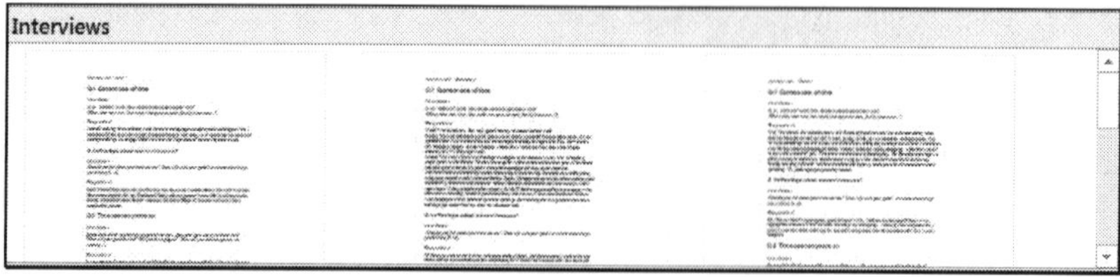

Sorting Options for a List

There are several ways to sort a list in the List View.

1. Click on any empty space in the List View.
2. Go to **Home | Workspace → 'Sort by' → <select>.**

These options are available:

Customizing the Item List

You can customize the columns associated with Project Items. The **Customize Current View** dialog box allows you to remove unnecessary columns or add additional ones.

1. Click on any empty space in the List View.
2. Go to **Home | Workspace → 'Customize...'**

alternatively

2. Right-click and select **List View → Customize...**

Tip: Some videos begin with a black frame, making the List View thumbnail a black square. But thumbnails of video items can display the specific frame that you want.

1. Move the playhead the frame you want to display.
2. Click in the video frame.
3. Go to **Media | Selection | Assign Frame as Thumbnail.**

The selected frame is displayed as a thumbnail in the List View and when using the Video tab for a Code that the Video Item is coded at.

The **Customize Current View** dialog box appears:

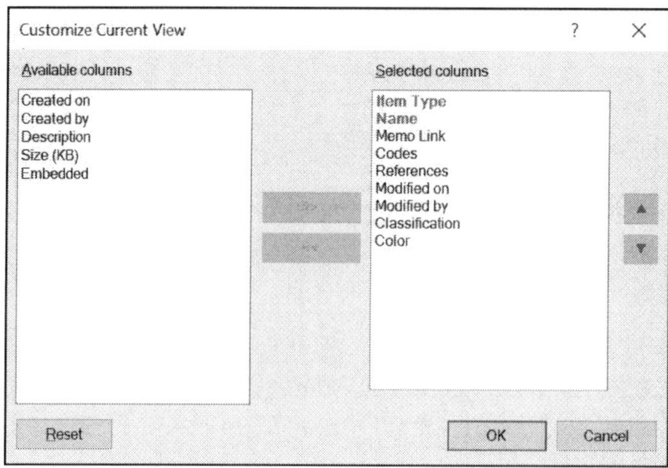

The detailed layout of this dialog box varies depending on which type of items is shown.

To reset all customizations for all types of items go to **Home | Workspace → Reset All Customizations** or alternatively right-click and select **List View → Reset All Customizations**.

Printing the Item List

Printing the Item List can be a valuable contribution to discussions in project team meetings:

1 Go to **File → Print → Print List...**
or right-click and select **Print → Print List...**

2 Select printer and printer settings, then **[OK]**.

Exporting the Item List

Exporting your item list as an Excel spreadsheet or a text document is also possible:

1 Go to **Share | Export → Export List**
or right-click and select **Export List...**

2 Select file name, location, and file type: XLS, .XLSX, .TXT, .DOC, .DOCX, or .RTF, then **[OK]**.

Deleting an Item

You can delete items from the List View. When you delete a parent Code you also delete its child Codes. Likewise, deleting a Classification also deletes its Attributes.

1 Select the appropriate folder or its subfolder.

2 Select the item or items in the List View that you want to delete.

3 Right-click and select **Delete**
or **[Del]**.

4 Confirm with **[Yes]**.

The Detail View

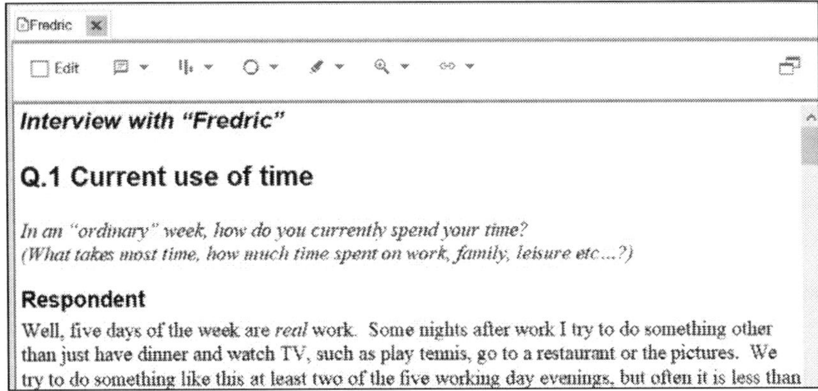

Fredric
Edit
Interview with "Fredric"
Q.1 Current use of time
In an "ordinary" week, how do you currently spend your time?
(What takes most time, how much time spent on work, family, leisure etc...?)
Respondent
Well, five days of the week are real work. Some nights after work I try to do something other than just have dinner and watch TV, such as play tennis, go to a restaurant or the pictures. We try to do something like this at least two of the five working day evenings, but often it is less than

The above image is an example of an open Project Item, which can include documents, audio clips, videos, pictures, Memos, or Codes.

A new feature is the Top Panel always displayed on the Detail View with the following functions from left to right:

Edit/Read Only
Annotations
Coding Stripes
Code
Highlight
Zoom
See Also Links
Undock/Dock

All of these functions will be explained in detail later on.

> **Did you know?** Read Only mode doesn't mean that a project item is *locked* from data analysis. You can still code and create links (but not hyperlinks) in a Read Only Source Item.

Each time a Source Item is opened it is Read Only and a context dependent menu Ribbon is opened. The item is made instantly editable by clicking on the 'Click to edit' link at the top of an open item. Alternatively, you can go to **Document | Edit** or **[Ctrl]** + **[E]** which is a toggling function.

Each time the Edit mode is activated a new dependent ribbon tab, **Edit**, is opened.

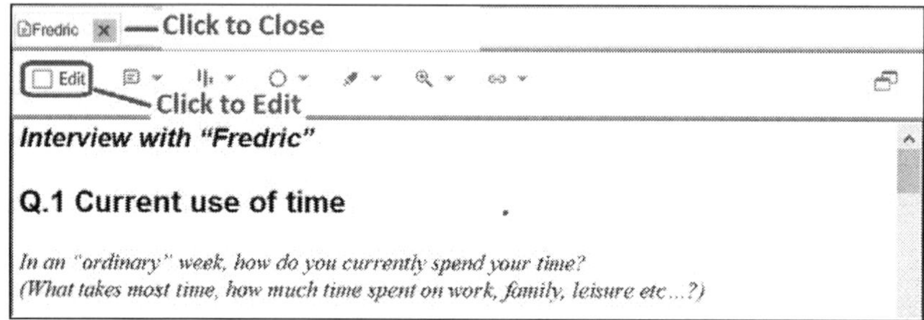

> **Tip:** When you have several open project items, you can undock these items as separate windows:
>
> 1 Right-click the upper tabs and select **Undock All**.
>
> Conversely, if you want to dock your open items then:
>
> 1 Go to **Home | Workspace | Dock**.
>
> While any window can be closed by clicking the x on the tab several windows can be closed simultaneously:
>
> 1 Right-click the upper tabs and select **Close All** or **Close All But This**.

Each item has its own tab when several items are opened at the same time. By default, Project Items are 'docked' inside the Detail View. You can undock an open item as a standalone window:

1 Go to **Home | Workspace → Undock**.

Any undocked item can be docked again:

1 Select the undocked item.
2 Go to **Home | Workspace → Dock**.

As an alternative you may also use the **Undock/Dock** button in the Top Panel of the Detail View:

Any undocked window can preferably be maximized with the conventional Maximize button.

Undocking items can only take place during an open work session; when you reopen a project all undocked windows are closed. However, you can go to **File → Options** and in the **Application Options** dialog box, select the **Display** tab, under the Detail View Defaults section, beside Window, you can select *Floating* (see page 41) so that an item window is always opened in undocked mode.

Copying, Cutting, and Pasting

Standard conventions for copying, cutting, and pasting text and images prevail in NVivo. In addition, NVivo can also copy, cut, and paste complete Project Items like Files, Codes, Cases, Queries etc. However, it is not possible to paste Codes into folders meant for Files and vice versa (this would breach the software's folder template conventions). It is only possible to paste an item into the folder appropriate for that type of folder (e.g., paste a Code within the Codes folder, a Query within the Queries folder, etc.). To cut and paste within NVivo:

1 Select an item (document, Code etc.)
2 Go to **Home | Clipboard → Cut**
or right-click and select **Cut**
or **[Ctrl]** + **[X]**.

alternatively

2 Go to **Home | Clipboard → Copy**
or right-click and select **Copy**
or **[Ctrl]** + **[C]**.
3 Select the appropriate folder or parent Code under which you want to place the item.
4 Go to **Home | Clipboard → Paste**
or right-click and select **Paste**
or **[Ctrl]** + **[V]**.

Paste Special

The normal **Paste** command includes all those elements. But after copying or cutting of some items (excluding Codes) you can decide which elements from the item that should be pasted:

1 Copy or cut the item or items that you want to paste into the new position.
2 Select the target folder.
3 Go to **Home | Clipboard → Paste Special...**

The **Paste Special Options** dialog box appears:

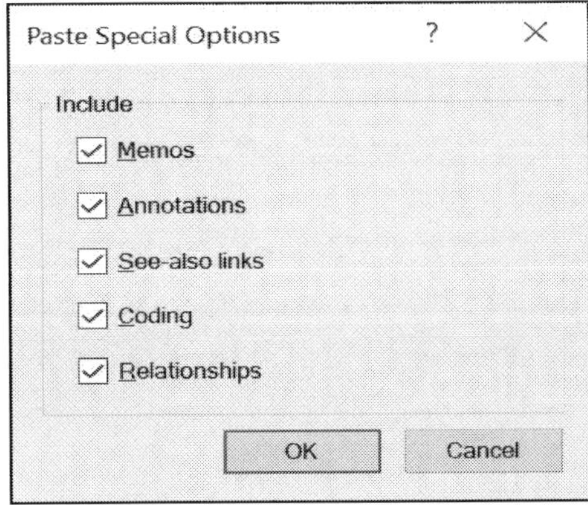

4 Select the item elements that you want to include. Additional context-based options may also appear: *Media content* and *Transcript* are valid for video and audio items and *Log entries* is valid for picture items.

5 Confirm with **[OK]**.

Undo

The undo-function can be made in several steps backwards. Undo only works for commands made after the last save:

1 Go to **Undo** on the **Quick Access Toolbar** or **[Ctrl]** + **[Z]**.

The arrow next to the undo-icon makes it possible to select which of the last five commands that shall be undone. When you select the first option only the last command is undone and when you select the last option all commands will be undone.

The option **Redo** (Undo - Undo) is available in Word but not in NVivo.

The Ribbons

Commands are organized into logical groups, collected under tabs. Each tab relates to a type of activity, such as creating new Project Items or analyzing your source materials.

The **Home**, **Create**, **Import**, **Create**, **Explore**, **Share**, and **Modules** tabs are always visible. The other tabs are 'contextual' which means that they are shown when needed. For example, the **Picture** tab is shown when a picture is opened.

Within each tab, related commands are grouped together. For example, the **Format** group on the **Home** tab contains commands for setting font size, type, bold, italics and underline.

The ribbon is optimized for a screen resolution of 1280 by 1024 pixels, when the NVivo window is maximized on your screen. When the NVivo window is not maximized and the ribbon is smaller, you may not see all the icons or text.

The instructions in this book apply certain conventions for commands and ribbon tabs, see Graphic Conventions, page 16.

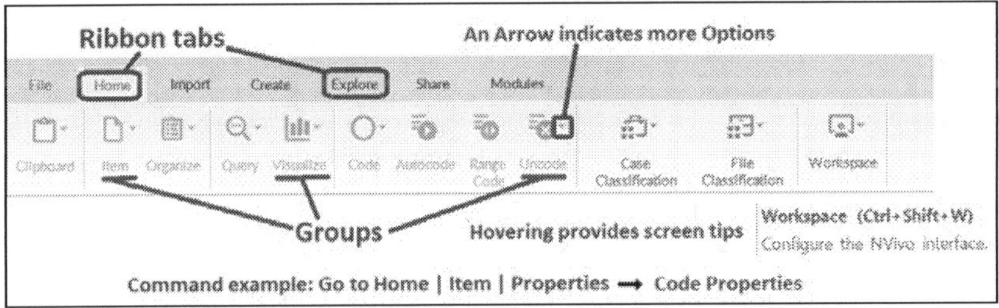

The **Quick Access Toolbar** is always visible and provides quick access to frequently-used commands. By default, the Save, Edit and Undo commands are available in Quick Access Toolbar. You can customize the Quick Access Toolbar by adding or removing commands. You can also move the Quick Access Toolbar above or below the ribbon by clicking the small arrow:

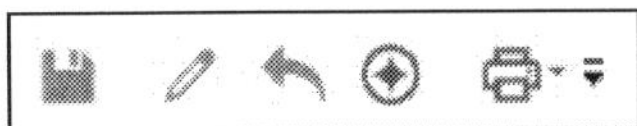

Select the options *Show Above the Ribbon* and *Minimize the Ribbon*. The menu tabs are shown again as soon as you point at any menu alternative.

The **Home** tab provides commands related to coding and exploring workflow (e.g., cut and paste):

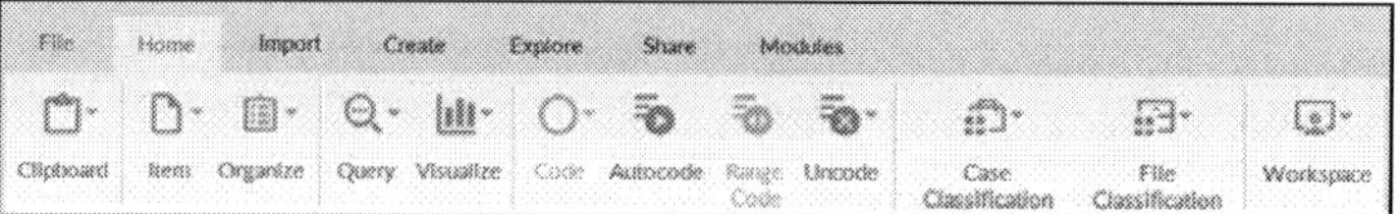

The **Import** tab provides commands related to importing new Project Items

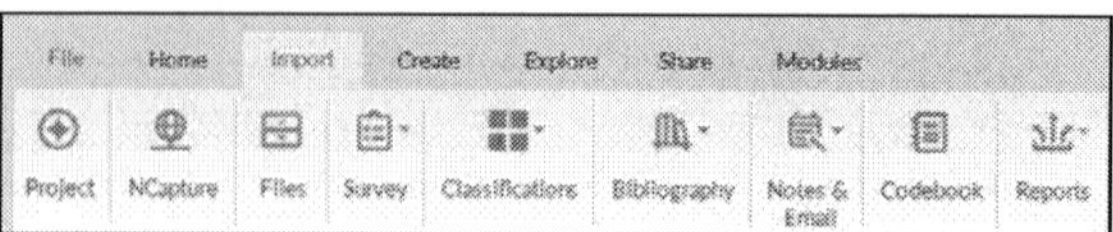

The **Create** tab provides commands related to creating memos, Codes or cases:

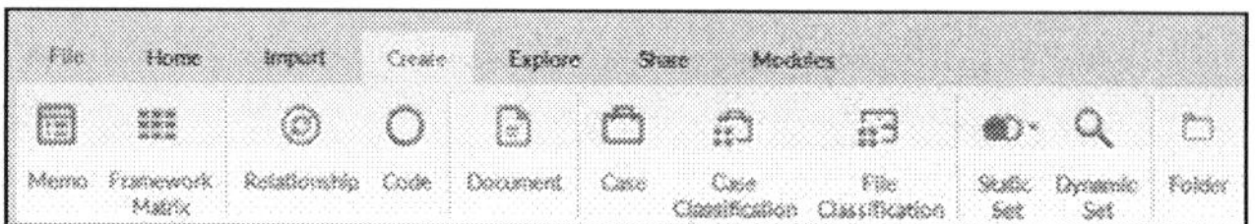

The **Explore** tab provides commands related to querying and visualizing your data:

The **Share** tab provides commands related to exporting and sharing your data:

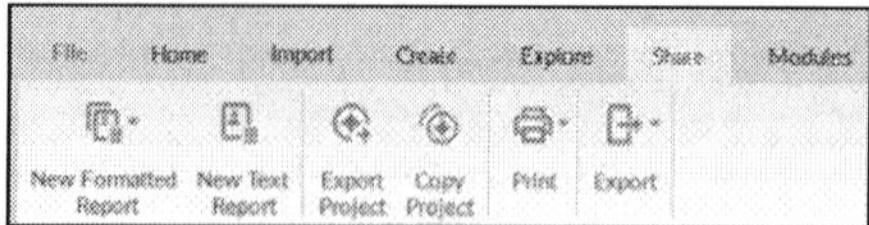

The **Modules** tab provides optional services:

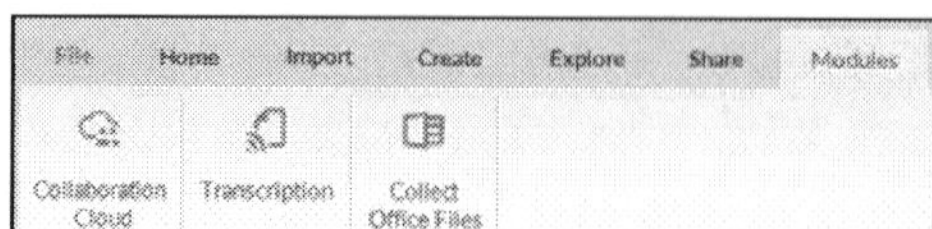

- ♦ -

The following tabs are context dependent, meaning they only become available depending on the Project Item type that is open.

The **Code/Case/Relationship/Sentiment** tabs provide commands related to Codes/Cases/Relationships/Sentiments, Text Search Queries and Coding Queries:

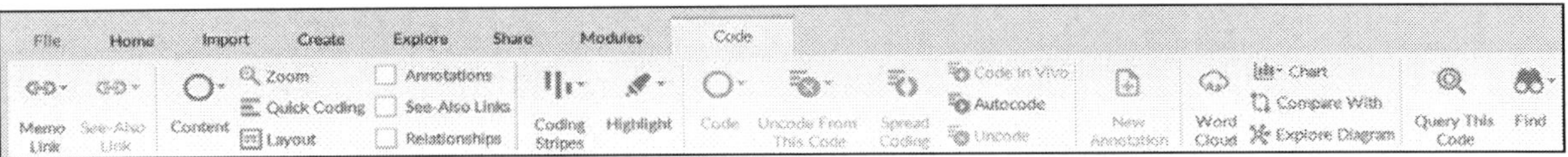

The **Document/Memo** tab provides commands related to text documents:

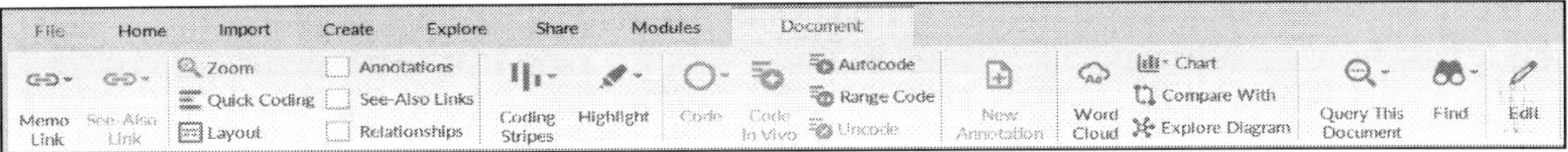

The **Edit** tab provides commands related to editing text documents:

The **PDF** tab provides commands related to PDF documents:

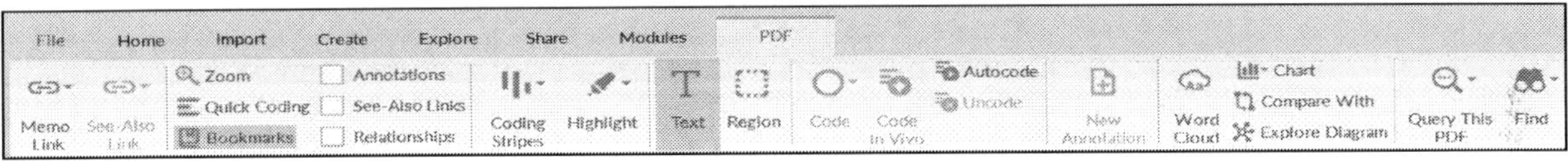

The **Framework Matrix** tab provides commands related to Framework Matrices:

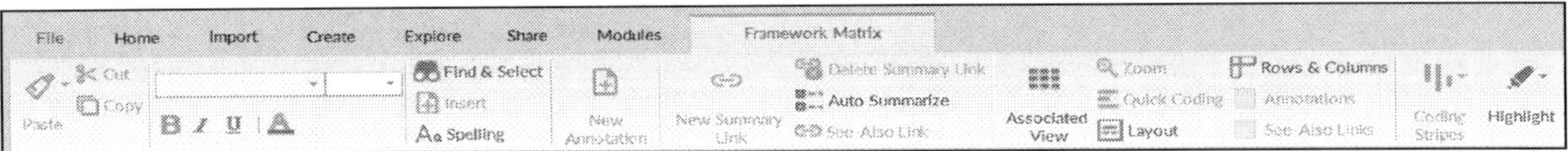

The **Audio/Video** tabs provide commands related to audio- and video items:

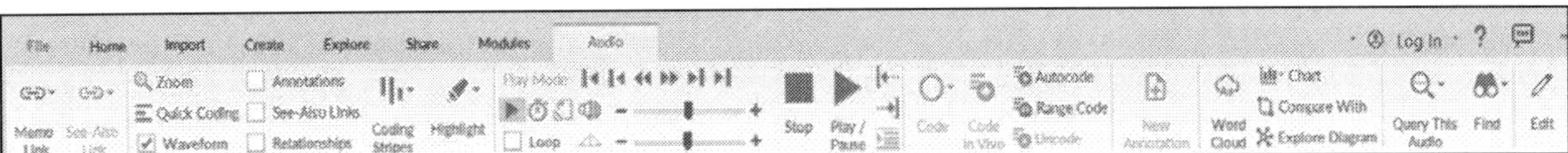

The **Edit** tab provides commands related to editing audio- and video items:

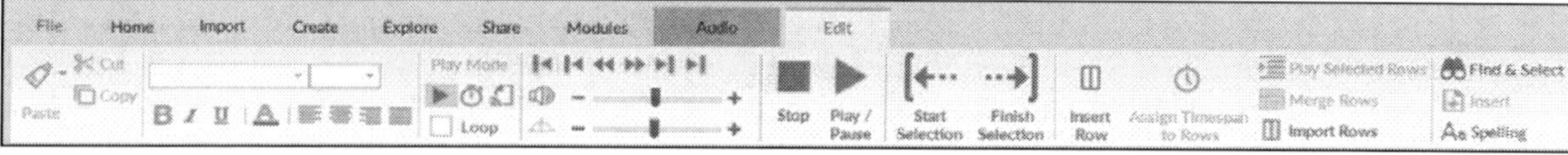

The **Picture** tab provides commands related to images:

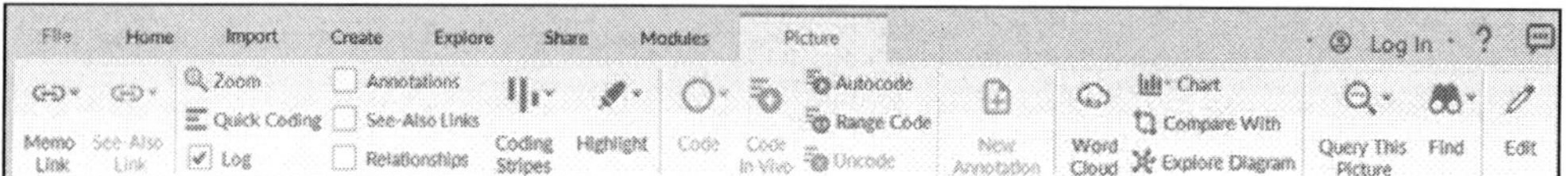

The **Edit** tab provides commands related to editing picture items:

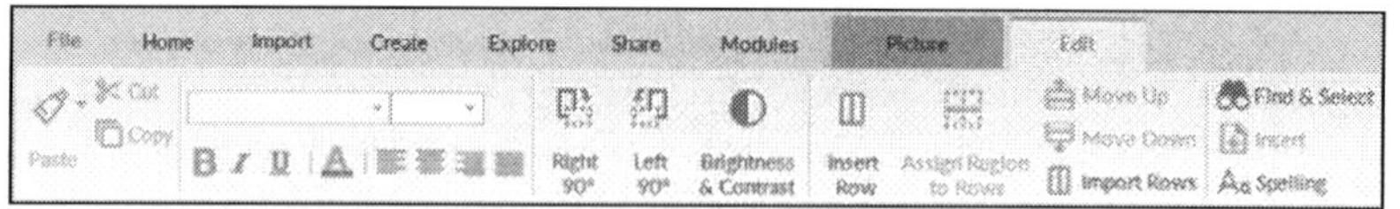

The **Word Frequency** tab provides commands related to the Word Frequency Queries:

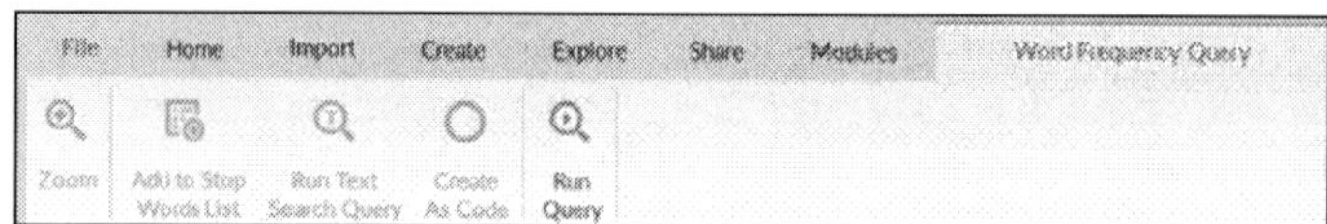

The **Matrix** tab provides commands related to the Matrix Coding Queries:

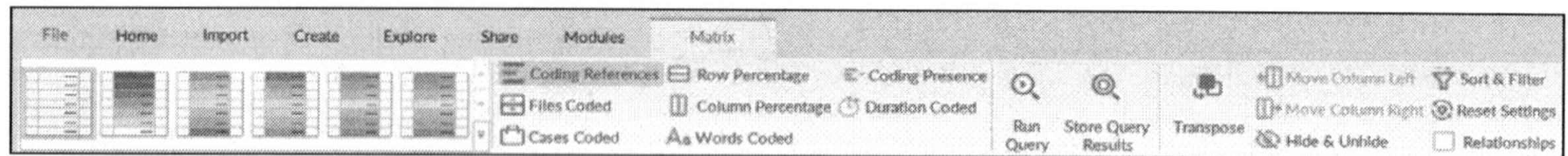

The **Crosstab** tab provides commands related to the Crosstab Queries:

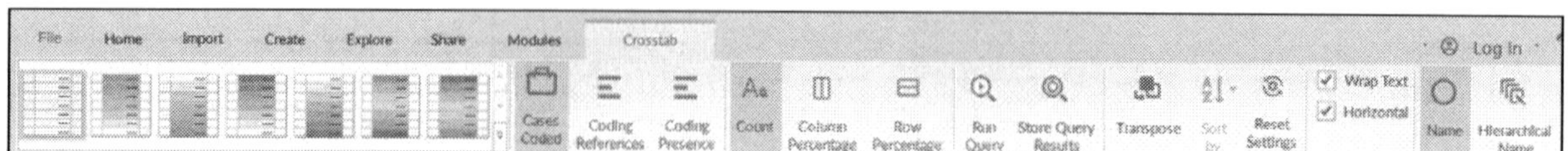

The **Formatted Report** tab provides commands related to the Report Designer:

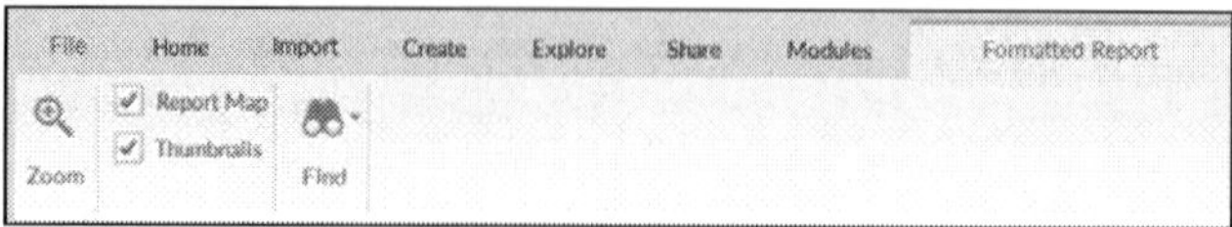

The **Designer** tab provides controls when working with Formatted Reports:

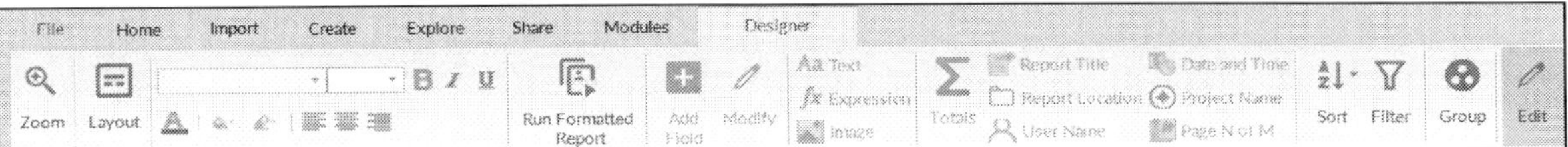

The **Mind Map** tab provides commands related to creating and modifying Mind Maps:

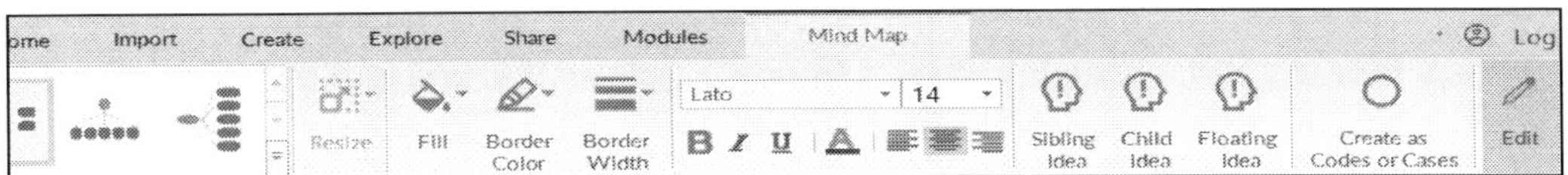

The **Project Map** tab provides commands related to creating and modifying Project Maps:

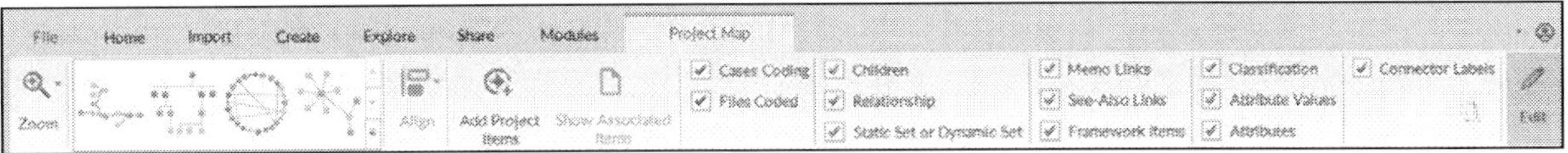

The **Concept Map** tab provides commands related to creating and modifying Concept Maps:

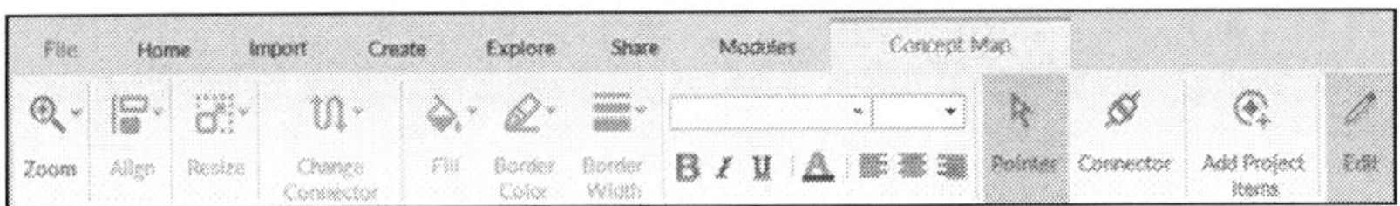

The **Chart** tab has commands creating and modifying Charts:

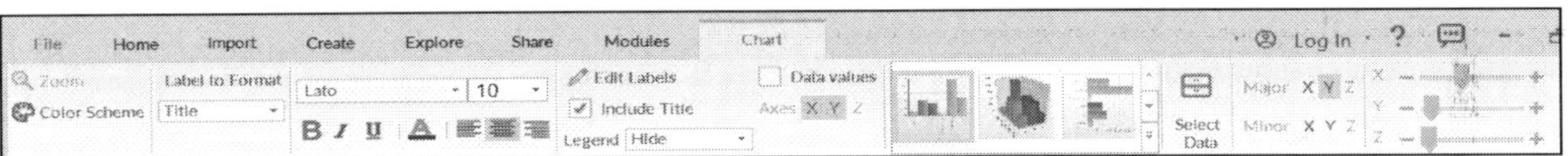

The **Hierarchy Chart** tab provides commands related to creating and modifying Hierarchy Charts:

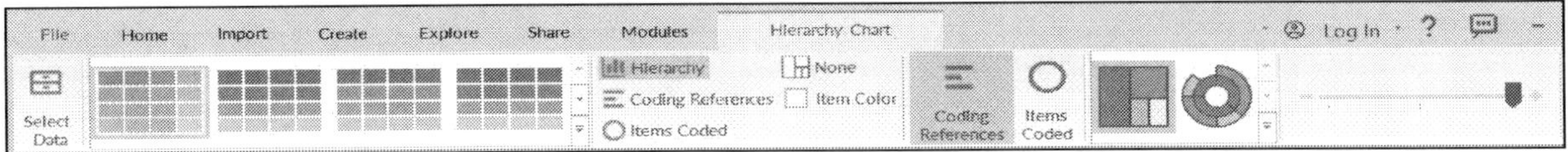

The **Word Tree** tab provides commands handling and modifying Word Trees:

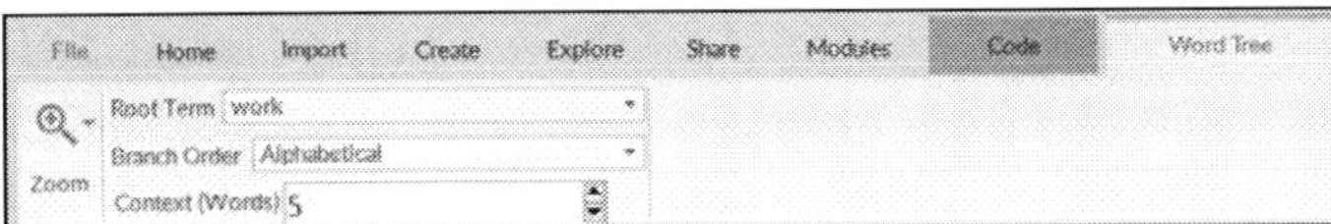

The **Cluster Analysis** tab provides commands related to conducting and formatting Cluster Analysis:

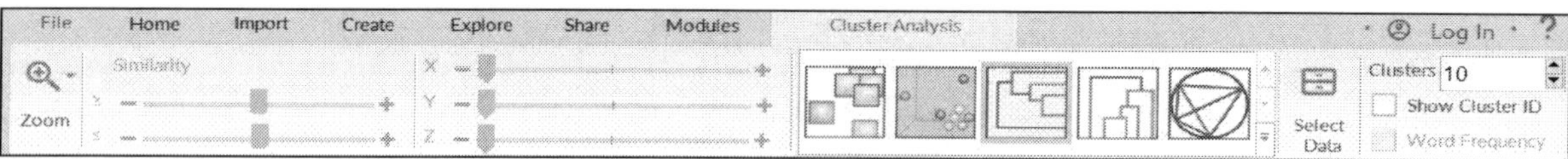

The **Comparison Diagram** tab provides commands related to modifying Comparison Diagrams:

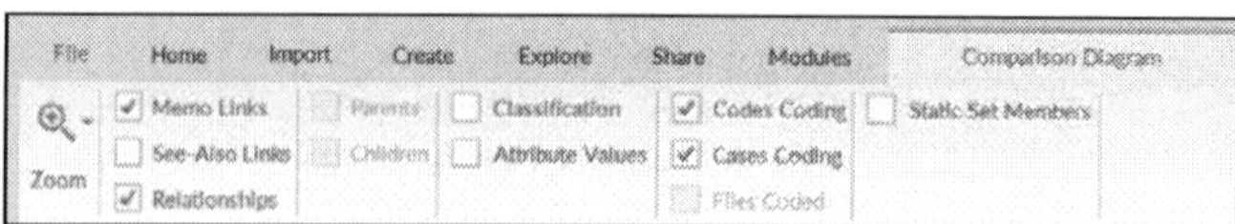

The **Explore Diagram** tab provides commands related to modifying Explore Diagrams.

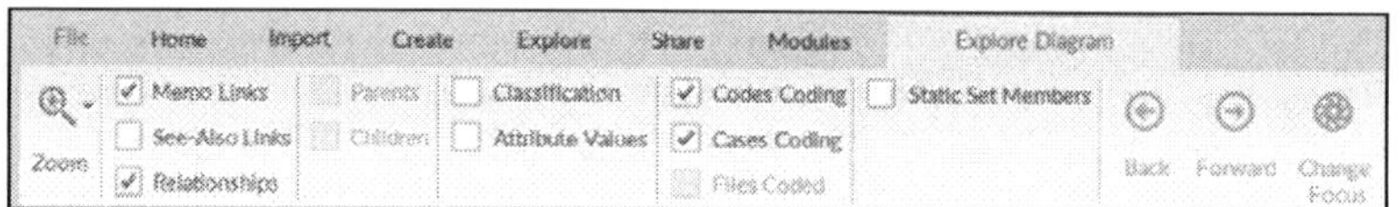

The **Sociogram** tab provides commands related to modifying Network Sociograms.

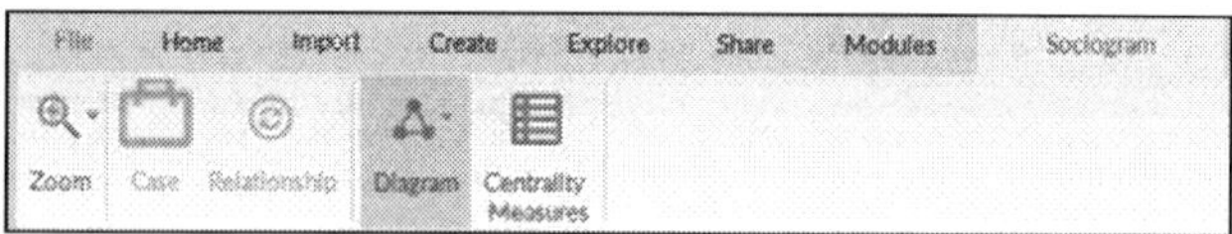

Common Analyze Functions on Several Tab Menus

Each of the following context dependent Tab menus have the frequently used menu groups in the rightmost part of the Tab menus:

Document, PDF (not Edit), Memo, Code (not Edit), Case (not Edit), External, and Relationship (not Edit).

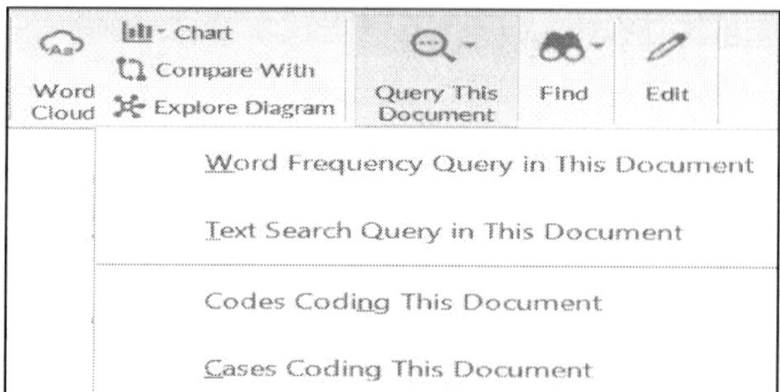

These options are shortcut menus for each opened item with default settings for the current project item. You will then have access to all other settings and can easily modify your analysis as soon as you once run these options.

Se Chapter 14, Queries, Chapter 26, Charts, and Chapter 27, Diagrams.

Application Options

NVivo project settings can be adjusted for an individual project or for the NVivo software overall. **Application Options** adjust settings for the software overall, and some changes you make only apply to new projects and will therefore have an effect on the **Project Properties** (see page 51) settings for future projects:

1 From the NVivo Welcome Screen or in an open project go to **File → Options**.

The **[Reset]** button will change the options back to the default settings and cannot be undone. Your username, initials, user interface language and server connections will be preserved.

The General Tab

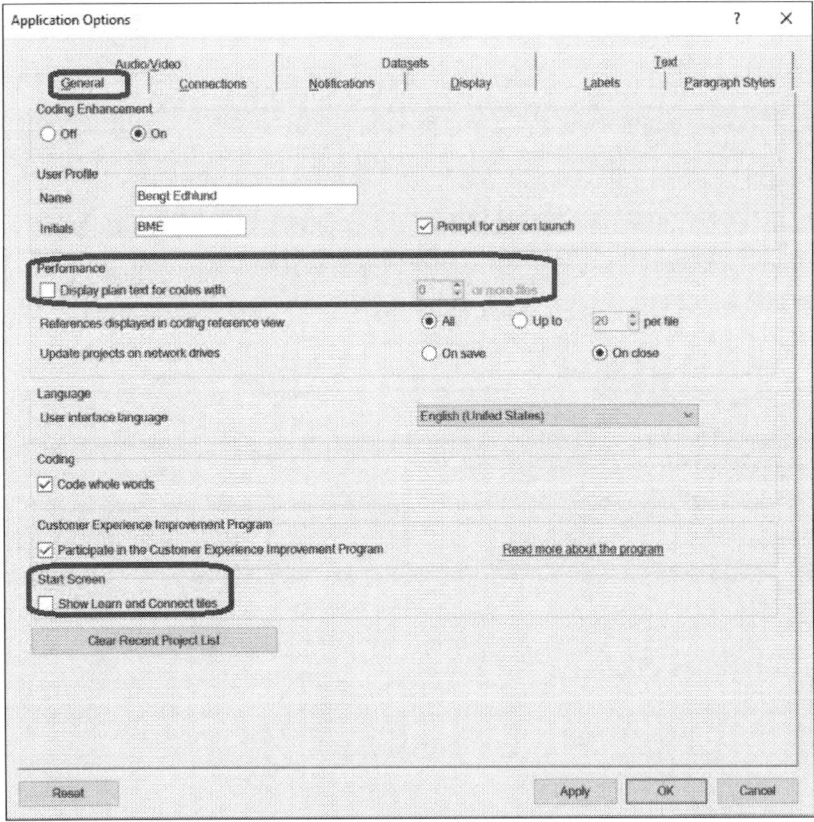

The **General** tab contains default options for working with the NVivo interface such as user interface language and coding properties.

Under Performance you can improve data handling by selecting *Display plain text for codes with <select> or more files.*

Settings made here take immediate effect in an ongoing project and will also become default for new projects. Here you can change the user interface language.

The Connections Tab

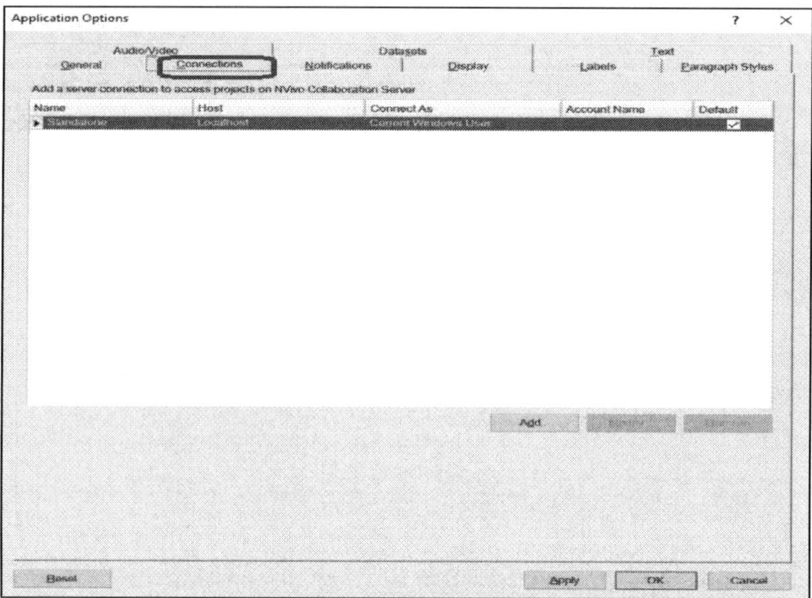

The **Connections** tab contains settings pertaining to NVivo for Teams – additional QSR proprietary teamwork software (see page 327).

The Notifications Tab

Tip: Why take a chance on losing valuable work? We recommend that a save reminder displays every 10 minutes, instead of the default 15.

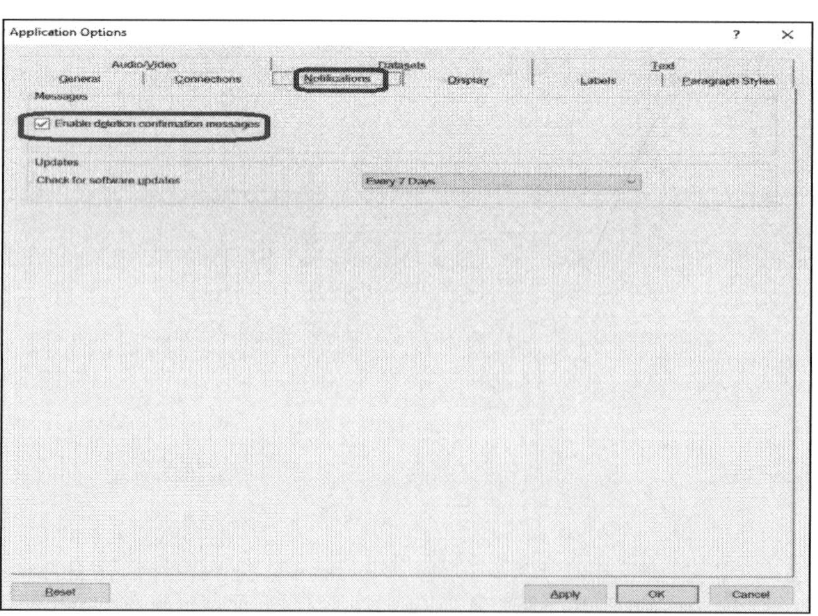

The **Notifications** tab contains default options for save reminders and software update checks.

All settings under this tab take immediate effect on an ongoing project.

The Display Tab

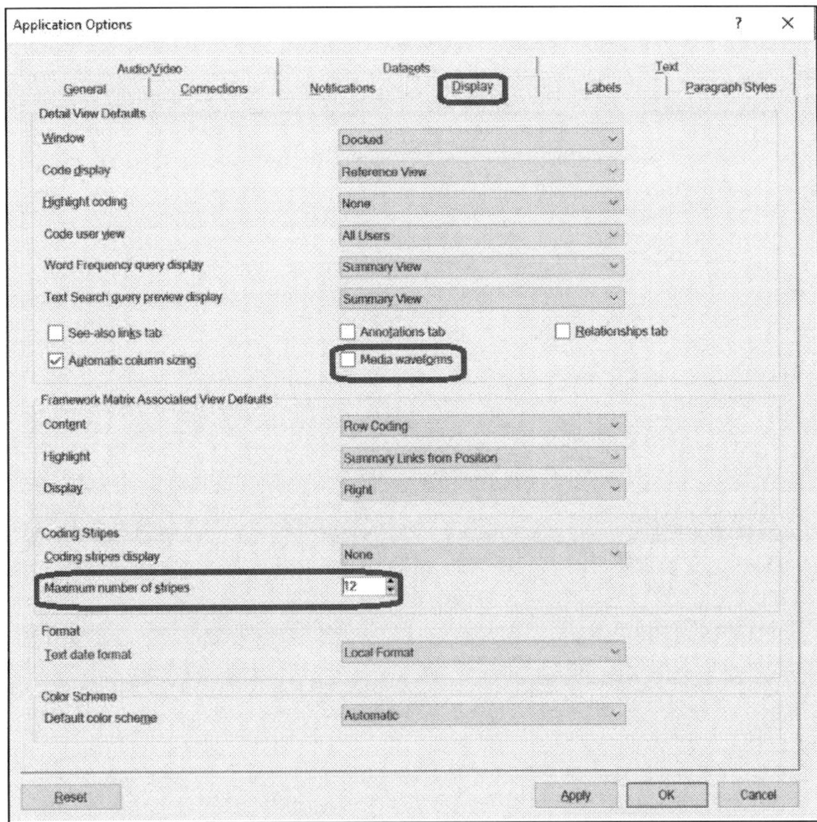

The **Display** tab contains default options for visual cues in NVivo such as coding stripes, highlighting, and tabs.

We suggest unchecking the display of Media waveforms as the waveform often disturbs other graphic information like coding stripes, links and selections.

We also suggest increasing the maximum number of coding stripes beyond the default number which is 7. The number of stripes cannot be extended beyond 200.

In case you prefer always to open your windows undocked, then set Detail View as Window *Floating*.

For settings related to Framework Matrix, see page 257.

All settings under this tab take immediate effect on an ongoing project.

The Labels Tab

The **Labels** tab allows you to customize the names of attributes, values and the Associated relationship type.

Settings made here will take effect next time a project is created. If you want to make changes in the current project, use **Labels** tab in **Project Properties** dialog box (see page 53).

The Paragraph Styles Tab

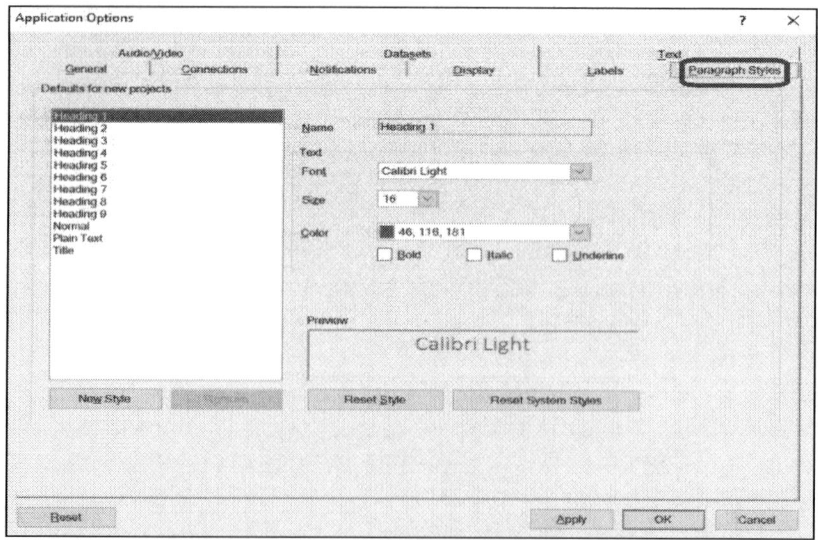

The **Paragraph Styles** tab contains default options for NVivo styles (see page 76). Changes made under Application Options will be available next time a new project is created. Existing project settings can be modified under the **Paragraph Styles** tab in **Project Properties** (see page 55).

The Audio/Video Tab

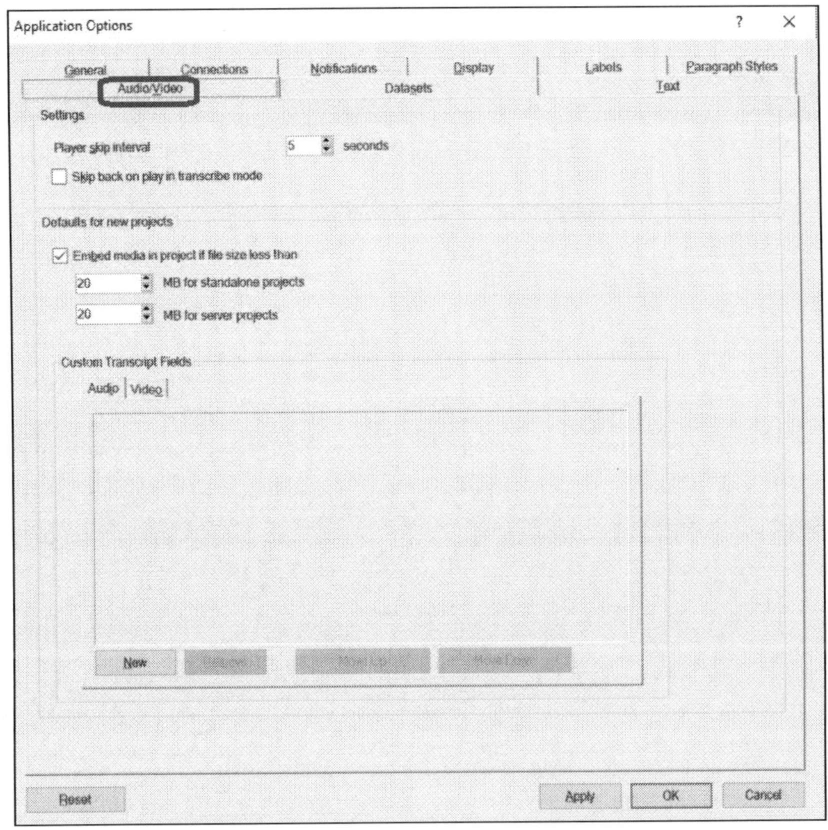

The **Audio/Video** tab contains settings for the skip interval for skipping forward and skipping backward. The threshold value for embedding is set here. These settings have an immediate effect on an open project. You can also create custom transcript fields (or columns) for audio and video items. However, these fields will come into effect for new projects. To create custom transcript fields in an existing project go to **File → Project Properties**, and select the **Audio/Video** tab, see page 56).

> **Tip:** Settings for the threshold value of embedded audio and video files are set under: ***Embed media in project if file size less than <value> MB.*** Max is 40 MB for single users. Embedded or not, you can always code, link and create transcript rows in a media item.

The Datasets Tab

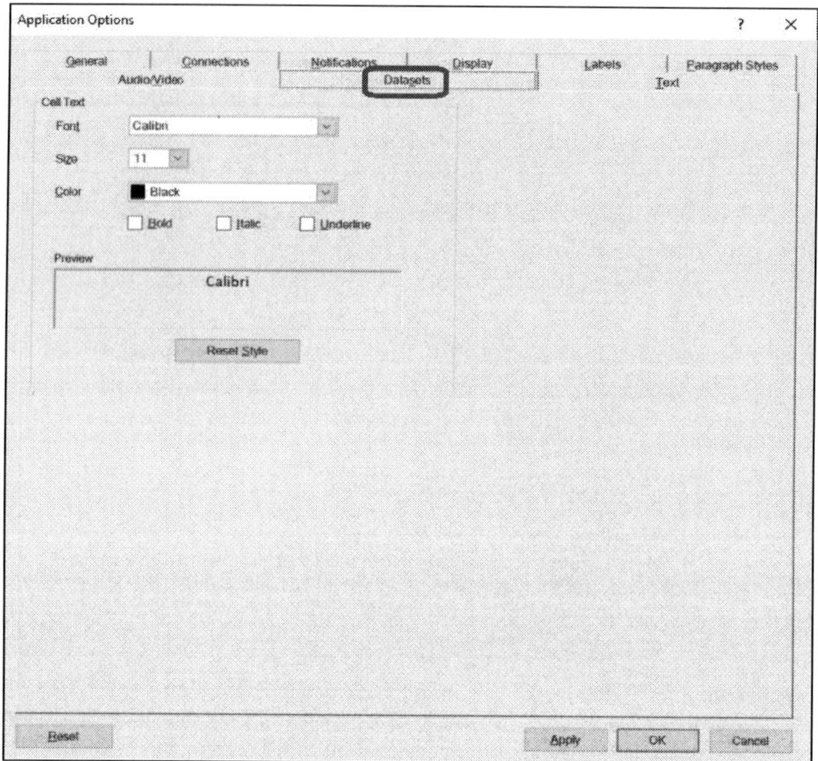

The **Datasets** tab allows you to adjust the font, size and color of cell text. Modifications made here will take effect next time a Dataset is opened.

The Text Tab

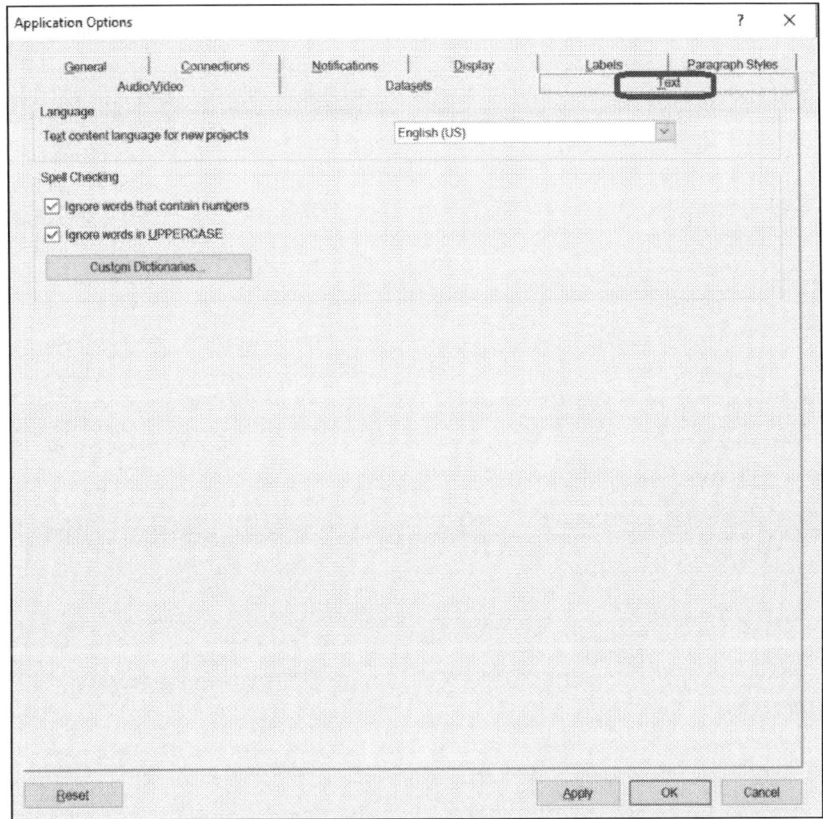

The **Text** tab allows you to make settings for the content language and the spell checking dictionaries that you want to use. The setting of language does not have an effect on the ongoing project. For the next new project the chosen language will be default. If you want to change content language for the current project go to the **General** tab of **Project Properties** dialog box (see page 51).

The supported languages are: Chinese (PRC), English (UK), English (US), French, German, Japanese, Portuguese and Spanish. If you use any other language then you can set the language as *Other*.

The button [**Custom Dictionaries...**] can be used to appoint one specific folder for each language which can include the custom dictionary, **<filename>.DIC**. This is a normal text-file and can be opened and edited with Notepad. If you already have a custom dictionary from before you can name it **<filename>.DIC** and store it in the defined folder. Even the setting *Other* can have its own custom dictionary.

Alternate Screen Layouts

NVivo offers alternate screen layouts to split the screen space for Detail View vertically instead of horizontally.

1 Go to **Home | Workspace → Right**.

The Right Detail View is very handy when coding with drag-and-drop (see page 167).

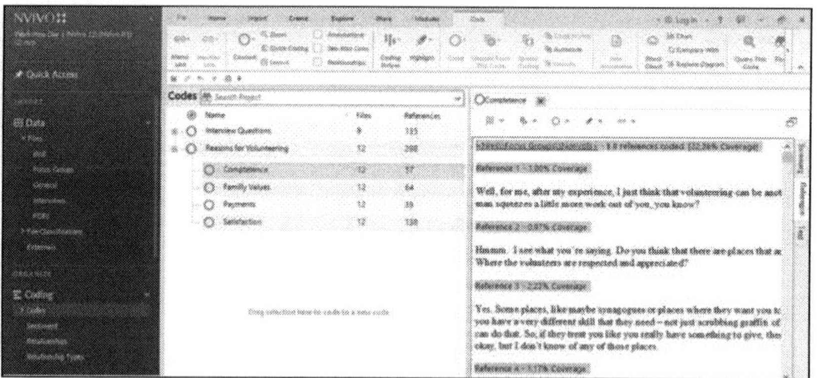

To revert to Bottom Detail View of the screen:

1 Go to **Home | Workspace → Bottom**.

Your **Detail View** setting preferences are now saved in between sessions.

For more screen space it is also possible to temporarily close the Navigation View.

1 Go to **Home | Workspace → Dashboard Mode**.

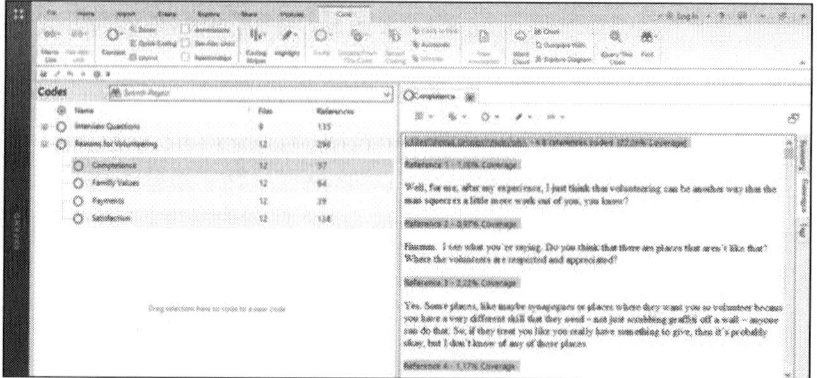

One option is hiding with the small arrow in the upper right corner of Navigation View:

Clicking on the left hand bar opens the Navigation View and you can select folders.

This setting is saved during current session and is saved even between sessions including the choice of folders. You can navigate to other folders by going with **[Ctrl]** + **[1** - 7] as follows:

[Ctrl] + [1] goes to folder **Data\\Files**
[Ctrl] + [2] goes to folder **Coding\\Codes**
[Ctrl] + [3] goes to folder **Cases\\Cases**
[Ctrl] + [4] goes to folder **Notes\\Memos**
[Ctrl] + [5] goes to folder **Sets\\Static Sets**
[Ctrl] + [6] goes to folder **Maps\\Maps**
[Ctrl] + [7] goes to folder **Reports\\Formatted Reports**

3. BEGINNING YOUR PROJECT

An NVivo project is a term used for all source documents and other items that altogether form your data analysis and findings. Importantly, an NVivo project is also a computer file that houses all those embedded Project Items.

NVivo can only open and process one project at a time. It is however possible to start the program twice and open one project in each program window. Cut, copy, and paste between two such program windows is limited to text, graphics and images and not Project Items like documents or Codes.

A project is built up of several items with different properties. There are internal sources (i.e., documents, memos), external sources (i.e., web sites), Codes, Queries and some other item types.

Creating a New Project

The Welcome screen will greet you each time you launch NVivo, and it is from here that you have the option to create a new project file (Blank Project):

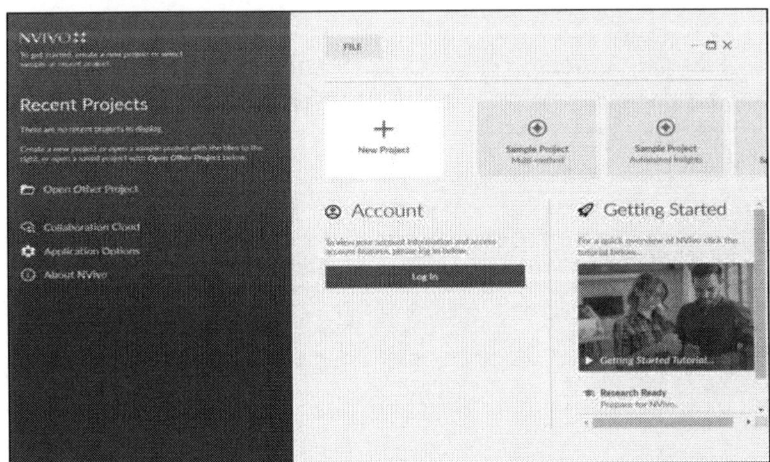

Your most recent projects are listed on the Welcome screen. You can also create a new project while navigating inside an existing project:

1 Go to **File → New**
or [**New Project**] on the Welcome screen
or this icon on the Quick Access Toolbar:

The **NEW PROJECT** – **STEP 1** dialog box appears:

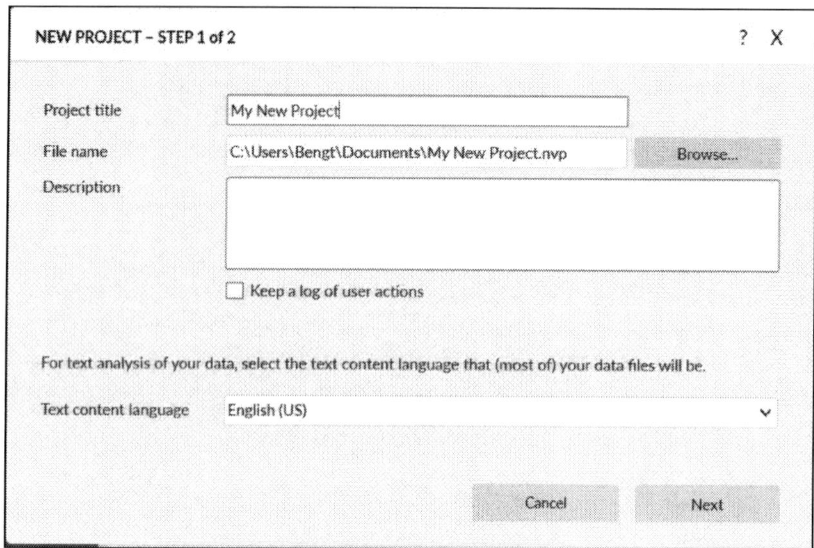

You must type a name for your project file, but the description is optional. The file path for your project is seen in the **File name** box. Click [**Browse...**] to select a new location for your project file. The default location of the project file is My Documents. The preferred location for ongoing project files is the native hard disk, the C-disk. About security backup, see page 62.

The name of a project can later be changed without changing the file name. Any open and saved NVivo project will be closed as NVivo opens a new or an existing project.

After having clicked [**Next**] the **NEW PROJECT** – **STEP 2** dialog box appears further explained on page 59:

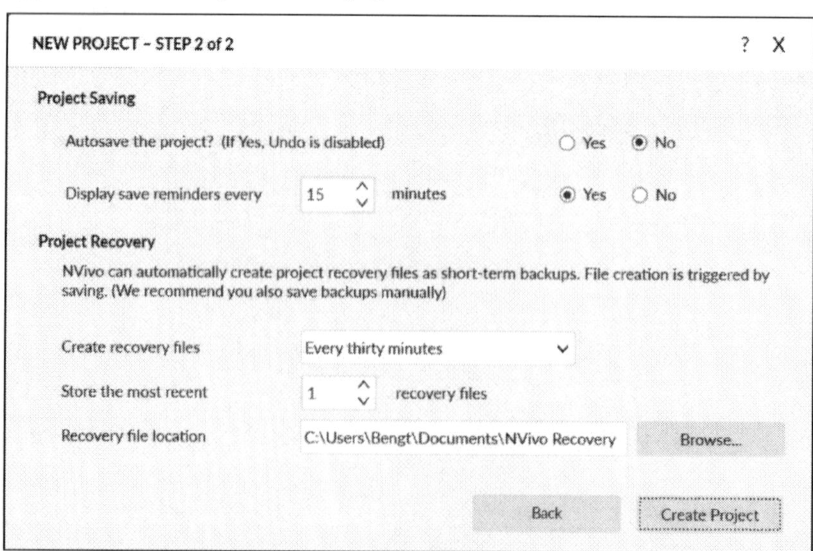

Sources & Project Size

NVivo is capable of importing and creating a variety of file types as data (e.g., text sources, tables, images, video, PDFs, etc.) Collectively, these items care called *Sources*. We'll discuss sources at length over the next few chapters, but for now it's important you understand that NVivo can either *import* Sources to a project file or *link* Sources externally to a Project file.

Files that are imported into NVivo are amalgamated by the software, which means that they become a part of the NVivo project. These are called *Internal Sources*. For example, any changes you make to imported sources (e.g., a text Source) are not reflected in the original document (e.g., a Microsoft Word text file).

Files that are linked into NVivo are only referenced by the software, which means that they exist independently of the NVivo project. These are called *External Sources* and cannot be coded, only the external item (the text inside NVivo) can be coded.

Audio- and video files are special as they can either be embedded or remain stored outside NVivo. If such files remain outside NVivo they can still be handled as if they were embedded, that is you can link and code, etc. Therefore, even not embedded media files are *Internal Sources*. It is the size of such files that decides if it should be embedded or not. A threshold value set by the user decides. The threshold value however, cannot exceed 40 MB (read more on page 98).

An NVivo Project file size is maximum 10 GB provided the storage is of type NTFS. Bear in mind that large Project Items (e.g., audio and video files) can be stored outside the project file. Linking to external files allows you to keep the project file size down. Using NVivo Collaboation Server (see Chapter 24, Collaborating with NVivo) allows for a maximum project file size of 100 GB or larger if storage space is available.

Project Properties

When a new project is created some settings from the **Application Options** dialog box are inherited. This dialog box opens by going to **File → Options**, and the settings that are inherited are found under these tabs: **Labels**, **Paragraph Styles, Audio/Video** and **Text**. Modifications and templates which are made in the **Project Properties** dialog box are only valid for your current project:

1 Go to **File → Info → Project Properties**.

The General Tab

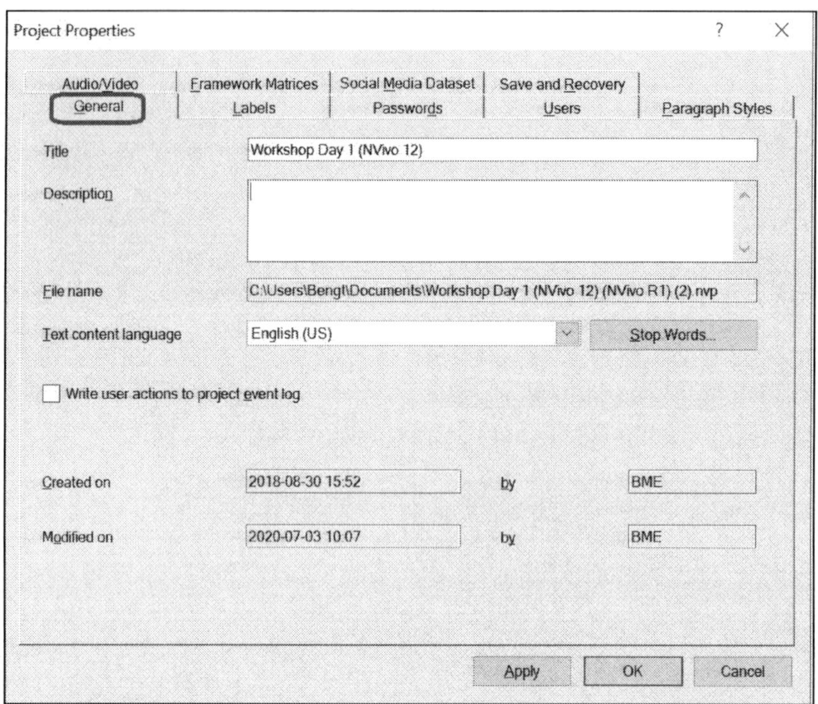

In this dialog box it is possible to modify your project name, but not the NVivo project file name. From the **Text content language** drop-down list, you will, if available, select the language of the data used in the project, otherwise select *English* or *Other*. Your content language will be the default language for spell check, as well as an important setting for Text Search Queries and Word Frequency Queries. For all languages except *Other* a default stop words list is built in. The stop words list can be edited using the [**Stop Words**] button or while using Word Frequency Queries (see Chapter 14, Queries). Such customized stop word lists are only valid for the current project. Even when the content language setting is *Other* you can build a customized stop words list.

> **Tip:** Your stop words list can be edited with the button [**Stop Words**]. Remember, customized stop words are only valid for the current project. Google on "stopwords swedish" or an applicable language to copy and paste other stop words lists.

Other language dependent functions are: Similar words (stemmed, synonyms, specializations, and generalizations), autocoding of Themes and Sentiments, Spell check (see pages 45 and 78).

The Description (max 512 characters) can be modified. *Write user actions to project event log* is optional. When activated you can open this log with **File → Info → Open Project Event Log** or delete with **File → Info → Clear Project Event Log**.

The Labels Tab

Under the **Labels** tab you can change some of your project's 'labels'. The **[Reset]** buttons reset to the values defined in the **Application Options** dialog box, under the **Labels** tab (see page 42).

The Passwords Tab

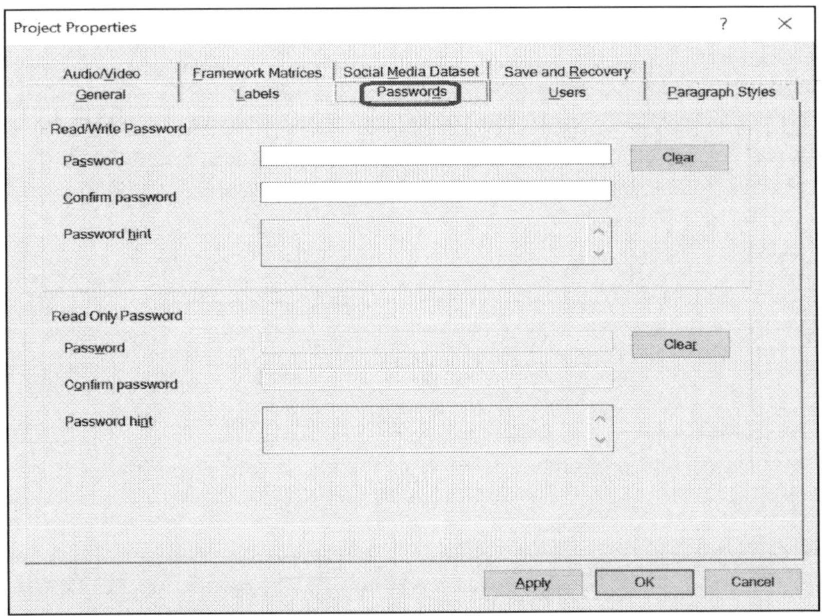

Under the **Passwords** tab you can define separate passwords for opening and editing your current project.

The Users Tab

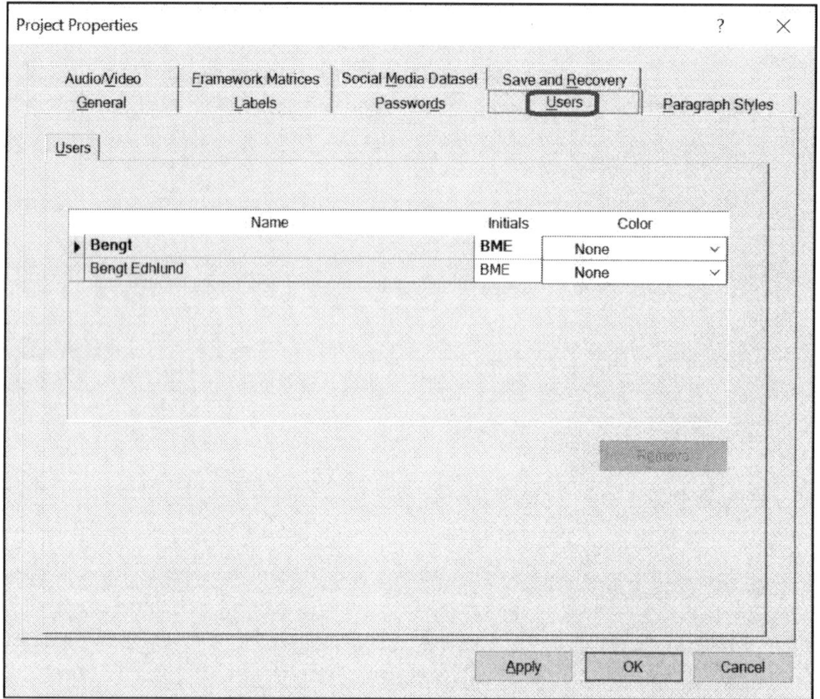

All users who have actively worked in the current project are listed here. The current user is identified by bold letters. You can replace a user with someone else on the list by selecting the user who shall be replaced (triangle) and using the [**Remove**] button. Select who will replace the deleted user by selecting from the list of users.

Users can also be given an individual color marking. Use the drop-down list in the Color column and select color. This color marking can be used when viewing coding stripes per user.

The Paragraph Styles Tab

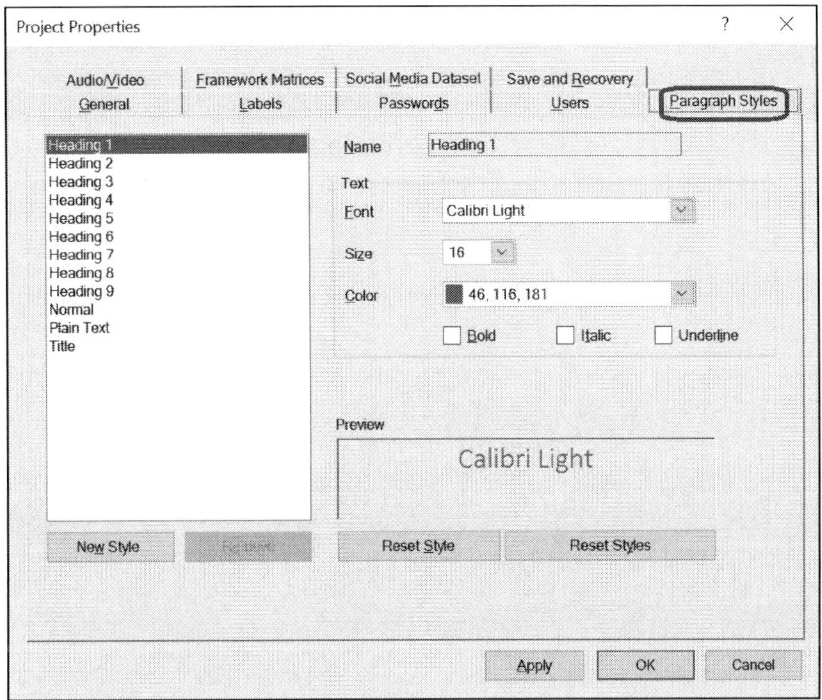

Under the **Paragraph Styles** tab, you can redefine your paragraph styles. The [**Reset Styles**] buttons reset to values defined in the **Application Options** dialog box, (see page 42).

The Audio/Video Tab

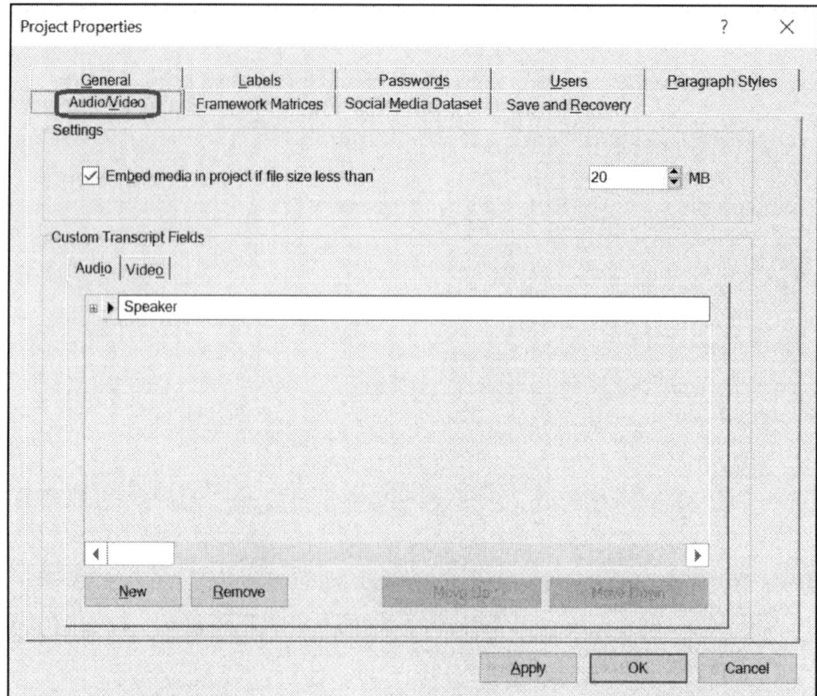

The settings for new projects are inherited from the **Application Options** dialog box, the **Audio/Video** tab (see page 43). Modifications made here are only valid for the current project.

When you need to create Custom Transcript Fields in your current project then you may use this dialog box. The [**New**] button defines more fields like Speaker, Affiliation with separate fields for Audio and Video.

The Framework Matrices Tab

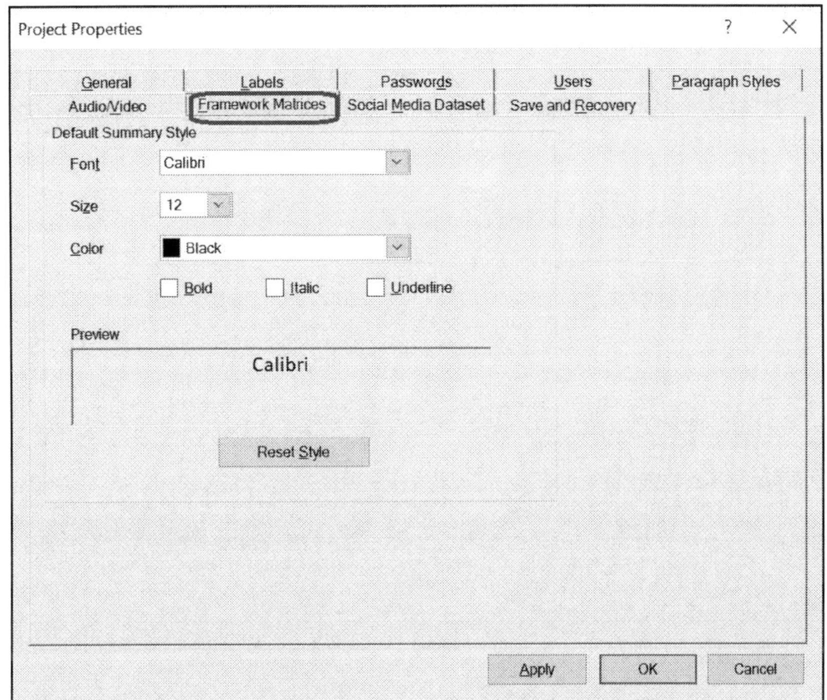

The settings here for new projects are inherited from the style Normal in the **Application Options** dialog box, the **Paragraph Style** tab (see page 42). Modifications made here are only valid for the Framework Matrices summaries in the current project.

The Social Media Dataset Tab

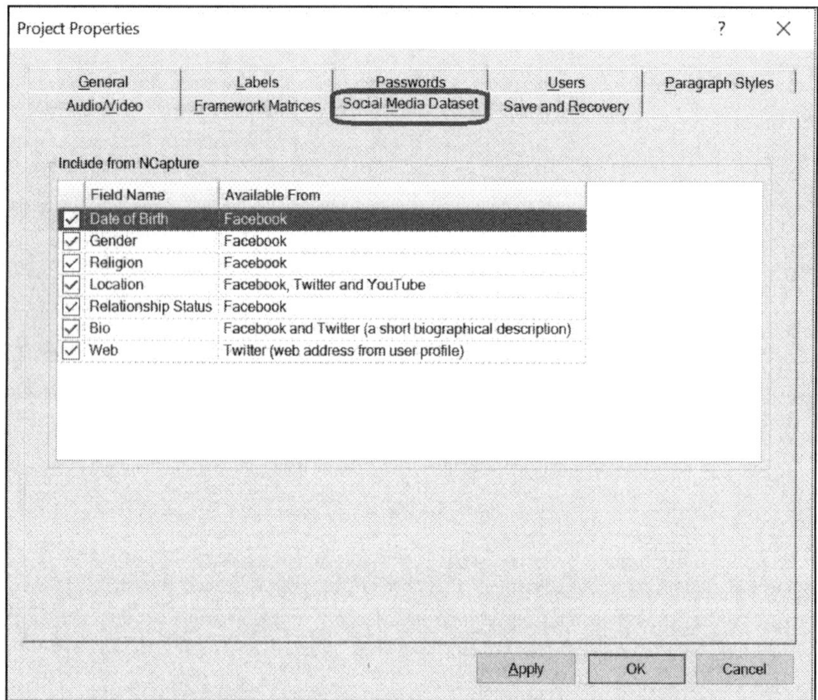

The **Social Media Dataset** tab: Social Media Datasets can be imported via NCapture files containing Facebook, Twitter, LinkedIn or YouTube data. This tab allows you to toggle the types of data you wish to capture from each social networking site.

The Save and Recovery Tab

Please note, that these settings are the same as dialog box **NEW PROJECT - STEP 2**, see page 50.

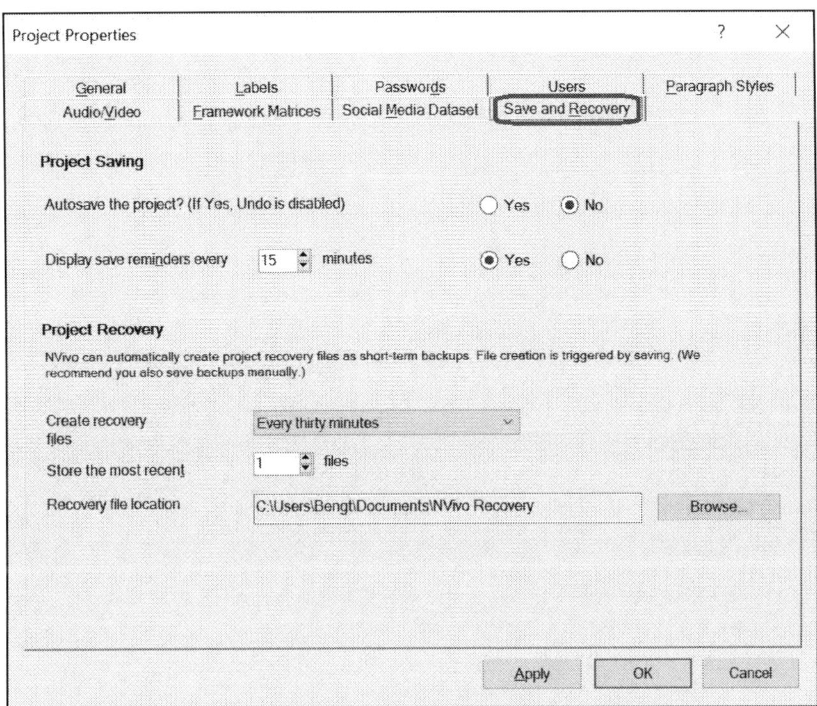

The **Project Recovery** section allows you to set the frequency of recovery files and the number of such files.

As you update and save your project, these settings will let NVivo create a 'project recovery file' to protect against loss of data. This is useful in situations where your project is compromised and you cannot open it—you will have the option to restore it from the project recovery file.

In case your project file will be damaged or corrupt and will not open normally, you will be presented with an option to recover from a project recovery file. This is the only way to open a recovery file. In case your current project file is lost then a dummy corrupt file will be needed and you need to ask your support for assistance.

Importing Projects

Projects and project items can be imported to an open project:

1. Open the project into which you wish to import a project.
2. Go to **Import | Project**.

The **Import Project** dialog box appears:

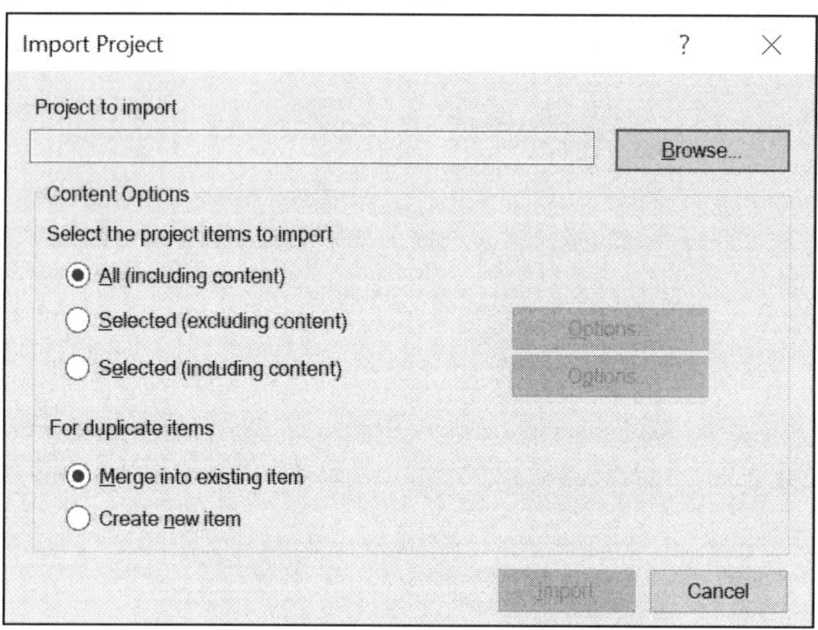

3. The [**Browse...**] button opens a file browser. Search for the project file to be imported.
4. Select the item options that you need for the import.
5. Confirm with [**Import**].

> **Tip:** For users who don't have access to NVivo for Teams, merging projects is a useful function for teams collaborating on the same project. Users can independently make changes to their project and, later, import their changes into a project 'master' file.

It is possible to import data from NVivo (*.NVP) and NVivo for Mac (*.NVPX) projects. However, the import of data from NVivo for Mac requires a Project Converter to be installed.

The options of this dialog box are very important to understand. When you need to merge two projects you simply first create a new project and then import one project after another applying the default settings of the **Import Project** dialog box.

When you for example need to import only folders, Codes, and Cases but not content (data) then you select *Selected (excluded content)* and the [**Options...**] button opens the **Import Options** dialog box:

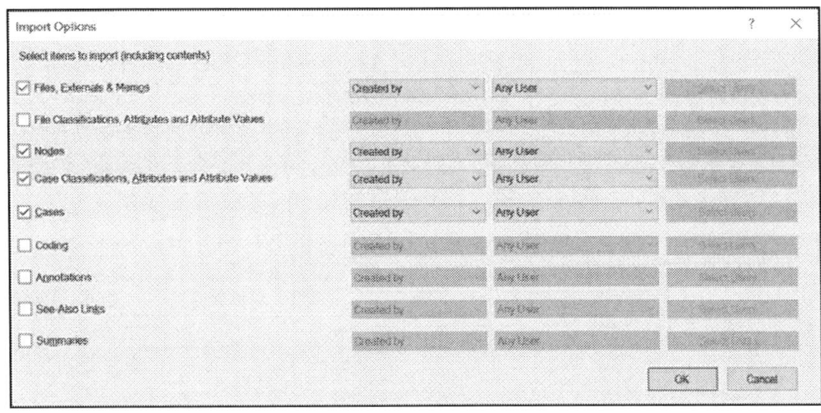

After choosing the applicable options, click [**OK**] and then [**Import**]. The result of such import can be used as a project template and is an easy way to inherit Code and folder structures from one project to another.

An **Import Project Report** is now shown each time an import has taken place listing all imported items.

Exporting Project Data

All Project Items (except folders) can be exported in various file types. For example, project Memos can be created in NVivo and then exported as .DOC or .DOCX files so they can be shared with collaborated over email:

1 Open a project.
2 Go to **Share | Export Project**.

The **Export Project Data** dialog box appears:

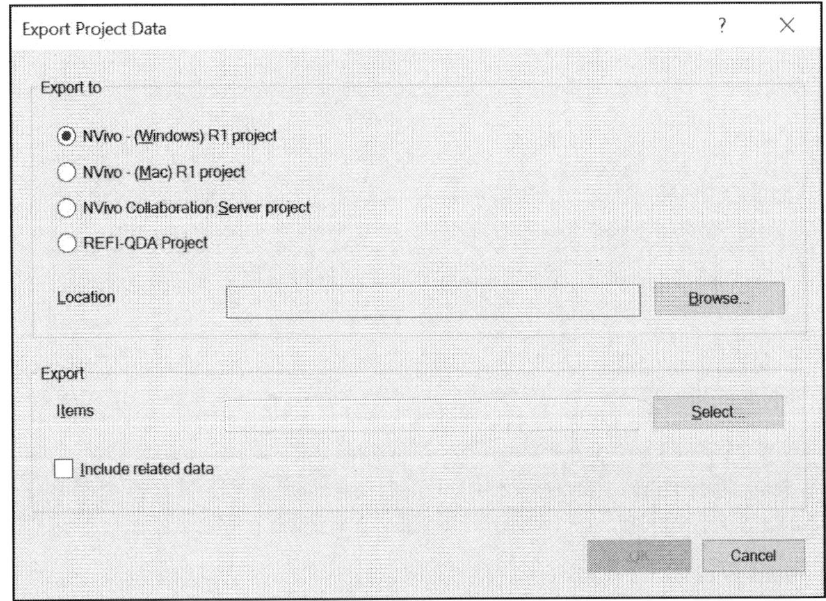

At **Export items** and the [**Select**] button you decide what items that shall be exported and at **Export to** and the [**Specify**] button you decide the name and location of the exported project data.

The option *NVivo (Mac)* requires a Project Converter to be installed.

The option *REFI-QDA* allows project transfer between participating qualitative data analysis (QDA) programs using the QDPX file standard. Projects can be exported into the QDPX file type from one program and opened in another.

Saving Projects

You can save the project file at any time during a work session. The complete project is saved; it is not possible to save single Project Items.

1 Go to **File → Save**

or the icon  on the Quick Access Toolbar.

If the option ***Enable project save reminders every 15 minutes*** has been chosen (see page 40) the following message will show:

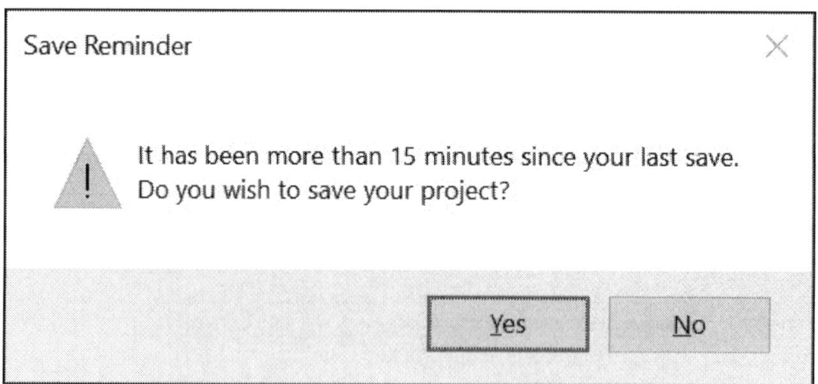

2 Confirming with [**Yes**] saves the whole project file.

Security Backup

Security backup of your NVivo project is important yet easy since the whole project is one file and not a structure of files and folders. Use Windows native tools for backup copies and follow the backup routines that your organization applies. The command **File → Copy Project** creates a copy of the project at the location that you decide while the current project remains.

It is advisable to include the current date in the file name of the backup copy so you can easily identify and open earlier versions of your project.

When you need to access such backup copy of your project file either copy the file to your local drive or create a new project and import the backup project. Never open a project file from a USB memory or any cloud service.

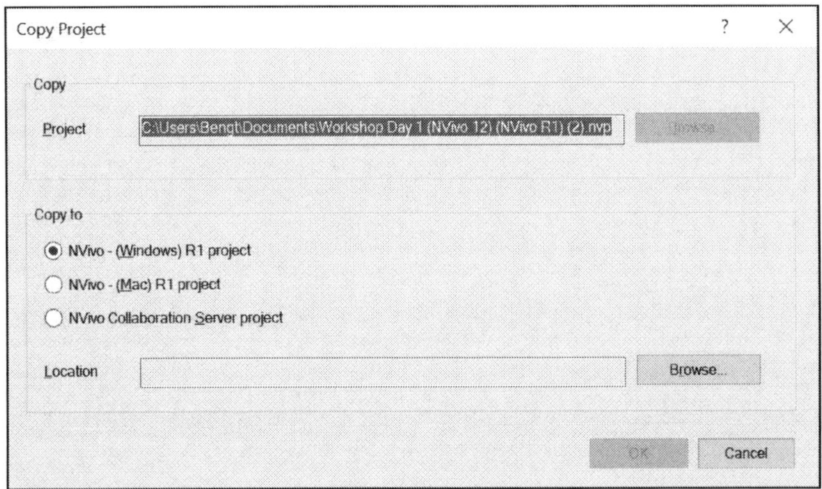

The option *NVivo Mac* requires a Project Converter to be installed.

Closing NVivo

After each work session save your project file and close NVivo. Close with:

File → Close
or the **X** in the upper rightmost corner of the screen
or **[Alt]** + **[F4]**.

4. HANDLING TEXT SOURCES

The Folder Structure for Data

The project folder structure for all types of source items are: Files, File Classifications, and Externals. The default folders as shown in the Navigator are:

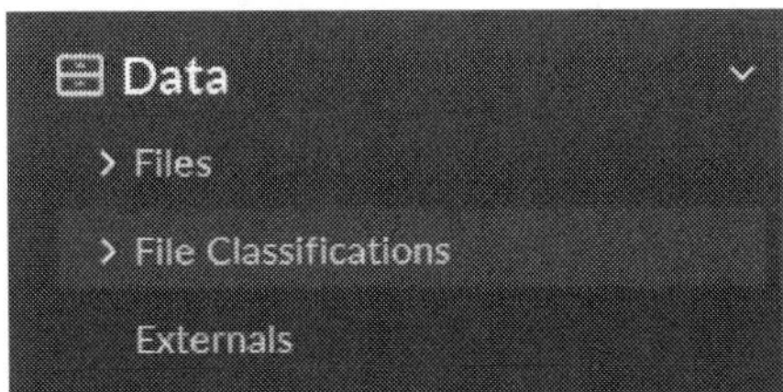

These folders and the names are not possible to delete, move, or rename. The folder names are depending on the user interface language setting, see page 39. However, the user can create subfolders to the default folder **Data\\Files** and **Data\\Externals** and create items shown the Navigator as items in the folder **Data\\File Classifications**.

Documents

From interview transcripts to government white papers, text data makes up the majority of qualitative research data. Text items can be easily imported from files created outside NVivo, like Word documents or text notes from Evernote. Text items can also be created by NVivo as most word processing tools and functions are incorporated in NVivo software, which we'll discuss in the next chapter.

Importing Documents

This section is about text-based sources that can be imported and these file types are: .DOC, .DOCX, .RTF, .TXT, and text-only Evernote export files (.ENEX). When text files are imported into NVivo, they become Project Items within the Source folder:

1 Go to **Import | Files**
  Default folder is **Data\\Files** or its currently open subfolder.
  Go to 4.

alternatively

1 Select the **Data\\Files** folder or its subfolder.
2 Go to **Import | Files**.
  Go to 4.

alternatively

2 Click on any empty space in the List View.

3 Right-click and select **Import Items...**
or **[Ctrl]** + **[Shift]** + **[I]**
Go to 4.

alternatively

3 Drag and drop your file's icon from an outside folder into its new folder. This option imports directly and leaves out the **Import Files** dialog box.

In all other cases, the **Import Files** dialog box appears:

Import Files
Import
\\Alfa\c\AAA\NVIVO_EXERCISES\INTERVIEWS\Anna.doc
Browse...
Create a case for each imported file
Import
Cancel

4 The [**Browse...**] button gives access to a file browser and you can select one or several documents for a batch import. To select multiple documents, use [**Shift**] + left click or if you want to import all use [**Ctrl**] + [**A**].

5 When the documents have been selected, confirm with [**Open**].

When you have selected *Create a case for each imported file* the dialog box **Import Files** offers several options:

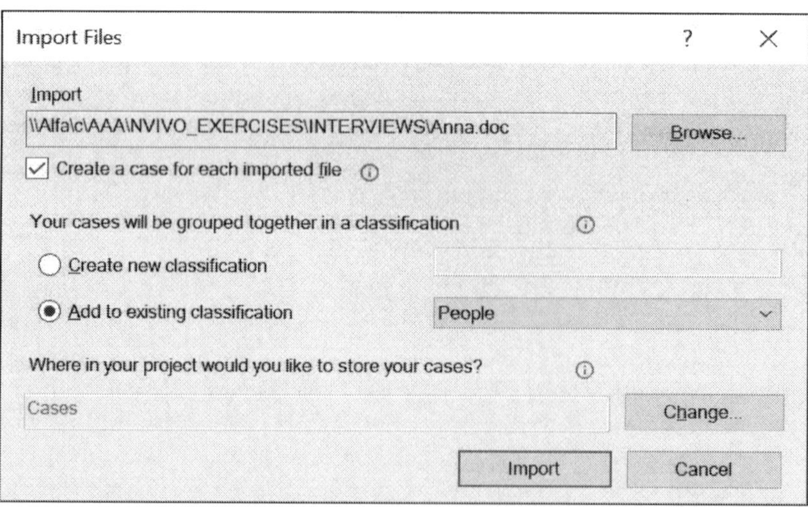

Each Source Item will be coded at a Case with the same name as the imported file and located in a folder or under the parent Case that has been selected with [**Change...**]. Also, you must assign the Cases to a Case Classification when importing (see Chapter 12, Classifications).

6 Confirm the import with [**Import**].

In this instance we are describing how to create a Case for each imported File. Therefore, we refer to Case Classifications and not as you might expect File Classifications which serves another purpose, see Chapter 12, Classifications.

When only *one* document has been imported, the **Document Properties** dialog box appears:

Document Properties			
General | Attribute Values			
Name	Anna		
Description			
Location	Files		
Size	30 KB	Color	None
Created on	2020-07-29 19:14	by	BME
Modified on	2020-07-29 19:14	by	BME
		OK	Cancel

Within this dialog box you can modify the name of the Source Item and optionally add a description.

7 Confirm with **[OK]**.

Creating a New Document

You can also create your own text items within NVivo, much the same as creating a Word document or text note in Evernote.

1 Go to **Create | Document**
Default folder **Data\\Files** or its currently opened subfolder.
Go to 4.

alternatively

1 Select the **Data\\Files** folder or its subfolder.

2 Go to **Create | Document**
Go to 4.

alternatively

2 Click on any empty space in the List View.

3 Right-click and select **New File → New Document...**
or **[Ctrl]** + **[Shift]** + **[N]**.

The **New Document** dialog box appears:

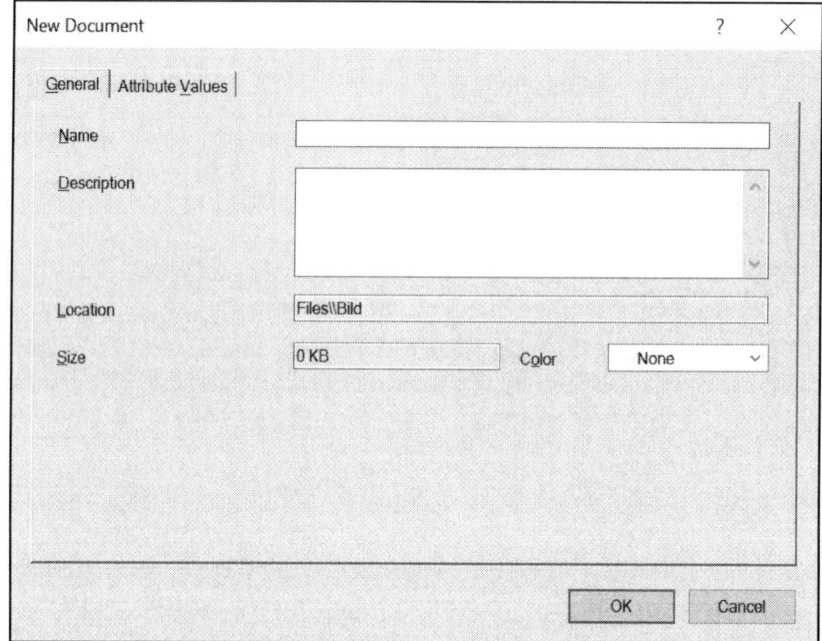

4 Type a name (compulsory) and a description (optionally), then **[OK]**.

A new text area opens in Detail View and you can create your document with all editing tools that NVivo offers.

Two new context dependent Ribbon menus, **Document** and **Edit**, have now opened and is opened each time a new document is created.

Here is a typical List View with some Source Items:

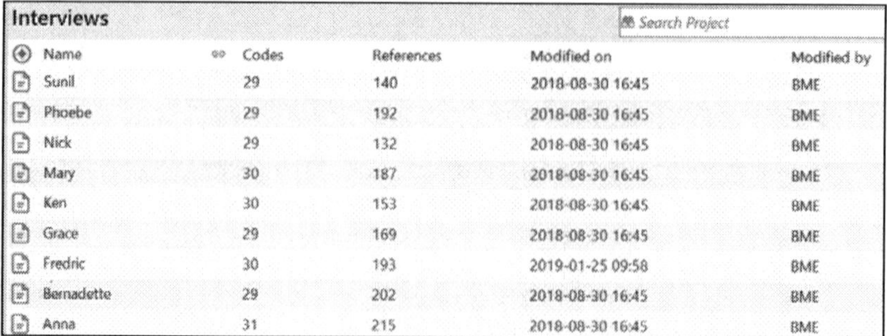

Interviews

Name	Codes	References	Modified on	Modified by
Sunil	29	140	2018-08-30 16:45	BME
Phoebe	29	192	2018-08-30 16:45	BME
Nick	29	132	2018-08-30 16:45	BME
Mary	30	187	2018-08-30 16:45	BME
Ken	30	153	2018-08-30 16:45	BME
Grace	29	169	2018-08-30 16:45	BME
Fredric	30	193	2019-01-25 09:58	BME
Bernadette	29	202	2018-08-30 16:45	BME
Anna	31	215	2018-08-30 16:45	BME

Opening a Document

Now that you have imported or created a list of Source Items, you can easily open one or more items anytime you see fit. All source items are always open in a write protected mode, see page 75.

1 Select the **Data\\Files** folder or its subfolder.

2 Select the document in the List View that you want to open.

3 Go to **Home | Item → 'Open' → Open Document...**
or right-click and select **Open Document...**
or double-click on the document in the List View
or **[Ctrl]** + **[Shift]** + **[O]**.

A new context dependent Ribbon menu, **Document**, has now opened and is opened each time a Document is opened.

Please note, NVivo allows you to open one document at a time, but several documents can stay open simultaneously.

Exporting a Document

As mentioned, you may wish at some point to export a text Source Item, such as a Memo you wrote inside NVivo but now need to email to a collaborator.

1 Select the **Data\\Files** folder or its subfolder.
2 Select the document(s) in the List View that you want to export.
3 Go to **Share | Export → Export**
or right-click and select **Export → Export <Item>**
or **[Ctrl]** + **[Shift]** + **[E]**.

The **Export Options** dialog box appears:

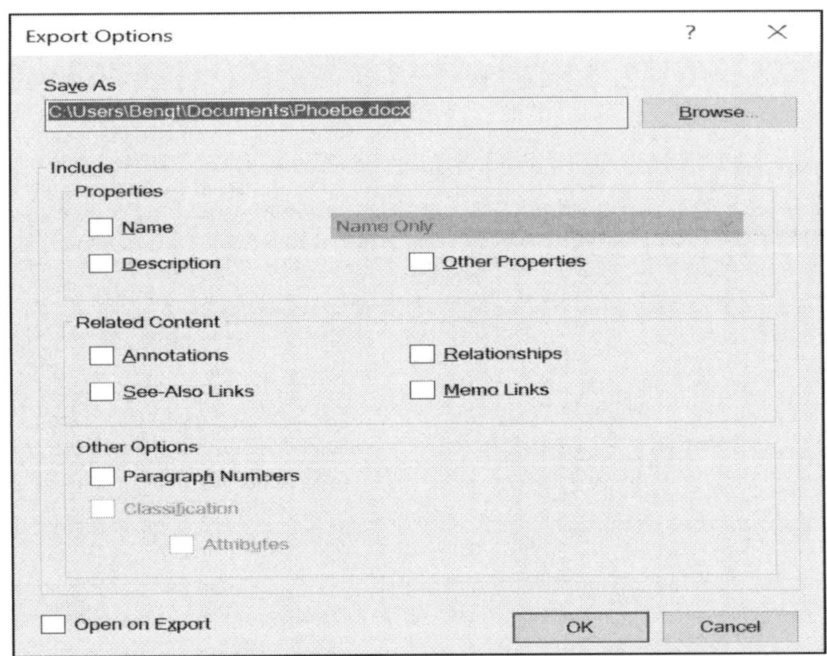

4 Select the options that you want. Confirm with **[OK]**.
5 Decide file name, location, and file type: .DOCX, .DOC, .RTF, .TXT, .PDF, or .HTML. Confirm with **[Save]**.

Remember, coding made on text items cannot be transferred when a Source Item is exported.

External Items

For any number of reasons, you may wish to refer to external items outside of your NVivo project (i.e., a web site, a file too large or a file type that is incompatible). NVivo allows you to create external items that can act as placeholders or links.

Creating an External Item

1. Select the **Data\\Externals** folder or its subfolder.
2. Click on any empty space in the List View.
3. Right-click and select **New External...**
   or **[Ctrl]** + **[Shift]** + **[N]**.

The **New External** dialog box appears:

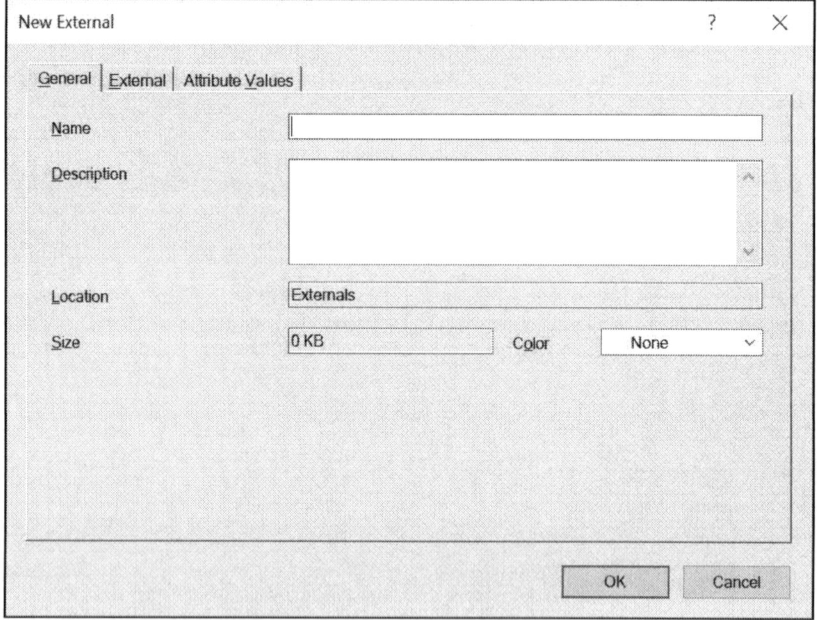

4. Type name (compulsory) and description (optional), then go to the **External** tab.

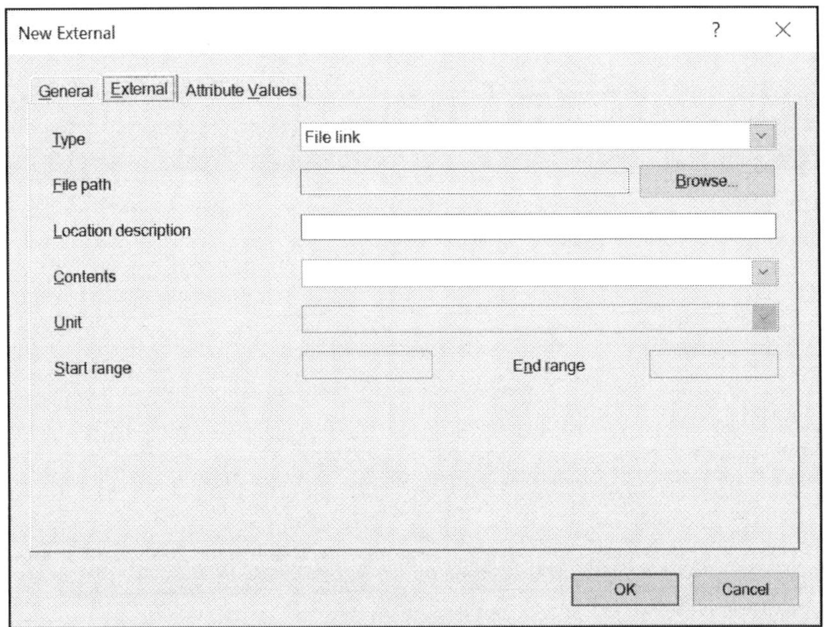

5. At **Type** select *File link* and then use the **[Browse...]** button to find the target file. Alternatively, at Type select *Web link* and type or paste the URL in the text box below. For non-digital items select *Other*.
6. At **Location description** type the location of the external file, like 'my computer' or physical place.
7. At **Contents** the options are *Audio*, *Image*, *Printed Document* or *Video*.

When you select Printed Document the **Unit** options are Chapter, Page, Paragraph, Section, Sentence, and Verse.

8. At **Start range** and **End range** you can put the first and the last page of an external document, like this:

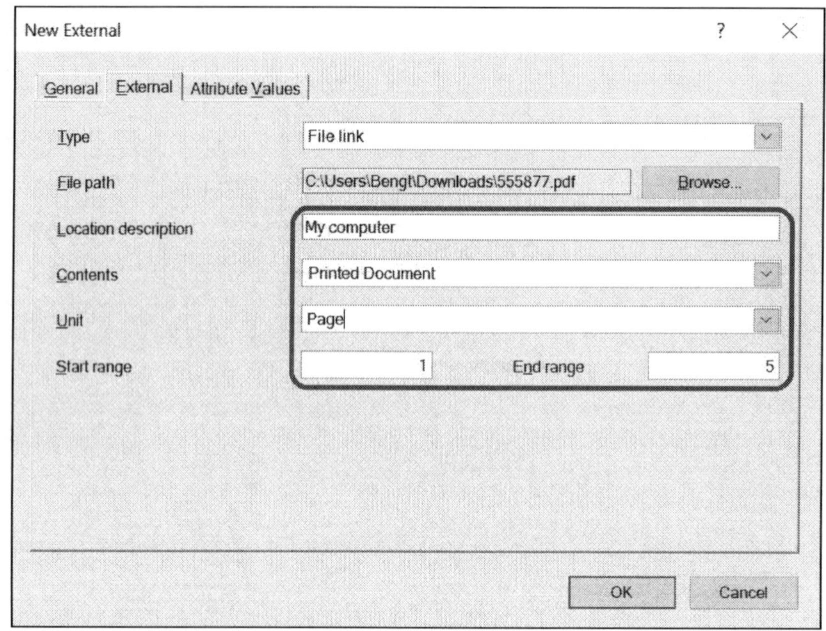

9 Confirm with **[OK]**.

Two new context dependent Ribbon menus, **External** and **Edit**, have now opened and is opened each time a new external is created.

The result can look like this. You can copy and paste text from an external PDF-document or text or image from an external Word-document. The external source item is not write-protected when created:

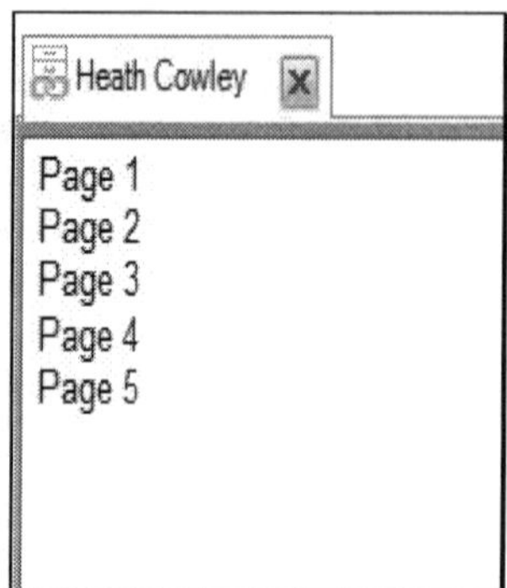

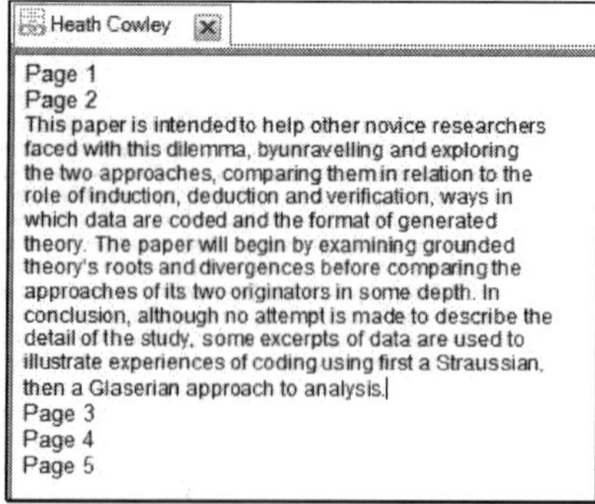

The text you enter or paste can be coded but not the content of the external file.

This is a typical List View of some external items:

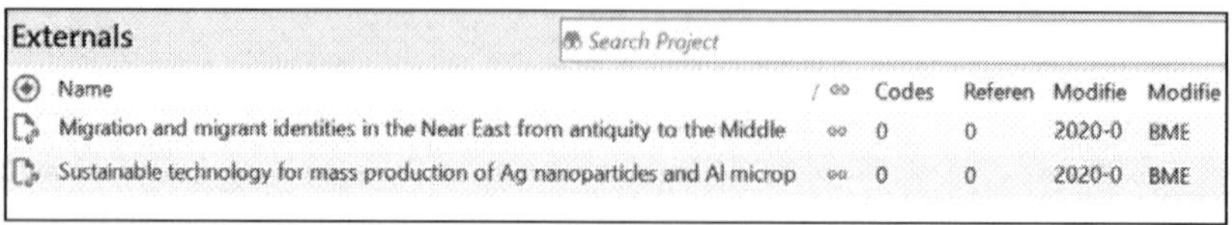

Opening an External Item

External items act identical to internal items within NVivo's Sources folder: they can contain text and that text can be edited and coded. To open an external item for viewing or editing:

1 Select the **Data\\Externals** folder or its subfolder.
2 Select the external item that you want to open.
3 Go to **Home | Item → 'Open' → Open External...**
  or right-click and select **Open External...**
  or double-click on the external item
  or **[Ctrl]** + **[Shift]** + **[O]**.

A new context dependent Ribbon menu, **External**, has now opened and is opened each time a Document is opened.

Remember, NVivo can only open one external item at a time, but several items can stay open simultaneously.

Opening an External Source

Unlike internal items, external items are necessarily linked to external sources, which can be opened through NVivo:

1 Select the **Data\\Externals** folder or its subfolder.
2 Select the external item in that has a link to the external file or URL that you want to open.
3 Go to **Home | Item → 'Open' → Open External File...**
  or right-click and select **Open External File...**

Editing an External Source or Link

1 Select the **Data\\Externals** folder or its subfolder.
2 Select the external item that you want to edit.
3 Go to **Home | Item → 'Properties' → External Properties...**
  or right-click and select **External Properties...**
  or **[Ctrl]** + **[Shift]** + **[P]**.

The **External Properties** dialog box appears.

4 Select the **External** tab and if you want to link to a new target file use **[Browse...]**. If you want to modify a web link change the URL.

Exporting an External Item

Similar to internal items, external items can be exported. However, the linked external file or the web link is not included in the exported item, only the external item text contents are exported.

1 Select the **Data\\Externals** folder or its subfolder.
2 Select the external item or items that you want to export.
3 Go to **Share | Export → Export**
  or right-click and select **Export → Export External...**
  or **[Ctrl]** + **[Shift]** + **[E]**.

The **Export Options** dialog box appears.

4. Select the options that you want. Confirm with [**OK**].
5. Decide file name, location, and file type: .DOCX, .DOC, .RTF, .TXT, .PDF, or .HTML. Confirm with [**Save**].

5. EDITING TEXT IN NVIVO

Whether you import a text document or create a new one, NVivo contains most of the functions of modern word processing software. Notwithstanding the fact that text document files are often imported, understanding how to edit text in NVivo is useful. Aside from its ability to edit existing source documents, you can use NVivo's word processing functionality to compose Memos, Externals, and Framework Matrix summaries.

Formatting Text

Remember, each time a Source Item is opened it is Read-Only. Therefore, click **Edit** in the top position of the Detail View or go to **Document | Edit** or **[Ctrl] + [E]**).

A new context dependent Ribbon menu, **Edit**, has now opened and is opened each time *an edit mode* is activated.

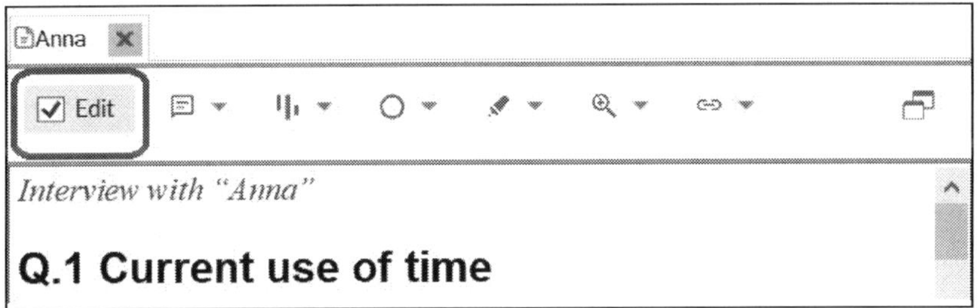

Selecting the whole document:

1 Position the cursor anywhere in the document.
2 Go to **Edit | Find & Select → Select All** or **[Ctrl] + [A]**.

You can also select any paragraph like his:

1 Position the cursor in the current paragraph.
2 Go to **Edit | Find & Select → Select Paragraph** or triple-click with the mouse.

> **Tip: Selecting Text**
> Select a passage of text by holding left-click and hover over it. Double left-clicking on a single word highlights just that word. And did you know that triple left-clicking on a single word selects the whole paragraph? Both of these shortcuts can be when coding.

Changing Fonts, Font Style, Size, and Color

1 Select the text you want to format.

2 Go to **Edit** | **'Format'** where these options appear:

3 Select the options you need with immediate effect.

Selecting a Style

1 Position the cursor in the paragraph you want to format.

2 Go to **Edit** | **'Format'** and select from the list of styles.

3 Confirm with [**OK**].

Resetting to previous style is possible as long as the project has not been saved after the last change:

1 Use the Undo function of the Quick Access Toolbar or [**Ctrl**] + [**Z**].

Aligning Paragraphs

Selecting Alignments

1 Position the cursor in the paragraph you want to format.

2 Go to **Edit** | **'Format'** and select from the list of alignment options.

Selecting Indentation

1 Position the cursor in the paragraph for which you want to change the indentation.

2 Go to **Edit** | **'Format'** and select increased or decreased indentation.

Creating Lists

1 Select the paragraphs that you want to make as a list.

2 Go to **Edit** and select a bulleted or numbered list.

Finding, Replacing and Navigating Text

Finding Text

1 Open a document and apply **Edit** mode.

2 Go to **Document** | **Find → Find...** or [**Ctrl**] + [**F**].

The **Find Content** dialog box appears:

3 Type a search word, then click **[Find Next]**.

The **Style** option makes it possible to search in a certain style.

Please note the option *Match case* which makes it possible to exactly match *UPPERCASE* or *lowercase* and the option *Find whole word* which switches off the free text search.

Searching and Replacing

1 Open a document.

2 Go to **Edit | Find & Select → Replace** or **[Ctrl]** + **[H]**.

The **Replace Content** dialog box appears:

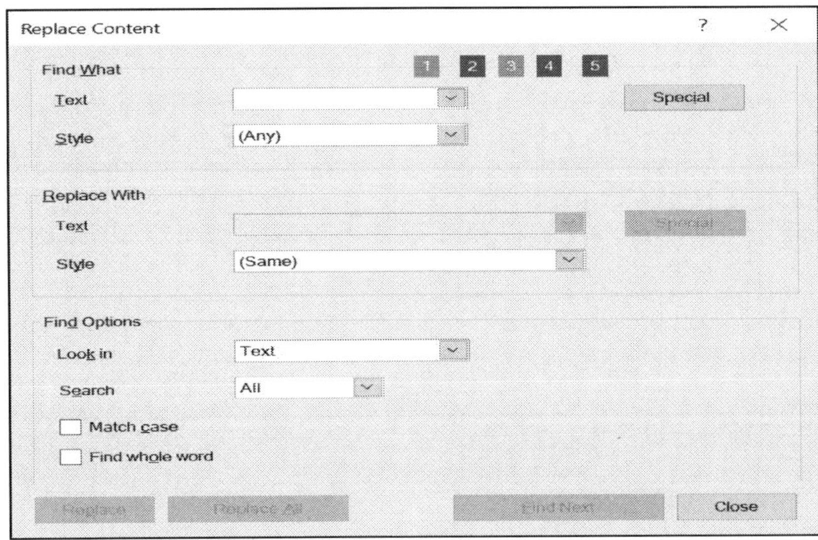

3 Type a find word and a replace word, then [**Replace**] or [**Replace All**].

The option Style near **Find What** makes it possible limit the search from All to any given style and the option Style near **Replace With** makes it possible to replace the found word as well as change the style from Same to any given style.

Please notice the option *Match case* which makes it possible to exactly match *UPPERCASE* and *lowercase* and the option *Find whole word* which switches off the double-sided auto truncation.

Spell Checking

NVivo comes with built-in dictionaries for English (UK), English (US), French, German, Portuguese and Spanish. If your source materials use specialized terms or abbreviations that are not in the built-in dictionary, you can add these words to a custom dictionary. Each of these languages can have its own custom dictionary.

When you spell check a source, NVivo flags words that are not in the built-in or custom dictionary. You can decide whether you want to ignore flagged words, correct them or add them to the custom dictionary.

You can spell check source content when the source is open in edit mode. You can spell check:

- Documents
- Memos
- Audio and video transcripts (the Content column only)
- Picture logs (the Content column only)
- Framework Matrices
- Externals

You can also spell check Annotations in any type of source, including non-editable source types such as Datasets and PDFs. You can also spell check annotations displayed in Detail View of a Code.

You can set your spell check preferences in **Application Options** (see page 45)—for example, you can choose whether or not to flag all uppercase words (e.g. USA) as spelling mistakes.

1 Open a Source Item in Edit mode.
2 Go to **Edit | Spelling**
or [**F7**].

The **Spelling: <Language>** dialog box appears:

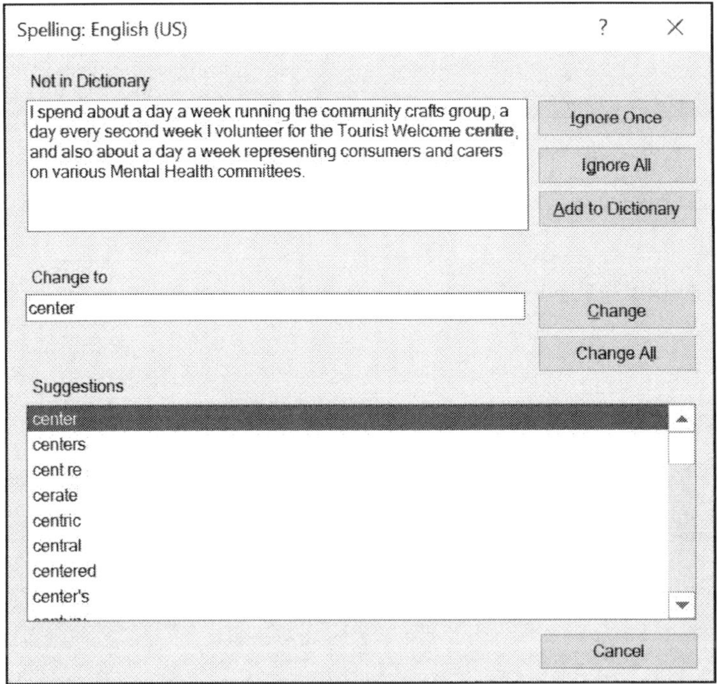

The meanings of these buttons are:

[Ignore Once]	Ignore and move to next
[Ignore All]	Ignore all instances in the whole source and move to next
[Add To Dictionary]	The word is added to the custom dictionary and will not be flagged from now on
[Change]	Changes the spelling to the highlighted suggested word
[Change All]	Changes the spelling to the highlighted suggested word at all instances in the whole source and move to next
[Cancel]	Stops the spell checking

When you want to spell check any Annotation, open the annotations window and keep the cursor within the annotation. If you have more than one annotation in the same source the spell checker will run through all of them. The source itself need not be in edited mode when you spell check an annotation.

For more on settings for content languages and dictionaries (see page 45).

Go to a Certain Location

'Go To' options vary depending on the source type (e.g., Documents, PDFs, Datasets, Pictures, and Audio or Video). Possible Go To options include Paragraph, Character Position, See Also Link and Annotation (above), as well as Dataset Record ID, Log Row, Page, Source, Time, and Transcript Row.

1 Go to **Edit | Find and Select → Go To...**
or **[Ctrl]** + **[G]**.

The **Go To** dialog box appears:

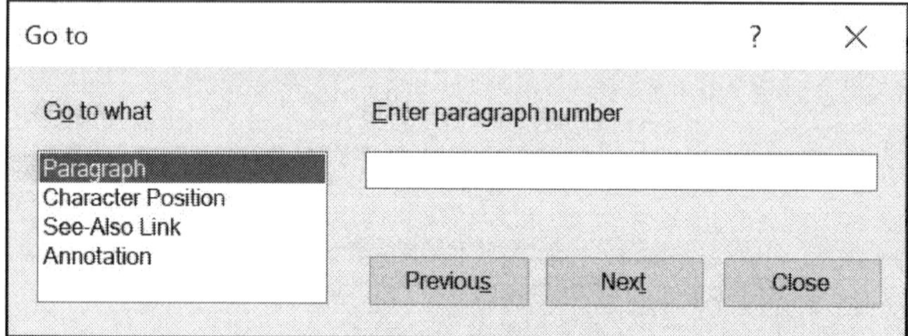

2 Select option at **Go to what** and when required, a value.
3 Click on **[Previous]** or **[Next]**.

Creating a Table

1 Position the cursor where you want to create a table.
2 Go to **Edit | Insert → Insert Text Table...**

The **Insert Text Table** dialog box appears:

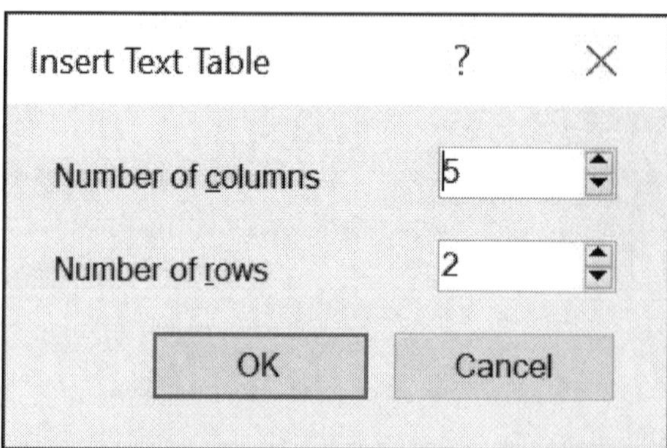

3 Select number of columns and number of rows in the table.
4 Confirm with **[OK]**.

Inserting Page Breaks, Images, Dates, and Symbols

Inserting a Page Break

1 Position the cursor where you want to insert a page break.
2 Go to **Edit | Insert → Insert Page Break**.

A page break is indicated with a dotted line on the screen.

Inserting an Image

1 Position the cursor where you want to insert an image.
2 Go to **Edit | Insert → Insert Image...**
3 Select an image with the file browser. Only .BMP, .JPG and .GIF file types can be inserted.
4 Confirm with [**Open**].

Inserting Date and Time

1 Position the cursor where you want to insert date and time.
2 Go to **Edit | Insert → Insert Date/Time** or [**Ctrl**] + [**Shift**] + [**T**].

This command can also be used in any Description box.

Inserting a Symbol

1 Position the cursor where you want to insert a symbol.
2 Go to **Edit | Insert → Insert Symbol...** or [**Ctrl**] + [**Shift**] + [**Y**]
3 Select a symbol from the **Insert Symbol** dialog box, confirm with [**Insert**].

Zooming

1 Open a document.
2 Go to **Document | Zoom → Zoom...**

The **Zoom** dialog box appears:

> **Tip:** Our preferred method of zooming in NVivo is [**Ctrl**] + mouse wheel. [**Ctrl**] + moving the mouse wheel forward allows zooming in; [**Ctrl**] + moving the mouse wheel backward allows zooming

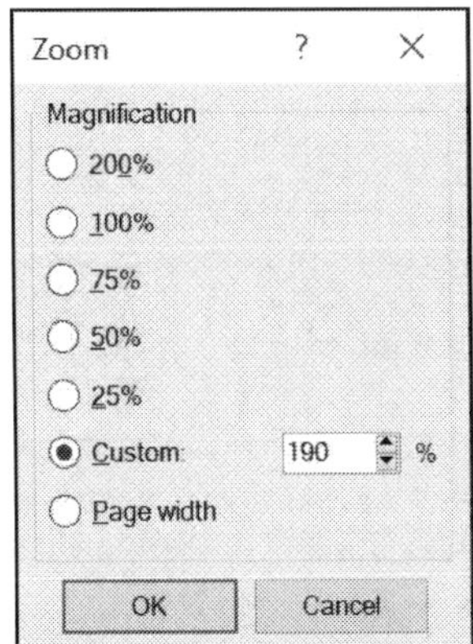

3 Select a certain magnification and confirm with [**OK**].

Alternatively, you may also use the Zoom-slider in the status bar below on the screen.

Alternatively, **[Ctrl]** + your mouse wheel allows zooming in or out. You can also zoom in or out in predetermined steps:

1 Open a document.
2 Go to **Document | View | Zoom → Zoom In** or **Document | View | Zoom → Zoom Out**.

Print Previewing

1 Open a document.
2 Go to **File → Print → Print Preview**.

The **Print Options** dialog box appears:

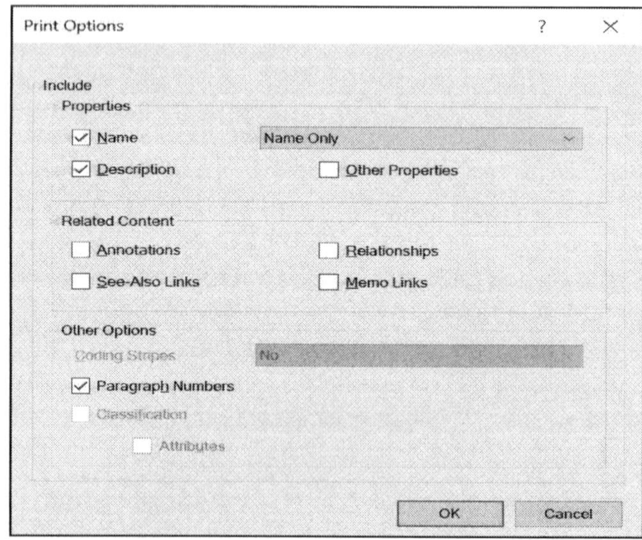

3 Select option for the preview.
4 Confirm with **[OK]**.

As you can see from the dialog box we have selected the options Name, Description, and Paragraph Numbers. This can be of great importance when working in a team. Also the page breaks are shown here and on screen only hard page breaks are shown.

result can look like this:

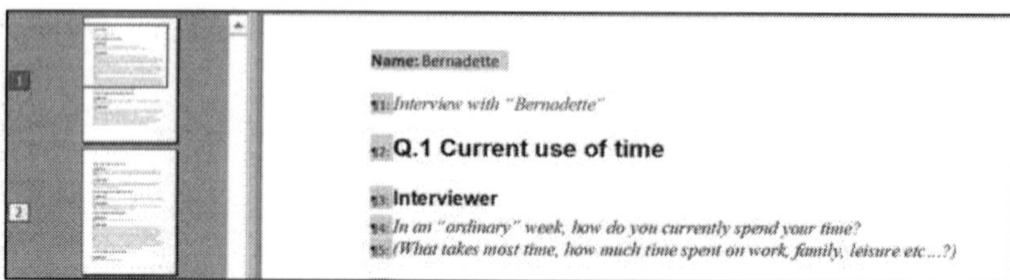

Name: Bernadette
Interview with "Bernadette"
Q.1 Current use of time
Interviewer
In an "ordinary" week, how do you currently spend your time?
(What takes most time, how much time spent on work, family, leisure etc...?)

In the Print Preview window there are numerous possibilities to navigate, zoom, and change the view. The thumbnails can be hidden with **View → Thumbnails** which is a toggling function. Print all pages with **File → Print** or **[Ctrl]** + **[P]**.

Printing a Document

1 Open a document.
2 Go to **File → Print → Print...**
  or **[Ctrl]** + **[P]**.

The **Print Options** dialog box now shows.

3 Select options for the printout.
4 Confirm with **[OK]**.

Printing with Coding Stripes

When you need to print a document with coding stripes (see page 193), you must first display the coding stripes on the screen. Then you need to select the option *Coding Stripes* in the **Print Options** dialog box:

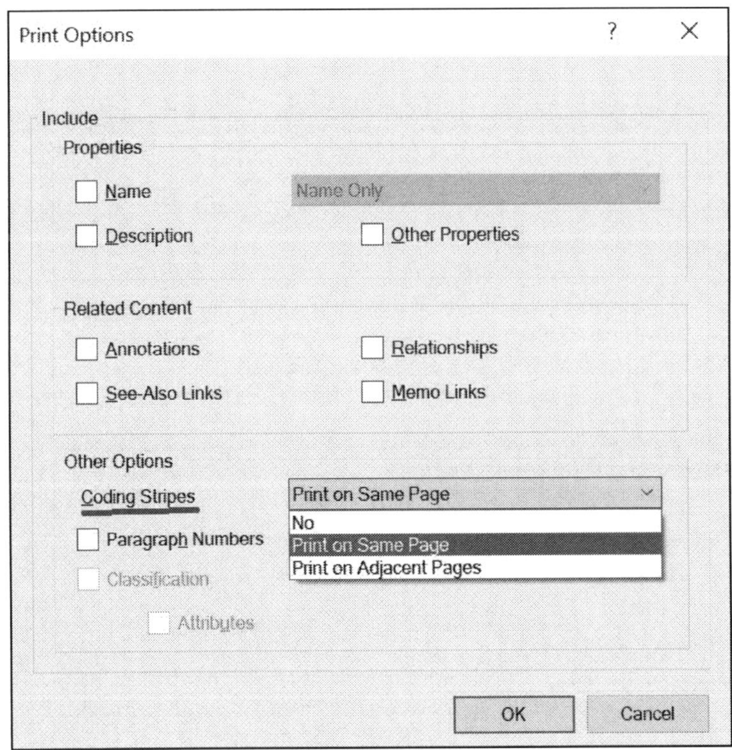

> **Tip:** NVivo is powerful software for organizing and analyzing text documents, but it is weak as a standalone word processor. A best practice we recommend is creating a document in Word (or your preferred word processing software) and then importing the text into NVivo.

The print options are: *Print on Same Page*:

Or *Print on Adjacent Pages*:

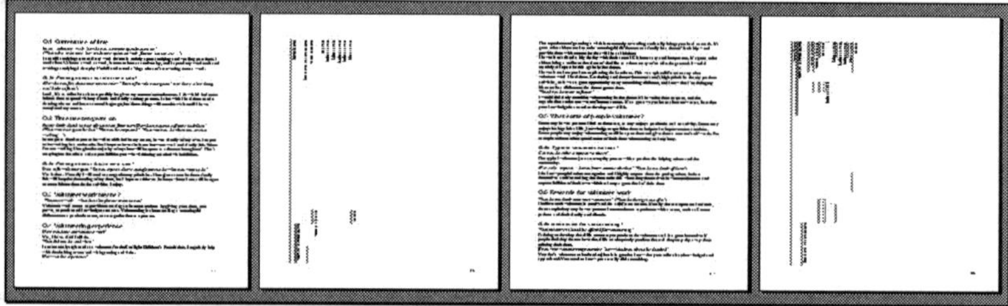

Page Setup

1 Open a document.
2 Open **File → Print → Print Preview**.
3 Click **[OK]**.
4 Go to **File → Page Setup...**

The **Page Setup** dialog box appears:

Tip: Make it a PDF!
If you find NVivo is mishandling your formatting, try converting your text document to a PDF. NVivo is also a powerful tool for handling PDF files with special formatting, like multiple columns. What about if you want to import a PowerPoint presentation into NVivo? Make it a PDF!

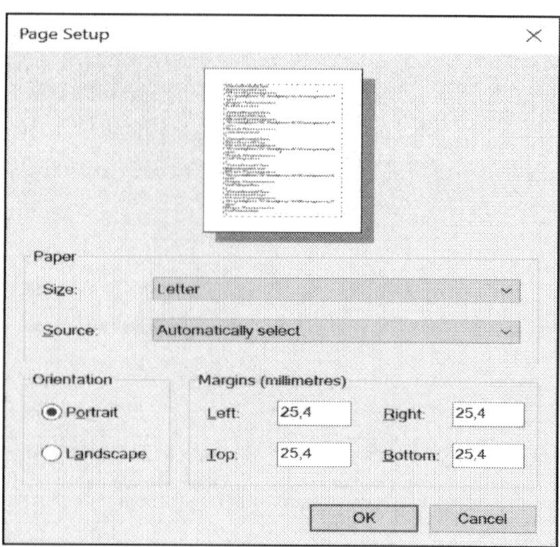

5 Decide the settings for paper size, orientation and margins, then **[OK]**.

Limitations in Editing Documents in NVivo

NVivo has certain limitations in creating advanced formatted documents.

Some of these limitations are:

- NVivo cannot merge two documents by any other means than copying/cutting and pasting text.
- It is difficult to format an image (change size, orientation, and move).
- It is difficult to format a table.
- It is difficult to format a paragraph (hanging indent, first line different, line spacing).
- Copying from a Word document to NVivo loses some paragraph formatting.
- Footnotes and endnotes in a Word document are lost after importing to NVivo. Word footnotes can however be manually replaced by NVivo Annotations (see page 127).
- Headers and footers are lost after import to NVivo.
- Page numbers are lost after import to NVivo but may be replaced by Insert page field in Word.
- Bookmarks and Comments are lost after import to NVivo.
- Field codes do not exist in NVivo and these are converted to text after importing to NVivo.
- NVivo cannot apply several columns, except when used in a table. When a multi-column document is imported it is displayed on the screen as single column. The multi-column design is restored when such document is exported or printed.

Often it is preferable to create a document in Word and then import to NVivo. Simply because Word is a dedicated and advanced word processor.

Tip: Formatting your Word documents for NVivo:

1 Give your Word documents meaningful file-names. If you write an interview per document, it is advantageous if the file-name is the name of the interviewee (real name or a code name). After importing to NVivo, both the Source Item and the Case will be given this name. Put all interviews of same kind in the same folder, and consider the sort order. If you are using numbers in the file names then you should apply a similar series of names, with the same number of characters, like 001, 002, .. 011, 012, .. 101, 102, etc.

2 Use Word's paragraph styles to enable autocoding. For structured interviews you should create document templates with subject headings and paragraph styles.

3 Whenever needed you can use Find and Replace and create headings with appropriate paragraph styles.

4 Divide the text into logical, appropriate paragraphs using the hard carriage return (ENTER on your keyboard). This facilitates the coding that can take place based on a keyword and the command 'Spread Coding to Surrounding Paragraph'. Remember triple-clicking!

6. HANDLING PDF ITEMS

Of particular interest to researchers who are conducting literature reviews, PDF documents will retain the original layout after import to NVivo and appear exactly as they were opened in Acrobat Reader. These PDFs can be coded, linked and searched as any other Source Item. One limitation is that PDF text cannot be edited nor can hyperlinks be created. Hyperlinks made in the original PDF, however, will function normally in NVivo.

Apart from bibliographic data with PDF articles downloaded from EndNote, web pages and Evernote files can now be imported into NVivo as PDF sources. This new feature allows web pages and Evernote files to be organized, coded and queried the same as any imported .PDF file (See Chapters 14, 19 and 21).

Importing PDF Items

1 Go to **Import | Files**.
Default folder is **Data\\Files** or its currently open subfolder.
Go to 4.

alternatively

1 Select the **Data\\Files** folder or its subfolder.
2 Go to **Import | Files**.
Go to 4.

alternatively

2 Click on any empty space in the List View.
3 Right-click and select **Import Items...**
or **[Ctrl]** + **[Shift]** + **[I]**.
Go to 4.

alternatively

3 Drag and drop your file's icon from an outside folder into its new folder. This option imports directly and leaves out the **Import Files** dialog box.

In all other cases, the **Import Files** dialog box is shown:

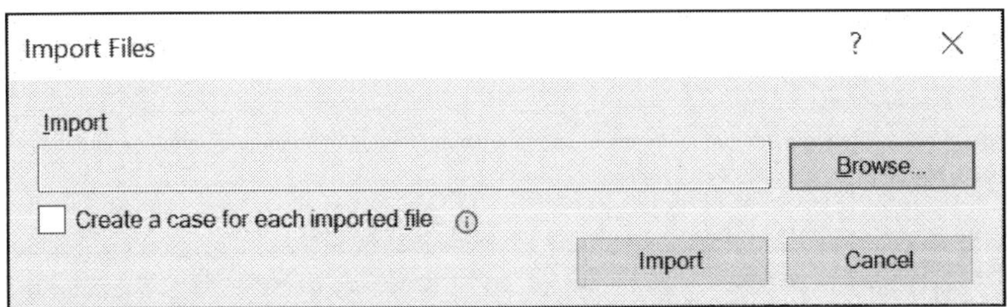

4 The [**Browse**] button gives access to a file-browser and you can select one or several PDFs for a batch import. To select multiple documents, use [**Shift**] + left click or if alternatively [**Ctrl**] + [**A**].

5 When the PDFs have been selected, confirm with [**Open**].

When you have selected *Create a case for each imported file* the dialog box offers several options:

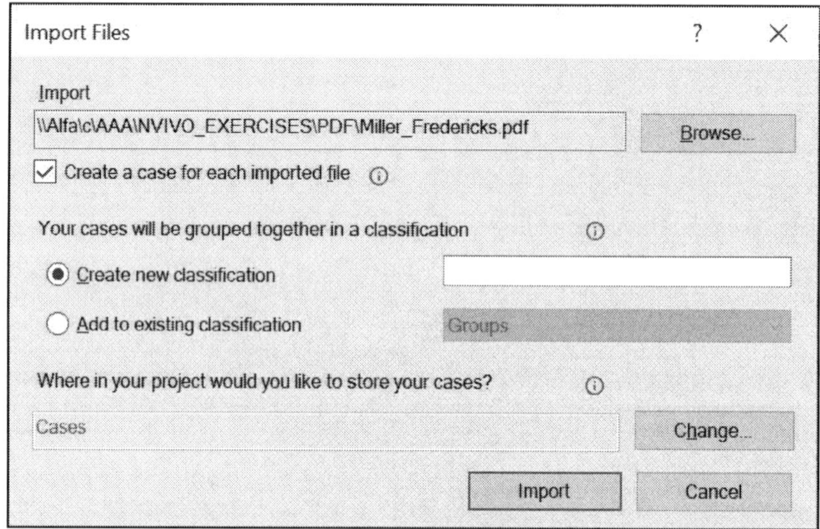

Each Source Item will be coded at a Case with the same name as the imported PDF file and located in a folder or under a parent Case that has been selected. Also, you must assign the Cases to a Classification when importing (see Chapter 12, Classifications).

6 Confirm the import with [**Import**].

In this instance we are describing how to create a Case for each imported File. Therefore, we refer to Case Classifications and not as you might expect File Classifications which serves another purpose, see Chapter 12, Classifications.

When only one PDF has been selected the **PDF Properties** dialog box appears:

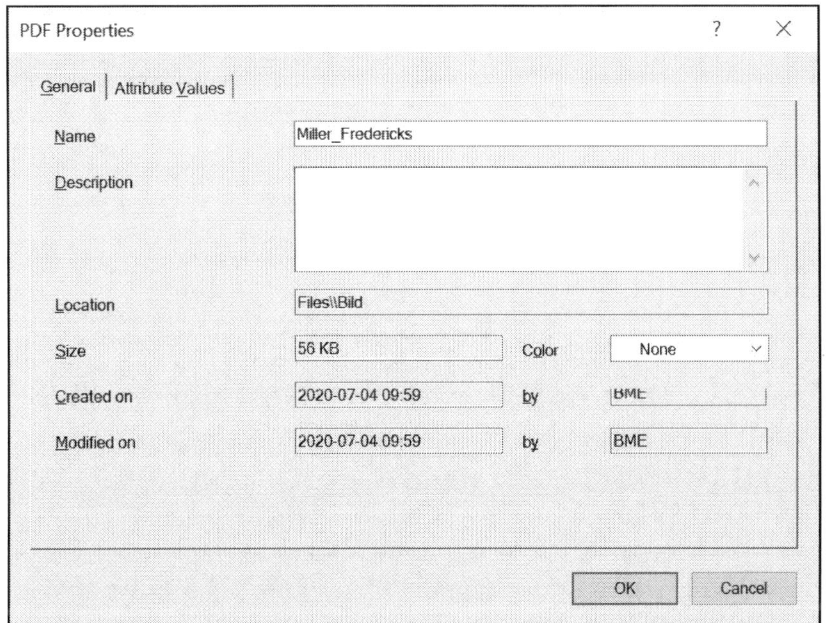

This dialog box will make it possible to modify the name of the PDF item and optionally add a description.

7 Confirm with **[OK]**.

Opening a PDF Item

1 Select the **Data/Files** folder or its subfolder.

2 Select the PDF in the List View that you want to open.

3 Go to **Home | Item → 'Open' → Open PDF...** or right-click and select **Open PDF...** or double-click on the PDF in the List View or **[Ctrl]** + **[Shift]** + **[O]**.

Please note, that you can only open one PDF at a time, but several PDFs can stay open simultaneously.

A new context dependent Ribbon menu, **PDF**, has now opened and is opened each time a PDF item is opened.

Sticky Notes in PDFs are very useful. You can create those with Acrobat Pro but also with recent versions of EndNote. Unfortunately, NVivo cannot open these Notes. NVivo applies instead its link-tools, as a standard for all types of source items. Annotations serve the same purpose as the Sticky Notes.

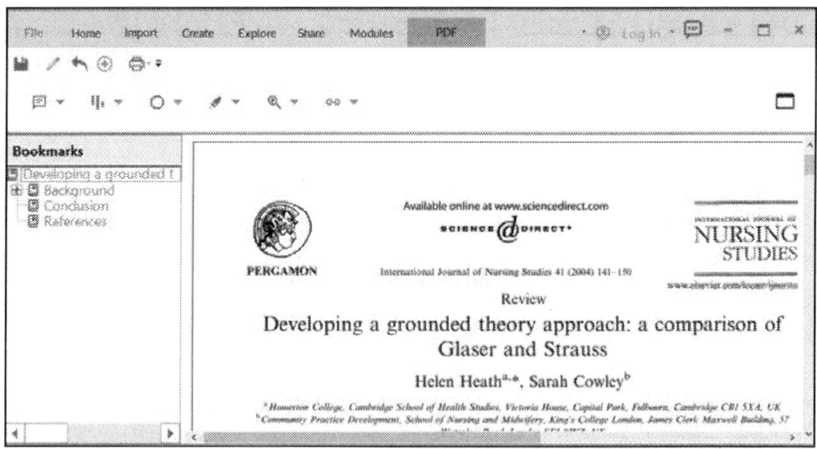

In this view you can code, link (See Also links, Annotations, Memo links) and search and query as with any other Source Item.

Selection Tools for PDF Items

There are two different selection tools for PDFs, Text or Region. Text Selection Mode is used for selecting any text in the PDF and is made as for any other selections within a Source Item. Selection Mode Text is default and is always active each time you open a PDF item. Scanned text documents will not inherently allow selectable text; ensure you use software like Adobe Acrobat to recognize scanned text (OCR, Optical Character Recognition) so text selection is possible in NVivo.

Region Selection Mode is used when you need to select an image, a table or any graph that is in the PDF document. When you need to select an image, a table or any graph:

1. Open a PDF Source Item.
2. Go to **PDF | Region**
   or point at the PDF right-click and select **Selection Mode → Region**.
3. With the mouse-pointer (which is now a cross) you define two diagonal corners of any rectangular area. Any text within such area will be interpreted as image not text.

To return to Selection Mode Text:

1. Go to **PDF | Text**
   or point at the PDF, right-click and select **Selection Mode → Text**.

Selections made can now be used when coding and linking. Only hyperlinks cannot be created in a PDF Source Item. See page 195 on how a Code that codes a PDF item is shown.

Exporting a PDF Item

Like most NVivo items, PDF sources can also be exported:

1. Select the **Data\\Files** folder or its subfolder.
2. Select the PDF or PDFs in the List View that you want to export.
3. Go to **Share | Export → Export**
   or right-click and select **Export → Export PDF...**
   or **[Ctrl]** + **[Shift]** + **[E]**.

Please also study page 248 regarding PDF items classified with Bibliographic ID created by a reference handling software and export of bibliographic data.

> **Tip: Working with PDF text documents.** NVivo's functionality to work with PDF text documents can be a dream come true for researchers working on literature reviews. While many academic articles can be downloaded as functional PDF text documents, book chapters or other types of print material must often be scanned by researchers themselves. We recommend Adobe Acrobat Pro or ABBYY FineReader as software that will take scanned documents and recognize their text (a process called OCR, Optical Character Recognition).

The **Export Options** dialog box appears:

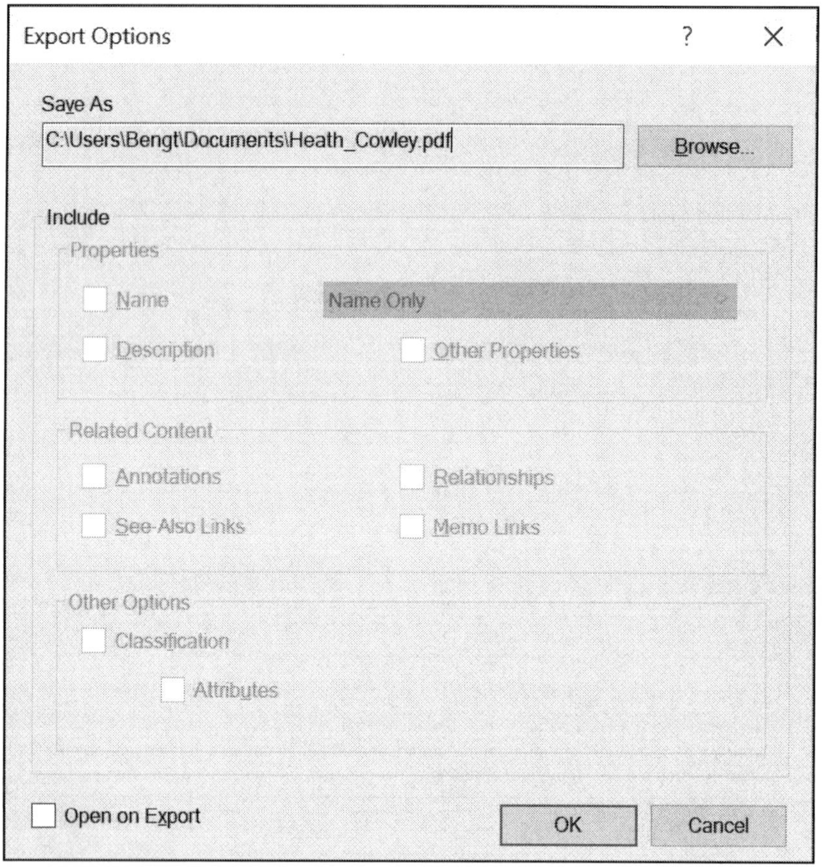

Export Options ? ×

Save As

C:\Users\Bengt\Documents\Heath_Cowley.pdf Browse...

Include

Properties

Name Name Only

Description Other Properties

Related Content

Annotations Relationships

See-Also Links Memo Links

Other Options

Classification

Attributes

Open on Export OK Cancel

4 Select the options that you want. Confirm with **[OK]**.
5 Decide file name, location, and file type: .PDF or .HTML. The PDF file type is only available when none of the above options have been selected. Finally confirm with [**Save**].

Please note, that any coding made on such items cannot be transferred when the Source Item is exported.

Tip: Using Word documents instead of PDFs. In our experience it is easier to work with Word files (.doc or .docx) than working with PDFs in NVivo. While it is not always possible to save your PDF files as Word documents, recent versions of Adobe Acrobat (X or XI) allow for PDF files to easily be saved as fully formatted Word files. Furthermore, Microsoft Word 2013 will allow for PDF files to be opened and saved as fully formatted Word files. *Also, when you scan documents solely with the purpose of importing them to NVivo then create them as Word documents, which is the preferred file type.*

Importing emails

NVivo supports importing emails directly from Microsoft Outlook. You can use the ribbon menu or simply drag and drop directly from Outlook. Emails are imported as PDF files. Emails from Outlook has the file type .MSG and includes email metadata such as sender, received date, etc. These data are imported as attributes and values under the File Classification *Email Message.*

1 Go to **Import | Notes & Email | Outlook...**
Default folder is **Data/Files** or its currently opened subfolder.
Go to 4.

alternatively

1 Select the **Data\\Files** folder or its subfolder.
2 Go to **Import | Notes & Email | Outlook...**
Go to 4.

alternatively

2 Click on any empty space in the List View.
3 Right-click and select **Import from → Import from Outlook...**
or **[Ctrl]** + **[Shift]** + **[I]**.
Go to 4.

alternatively

3 Drag and drop your file's icon from an outside folder into its new folder. This option imports directly and leaves out the **Import Files** dialog box.

In all other cases, the **Import Files** dialog box is shown:

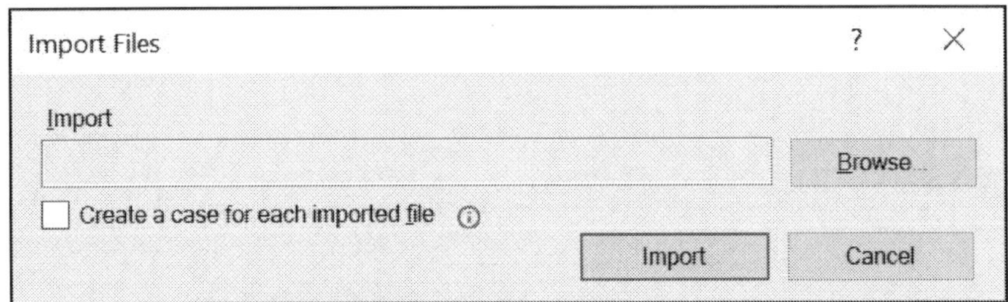

4 The **[Browse]** button gives access to a file-browser and you can select one or several emails for a batch import.
5 When the emails have been selected, confirm with **[OK]**.

When you want to import an attachment to an email open the email in Outlook and drag the attachment to the List View of the chosen source folder. Depending on the attached file type the **Properties** dialog will open.

7. HANDLING AUDIO- AND VIDEO-ITEMS

So far, we have mainly focused on text data, but NVivo has a variety of useful functions for researchers interested in working with audio and video data. NVivo provides two primary functions for handling audio and video source data. First, audio and video data can be imported into NVivo as a data source, which can be organized, coded and queried similar to text source data. But second, and perhaps more importantly for some researchers, NVivo contains a full functioning transcription utility for importing, creating, and exporting text transcripts. Instead of outsourcing transcription to third-party vendors or spending funds on specialized transcription software, NVivo gives researchers a very useful option for transcribing their own audio and video files within the software.

NVivo can import the following audio formats: .MP3, .M4A, .WAV, and .WMA and the following video formats: .MPG, .MPEG, .MPE, .MP4, .MOV, .QT, .3GP, .MTS, and .M2TS. Several of these media formats are new to NVivo to allow users to import more media content form their smart phones. Media files less than 40 MB can be imported and embedded in you NVivo project.

Files larger than 40 MB must be stored as external files. Importantly, external files can be handled the same way as an audio or video embedded item. NVivo contains an on-board audio and video player for external files, so even though a large video file may not be embedded in your project, you can still view, transcribe, code, and query the file using the NVivo player. But remember, if you open your NVivo project on another computer the external file references will no longer work, unless you assemble copies of those files in identically named file folders on the new computer you are using.

Even the not embedded media items are located under the **Data\\Files** folder or its subfolders as they are managed in all respects as if they were embedded.

The threshold value for audio and video files that can be stored as external files can be reduced for all new projects with **File → Options...**, select the **Audio/Video** tab, section **Default for new projects** (see page 43). To adjust values for the current project, use **File → Info → Project Properties...**, select the **Audio/Video** tab, section *Settings* (see page 56). To adjust for the current Audio/Video item, go to **Home | Item → 'Properties' → Audio/Video Properties** and the dialog box **Audio/Video Properties** and the **Audio/Video** tab (see page 98).

Importing Media Items

Importing media files follows a similar, simple protocol as importing text files or PDFs:

1 Go to **Import | Files**.
Default folder is **Data\\Files** or its currently open subfolder.
Go to 4.

alternatively

1 Select the **Data\\Files** folder or its subfolder.
2 Go to **Import | Files**.
Go to 4.

alternatively

2 Click on any empty space in the List View.
3 Right-click and select **Import Items...**
or **[Ctrl]** + **[Shift]** + **[I]**.
Go to 4.

alternatively

3 Drag and drop your file's icon from an outside folder into its new folder. This option imports directly and leaves out the **Import Files** dialog box.

In all other cases the **Import Files** dialog box appears:

4 The **[Browse...]** button gives access to a file browser and you can select one or several media files for a batch import.
5 When the file or files have been chosen, confirm with **[Import]**.

> Importing media files is sometimes not possible caused by the absence in your computer of an uptodate device called *Codec*. Often the problem is solved by upgrading with an appropriate Codec package. If so contact us for assistance.

When you have selected *Create a case for each imported file* the dialog box offers several options:

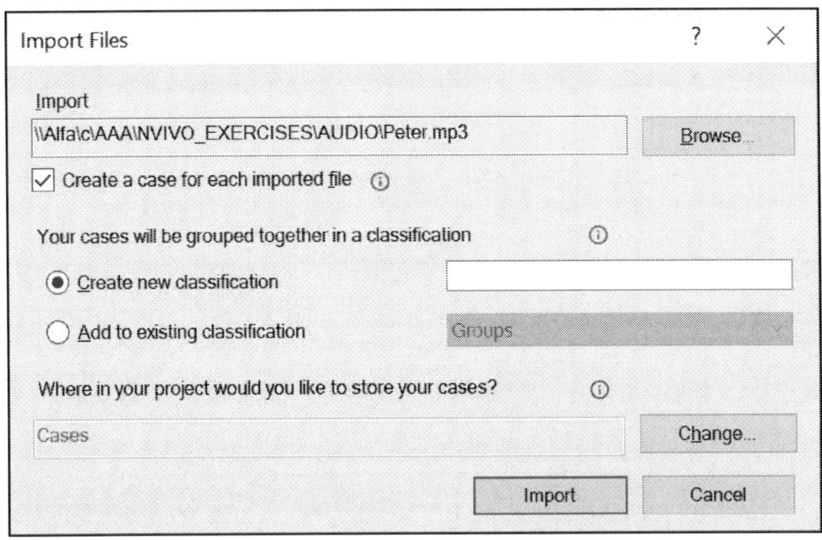

Where in your project would you like to store you cases? Each Source Item will be coded at a Case with the same name as the imported file and located under in a folder or under a parent Case that has been selected with **[Change...]**. Also you must assign the Cases to a Case Classification when importing (see Chapter 12, Classifications).

6 Confirm the import with **[Import]**.

When only one media file is imported the **Audio/Video Properties** dialog box is shown:

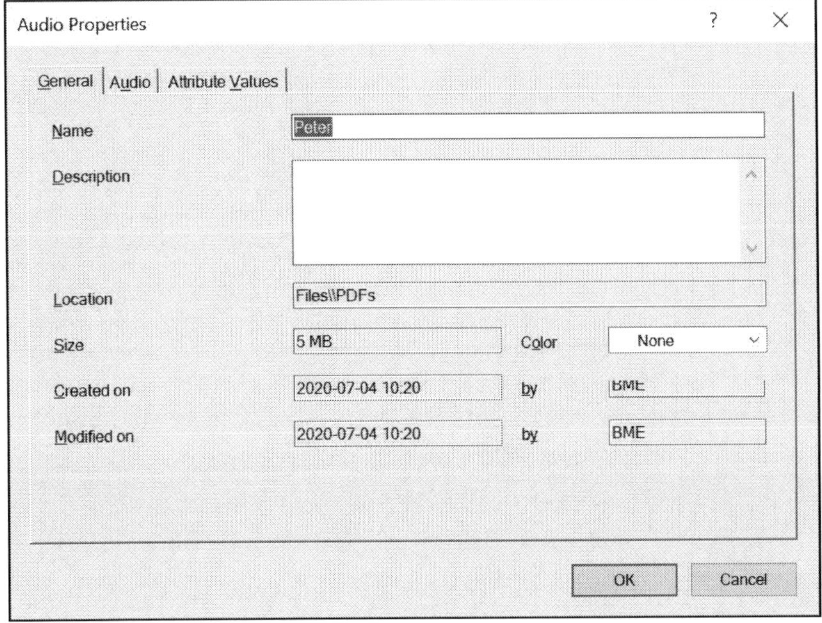

This dialog box will make it possible to modify the name of the item and optionally add a description.

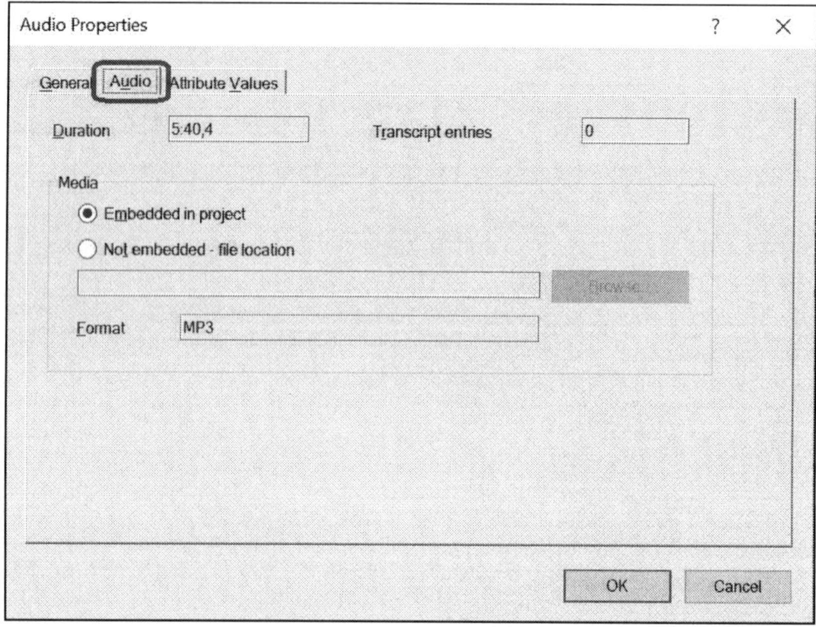

When the **Audio/Video** tab has been chosen you can let the audio file be stored as an external file even if the size is below the limit for embedding. After an audio- or video file has been imported you can change the properties from embedded item to external storage and vice versa by using **Audio (Video) Properties**. An embedded item cannot exceed 40 MB.

7 Confirm with [**OK**].

Creating a New Media Item

Instead of importing an audio or video item, a new media item can also be created:

1. Select the **Data\\File** folder or its subfolder and point at an empty place in the List.
2. Right-click and select **New File → New Audio.../New Video...**

The **New Audio/New Video** dialog box appears:

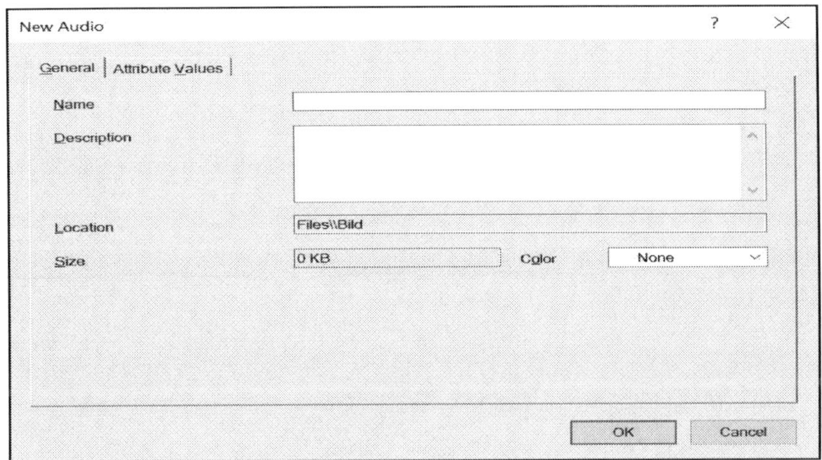

3. Type name (compulsory) and a description (optional), then [**OK**].

Two new context dependent Ribbon menus, **Audio/Video** and **Edit**, have now opened and is opened each time a new media item is created.

When you create a new media item it initially has no media file or transcript. Instead these pieces of information can be imported separately. From the open media item, go to **Edit | Media Content** or **Edit | Import Rows** (see page 105). From here, select the required contents.

Here is a typical List View with some audio and video items:

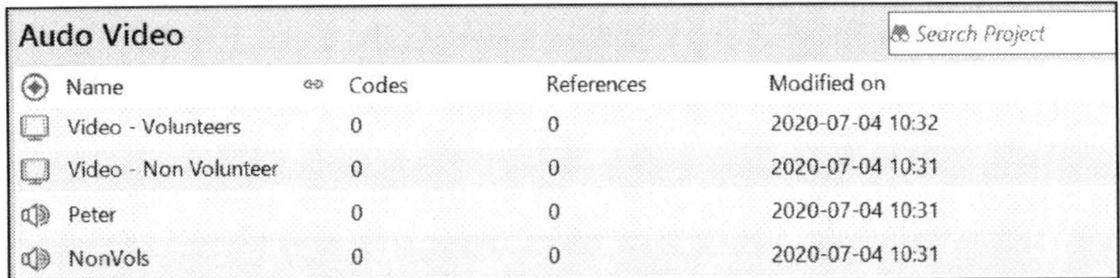

Audo Video

Name	Codes	References	Modified on
Video - Volunteers	0	0	2020-07-04 10:32
Video - Non Volunteer	0	0	2020-07-04 10:31
Peter	0	0	2020-07-04 10:31
NonVols	0	0	2020-07-04 10:31

Opening a Media Item

Now that you've created and imported some media items, you'll want to open them to access their data. Crucially, when handling media items you will have access to the **Audio** or **Video** ribbons, one of NVivo's context-dependent ribbons:

1 Select the **Data\\Files** folder or its subfolder.
2 Select the media in item in in the List View that you want to open.
3 Go to **Home | Item → 'Open' → Open Audio/Video...**
or right-click and select **Open Audio/Video...**
or double-click on the media item in the List View
or **[Ctrl]** + **[Shift]** + **[O]**.

A new context dependent Ribbon menu, **Audio/Video**, has now opened and is opened each time a media item is opened.

Please note, NVivo only allows you to open one media item at a time, but several items can stay open simultaneously.

An open audio item, showing the waveform, may look like this:

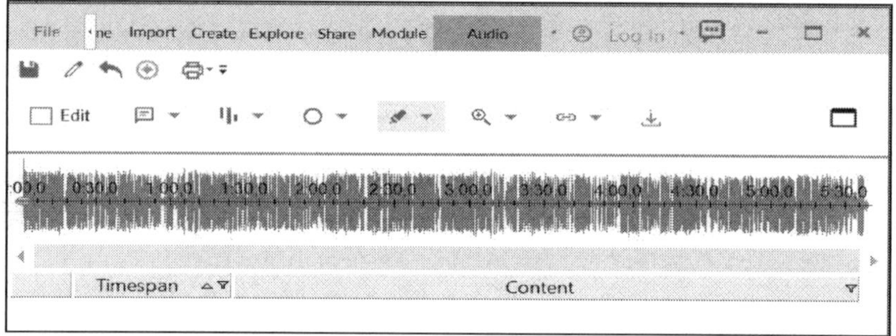

Provided a soundcard and speakers are connected to the computer you can now play and analyze the audio item.

Creating Custom Transcript Fields

When you import transcripts, see page 105, then the transcript file may have defined the Custom Transcript Fields. Otherwise, if you have defined those fields with **Application Options**, the **Audio/Video** tab, page 43, then all new projects will have them. If you need to define or edit the Transcript Fields for the current project, then use **Project Properties**, the **Audio/Video** tab, see page 56.

A practical measure is to use split panes by selecting one or more rows, right-click and apply **Split Panes** which separates the default fields from the Custom Transcript Fields. This makes it easier to adjust the column widths. This example is with hidden waveform as described on page 41:

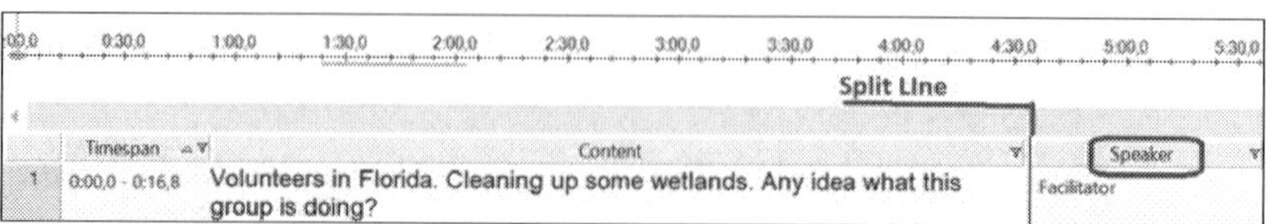

Play Modes

NVivo offers three Play Modes for working with media items, with each having a special function relating to transcription. *Normal Mode* simply plays your media item; *Synchronize Mode* plays your media item while scrolling through the corresponding rows of your transcript; and *Transcribe Mode* creates a new time interval each time you play your media item, and ends that interval when you stop.

Go to **Audio/Video | Playmode** to view or change playmode options.

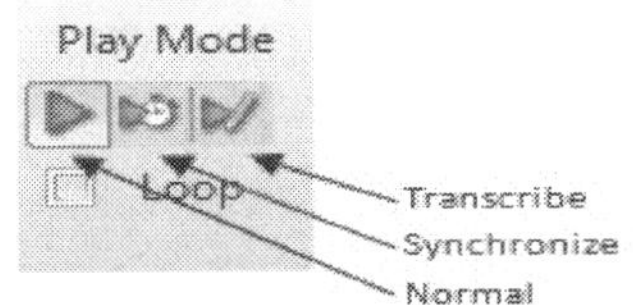

Playmode *Normal*

When a media item is opened the play mode is always *Normal*.

1 Go to **Audio/Video | Play/Pause** or **[F4]**.

Only the selected section will be played if there is a selection along the timeline. The selection disappears when you click outside the selection.

1 Go to **Audio/Video | Stop** or **[F8]**.

Rewind, Fast Forward etc.

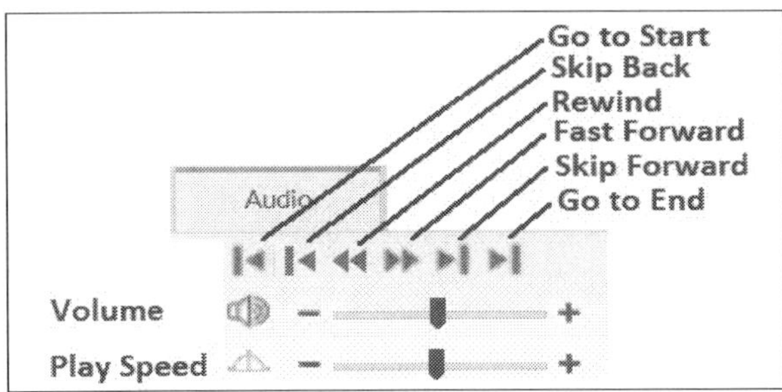

1 Go to **Audio/Video | 'Player' → Go to Start.**
2 Go to **Audio/Video | 'Player' → Skip Back** or **[F9]**.
3 Go to **Audio/Video | 'Player' → Rewind.**
4 Go to **Audio/Video | 'Player' → Fast Forward.**
5 Go to **Audio/Video | 'Player' → Skip Forward** or **[F10]**.
6 Go to **Audio/Video | Go to End.**

The *Skip* interval is determined by the setting under **File → Options**, the **Audio/Video** tab (see page 43). You can set loop playing at **Audio/Video | Play Mode**.

> **Tip:** We recommend hiding the waveform to make it easier to view a selection and other markings along the timeline. Go to **Audio/Video) | View | Waveform**, which is a toggling function. Each media item retains its individual setting during the ongoing session.
>
> You may set a default for viewing the waveform by going to **File → Options**, the **Display** tab and deselect *Waveform*.

Volume and Speed

1 Go to **Audio/Video | 'Player' → Volume**. This slider also allows mute.

2 Go to **Audio/Video | 'Player' → Play Speed**. There are fixed positions and continuous slider.

Play Mode *Synchronized*

You can play any media item synchronized so the transcription text row is highlighted and always visible (by automatic scrolling).

1 Go to **Audio/Video | Play Mode → Synchronize**.

2 Play.

Play Mode *Transcribe*

You can link audio timeline intervals with rows of text (e.g., written comments, direct transcripts or translations). In NVivo, the practice of linking time segments of audio or video with rows of text is called *transcription*. While *transcription* can be used to create verbatim transcripts of your audio files, some researchers find it faster to write short-hand transcripts.

Transcription requires several steps. First, you need to define an interval that will correspond with the row of the text. Next, the audio timeline interval and the text row need to be linked. From there, you have a transcript ready to code and link.

1 Go to **Audio/Video | Play Mode → Transcribe**.

2 Play.

Timeline intervals can be defined in a number of ways, such as by selecting portions of the timeline with your mouse when audio is paused, or by using keyboard commands to mark the start and end of an interval while audio is playing (our preferred method!). See page 104.

Selecting a Time Interval in Play Mode *Normal*

NVivo acts like a simple audio file player when in Normal Play Mode. There ar*e two ways* to select a time interval that *can be used for* coding or for creating a transcription row. Please note that these methods will work in *any* Play Mode:

1 Use the left mouse button to define the start of an interval, then hold the button, drag along the timeline, and release the button at the end of the interval.

alternatively

1 Play the media item, possibly at low speed, see above.

2 Determine the start of an interval by going to **Edit | Start Selection** (only in Edit mode) or **Audio/Video | Start Selection** or **[F11]**.

3 Determine the end of an interval by going to **Edit | Stop Selection** (only in Edit mode) or **Audio/Video | Stop Selection** or **[F12]**.

The result is a selection (a blue frame) along the timeline. Now you can code or link from this selection. To proceed with creating the next selection you need to click outside the previous selection. Retaining the current selection will limit the play interval.

Creating a Transcript Row from a Time Interval in Normal Play Mode

Once you have selected a time interval, there are several methods to create a new row. Please note that these methods will work in *any* Play Mode:

1 Make a selection along the timeline.

2 Go to **Edit | Insert Row** or right-click and select **Insert Row** or **[Ctrl]** + **[Ins]**.

The result is a transcript row corresponding to the selected time interval called *Timespan*, with the textbox in the column called *Content*:

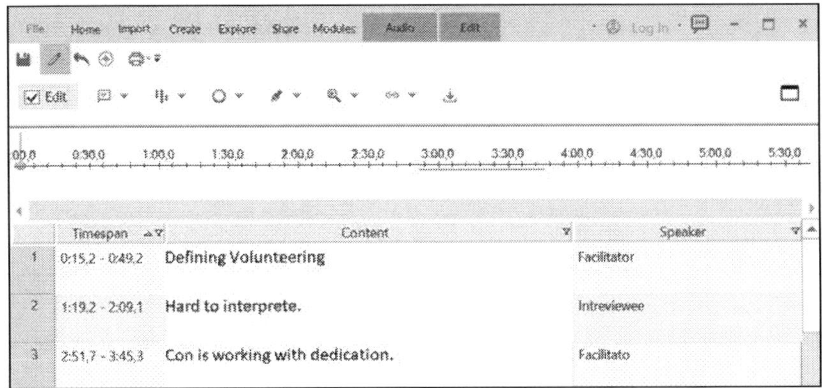

Should you need to adjust a timespan you can do as follows:

1. Select a transcript row by clicking in the row item number (the leftmost column). The corresponding timespan along the timeline is then marked with a purple guiding line.
2. Make a new modified selection along the timeline.
3. Go to **Edit | Assign Timespan to Rows** or right-click and select **Assign Timespan to Rows**.

As an alternative you can also modify the timespan directly in the transcript row by typing a new start time and a new stop time. From there you can then make a new selection along the timeline:

1. Select a transcript row by clicking in the row item number (the leftmost column).
2. Go to **Edit | Find & Select → Select Media from Transcript**.

Creating a Transcript with Play Mode *Transcribe*

As experienced NVivo users and trainers, we believe that Transcribe Mode is the best method for researchers who are using media files to create verbatim transcripts, real-time summaries, or notes on extra-linguistic cues or vocal intonation. Transcribe Mode allows you, using basic keyboard shortcuts, to quickly and easily generate text to accompany your media data.

1. Go to **Audio/Video | Play Mode → Transcribe.**
   Play and determine start of an interval by going to
   Edit | Start/Pause
   or **Audio/Video | Start/Pause**
   or **[F4]**.
2. Determine end of an interval by going to
   Edit | Stop
   or **Audio/Video | Stop**
   or **[F8]**.

While transcribing you can pause the audio if you need time to finish writing. We recommend going to **File → Options**, the **Audio/Video** tab and turning on the setting *Skip back on play in transcribe mode.* This will automatically rewind an interval you have created back to its beginning after you pause your transcription.

At any time you can also create the beginning of a new interval with **[F11]** and then end it with **[F12]**. You will also get a new transcript row but you need to pause with a separate command.

Merging Transcript Rows

Sometimes there is a need of cleaning up or reducing the number of transcript rows by merging several rows:

1. Open a media item in edit mode.
2. Select two or more transcript rows by holding down the **[Ctrl]** key and left-clicking in the item number column of the transcript rows.
3. Go to **Edit | Merge Rows**.

The merged row now covers the timespan from the first to the last selected timeslots.

Importing Transcripts

In the event your transcripts are existing text files on your computer (perhaps you are fortunate enough to be using a transcription service for your project), it is possible to import text material as a transcript for its original audio file. NVivo allows you to correspond your transcript text with the audio file by using either *Timestamps*, *Paragraphs*, or *Tables*. The filet type of your imported text file needs to be .DOC, .DOCX, .RTF, or .TXT.

The *Timestamp* Style format:

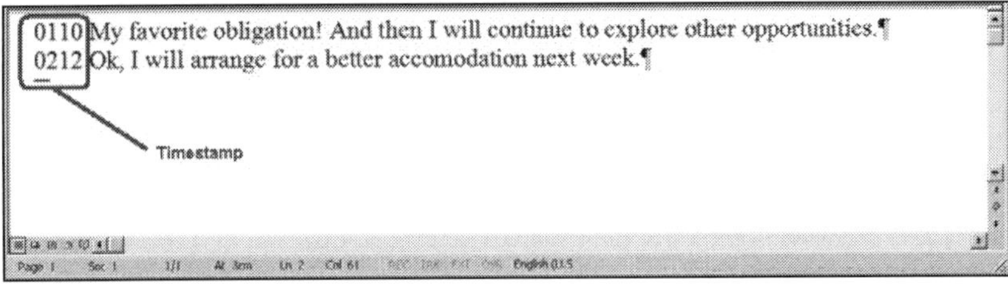

The *Paragraph* Style format:

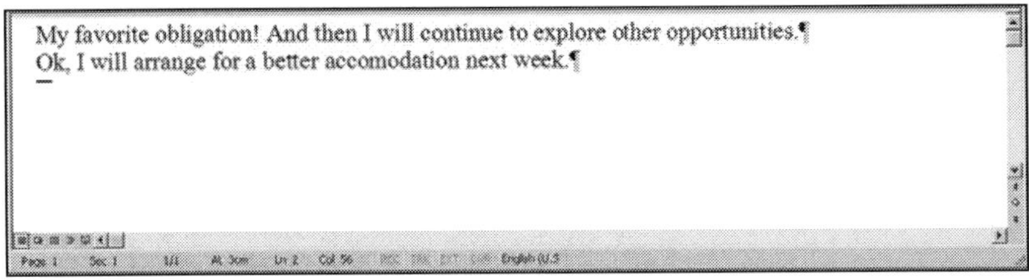

The *Table* Style format:

Timespan	Content	Speaker
0110	My favorite obligation! And then I will continue to explore other opportunities.	Ruth
0212	Ok, I will arrange for a better accomodation next week.	Edgar

To import a transcript file:

1 Open the media item in edit mode.

2 Go to **Edit | Import Rows**.

The **Import Transcript Entries** dialog box appears:

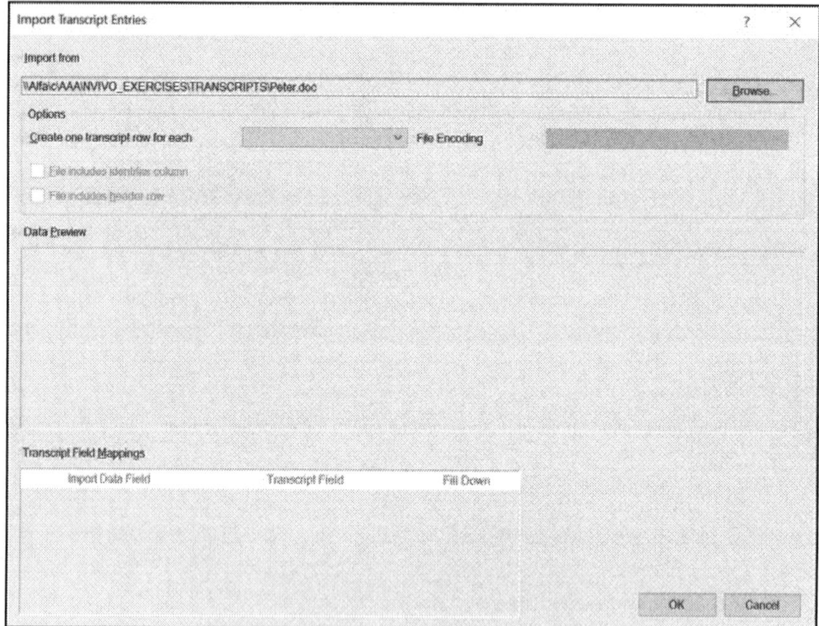

3 The [**Browse...**] button gives access to a file browser and you can select the file you want to import.

4 Once a file is selected at *Options, Create one transcript row for each* you need to select an alternative that corresponds to the appropriate style format.

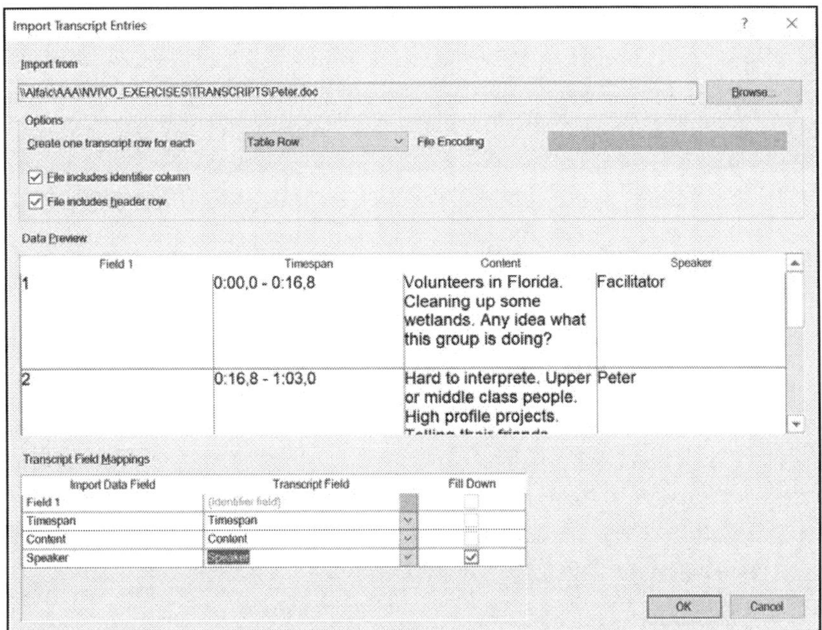

5 When Data Preview displays a correct image of the transcript then you need to set the Transcript Field Mappings so that imported data are mapped to the proper columns in the media item.

6 Confirm with [**OK**].

Note, when more columns are included in the imported file these columns will also be created in NVivo:

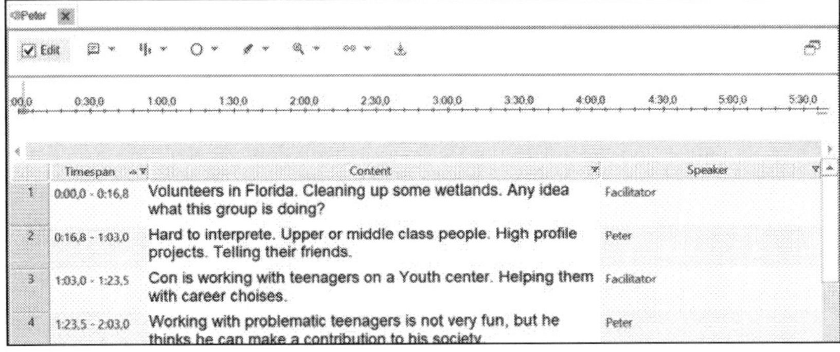

Transcript Display Options

Transcript rows can also be hidden:

1 Right-click on one or more rows.

2 Select **Row → Hide Row**.

Revert to show by **Row → Unhide Row** or **Show All Rows**.

Transcript columns can also be hidden.

1 Right-click on one or more columns.
2 Select **Column → Hide Column**.

Revert to show by **Column → Unhide Column** or **Show All Columns**.

In the column heads there is also a filter function (the funnel) that can hide or unhide certain rows or use **Column → Filter Column**. Filters are cleared by **Column → Clear Filter on Column** or **Clear All Column Filters**.

You may also hide/unhide the video player in a video item:

1 Go to **Video | Video Player**.

This is a toggling function.

NVivo Transcription Service

With NVivo a new, highly automated multi-language transcription service is introduced.

1 Go to **Modules | Transcription** or right-click and select **Transcription**.

You will be asked to login or create a new account at *myNVivo*. You will also be asked to transfer a reasonable amount to your account. As we write the price is around 28 EUR per hour of your audio or video file.

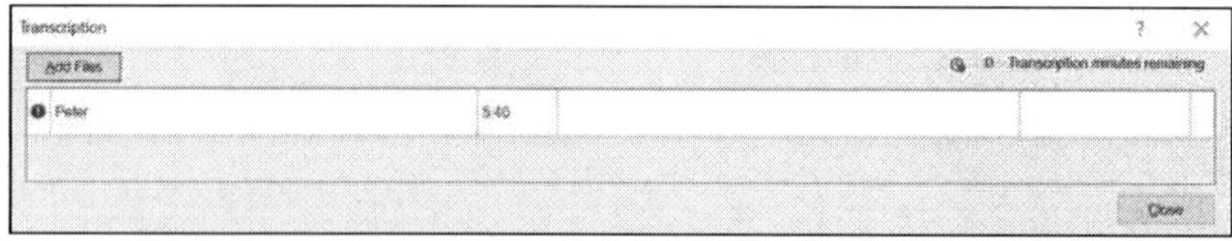

The [**Add Files**} button lets you select the audio/video file that you want to be transcribed. Provided your account covers the cost the file will be uploaded and when transcription is completed the text file will be returned and integrated as transcript rows in your audio or video item in NVivo.

Such automated transcription service may need minor or major editing. It is always possible to edit directly in audio or video transcript rows. However, we find it often more easy and productive to use Word instead. Therefore you can also use the NVivo Transcription service independent from NVivo by logging in to:

`https://account.mynvivo.com/login`

And when your editing is finished you can import the Word file to NVivo. This latter method also confirms that you can use NVivo Transcription also for older versions of NVivo.

Coding a Media Item

With your newly created time intervals or transcript rows, you may want to begin coding data to correspond with project Codes (Chapter 10, Introducing Codes). Coding a media item can be done in two ways:

1. Coding the transcript row or words in the transcript text
2. Coding a timeslot along the timeline

These coding principles are the same for media items as for any text material: select a text or an interval that to code and then select the Code or Codes at which you will be coding.

If you want to code a whole transcript row, select the row by clicking the item number column, then right-click and select the Code or Codes that you want to code to.

If you want to code a certain timeslot along the timeline, make a selection and then select the Code or Codes, see Chapter 10, Introducing Codes and Chapter 13, Coding.

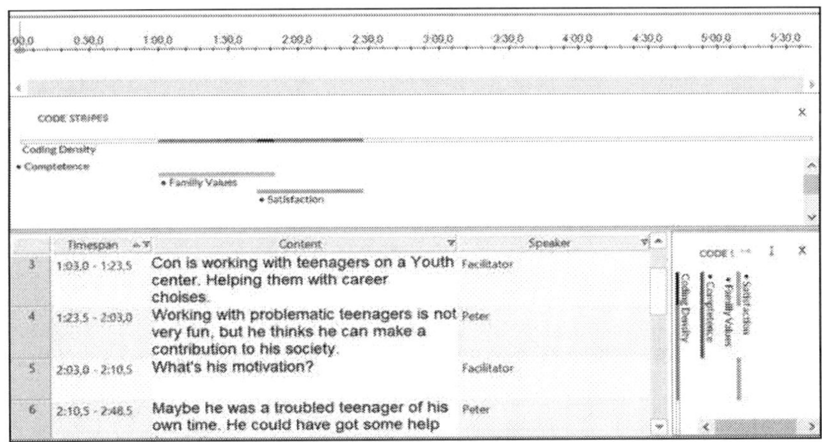

Shadow Coding

Shadow Coding is a special feature related to coding of media items. Shadow Coding means that when a text or a row in a transcript has been coded the corresponding interval of the timeline displays the coding faintly, like a shadow. Shadow coding can only be shown with coding stripes turned on (see page 193). Coding stripes are filled colored lines and shadow coding stripes are the same color, but lighter - hence the name shadow coding.

The media item above is coded at the Codes *Management* and *Public Service*. Both the transcript row and the timeslot are coded at the Code *Management*. Therefore, the item has 'double' coding stripes. The Code *Public Service* is only coded at the transcript row. Shadow coding has no use other than being a visual aid when studying coding stripes. Shadow coding can be switched on and off with **Audio/Video | Coding Stripes →Shadow Coding**.

Working with the Timeline

Sometimes there is a need of selecting a timespan from an existing transcript:

1. Open a media item with transcript rows.
2. Select a transcript row.
3. Go to **Edit | Find & Select → Select Media from Transcript**.

Now there is an exact selection and you can play, code or link from this selection.

Playing an interval from a transcript row:

1. Open a media item with transcript rows.
2. Select a transcript row.
3. Go to **Edit | Play Selected Rows** or right-click and select **Play Selected Rows**.

Only the selected interval will be played.

When you open a Code that codes both a row and a timeslot then click on a coding stripe, open the **Audio** tab and it looks like this. Playing from here only plays the coded timeslot(s).

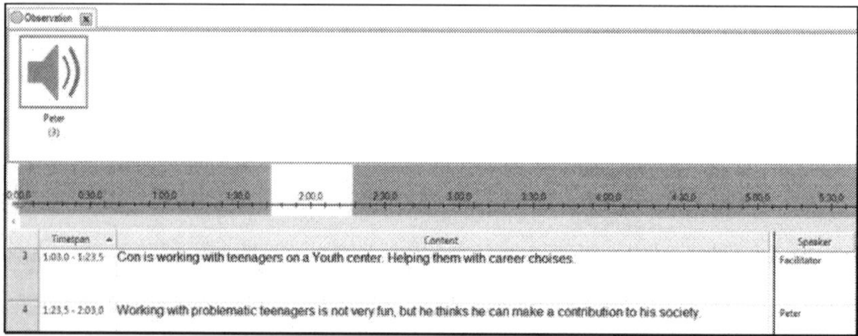

About autocoding of transcripts, see page 182.

Linking from a Media Item

An audio item can be linked (Memo Links, See Also Links and Annotations) in the same manner as any other NVivo item. However, hyperlinks cannot be created from an audio item. Links can be created from a selected timespan or from the transcript.

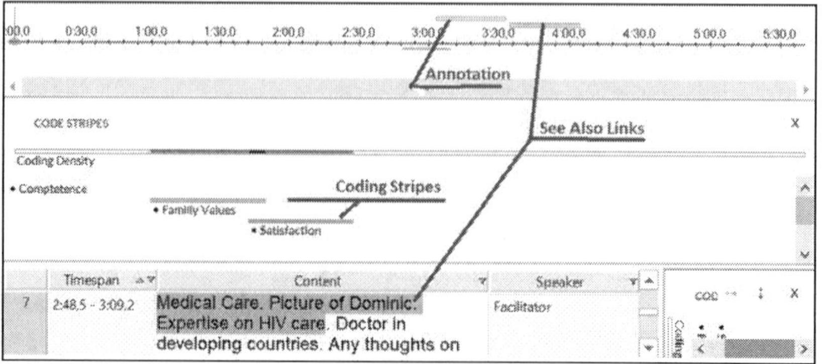

A Memo Link is shown in the list view. A See Also Link or an Annotation that refers to a timespan are shown above the timeline as a filled pink line and a filled blue line respectively. Coding stripes are shown below the timeline, see Chapter 9, Memos, Links, and Annotations.

Exporting a Media Item

Like any Source Item in NVivo, media items can be exported:

1 Select the **Data\\Files** folder or its subfolder.
2 Select the media item or items that you want to export.
3 Go to **Share | Export → Export** or right-click and select **Export → Export Audio/Video/Transcript...** or **[Ctrl]** + **[Shift]** + **[E]**.

The **Export Options** dialog box appears:

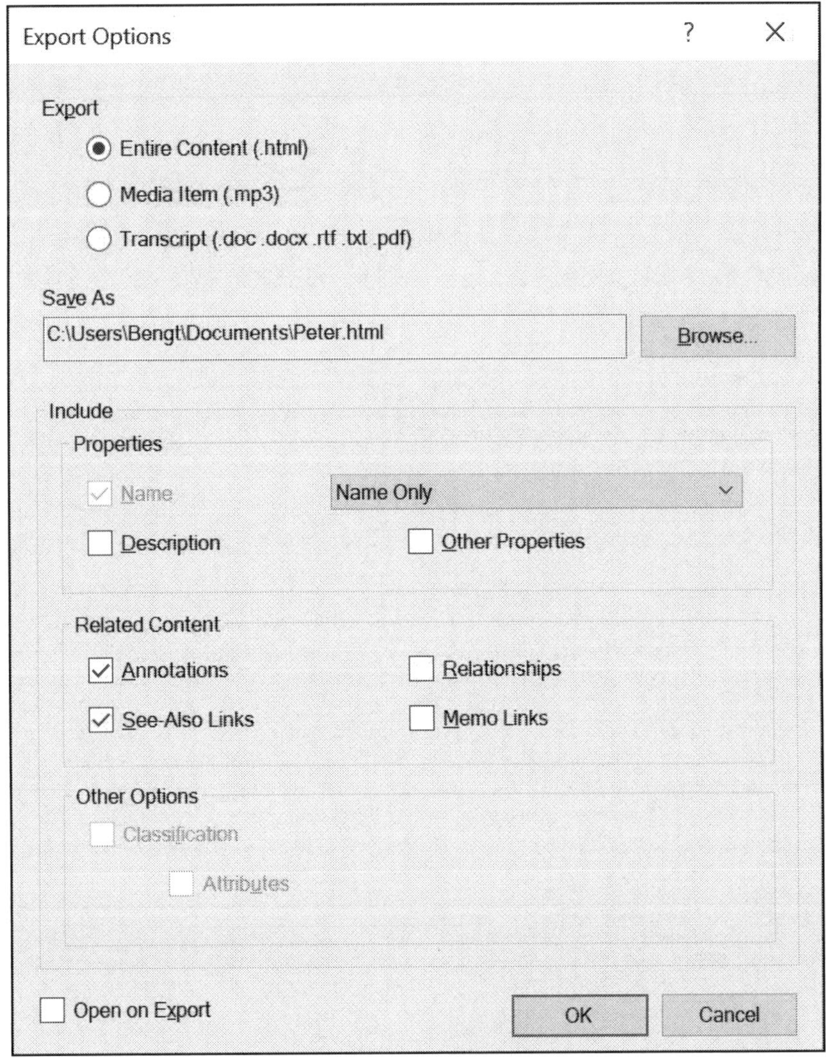

4 Select applicable options for the export of the media file, the transcript, or both. Confirm with [**OK**].
5 Decide the file name, location, and file type: .HTM, or .HTML. Confirm with [**Save**].

When you select *Entire Content* the result is a web page and the media file and other supporting files are stored in a folder called 'Filename_files'. If you also select the option *Open on Export* then the web browser opens and the result is shown instantly.

- ♦ -

A media item can also be printed with the normal command **File → Print → Print** or [**Ctrl**] + [**P**]. A transcript and its coding stripes can similarly be printed.

8. HANDLING PICTURE ITEMS

In the same way that NVivo associates media sources with timespans which correspond to text (e.g., transcription rows), handling pictures in NVivo is about defining a Region of the picture which then can be associated with a written note, called a Picture Log. Both a Region and a Picture Log can be coded and linked. NVivo can import the following picture formats: .BMP, .GIF, .JPG, .JPEG, .TIF, and .TIFF.

Importing Picture Items

NVivo can easily import a number of the most common image types. Plenty of free online image converter websites exist in the event you find you possess an image file that is a different format than NVivo accepts:

1 Go to **Import | Files**.
  Default folder is **Data\\Files** or its currently open subfolder.
  Go to 4.

alternatively

1 Select the **Data\\Files** folder or its subfolder.
2 Go to **Import | Files**.
  Go to 4.

alternatively

2 Click on any empty space in the List View.
3 Right-click and select **Import Items...**
  or **[Ctrl]** + **[Shift]** + **[I]**.
  Go to 4.

alternatively

3 Drag and drop your file's icon from an outside folder into its new folder. This option imports directly and leaves out the **Import Files** dialog box.

In all other cases the **Import Files** dialog box appears:

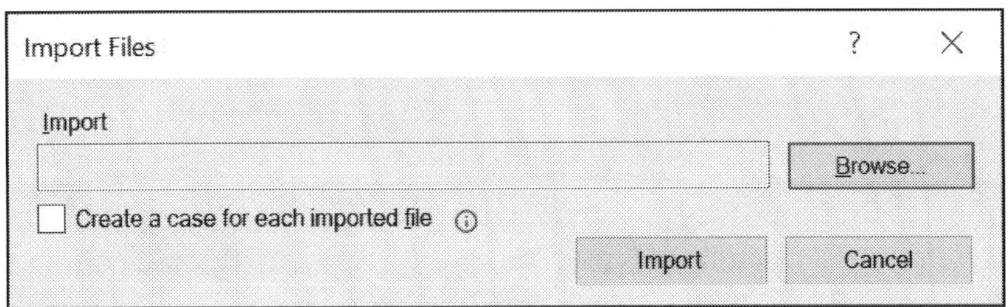

4 The **[Browse...]** button gives access to a file browser and you can select one or several picture files for import.
5 When the picture files have been selected, confirm with **[Import]**.

When you have selected *Create a case for each imported file* the dialog box offers several options:

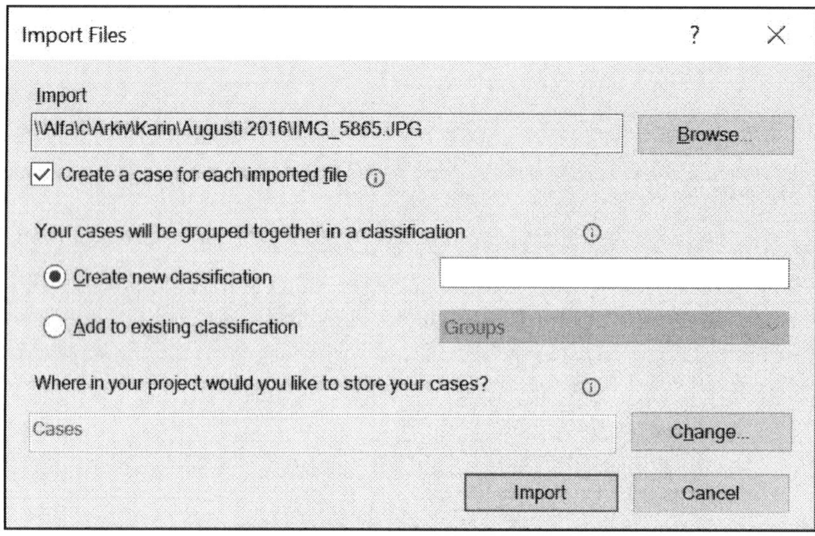

Each Source Item will be coded at a Case with the same name as the imported file and located in a folder or under a parent Case that has been selected. Also you must assign the Cases to a Classification when importing (see Chapter 12, Classifications).

6 Confirm the import with **[Import]**.

When only one picture file has been imported the **Picture Properties** dialog box appears:

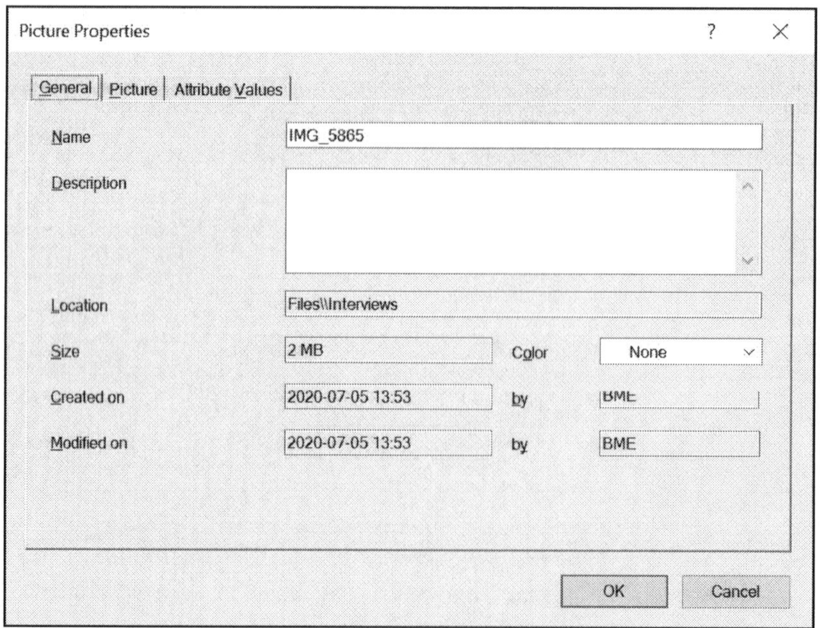

This dialog box makes it possible to modify the name of the item and optionally add a description. The **Picture** tab gives access to details and data from the imported picture:

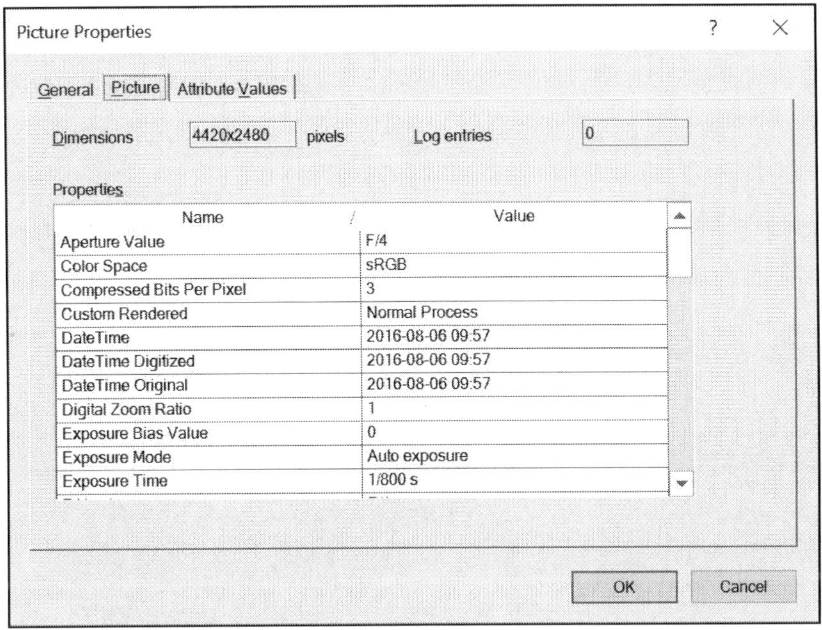

7 Confirm with **[OK]**.

Here is a typical List View of some picture items:

Images

Name	Codes	References	Modified on	Modified by
IMG_5867	1	1	2020	BME
IMG_5864	1	1	2020-07-05 13:56	BME
IMG_1982	0	0	2020-07-01 14:19	BME
Community	0	0	2019-05-25 08:01	BME

Opening a Picture Item

1 Select the **Data\\Files** folder or its subfolder.

2 Select the picture item in the List View that you want to open.

3 Go to **Home | Item → 'Open' → Open Picture...**
or right-click and select **Open Picture...**
or double-click the picture item
or **[Ctrl]** + **[Shift]** + **[O]**.

The context dependent ribbon menu **Picture** has now opened and is opened each time a Picture item is opened. Remember that NVivo can only open one picture item at a time, but several picture items can stay open simultaneously.

An open picture item can look like this:

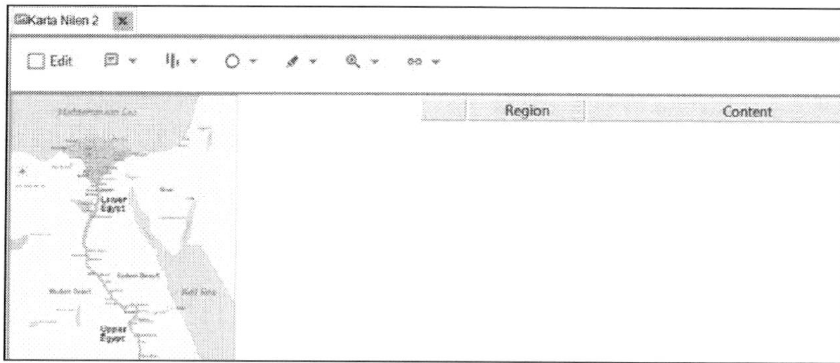

The handling of pictures is about defining a Region of the picture which then can be associated with a written note, a Picture Log. Both a Region and a Picture Log can be coded and linked.

Selecting a Region and Creating a Picture Log

The following instruction requires Edit mode which is achieved with *Click to edit* or **[Ctrl]** + [E] and a new context dependent Ribbon menu, **Edit**, opens and is opened each time a picture item is set to Edit mode.

1 Select a corner of the Region with the left mouse button, then drag the mouse pointer to the opposite corner and release the button.

2 Go to **Edit | Insert Row** or **[Ctrl]** + **[Ins]**.

The result can appear like this and the Picture Log can be typed in the cell below the column head Content:

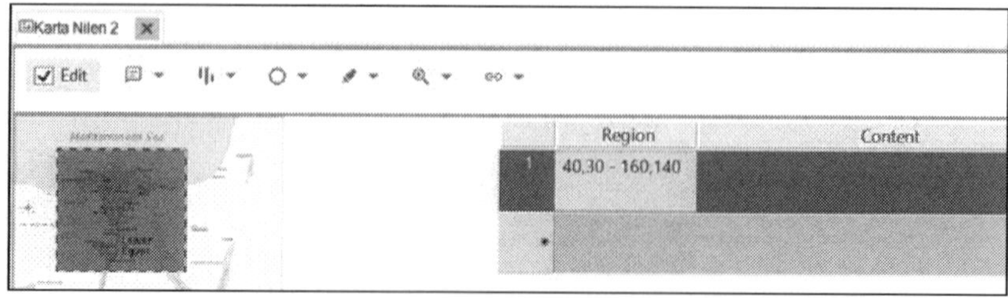

Sometimes you may need to redefine a Region and a Picture Log:

1 Select the row of the Picture Log that you wish to redefine. When selecting a Row the corresponding Region is highlighted.

2 Select a new Region (redefine a highlighted area).

3 Go to **Edit | Assign Region to Rows**.

alternatively

3 Right-click and select **Assign Region to Rows**.

In this way you adjust both a Region and a Row of the Picture Log.

As an alternative you can use a Row from which you can select a new Region:

1 Select a Row of the Picture Log. Corresponding region will be highlighted.
2 Go to **Edit | Find & Select → Select Region from Log**.

alternatively

2 Right-click and select **Select Region from Log**.

You can also hide the Picture Log:

1 Select one or more Picture Log rows.
2 Right-click and select **Row → Hide Row**.

Revert to show by **Row → Unhide Row**
or **Show All Rows**.

Editing Pictures

NVivo offers some basic functions for easy editing of picture items. The following functions are menu options after a picture item has been opened in Edit mode:

Edit | Right 90°
Edit | Left 90°
Edit | Brightness & Contrast

Coding a Picture Item

You can code a Picture Log, a selected text element or a Region of a picture item. The act of coding is in principle the same way you would code other elements of your NVivo project. In short you select data to be coded and then you select the Code or Codes that the data will be coded at, see Chapter 10, Introducing Codes and Chapter 13, Coding.

If you need to code a row of the picture log, select the row by clicking the leftmost column of the row, right-clicking and selecting a Code or Codes.

If instead (or in addition) you need to code a Region, select the Region and select a Code or Codes as usual.

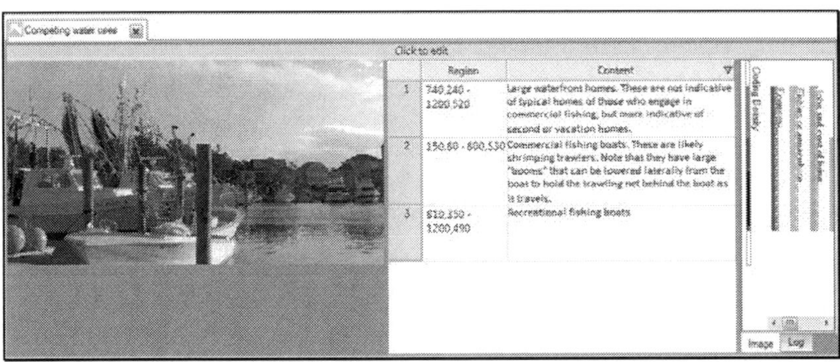

Coding stripes for a picture item are always shown in a window to the left and in a position levelled with the region. Coding stripes from a coded region are colored and filled while coding stripes from a coded picture log are lighter colored. (Same look as Shadow coding stripes.)

The above example shows a picture item that has been coded at the Code *Waterfront*. Both the region and the picture log have been directly coded and therefore 'double' coding stripes are shown.

We would also like to show when the Code *Waterfront* has been opened. After having clicked the **Picture** tab to the right you will see both the coded region of the picture and the corresponding Picture Log.

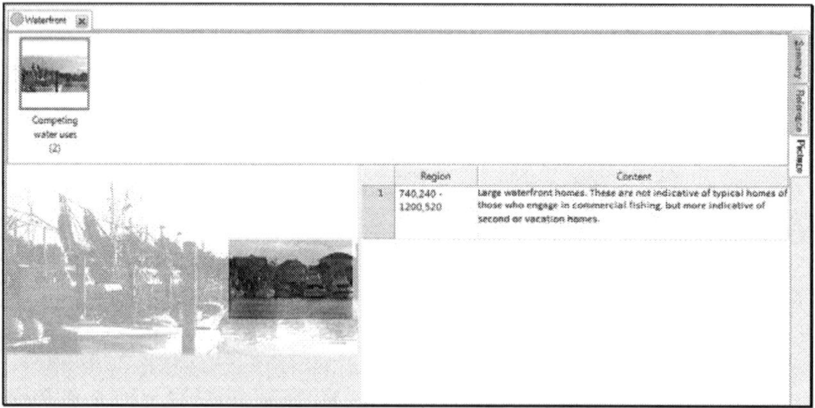

Linking from a Picture Item

A picture item can be linked (Memo Links, See Also Links and Annotations) in the same manner as any other NVivo item. However, hyperlinks cannot be created from a picture item. Links can be created from a selected region or from the Picture log. A Memo Link is not shown elsewhere than in the list view. See Also Links or Annotations are shown as pink and blue frames respectively:

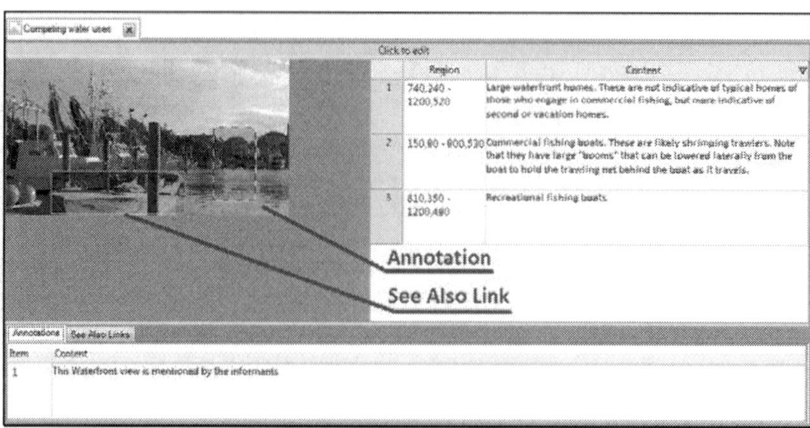

See also Chapter 9, Memos, Links, and Annotations.

Exporting a Picture Item

1 Select the **Data** **Files** folder or its subfolder.
2 Select the picture item or items in that you want to export.
3 Go to **Share | Export → Export**
or right-click and select **Export → Export Picture/Log...**
or **[Ctrl]** + **[Shift]** + **[E]**.

The **Export Options** dialog box appears:

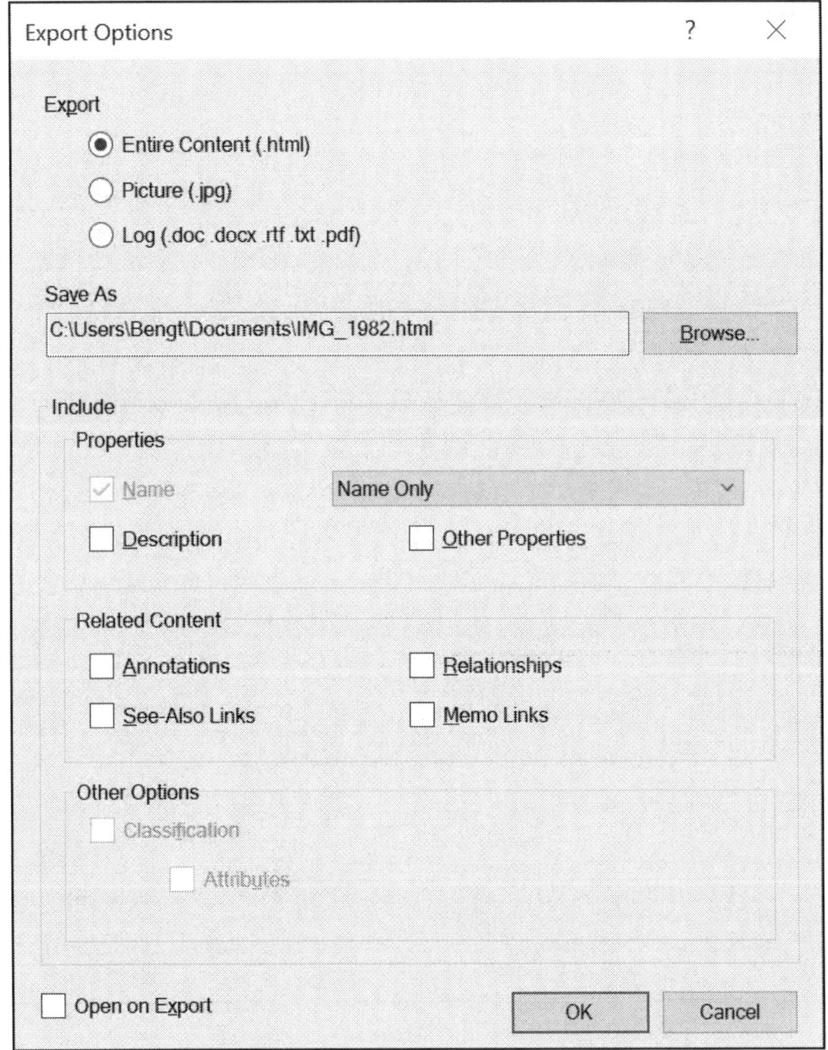

4 Select applicable options, which allows for the export of the picture file or the picture log. Confirm with **[OK]**.
5 Decide file name, location, and file type. Confirm with **[Save]**.

When you select *Entire Content* the result is a web page with the picture file in a folder called 'Filename_files'. Your web browser will open and the result is instantly shown if you also check the option *Open on Export*.

- ♦ -

A picture item can also be printed with the normal command **File → Print → Print** or **[Ctrl]** + **[P]**. The picture, and optionally the transcript and the coding stripes can be printed.

9. MEMOS, LINKS, AND ANNOTATIONS

The Folder Structure for Notes

The project folder structure for all types of notes and certain analytic tools are: Memos, Framework Matrices, Annotations, and See Also Links. The default folders as shown in the Navigator are:

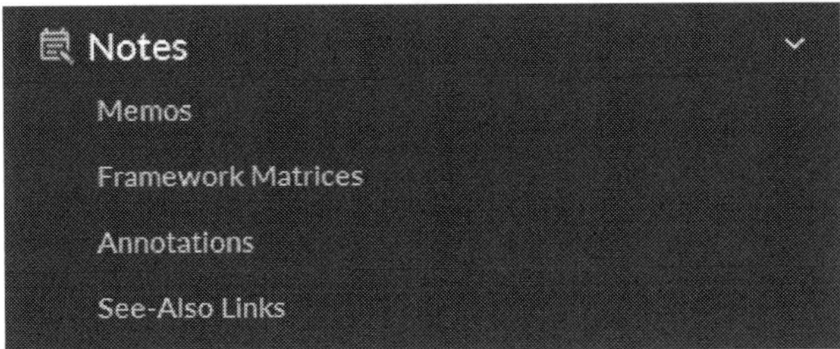

These folders and the names are not possible to delete, move, or rename. The folder names are depending on the user interface language setting, see page 39. However, the user can create subfolders to the default folder **Notes\\Memos** and **Notes\\Framework Matrices**.

Memos, Memo Links, See Also Links, Hyperlinks and Annotations are NVivo tools that allow you to create connections and track your ideas across your data. While similar in function, each of these four tools operates differently, with Memos and Memo Links being closely related.

Exploring Links in the List View

Memo Links, See Also Links, and Annotations (but not Hyperlinks) can be opened and viewed in the List View like any other Project Item.

1 Select any of the following folders:
Notes\\Memos
Notes\\Framework Matrices
Notes\\Annotations
Notes\\See Also Links

Next you will see the selected list of links in the List View.

Right-clicking a **Memo** item in the List View will open a menu with the options: Open Linked Item, Open Linked Memo and Delete Memo Link. Exporting and printing the whole list of items are also available options.

Double-clicking **Framework Matrices** or any of its sub-folders opens the List View of user created Framework Matrices, see details in Chapter 17, About the Framewok Method.

Double-clicking an **Annotation** item in the List View opens the source and its Annotation in the Detail View. Right-clicking on an Annotation will open a menu with the options: Open Source and

Delete. Exporting and printing the whole list of items are also available options.

Double-clicking a **See Also Link** in the List View opens the **See Also Link Properties** dialog box. Right-clicking on such item will open a menu with the options: Open From Item, Open To Item, Edit See Also Link... and Delete. Exporting and printing the whole list of items are also available options.

This Chapter also describes how to handle **hyperlinks**.

Memos

Memos are a type of source that allows you to record research insights in a source document that can be linked to another item in your project. Any Source or Code can have one Memo linked to it, called a Memo Link. For example, Memos can be notes, instructions or field notes that have been created outside NVivo. A memo cannot be linked to another memo with a Memo Link.

A memo can be imported from an external source or with NVivo.

Importing a Memo

As with other Project Items you can import them or create them with NVivo. The following file types can be imported as memos: .DOC, .DOCX, .RTF, and .TXT.

1 Go to **Import | Notes & Email | Memos**.
Default folder is **Notes\\Memos** or its currently open subfolder.
Go to 4.

alternatively

1 Select **Notes\\Memos** folder or its subfolder.

2 Go to **Import | Notes & Email | Memos**.
Go to 4.

alternatively

2 Click on any empty space in the List View.

3 Right-click and select **Import Memos...**
or **[Ctrl]** + **[Shift]** + **[I]**.
Go to 4.

alternatively

3 Drag and drop your file's icon from an outside folder into its new folder. This option imports directly and leaves out the **Import Memos** dialog box.

In all other cases the **Import Memos** dialog box appears:

Import Memos

Import

\\Alfa\c\AAA\NVIVO_EXERCISES\MEMOS\Double standards.doc

Browse...

Create a case for each imported file

Import Cancel

4 The [**Browse...**] button gives access to a file browser and you can select one or several documents for a batch import.

5 When selected, confirm with [**Import**].

When you have selected *Create a case for each imported file* the dialog box offers several options:

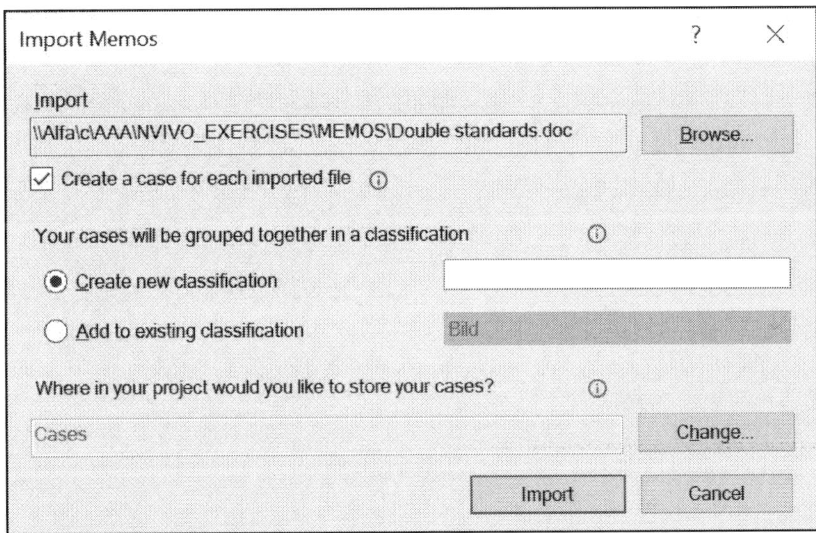

Each Source Item will be coded at a Case with the same name as the imported file and located in a folder or under a parent Case that has been selected. Also you must assign the Cases to a Classification when importing (see Chapter 12, Classifications).

6 Confirm the import with [**Import**].

Creating a New Memo

1 Go to **Create | Memo**.
Default folder is **Notes\\Memos** or its currently open subfolder.
Go to 4.

alternatively

1 Select **Notes\\Memos** folder or its subfolder.

2 Go to **Create | Memo**.
Go to 4.

alternatively

2 Click on any empty space in the List View.
3 Right-click and select **New Memo...**
or **[Ctrl]** + **[Shift]** + **[N]**.

The **New Memo** dialog box appears:

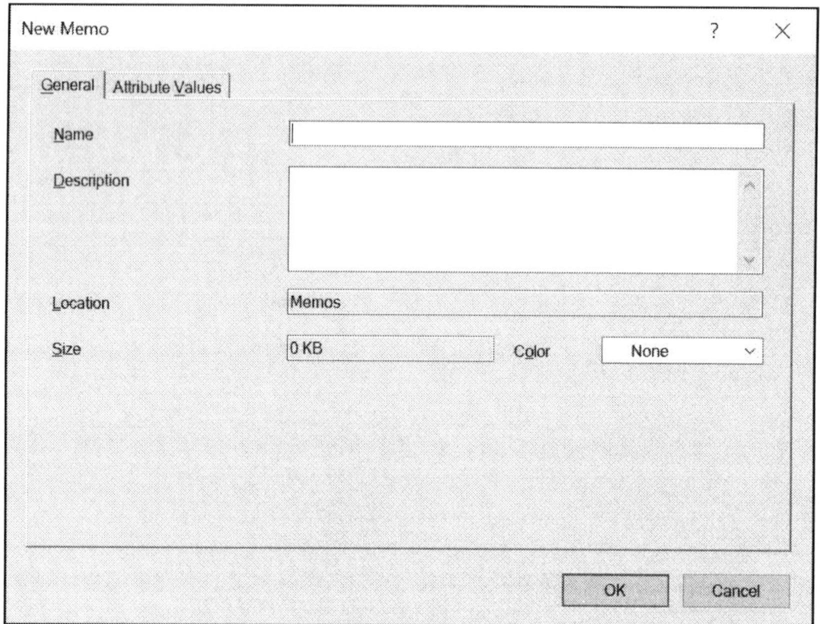

5 Type a name (compulsory) and a description (optional), then **[OK]**.

A new text area opens in Detail View and you can create your memo with all editing tools that NVivo offers.

Two new context dependent Ribbon menus, **Memo** and **Edit**, have now opened and opens each time a new memo is created.

Here is a typical List View with some memos (with linked items):

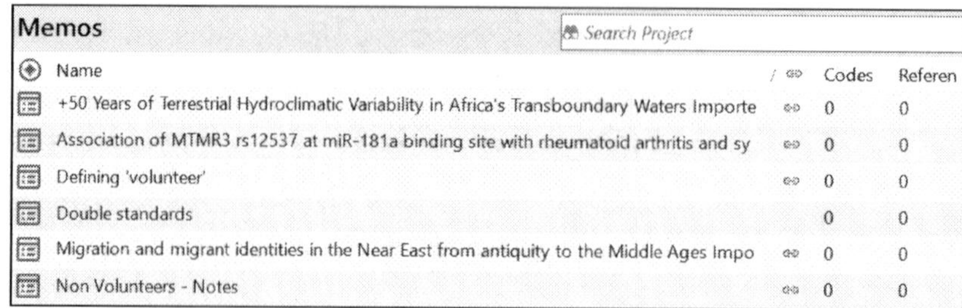

Memos

Name	Codes	Referen
+50 Years of Terrestrial Hydroclimatic Variability in Africa's Transboundary Waters Importe	0	0
Association of MTMR3 rs12537 at miR-181a binding site with rheumatoid arthritis and sy	0	0
Defining 'volunteer'	0	0
Double standards	0	0
Migration and migrant identities in the Near East from antiquity to the Middle Ages Impo	0	0
Non Volunteers - Notes	0	0

Opening a Memo

1. Select the **Notes\\Memos** folder or its subfolder.
2. Select a memo in the List View that you want to open.
3. Go to **Home | Item → 'Open' → Open Memo...**
   or right-click and select **Open Memo...**
   or double-click on the memo in the List View
   or **[Ctrl]** + **[Shift]** + **[O]**.

A new context dependent Ribbon menu, **Memo**, has now opened and is opened each time a memo is opened.

Please note, you can only open one memo at a time, but several memos can stay open.

Creating a Memo Link

Memo Links truly distinguish Memos from other types of NVivo sources. Memo Links are an optional component of Memos.

1. In the List View select the source (File) from which you want to create a Memo Link. You cannot create a Memo Link to a memo that is already linked.
2. Right-click and select **Memo Link → Link to Existing Memo...**

The **Select Project Item** dialog box is shown. Only unlinked memos can be selected, linked memos are dimmed.

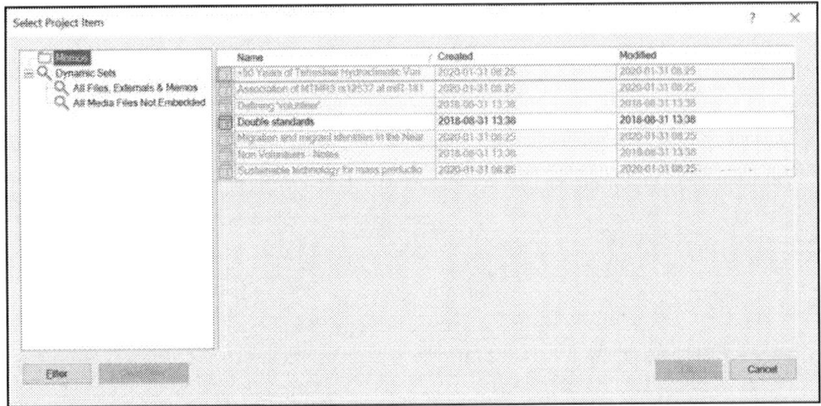

3. Select the memo that you want to link to and confirm with **[OK]**.

The Memo Link is shown in the List View with one icon for the memo and one icon for the linked item.

Creating a Memo Link and a New Memo Simultaneously

NVivo makes it easy to create a Memo Link and a new Memo simultaneously:

1 In the List View select the item (File) from which you want to create a Memo Link and a new Memo.
2 Right-click and select **Memo Link → Link to New Memo...** or **[Ctrl]** + **[Shift]** + **[K]**.

The **New Memo** dialog box is shown and you continue according to page 124.

Opening a Linked Memo

A Memo can be opened as outlined above, but a linked Memo can also be opened in the event where a Memo Link is in place.

1 In the List View select the item from which you want to open a Linked Memo.
2 Right-click and select **Memo Link → Open Linked Memo** or **[Ctrl]** + **[Shift]** + **[M]**.

Deleting a Memo Link

1 In the List View select the item from which you want to delete a Memo Link.
2 Right-click and select **Memo Link → Delete Memo Link**.

The **Delete Confirmation** dialog box appears:

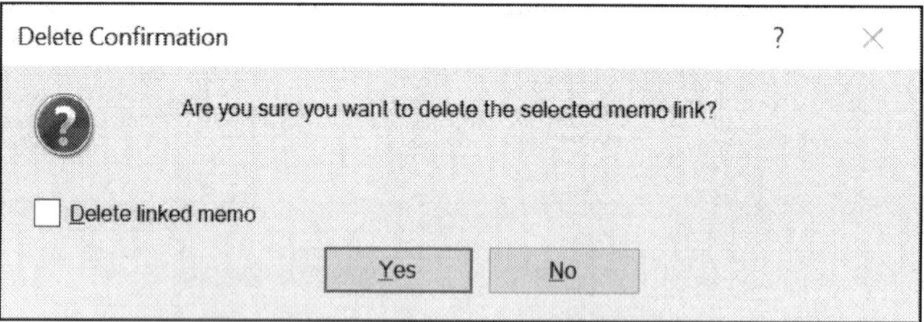

3 If you select *Delete linked memo* then also the Memo will be deleted, otherwise only the Memo Link will be deleted. Confirm with **[Yes]**.

Exporting a Memo

As mentioned, you may wish at some point to export a Memo you wrote inside NVivo but now need to email to a collaborator.

1 Select the **Notes\\Memos** folder or its subfolder.
2 Select the memo (s) in the List View that you want to export.
3 Go to **Share | Export → Export** or right-click and select **Export → Export Memo** or **[Ctrl]** + **[Shift]** + **[E]**.

The **Export Options** dialog box appears:

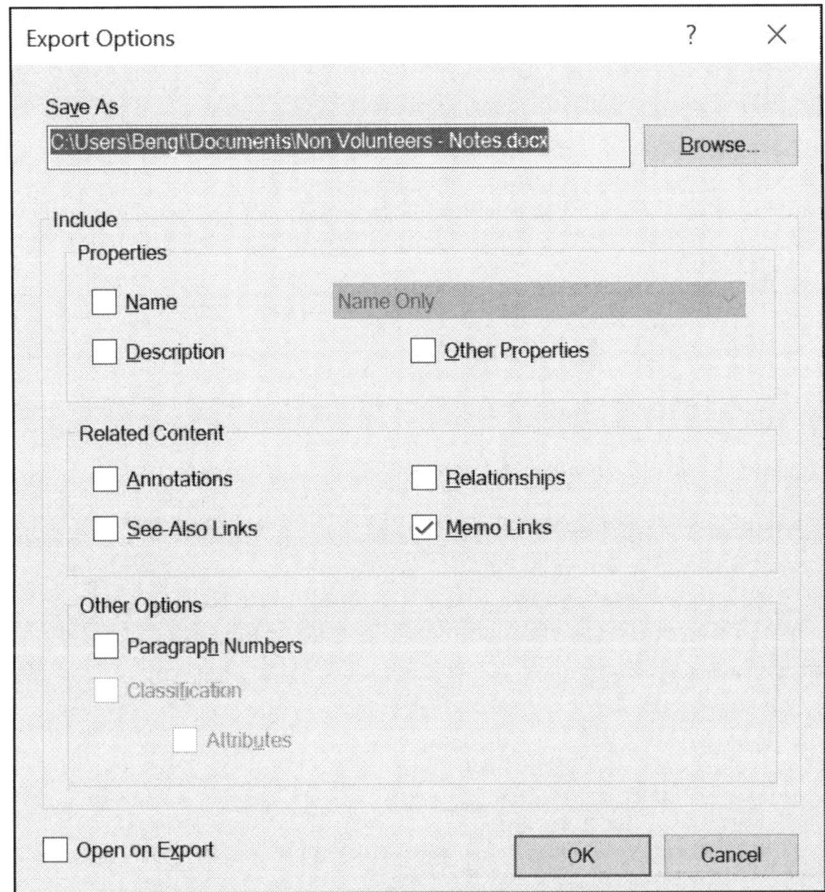

4 Select the options that you want. Confirm with **[OK]**.
5 Decide file name, location, and file type: .DOCX, .DOC, .RTF, .TXT, .PDF, or .HTML. Confirm with **[Save]**.

Remember, coding made on text items cannot be transferred when a Memo is exported.

Annotations

Annotations and See Also Links are similar but different. When you create an Annotation, the Annotations tab appears at the bottom of a Source or Code to a point of your choosing. An Annotation could be a quick note, a reference or an idea. Unlike Memos, which can only link to entire sources, Annotations link to specific segments of your data (e.g., text from a focus group transcript, or a segment of time from a video source). An Annotation in NVivo shares similarities with a footnote in Word, especially because annotations are numbered within each Project Item. Annotations cannot be coded.

Creating an Annotation

1. Open a Source Item (File) or a Code.
2. Select the text or other section area that you want to link to an Annotation.
3. Right-click and select **New Annotation**
   or **[Ctrl]** + **[Shift]** + **[A]**.
   or use the top toolbar of the Detail View where you can hide, unhide, add, or delete See Also links:

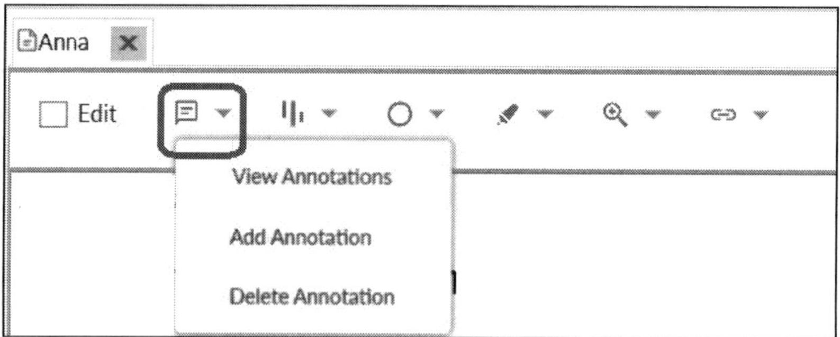

A new window will open where the Annotation can be typed. The linked area is then shown highlighted in blue.

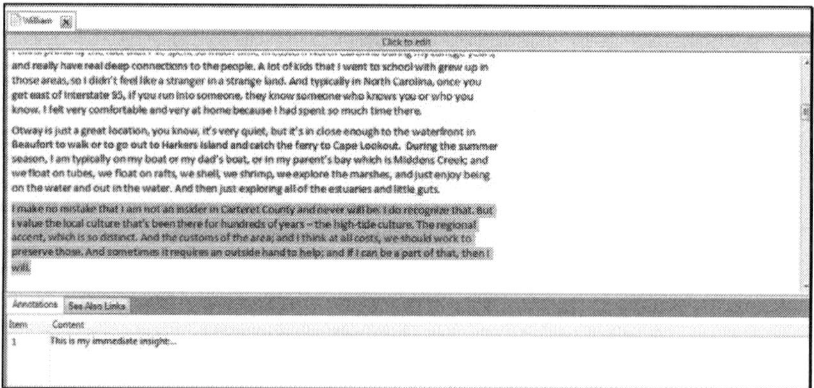

Hiding or Unhiding Annotations

When an NVivo item contains Annotations, you have the option of toggling the Annotations tab on or off.

1. Open the Project Item that contains Annotations.
2. Go to <**Type**> | **'View'** | **Annotations**.

This is a toggling function and is valid separately for each item.

Deleting an Annotation

1. Position the cursor on the link to an Annotation.
2. Right-click **Delete Annotation**.
3. Confirm with **[Yes]**.

See Also Links

See Also Links literally create connection points between different items from your NVivo project. See Also Links are links from a selection (text, picture region, or audio segment) in an item to another item or a certain selection from another item. Multiple See Also Links can be linked to the same item, unlike Memo Links which are a one-to-one relationship between a Memo and its attendant NVivo item.

Creating a See Also Link to Another Item

1. Open the item from which you want to create a See Also Link.
2. Select the section (text, picture) from which you want to create a See Also Link.
3. Right-click and select **Links → See Also Link → New See Also Link...**

The **New See Also Link** dialog box appears:

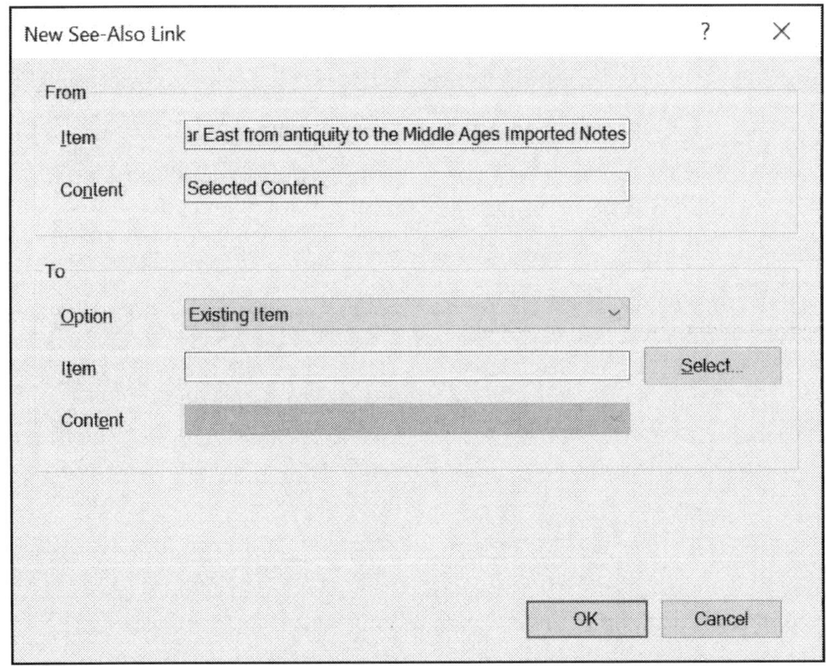

Under the **Option** drop down list, you can select what type of Project Item you will link. An item will be created if you select an option starting with **New** <..>. If you select the option Existing Item you go to the **[Select...]** button and use the **Select Project Item** dialog box to select an item to link to. When the item has been selected the link goes to the entire target item.

4. Confirm with **[OK]**.

For example, in this Source Item the See Also Links are indicated as a pink colored highlighting:

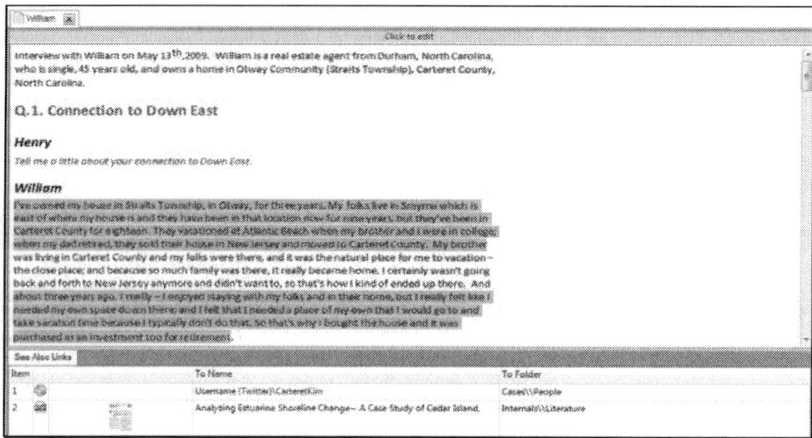

Creating a See Also Link to a Selection of Another Item

1 Open the target item that you want to link to.
2 Select the section (text, image) that you want to link to.
3 Copy with for example **[Ctrl]** + **[C]**.
4 Open the item from which you want to create a See Also Link.
5 Select the area (text, image) that you want to link from.
6 Go to **Home | Clipboard | Paste As See Also Link** or right-click and select **Paste As See Also Link**.

Opening a See Also Link

1 Position the cursor on the See Also Link or select the entire link.
2 Right-click and select **Links → Open To Item**.

The target item will open and if you have used the option *Selected Content* the selected area will be shown highlighted otherwise not.

Hiding or Unhiding See Also Links

You can view all the See Also Links from a certain item in a window below the open item. The links are shown as a list of items. Clicking on an item opens the link. Right-clicking and selecting **Open To Item...** also opens the link.

The top toolbar of the Detail View can hide or unhide the See Also links:

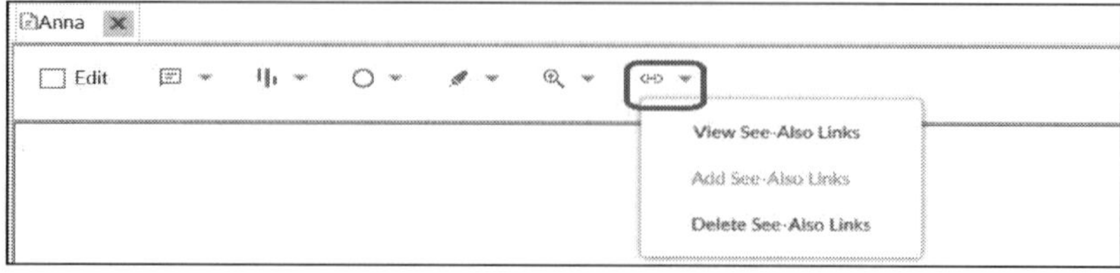

Opening a Linked External Source

Provided the See Also Link leads to an external item, you are able to open that external source (file or web site) directly. You may wish to create links to external sources rather than creating hyperlinks as you may reduce unnecessary modifications to the external sources.

1. Position the cursor on the See Also Link or select the entire link.
2. Right-click and select **Links → Open Linked External File**.

Deleting a See Also Link

1. Position the cursor on the See Also Link or select the entire link.
2. Right-click and select **Links → See Also Link → Delete See Also Link.**
3. Confirm with [**Yes**].

Hyperlinks

NVivo can create links to external sources in two ways:

- Hyperlinks from a Source Item (File).
- External items (see page 70).

Creating Hyperlinks

1. Select a section (text or image) in a Source Item (File) while in Edit mode.
2. Right-click and select **Links → Hyperlink → New Hyperlink...**

The **New Hyperlink** dialog box appears:

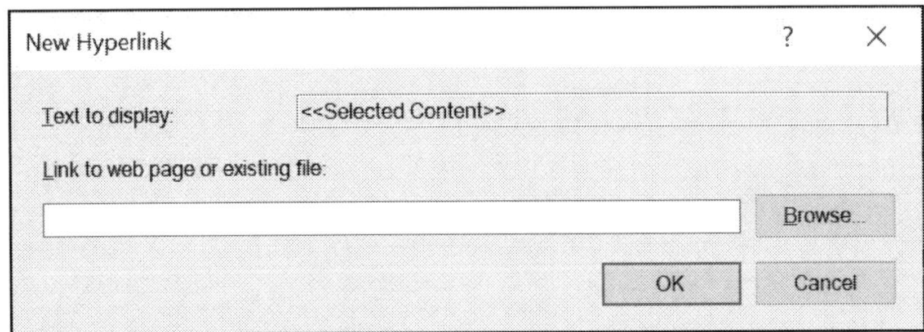

3. Paste a complete URL or use [**Browse...**] to find the target file in your computer or in your local network.
4. Confirm with [**OK**].

A Hyperlink is blue and underlined.

Opening a Hyperlink

The following two methods will open a Hyperlink:

1 Position the cursor on the link.
2 Right-click and select **Links → Hyperlink → Open Hyperlink**.

alternatively

2 Hold down the **[Ctrl]** key.
3 Click on the link.

This latter command will sometimes cause the external file (depending on the file type) to open as a minimized window. If so then either repeat this command or click on the Windows toolbar.

Deleting a Hyperlink

1 Position the cursor on the hyperlink while in Edit mode or point at the link in a Source Item while in Edit mode with the mouse pointer which will then become an arrow.
2 Right-click and select **Links → Hyperlink → Delete Hyperlink**.

The **Delete Hyperlink** dialog box appears:

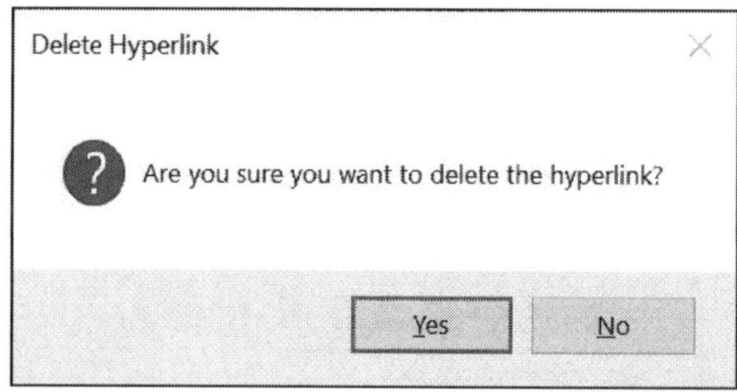

3 Confirm with **[Yes]**.

10. INTRODUCING CODES

The Folder Structure for Coding

The project folder structure for Coding are: Codes, Sentiment, Relationships, and Relationship Types. The default folders as shown in the Navigator are:

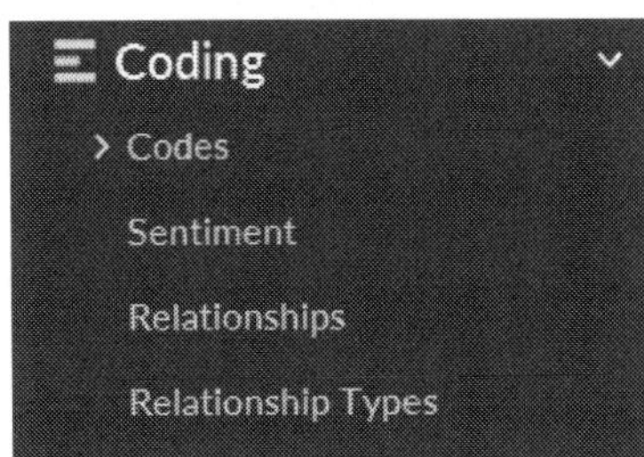

These folders and the names are not possible to delete, move, or rename. The folder names are depending on the user interface language setting, see page 39. However, the user can create subfolders to the default folder **Coding\\Codes**.

A Code[1] is a connecting point. In NVivo, Codes are the primary tool for organizing and labelling data. You can think of a Code as a 'container' of certain elements of your files. Codes can represent abstract concepts, such as topics, themes, and ideas. Codes can also represent tangible concepts, such as people, places, and things.

Codes can represent anything you would find useful to organize and classify elements of your project. Some researchers know very early what kind of Codes they will need to organize and categorize data. You can create Codes before you start to work with your data or you may need to brainstorm organizational categories, concepts and structures 'on the fly' as they work through their source material. The way you work with Codes varies largely depending on the methods used, the research situation and your personality.

> **Tip:** Some advice we offer coding newcomers is to record your thought processes in as much detail as possible when you are coding. The Description field of the **New Code** dialog box is an excellent place to capture why you have created that Code and how you think it relates to your coding hierarchy.

Early in your project, we recommend identifying a few Codes that you think will be useful. These early Codes can be coded as you work through your data for the first time (more on coding later). These early Codes can be moved, merged, renamed, redefined or even deleted later on as your project develops.

NVivo also has developed a system for organizing

[1] In previous software versions the term used was **Node**.

and classifying both Source Items (Files) and Codes, see Chapter 12, Classifications.

The terms *Parent Code*, *Child Code* and *Aggregate* are used when NVivo's Code system is described. A *Parent Code* is the next higher hierarchical Code in relation to its *Child Codes*.

An *Aggregate*[2] means that a Parent Code will take on all of the content of its immedate Child Codes. At any time you can activate or deactivate Aggregation with immediate effect. The Aggregate control is in the **New Code** dialog box or **Code Properties** dialog box.

Creating a Code

Manually creating a new Code can be done in a number of ways.

1 Go to **Create | Code**.
  Default folder is **Coding\\Codes** or its currently open subfolder.
  Go to 4.

alternatively

1 Select the **Coding\\Codes** folder or its subfolder.
2 Go to **Create | Code**.
  Go to 4.

alternatively

2 Click on any empty space in the List View.
3 Right-click and select **New Code...**
  or **[Ctrl]** + **[Shift]** + **[N]**

---

[2] *Aggregate* in NVivo has an imperfection in that the number of coded data segments (called references) is calculated as the arithmetic sum of the Child Codes' references. Instead, this should be the logical sum as some references may be overlapping.

The **New Code** dialog box appears:

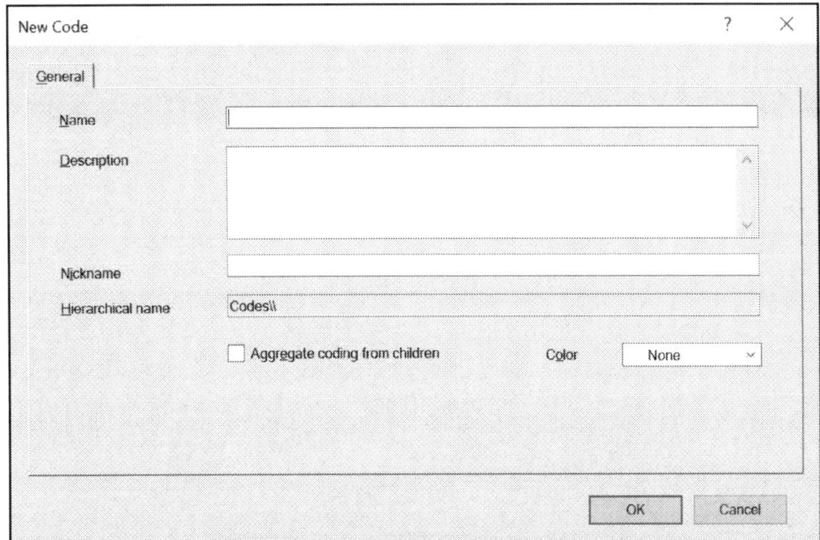

4 Type name (compulsory) and a description and a nickname (both optional), then **[OK]**.

A new context dependent Ribbon menu, **Code**, opens each time a new code is created or opened.

Here is a typical List View of some Codes:

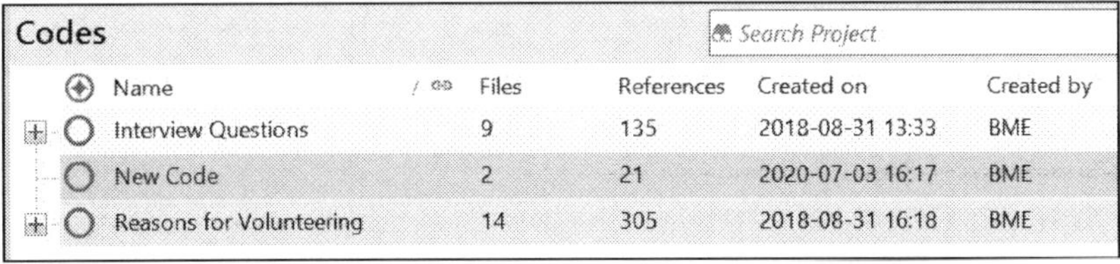

Please note, that a [+] sign to the left of the code symbol indicates that Child Codes exist. Clicking opens and closes the Child Codes.

Building Hierarchical Codes

As mentioned, Codes can be organized hierarchically. As a result, there are Code headings and subheadings in several levels of a coding hierarchy. Codes can therefore form a sort of structured vocabulary, such as the MeSH (Medical Subject Headings) used by the Medline/PubMed article database. Cases (see next Chapter) can also be organized hierarchically if required.

> **Tip:** Nicknames are only for Codes and Cases. A practical use when code names are very long. Use simple abbreviations. Must be unique within the project. Useful for the **Find** function and when coding with the Quick Coding Bar.

Creating a Child Code/Case

Assembling a Code hierarchy of Parent Codes and Child Codes is simple in NVivo:

1. Select the **Coding\\Codes** folder or its subfolder.
2. Select the Code to which you want to create a Child Code.
3. Go to **Create | Code**
   or right-click and select **New Code...**
   or **[Ctrl]** + **[Shift]** + **[N]**.

The **New Code** dialog box now is shown.

4. Type a name (compulsory) and a description and a nickname (both optional), then **[OK]**.

It is also possible to move Codes within the list view with drag-and-drop or cut (**[Ctrl]** + **[X]**) and paste (**[Ctrl]** + **[V]**). When you drag one Code icon on top of another Code icon you create a Child Code. You can also create a Child Code when you cut a Code, left-click a different Code, and then paste.

Here is a typical List View of some hierarchical Codes:

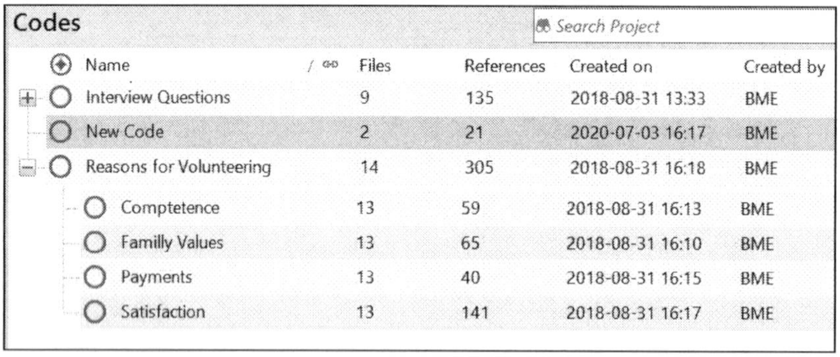

Codes — Search Project

Name	Files	References	Created on	Created by
+ Interview Questions	9	135	2018-08-31 13:33	BME
New Code	2	21	2020-07-03 16:17	BME
− Reasons for Volunteering	14	305	2018-08-31 16:18	BME
Comptetence	13	59	2018-08-31 16:13	BME
Familly Values	13	65	2018-08-31 16:10	BME
Payments	13	40	2018-08-31 16:15	BME
Satisfaction	13	141	2018-08-31 16:17	BME

Underlying items in the list can be opened or closed by clicking the + or - symbols, but also by using **Home | Workspace → Expand All (Selected) Codes/ Collapse All (Selected) Codes**.

These menu options are also available by right-clicking in the List View: **Expand/Collapse**.

A useful function is showing Child Code Headers. When these headers are displayed you can modify the column widths. Apply **Home | Workspace → Child Headers** (toggling).

> **Tip:** If you select *Append linked memos* a new memo will be created with the same name as the new code. If all merged codes have memos the new memo will append the contents from all its memos.

Merging Codes

Any Code can be merged into an existing Code. Merging two Codes simply combines the content of one Code into another.

1. Cut or copy one or more Code(s).
2. Select a target Code.

3 Go to **Home | Clipboard → Merge Into Selected Code** or right-click and select **Merge Into Selected Code** or **[Ctrl]** + **[M]**.

The **Merge Into Code** dialog box is shown:

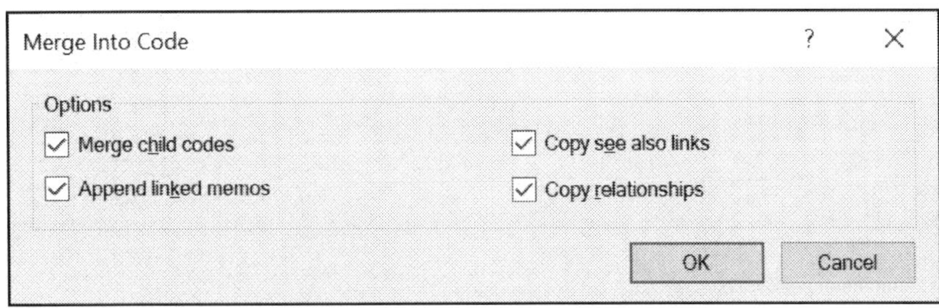

4 Select the applicable options, then click **[OK]**.

Alternatively, you can merge two (or more) Codes into a new Code:

1 Cut or copy two or more Codes.
2 Select the folder under which you want to place the new Code.
3 Go to **Home | Clipboard → Merge Into New Code...** or right-click and select **Merge Into New Code...** Go to 5.

alternatively

3 Select the Parent Code under which you want to place the new Code.
4 Go to **Home | Clipboard → Merge Into New Child Code** or right-click and select **Merge Into New Child Code...**

The **Merge Into Code** dialog box appears:

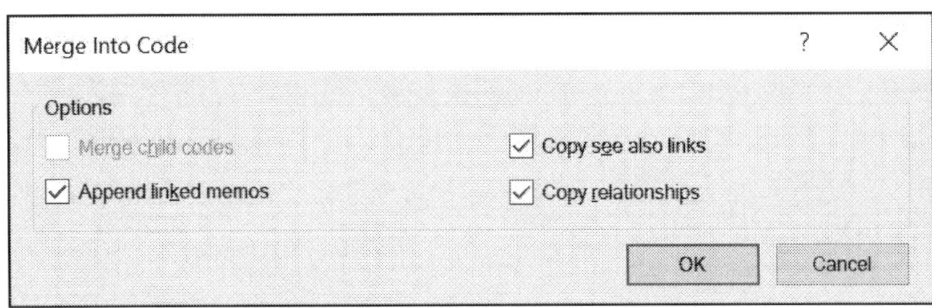

5 Select the applicable option(s), then click **[OK]**.

The **New Code** dialog box appears:

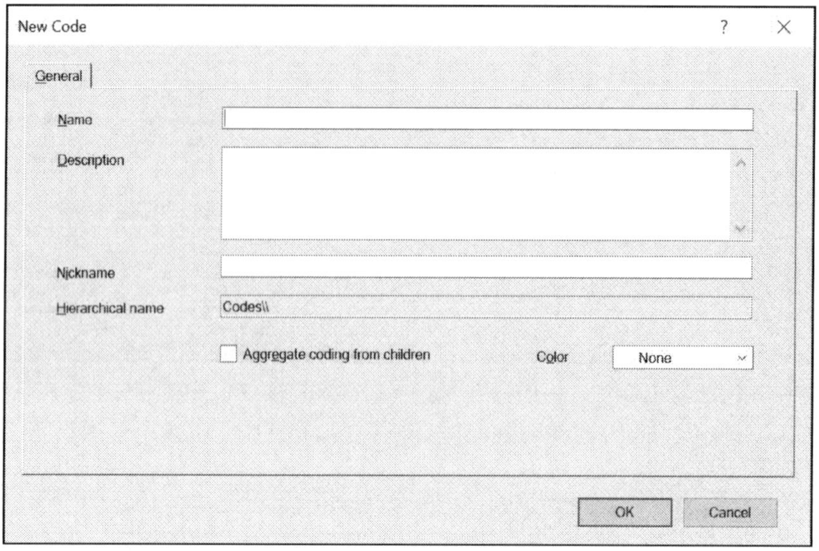

6 Type name (compulsory) and description and a nickname (both optional), then **[OK]**.

Relationships

Relationships are Codes that indicate that two Project Items (Source Items or Codes) are related, such as the hypothesis *Poverty* **influences** *Public Health.* Data supporting that hypothesis could be coded at such relationship Code, which represents the relationship between the Codes *Poverty* and *Public Health.*

Different relationship types are defined by the user and are stored under **Coding\\Relationship Types** folder. Relationships are then created as associative, one way, or symmetrical (see below). The Relationships folder is not allowed to have subfolders and Relationships cannot be arranged hierarchically. Classifications cannot be assigned to Relationships.

Creating a Relationship Type

Before creating relationships amongst your data, you must create some relationship types. In the above example (*Poverty* **influences** *Public Health),* the relationship type is titled **influences**.

1 Select the **Coding\\Relationship Type** folder.
2 Click on any empty space in the List View.
3 Right-click and select **New Relationship Type...** or **[Ctrl]** + **[Shift]** + **[N]**.

The **New Relationship Type** dialog box appears:

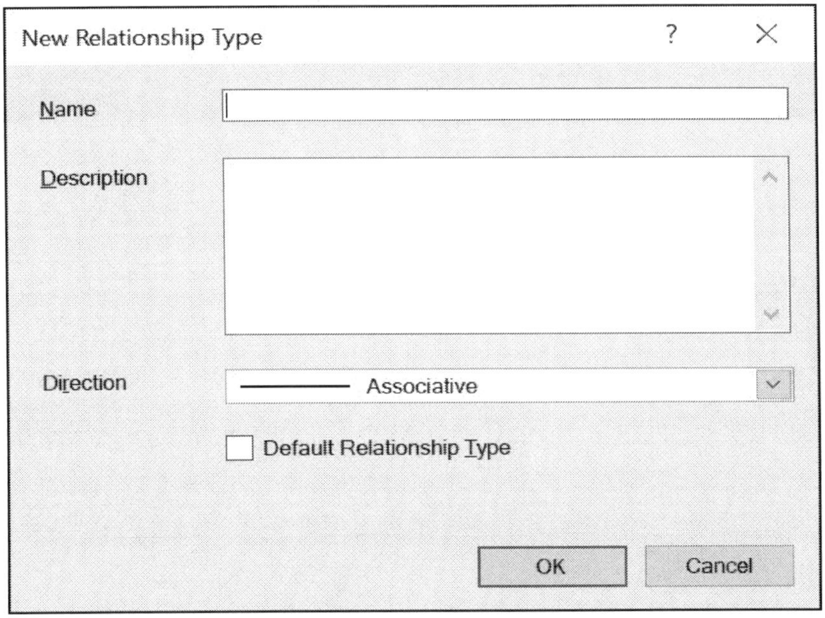

4 Select *Associative, One Way* or *Symmetrical* from the drop-down list at **Direction**.

5 Type a name (compulsory) and a description (optional), then [**OK**].

The Relationship Types in the List View, may look like this:

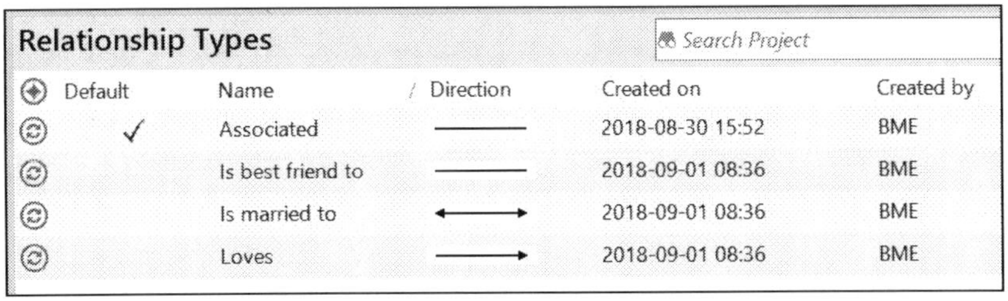

Relationship Types

Default	Name	Direction	Created on	Created by
✓	Associated	———	2018-08-30 15:52	BME
	Is best friend to	———	2018-09-01 08:36	BME
	Is married to	←——→	2018-09-01 08:36	BME
	Loves	——→	2018-09-01 08:36	BME

Creating a Relationship

Now that you have defined a relationship type, it's time to begin creating Relationships between items in your NVivo project.

1 Go to **Create | Relationship**.
Default folder is **Coding\\Relationships**.
Go to 4.

alternatively

1 Select the **Coding\\Relationships** folder.

2 Go to **Create | Relationship**.
Go to 4.

alternatively

2 Click on any empty space in the List View.

3 Right-click and select **New Relationship...** or **[Ctrl]** + **[Shift]** + **[N]**.

The **New Relationship** dialog box appears:

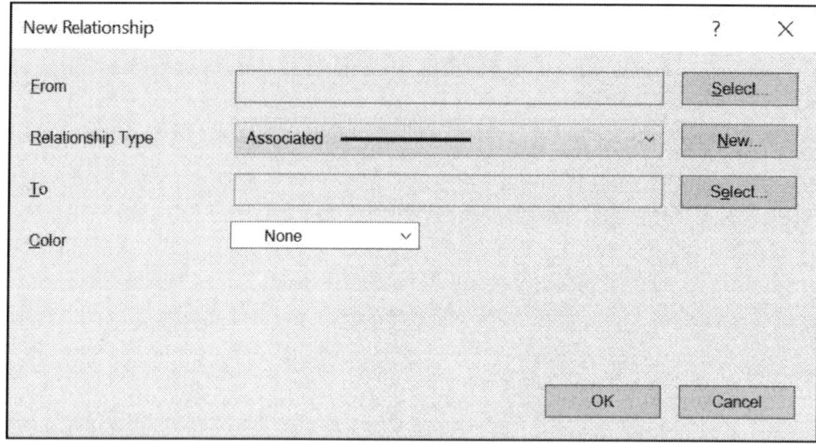

A Relationship defines a relation between two Project Items, Source Items or Codes.

4 Use the **[Select...]** buttons to find the two items that will be connected by this Relationship.

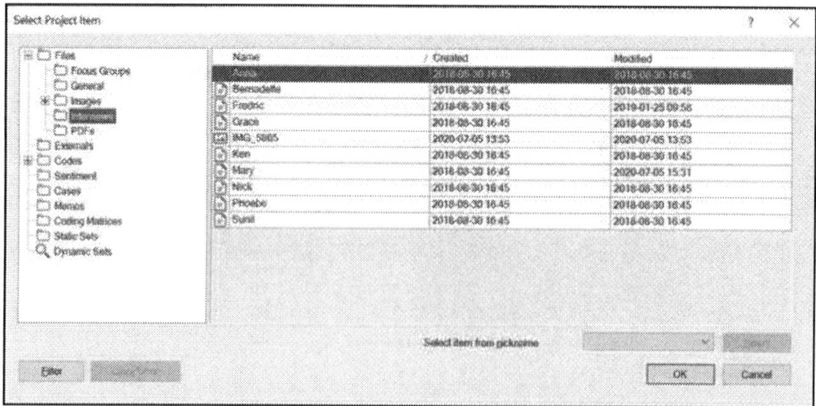

5 Select one From-item and one To-item. Confirm with **[OK]**.

6 Select a Relationship Type with the drop-down list.

The **New Relationship** dialog box will then look like this to represent a much more concrete relationship: that *Anna* **is married to** *Raul*:

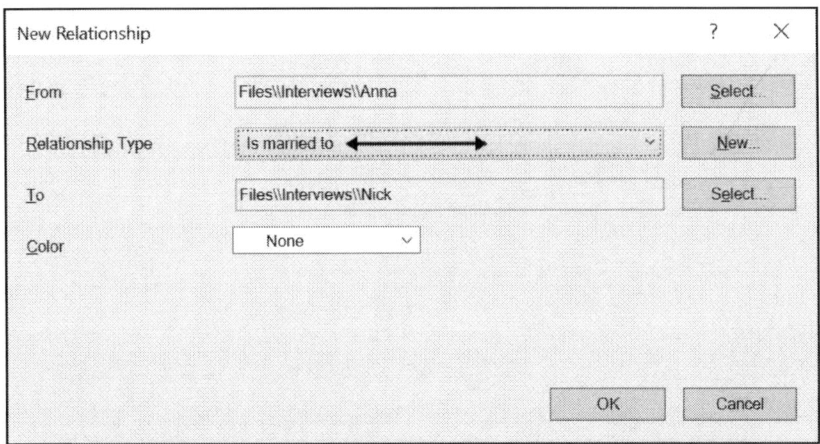

A new context dependent Ribbon menu, **Relationship**, has now opened and is opened each time a Relationship is created or opened.

Using the **[New...]** button you can create a new Relationship type, see page 138.

7 Confirm with **[OK]**.

The List View with Relationships may look like this:

Relationships

From Name	From F	Type	To Name	To Fold	Directio	Files	Referen	Created on	Created
Interviewees\F	Cases	Is best friend to	Interviewees\M	Cases	——	0	0	2018-09-01	BME
Interviewees\	Cases	Is married to	Focus Group M	Cases	←→	0	0	2018-09-01	BME
Anna	Files\\I	Is married to	Nick	Files\\I	←→	0	0	2020-07-06	BME
Interviewees\	Cases	Loves	Focus Group M	Cases	——→	0	0	2018-09-01	BME

Using the Quick Coding Bar on Relationships

NVivo has improved the Quick Coding bar to facilitate the creation of new Relationships and new Relationship Types. When you have found a section in your sources that verifies a relationship of some kind you select this text accordingly. Then with the Coding bar you first select Relationships in the **In** scroll bar:

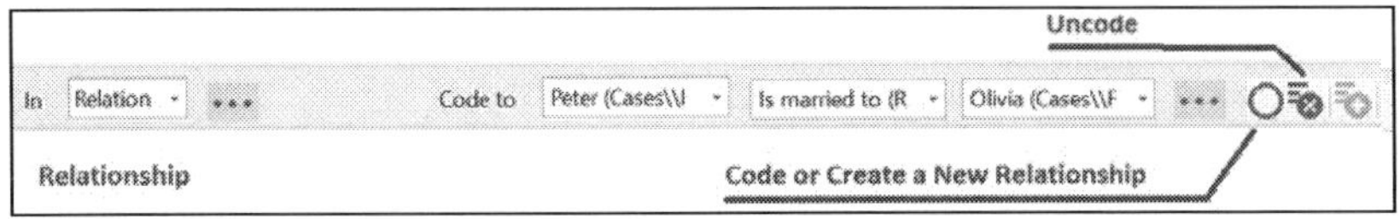

Then you select a From Case and a To Case and a proper Relationship Type. You can also as an alternative create new items by typing new names in the Coding bar and finally confirm with the Code button. The default direction will be *Associated* and can easily be changed later on.

Viewing a Relationship from a Related Item

1 Open an item in the List View that has a relationship.
2 Go to **<item type> | Relationships**
which is a toggling function.

A new window will open and the relationship will show:

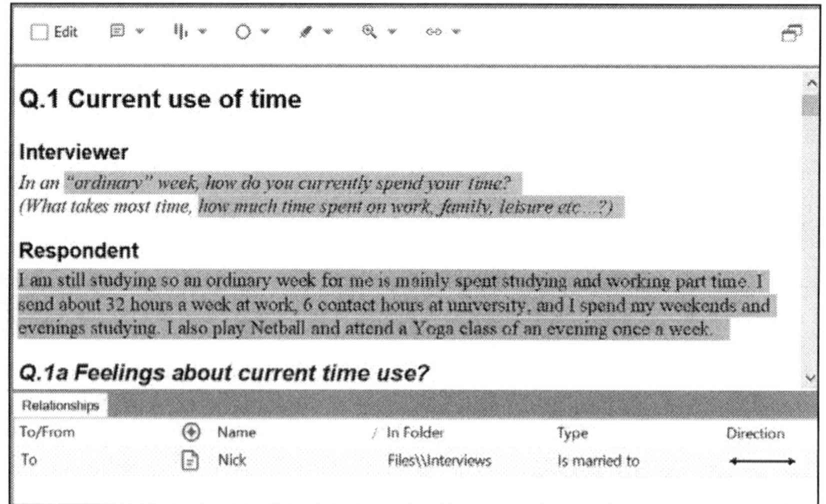
Edit
Q.1 Current use of time
Interviewer
In an "ordinary" week, how do you currently spend your time?
(What takes most time, how much time spent on work, family, leisure etc...?)
Respondent
I am still studying so an ordinary week for me is mainly spent studying and working part time. I send about 32 hours a week at work, 6 contact hours at university, and I spend my weekends and evenings studying. I also play Netball and attend a Yoga class of an evening once a week.
Q.1a Feelings about current time use?
Relationships
To/From
Name
In Folder
Type
Direction
To
Nick
Files\\Interviews
Is married to

Exporting a Code

All Project Items (except folders) can be exported in various file types:

1 Select the item(s) that you want to export, like a Code.
2 Go to **Share | Export → Export**
or right-click and select **Export → Export Code**
or **[Ctrl]** + **[Shift]** + **[E]**.

The **Export Options** dialog box appears:

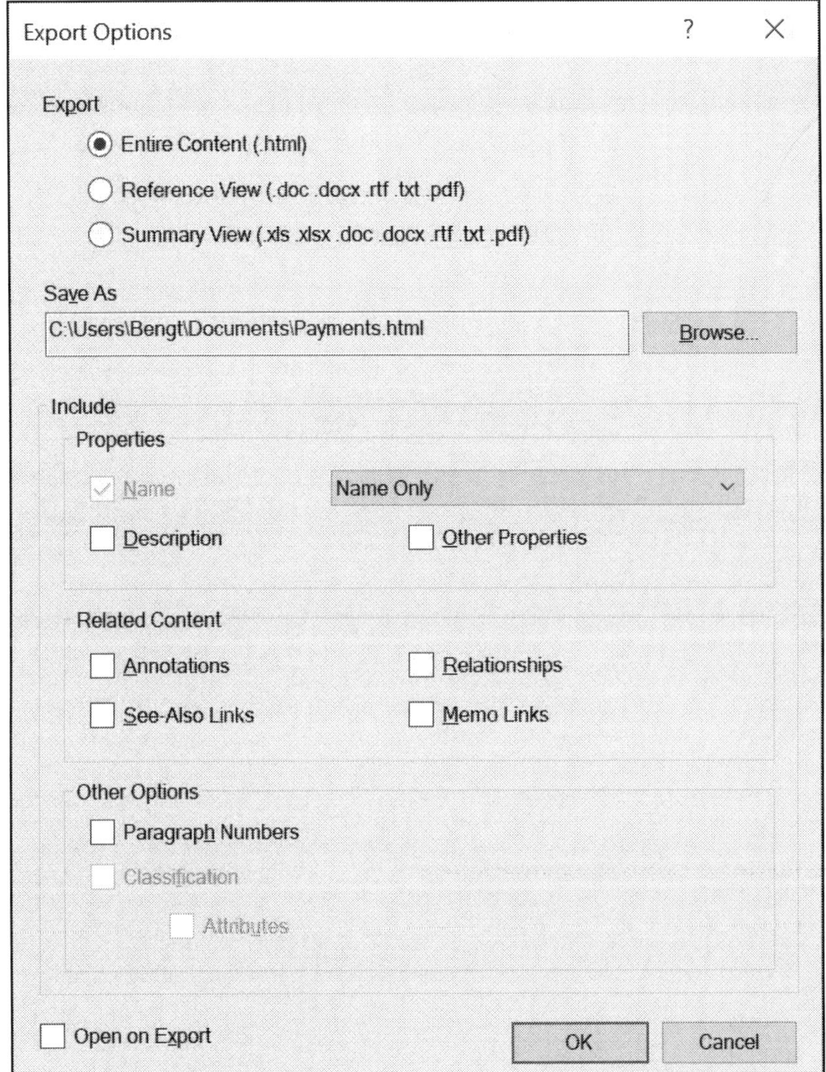

3 Select options, file name, location, and file type. Confirm with **[OK]**.

The option *Entire Content* creates a HTML-page with several files and folders that can be uploaded to a Web-server.

Converting a Relationship to a Code or a Case

By copying a Relationship and then pasting it into the **Coding\\Codes** or **Cases\\Cases** folder the result will be a new Code with the same name as the from item of the Relationship.

11. INTRODUCING CASES

The Folder Structure for Cases

The project folder structure for **Cases** are: Cases and Case Classifications. The default folders as shown in the Navigator are:

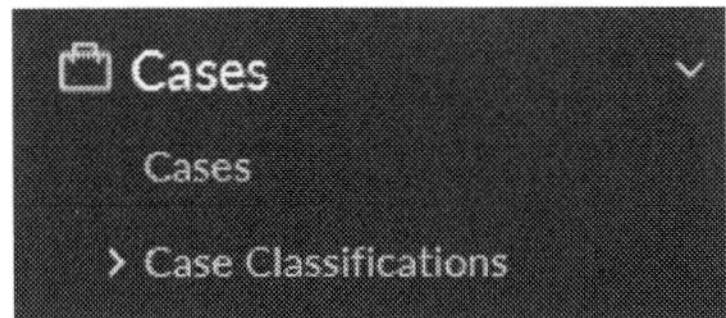

These folders and the names are not possible to delete, move, or rename. The folder names are depending on the user interface language setting, see page 39. However, the user can create subfolders to the default folder **Cases\\Cases** and create items shown the Navigator as items in the folder **Cases\\Case Classifications**.

In our work, we find it useful to make a distinction between Codes and Cases[3]. Codes are containers based on themes, your ideas and insights about your project. A Code therefore represents a theme or a topic common to the whole project. Codes are often represented by a Code hierarchy.

Cases are containers based on cases, the tangible elements of your project, like your participants or research settings. Importantly, Cases have the ability to be labeled with customized meta-data called Case Classifications. A Case is understood as a member of a group of items which are classified with Attributes and Values reflecting demographic or descriptive data. Cases can be people (Interviewees, Survey Participants, etc.), places (Villages, Schools, etc.) or any other groupings with similar properties.

Let's consider the example of interviews, which are a method of data collection used in many qualitative studies. The interview transcript would be the NVivo File. Concepts discussed during the interview could be assigned to Codes and the interviewees could be assigned to aCases. From there, demographic characteristics like gender, age, and education level can then be applied to the Case in the form of Attributes and Values (we expand on this in Chapter 12, Classifications) The research design of many qualitative studies is often based on the intersection between Cases and Codes. We will illustrate this when we describe Coding Matrices (see page 211) and Framework Matrices (see page 251).

---

[3] In previous software versions the term used was **Case Node**.

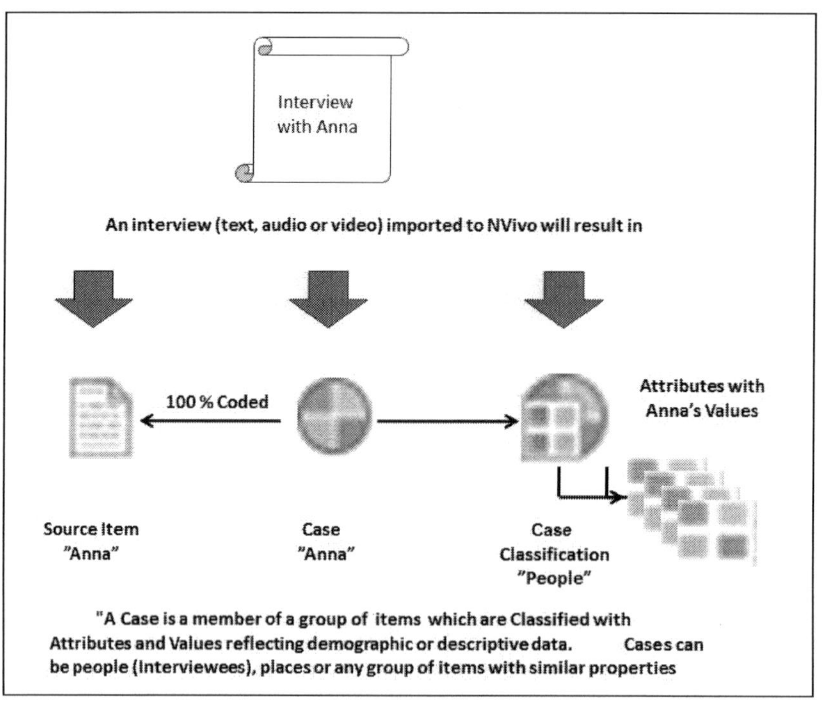
Interview
with Anna
An interview (text, audio or video) imported to NVivo will result in
100 % Coded
Attributes with
Anna's Values
Source Item
"Anna"
Case
"Anna"
Case
Classification
"People"
"A Case is a member of a group of items which are Classified with
Attributes and Values reflecting demographic or descriptive data. Cases can
be people (interviewees), places or any group of items with similar properties

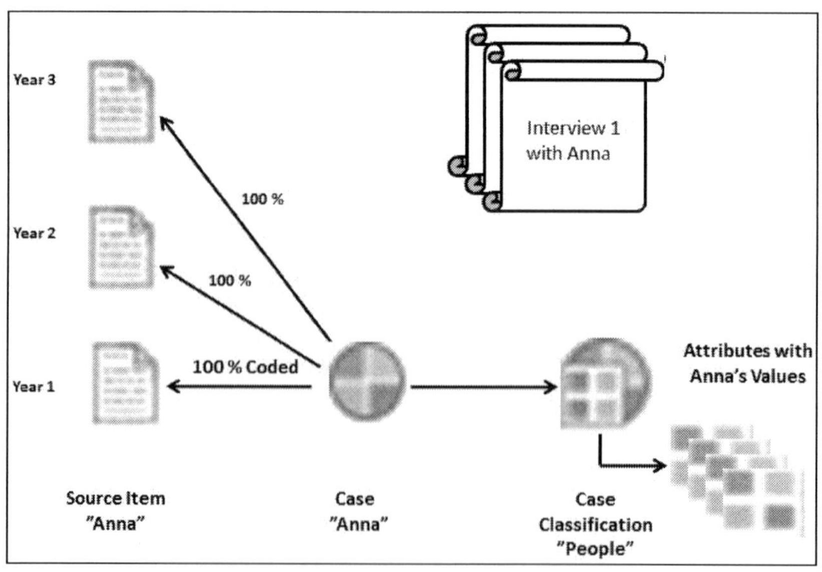
Year 3
Year 2
Year 1
Interview 1
with Anna
100 %
100 %
100 % Coded
Attributes with
Anna's Values
Source Item
"Anna"
Case
"Anna"
Case
Classification
"People"

Creating a Case

Manually creating a new Case can be done in a number of ways.

1 Go to **Create | Case**.
Default folder is **Cases\\Cases** or its currently open subfolder.
Go to 4.

alternatively

1 Select the **Cases\\Cases** folder or its subfolder.
2 Go to **Create | Case**.
Go to 4.

alternatively

2 Click on any empty space in the List View.
3 Right-click and select **New Case...**
or **[Ctrl]** + **[Shift]** + **[N]**

The **New Case** dialog box appears:

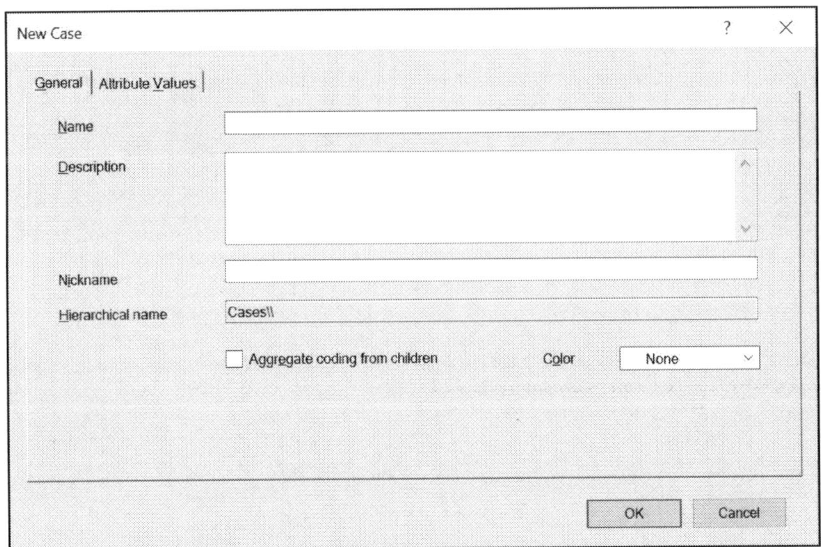

4 Type name (compulsory) and a description and a nickname (both optional), then **[OK]**.

A new context dependent Ribbon menu, **Case**, opens each time a Cases is created or opened.

Please note, that Cases can be connected to certain Attribute Values, by going to the **Attributes Vales** tab and selecting a Case Classification, such as People in the screenshot below:

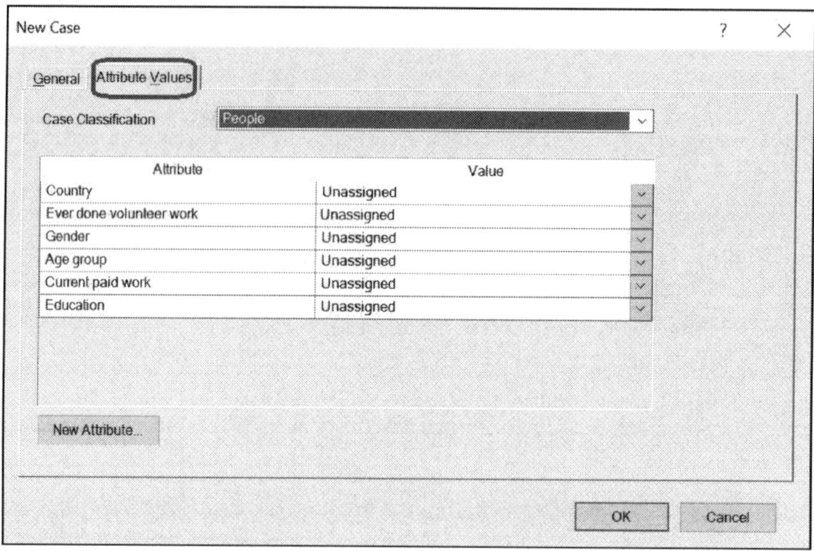

Here is a typical List View of some Cases:

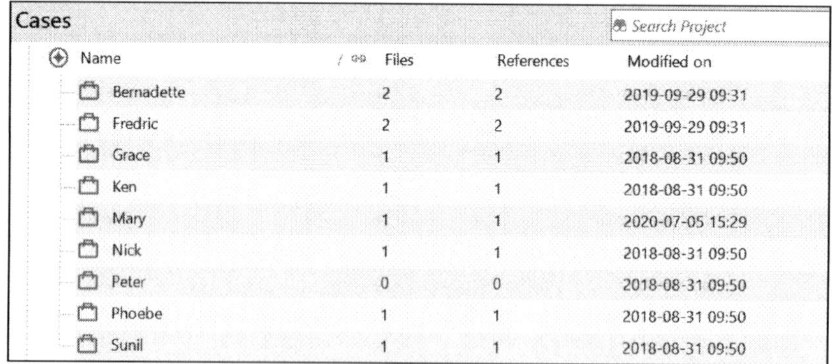

Name	Files	References	Modified on
Bernadette	2	2	2019-09-29 09:31
Fredric	2	2	2019-09-29 09:31
Grace	1	1	2018-08-31 09:50
Ken	1	1	2018-08-31 09:50
Mary	1	1	2020-07-05 15:29
Nick	1	1	2018-08-31 09:50
Peter	0	0	2018-08-31 09:50
Phoebe	1	1	2018-08-31 09:50
Sunil	1	1	2018-08-31 09:50

12. CLASSIFICATIONS

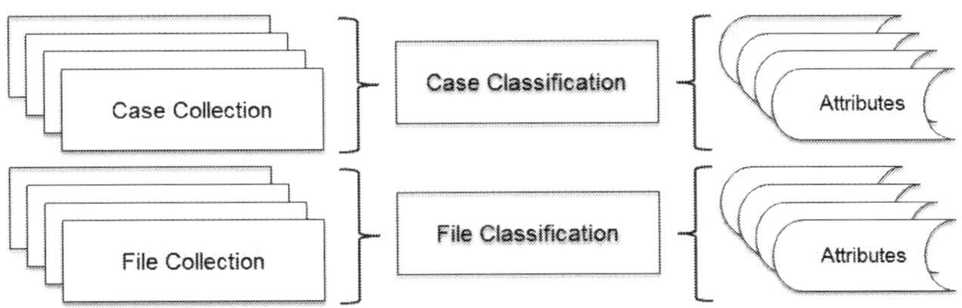

Case and File Classifications

Files, Codes, Cases, Classifications, Attributes, and Values are related in the following way.

Files hold primary or secondary data. They can be text sources, media sources or picture sources. Are in earlier literature named Source Items.

Codes represent a topic, a phenomenon, an idea, a value, an opinion, a case, or any other abstraction or tangible object thought to be important for the current study. Codes are *not* classified.

Cases represent information that is generated from a certain source like an informant, a place, an organization or any other source that is subject to the current study.

Attributes represent characteristics or properties of a File or a Case which has or will have an impact when analyzing data. Each such attribute has a set of ***Values***. Attributes and values hold the demographic data of the study. For example, if gender is your attribute, the possible values are male or female.

Classifications are defined by NVivo as a collective name for a certain set of Attributes that will be assigned to certain Files or Cases. Think of Classifications as an easy way to replicate a group of related attributes. Classifications are not applied on Codes.

Classifications fall into two types: Case Classifications and File Classifications. We will explore how to create Classifications, how they are associated with Files and Cases and how individual values are handled. Attributes cannot be created without the existence of Classifications. This chapter presents examples of how to create a Case Classification, but the procedures are similar for File Classifications.

Case Classifications

An example: You are part of a study looking at the experiences of pupils, teachers, politicians and schools. There are reasons to create individual Case Classifications for each of these four groups:

- Attributes for pupils could be: Age, gender, grade, number of siblings, social class.
- Attributes for teachers could be: Age, gender, education, number of years as teacher, school subject.
- Attributes for politicians could be: Age, gender, political preference, number of years as politician, other profile.
- Attributes for schools could be: Size, age, size of the community, political majority.

Each of these four groups needs its own set of attributes, with each attribute requiring its own set of values. Case Classifications allow you to quickly assign the appropriate list of attributes to groups of Cases.

File Classifications

In NVivo, Classifications are also applied to Files or Source Items with attributes and values. File Classifications, for example, could be applied to research on art history where imported image Files may need attributes like the time period of the art work, the place of origin, and other relevant conditions. File Classifications can also be applied to research that is the result of a literature review, with attributes like journal name, type of study, keywords, publication date, name of authors etc. (See Chapter 16: Handling Bibliographic Data)

Creating a Case Classification

Although NVivo includes some default Classifications (e.g., the Case Classification *Person* and the File Classification *Reference*), it is possible to create your own custom Classifications:

1 Go to **Create | Case Classification**.
Default folder is **Cases\\Case Classifications**.
Go to 4.

alternatively

1 Select the **Cases \\Case Classifications** folder.
2 Go to **Create | Case Classification**.
Go to 4.

alternatively

2 Click on any empty space in the List View.
3 Right-click and select **New Classification...**
or **[Ctrl]** + **[Shift]** + **[N]**.

The **New Classification** dialog box appears:

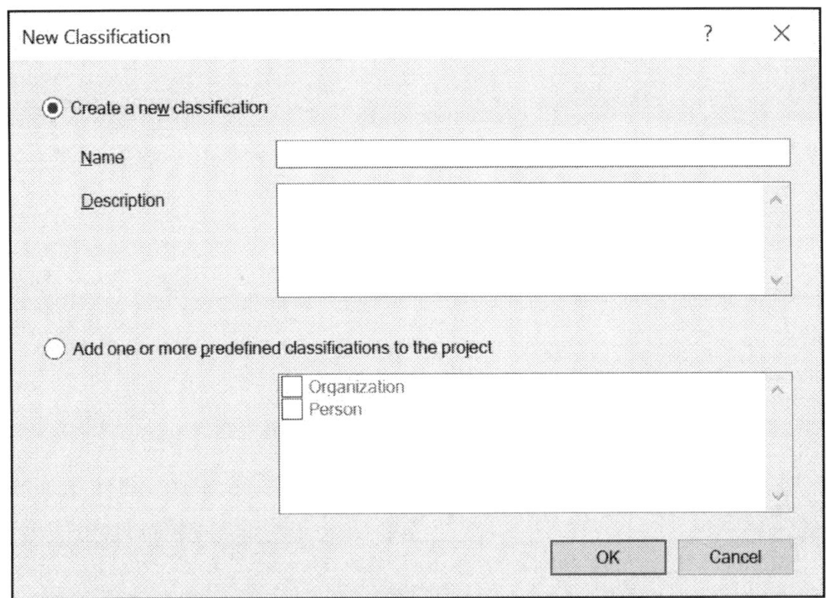

You can choose between creating your own new Classification and using one of NVivo's templates.

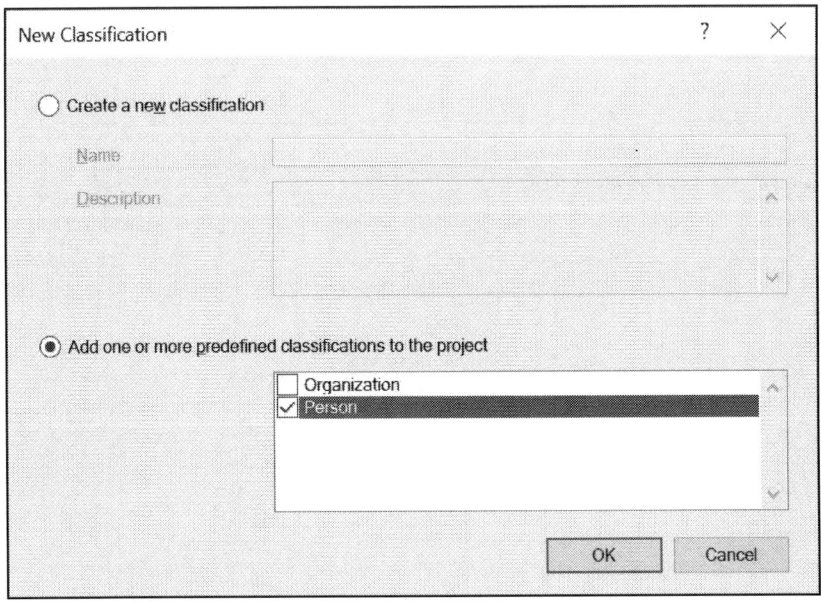

This example uses the template *Person.* You may also choose *Create a new classification.*

4 Click **[OK]**.

The result is shown like this in the List View:

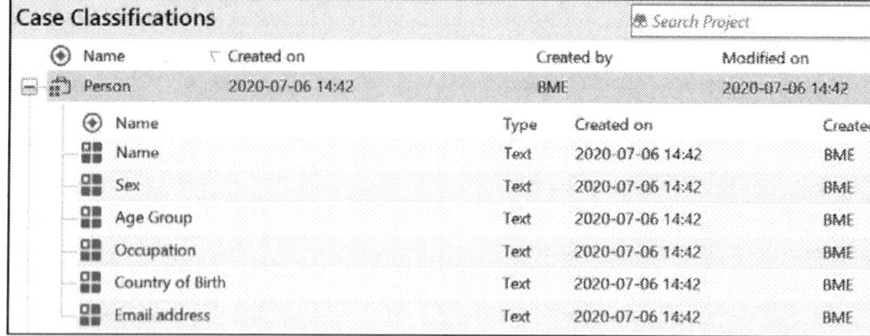

The attributes that have been created from this template have initially no other values than *Unassigned* and *Not Applicable*.

The classification can easily be edited. You can create new attributes and you can delete those not needed.

Customizing a Classification

A Classification can easily be edited. You can also easily create new attributes and delete those not needed.

1 Select a Classification in the List View.
2 Right-click and select **New Attribute...** or **[Ctrl]** + **[Shift]** + **[N]**.

The **New Attribute** dialog box appears:

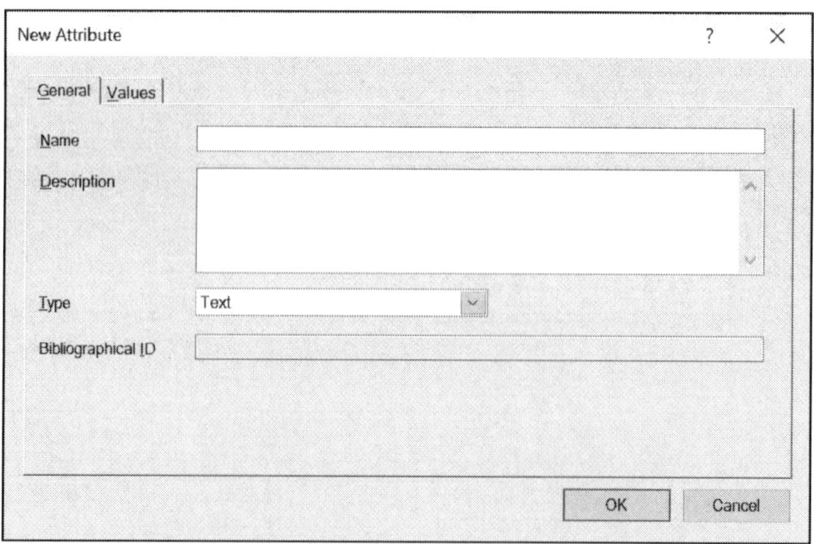

3 Type a name (compulsory) and a description (optional) and select the attribute type (Text, Integer, Decimal, Date/Time, Date, Time or Boolean), then **[OK]**.

The data type field indicates what kind of data will constitute an Attribute's Values. There are seven data types: **Text** data includes any text content (e.g., profession); **Integer** data includes a number without a decimal place; **Decimal** data includes a number with a decimal place; **Time** data is the time in hours, minutes and seconds; **Date/Time** data is a combination of the calendar date and time; and **Boolean** data are binary pairs (e.g., yes or no, 0 or 1).

You can also decide which values belong to the attribute. Use either the **New Attribute** dialog box or the **Attribute Properties** dialog box, under the **Values** tab:

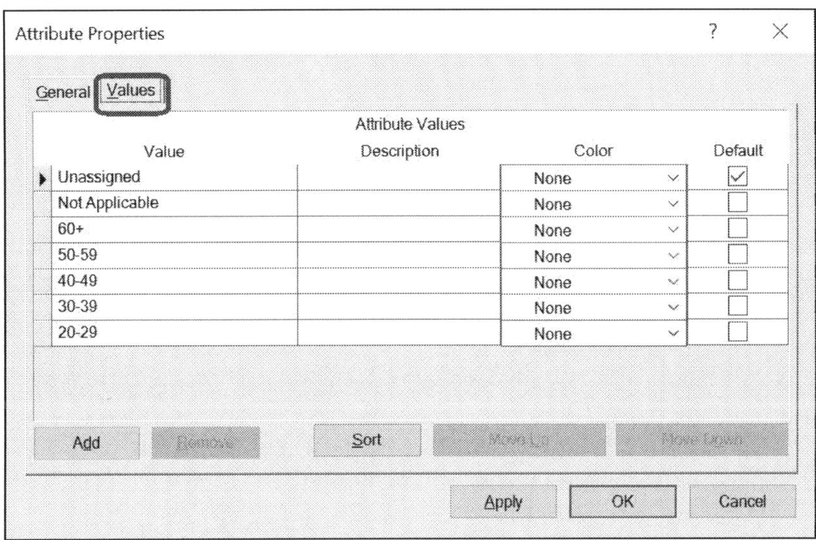

4 The [**Add**] button creates a text box in which you can type new values. Confirm with [**OK**]. To delete any value, you need to select this value, then click [**Remove**] and if this value has been assigned to any case you will be asked to replace the value by an existing one.

Finally, you need to assign the Classification to a Case.

1 Select one or several Cases that shall be assigned a Classification.
2 Right-click and select **Classification → <Name of Classification>**.

Alternatively, if you only select *one* Case:

1 Select the Case that shall be assigned a Classification.
2 Right-click and select **Case Properties** or [**Ctrl**] + [**P**].

The **Case Properties** dialog box appears:

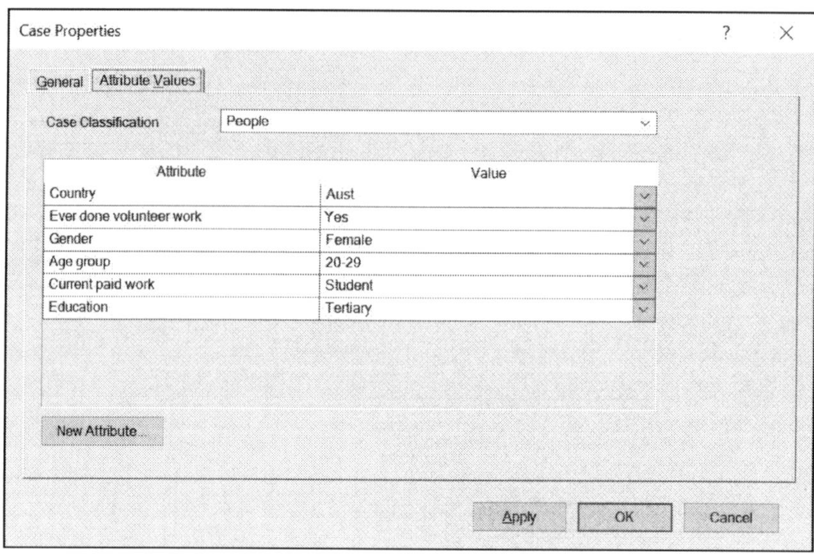

3 Use the **Attribute Values** tab. The **Classification** drop-down list will give you access to all Case Classifications in the project.

4 In the column *Value* you can use the drop-down list to set individual values to the current Case.

5 Confirm with [**OK**].

Working with the Classification Sheet

The overview of the attributes and values of Files or Cases is called a Classification Sheet. This sheet is a matrix where rows are Files or Cases and columns are Attributes. The cells contain the values.

While creating a Classification allows you to establish the Attributes and Values associated with classified items, the application of that metadata is done through the Classification Sheet. When a Classification Sheet is opened you can update values, along with sorting and filtering data.

1 Select a Case/File Classification in the List View.

2 Go to **Home | Item → 'Open' → Open Classification Sheet**.

alternatively

2 Right-click and select **Open Classification Sheet**
or key command [**Ctrl**] + [**Shift**] + [**O**]
or double-click.

alternatively

2 Select a classified Case (File) in the List View

3 Right-click and select **Open Classification Sheet**.

A new context dependent Ribbon menu, **Classification**, has now opened and is opened each time a Classfication is opened.

The navigation view looks like this. When you select the folder **Cases\\Case Classifications** then all classifications are shown in the List View:

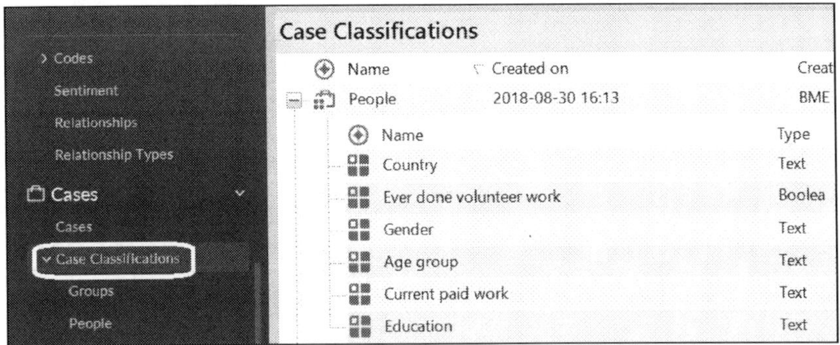

Below is a sample Classification Sheet. As you can see, each row is an item that has been classified with the Classification *People*, each column is an Attribute, and each cell contains the attribute's attendant value:

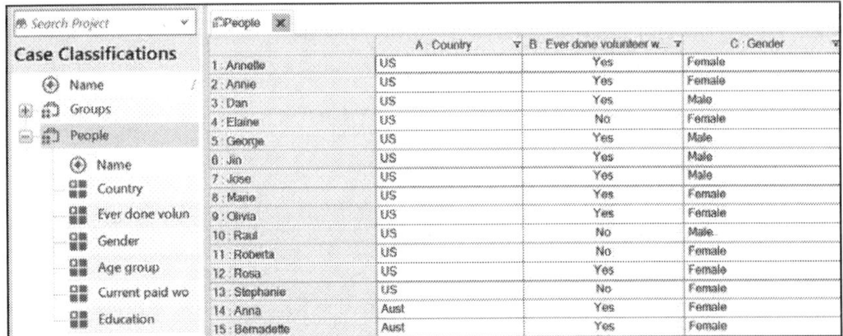

	A : Country	B : Ever done volunteer w...	C : Gender
1 : Annette	US	Yes	Female
2 : Annie	US	Yes	Female
3 : Dan	US	Yes	Male
4 : Elaine	US	No	Female
5 : George	US	Yes	Male
6 : Jin	US	Yes	Male
7 : Jose	US	Yes	Male
8 : Mario	US	Yes	Female
9 : Olivia	US	Yes	Female
10 : Raul	US	No	Male
11 : Roberta	US	No	Female
12 : Rosa	US	Yes	Female
13 : Stephanie	US	No	Female
14 : Anna	Aust	Yes	Female
15 : Bernadette	Aust	Yes	Female

When you select **Cases\\Case Classifications\\<name of Classification>** you will view all shortcuts of all classified items and attributes and values as child items to each case:

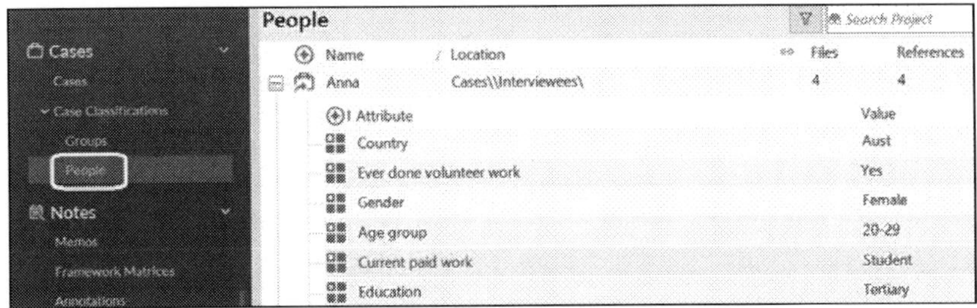

Once you have your Classification Sheet open, there are a number of options for editing, structuring, viewing and occluding aspects of your data.

Editing the Classification Sheet

Once you point at a cell in the Classification sheet there will be right side arrow in the cell. Clicking at the arrow lets you select any of the available values or overtype any value and a new value will be created. However, you cannot delete any value here.

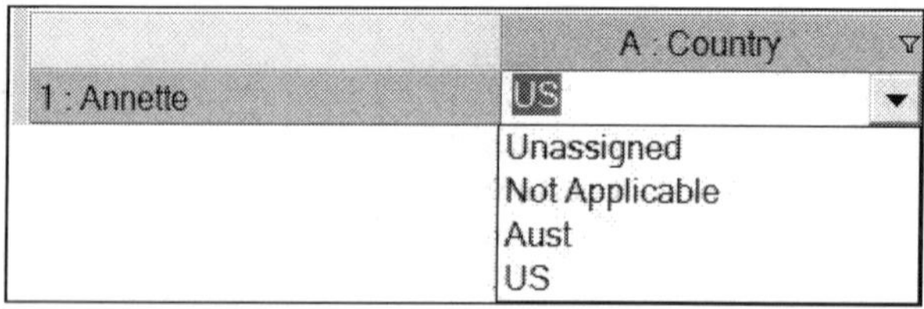

Hiding/Unhiding Row Numbers (Toggling Function)

1 Open a **Classification Sheet**.
2 Go to **Classification | Hide & Unhide → Row IDs**
  or right-click and select **Row → Row IDs**.

Hiding Rows

1 Open a **Classification Sheet**.
2 Select one row or several rows that you want to hide.
3 Go to **Classification | Hide & Unhide → Hide Row**
  or right-click and select **Row → Hide Row**.

Hiding/Unhiding Rows using Filters

1 Open a **Classification Sheet**.
2 Select a column.
3 Go to **Classification | Sort & Filter → Filter Column...**

alternatively

3 Click the 'funnel' in any column head
  or select a column, right-click and select **Column → Filter Column...**

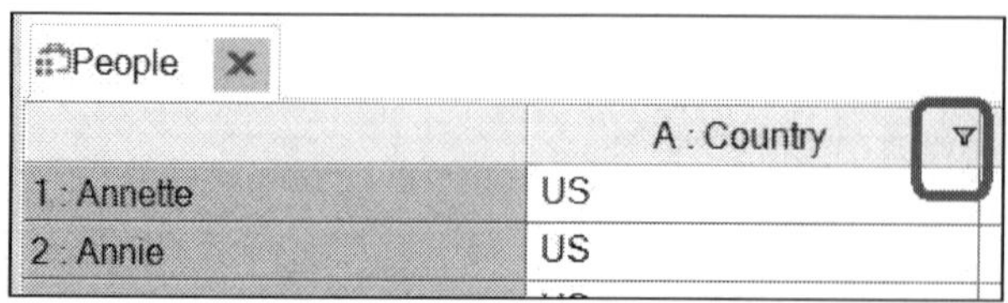

The **Classification Filter Options** dialog box appears:

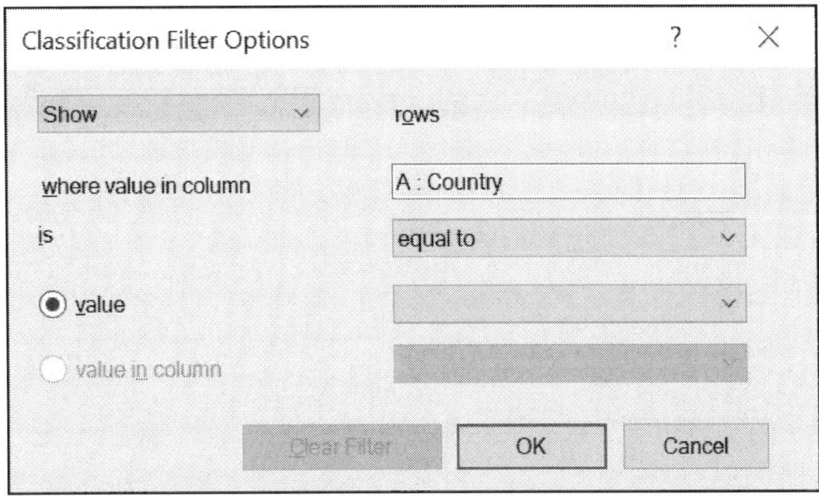

4 Select value and operator for hiding or unhiding. Confirm with [**OK**]. When a filter has been applied the funnel symbol turns *red*.

To reset a filter select [**Clear Filter**] in the Classification Filter Options dialog box or right-click and select **Column → Clear All Column Filters** or go to **Classifications | Sort & Filter → Clear All Column Filters**.

Unhiding Rows

1 Open a **Classification Sheet**.
2 Select one row on each side of the hidden row(s) that you want to unhide.
3 Go to **Classifications | Hide & Unhide → Unhide Row** or right-click and select **Row → Unhide Row**.

Unhiding All Rows

1 Open a **Classification Sheet**.
2 Go to **Classifications | Hide & Unhide → Show All Rows** or right-click and select **Row → Show All Rows**.

Hiding /Unhiding Column Letter /Toggling Function)

1 Open a **Classification Sheet**.
2 Go to **Classifications | Hide & Unhide → Column IDs** or right-click and select **Column → Column IDs**.

Hiding Columns

1 Open a **Classification Sheet**.
2 Select one column or several columns that you want to hide.
3 Go to **Classifications | Hide & Unhide → Hide Column** or right-click and select **Column → Hide Column**.

Unhiding Columns

1. Open a **Classification Sheet**.
2. Select a column on each side of the hidden column(s) that you want to unhide.
3. Go to **Classifications | Hide & Unhide → Unhide Column** or right-click and select **Column → Unhide Column**.

Unhiding All Columns

1. Open a **Classification Sheet**.
2. Go to **Classifications | Hide & Unhide → Show All Columns** or right-click and select **Column → Show All Columns**.

Transposing the Classification Sheet (Toggling Function)

Transposing means that rows and columns switch places.

1. Open a **Classification Sheet**.
2. Go to **Classifications | Transpose**
   or right-click and select **Transpose**.

Moving a Column Left or Right

1. Open a **Classification Sheet**.
2. Select the column or columns that you want to move. If you want to move more than one column, they need to be adjacent.
3. Go to **Classifications | Move Column Left/Move Column Right**
   or right-click and select **Column → Move Column Left/Move Column Right**
   or **[Ctrl] + [Shift] + [L]/ [Ctrl] + [Shift] + [R]**.

Resetting the Classification Sheet

1. Open a **Classification Sheet**.
2. Right-click and select **Reset Settings**.

Case Name Formats

Three case name formats can be applied: Name (normal), Hierarchical Name and Nickname. Applicable format can be set by opening a classification sheet and going to:
Classifications | Name
Classifications | Hierarchical Name
Classifications | Nickname.

Exporting Classification Sheets

A Classification Sheet can be exported as a tab delimited text-file or an Excel spreadsheet:

1 Select the Classification Sheet in the List View that you want to export.

2 Go to **Share | Export → Export** or right-click and select **Export → Export Classification Sheet...** or **[Ctrl]** + **[Shift]** + **[E]**.

The **Export Classification Sheets** dialog box appears:

> **Tip:** An easy way to convert an Excel worksheet to text is:
> 1 Select the whole worksheet
> 2 Copy
> 3 Open Notepad
> 4 Paste into Notepad
> 5 Save with a new name

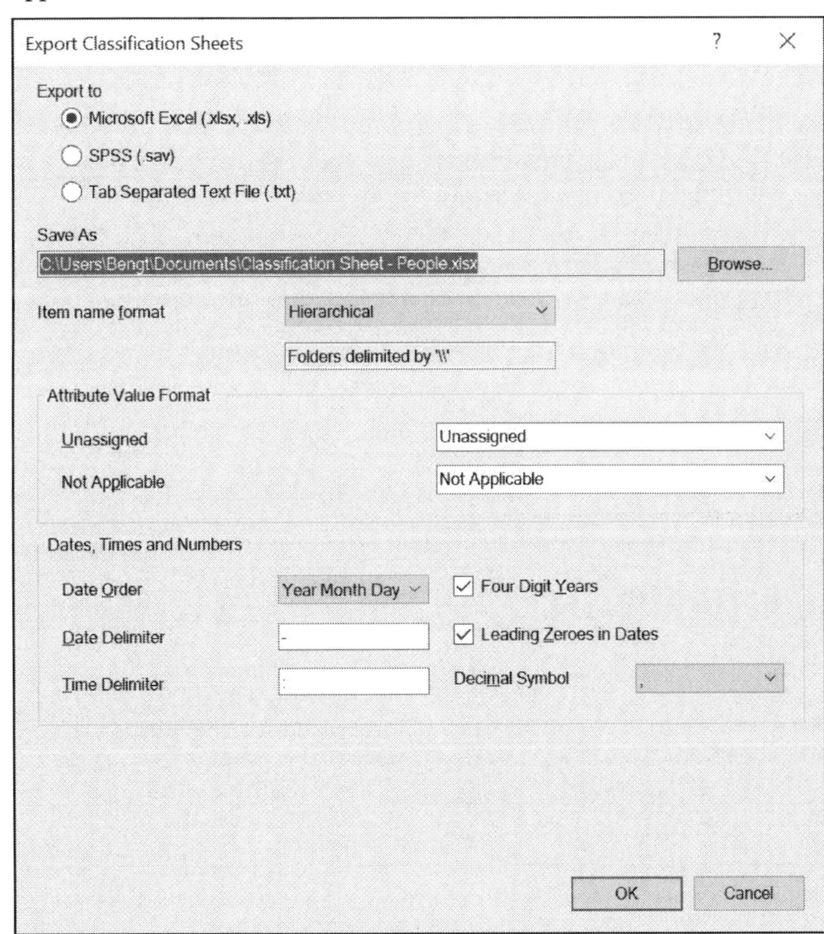

As you can see the available file types are Excel, SPSS, or TXT. With **[Browse...]** you can decide name and location.

3 Confirm with **[OK]**.

Importing a Classification Sheet

You can import a Classification Sheet as a tab-delimited text-file, an Excel spreadsheet, or an SPSS file type .SAV. All Codes, Attributes and Values are created from the imported file if they do not exist already.

1 Go to **Import | Classifications → Import Classification Sheets... / SPSS.**
  Default folder is **Cases\\Case Classifications**.
  Go to 4.

alternatively

1 Select the **Cases\\Case Classifications** folder.
2 Go to **Import | Classifications → Import Classification Sheets... / SPSS.**
  Go to 4.

alternatively

2 Click on any empty space in the List View.
3 Right-click and select **Import Classification Sheets.../ Import from SPSS...**

When you select SPSS then Windows file browser appears otherwise the **Import Classification Sheets Wizard – Step 1** appears:

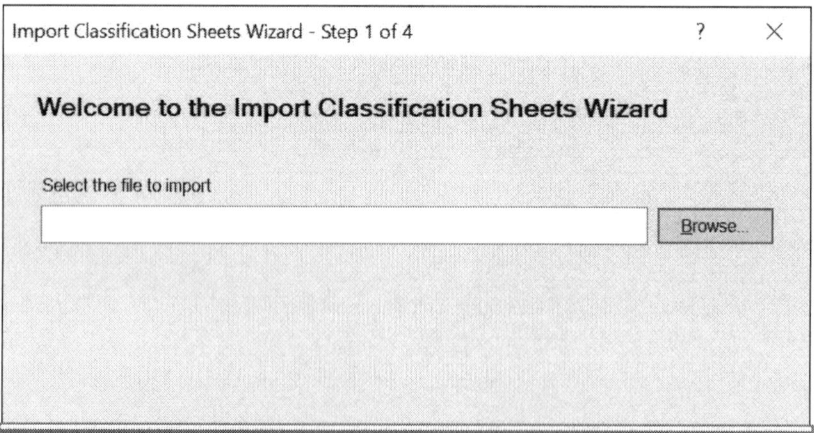

4 With **[Browse...]** you will find the file that you want to import.
5 Click **[Next]**.

The **Import Classification Sheets Wizard – Step 2** appears:

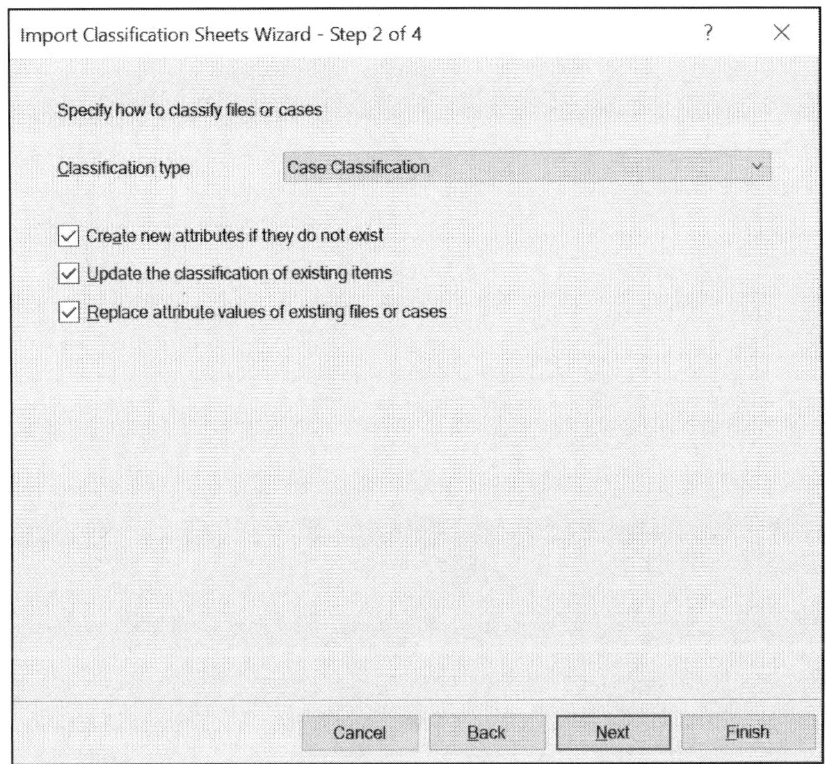

Here you decide if you want to create a new classification or use an existing one.

Create new attributes if they do not exist creates new attributes for the chosen classification.

Update the classification of existing iems replaces the classification of the Source Items or Codes that already exist in the location to be chosen.

Replace attribute values of existing files or cases that appear in this file determines if imported values shall replace the existing ones.

6 Click **[Next]**.

The **Import Classification Sheets Wizard - Step 3** appears:

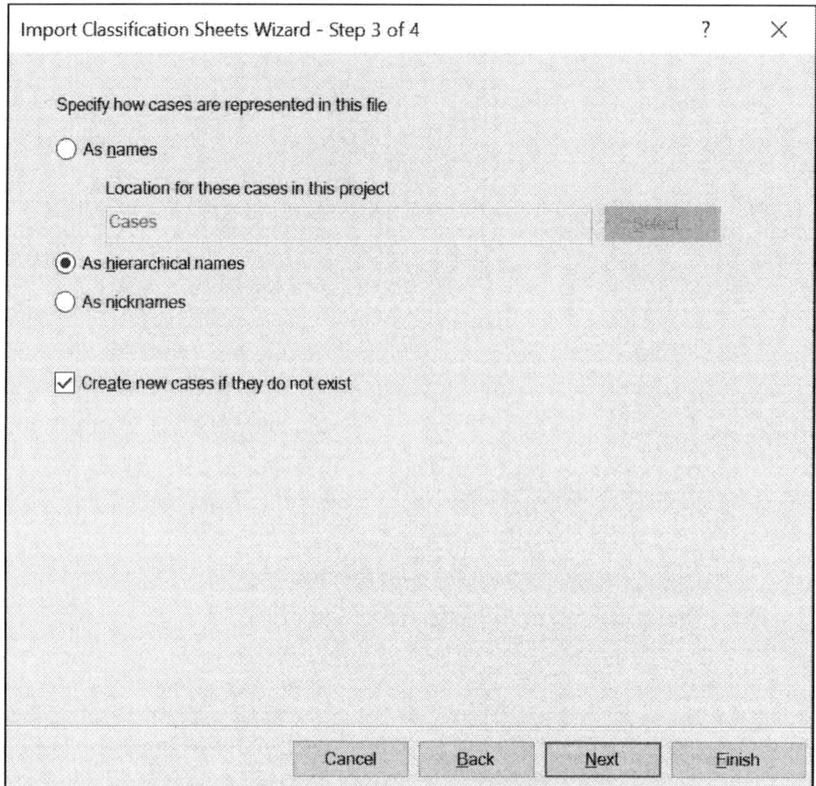

The option *As names* is selected when the first column of your file contains code names only. Requires that you use the [**Select**]-button to decide the location of the imported Codes.

The option ***As hierarchical names*** is selected when the first column of your file contains the full hierarchical name, see page 23.

The option ***As nicknames*** is selected when the first column of your file contains the code nicknames, see page 135.

7 Use *As names* and the [**Select**]-button to decide the location of the Codes when imported.

8 Click [**Next**].

The **Import Classification Sheets Wizard** – **Step 4** appears:

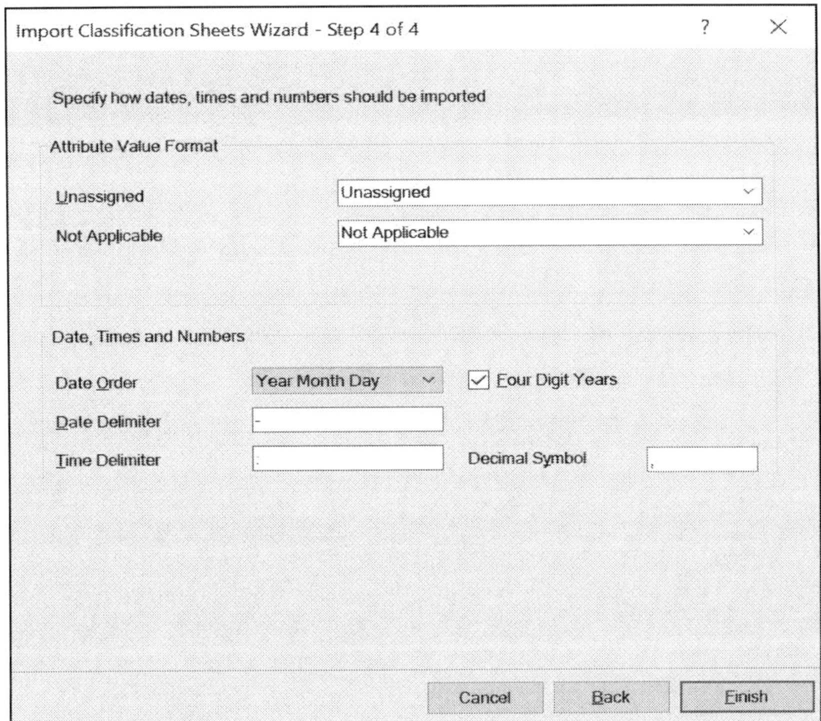

9 Decide the formats of unassigned values, dates, times and numbers.

10 Confirm with **[Finish]**.

The result, a Classification Sheet in NVivo, looks like this:

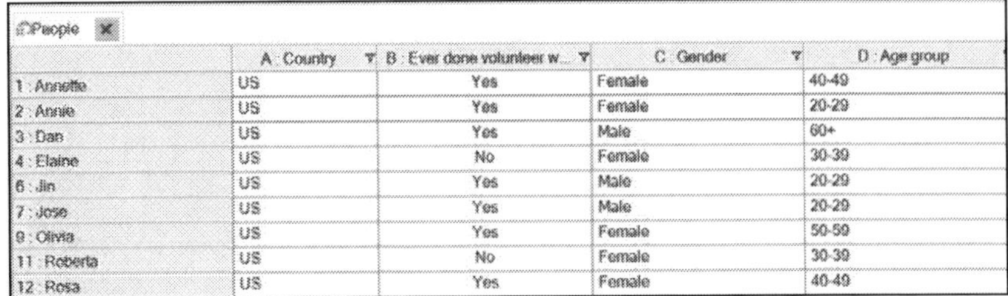

People

	A : Country	B : Ever done volunteer w...	C : Gender	D : Age group
1 : Annette	US	Yes	Female	40-49
2 : Annie	US	Yes	Female	20-29
3 : Dan	US	Yes	Male	60+
4 : Elaine	US	No	Female	30-39
6 : Jin	US	Yes	Male	20-29
7 : Jose	US	Yes	Male	20-29
9 : Olivia	US	Yes	Female	50-59
11 : Roberta	US	No	Female	30-39
12 : Rosa	US	Yes	Female	40-49

The Classification itself with its attributes can be displayed the List View:

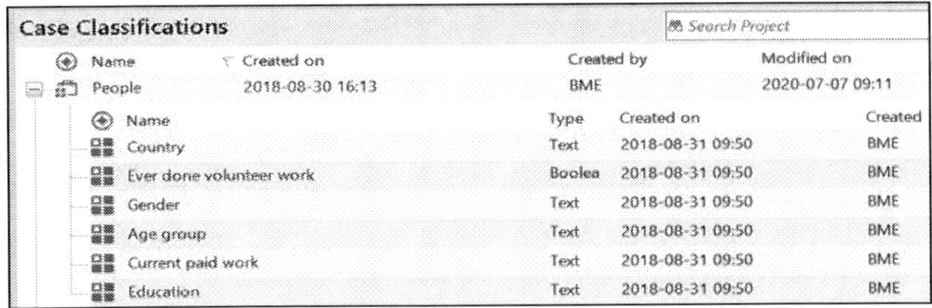

Case Classifications

Name	Created on	Created by	Modified on
People	2018-08-30 16:13	BME	2020-07-07 09:11

Name	Type	Created on	Created
Country	Text	2018-08-31 09:50	BME
Ever done volunteer work	Boolea	2018-08-31 09:50	BME
Gender	Text	2018-08-31 09:50	BME
Age group	Text	2018-08-31 09:50	BME
Current paid work	Text	2018-08-31 09:50	BME
Education	Text	2018-08-31 09:50	BME

13. CODING

Coding is the act of assigning a portion of your source material to one of your Codes. Coding can be carried out in two ways: *Manual Coding* (or just *Coding*) is conducted by the NVivo user; *Autocoding* is conducted by the NVivo software responding to pre-determined elements of text-based Files.

The item being coded can be any piece of data, even something as small as a single word from a document or a single frame from a video. However, a Description or an Annotation cannot be coded. Codes are the set of conceptual terms or case information that you will code to. One usually says that you are *coding* a certain source element at a certain Code.

As arguably the most important function of qualitative data analysis software, NVivo offers a variety of methods for coding data:

- The Quick Coding Bar
- Drag-and-drop
- Right-click/Menus/Keyboard Commands
- Autocoding by various principles
- Range coding
- In Vivo coding
- Coding by Query

Here follow some basic definitions used both in the NVivo commands and in our instructions:

Code implies that the entire content of a Source Item(s) or a selection is coded to a new or existing Code.

Code In Vivo implies that a selection creates a Code in the **Coding\\ Codes** folder named as the selected text (max 256 characters).

Autocode implies that the entire content of a Source Item(s) can be autocoded applying any of the applicable options.

Create As implies that the entire content of a Source Item(s) is created as a Set, Code or one or several Cases.

The Quick Coding Bar

The Quick Coding Bar can be moved around on the screen or be positioned in the lower part of the Detail View. You can toggle hiding/unhiding and docked/floating by going to **<Item Type>** | **View** | **Quick Coding** and the options **Hide, Docked** and **Floating**. Ideally, you will find the **Quick Coding Bar** useful enough to keep open each time you use NVivo – we do!

The **Quick Coding Bar** is active as long as a selection has been made in a Source Item or in a Code.

The drop-down list at **In** has four options: *Codes, Cases, Relationships* and *Nicknames*. The first time in a new work session you normally select *Codes* and then click on the first [...] button that now displays the **Select Location** dialog box. From here you can select among Code folders and parent Codes.

We have explained Codes and Relationships in this book, but Nicknames deserve some attention here. Nicknames are an opportunity for you to create 'shortcuts' to your most popular Codes. For example, giving your 5 most popular Codes' nicknames allows you to efficiently access them from the **Quick Coding Bar** without needing to browse through your coding hierarchy. Nicknames can also be useful for creating shortened versions of Codes with long names.

After selecting your Codes, Cases, Relationships, or Nickname, proceed to the drop-down list at **Code to**. This list contains all Codes at the selected location in alphabetic order. You can also use the second [...] button that opens the **Select Project Items** dialog box thus giving access to all Codes. You can select more than one Code to code to. You can also create a new Code by typing its name in the **Code to** text box at. The location of this new Code is determined by the setting in the left textbox **In**. Command **[Ctrl]** + **[Q]** positions the cursor in the right text box **Code to**, which will auto-complete Code names based on your typing – another shortcut.

The **Code to** drop-down also list saves the names of the last nine Codes used during an ongoing work session. You find this list below a divider and in the order they were last used.

After you have selected your Codes, the **Quick Coding Bar** can perform the following functions:

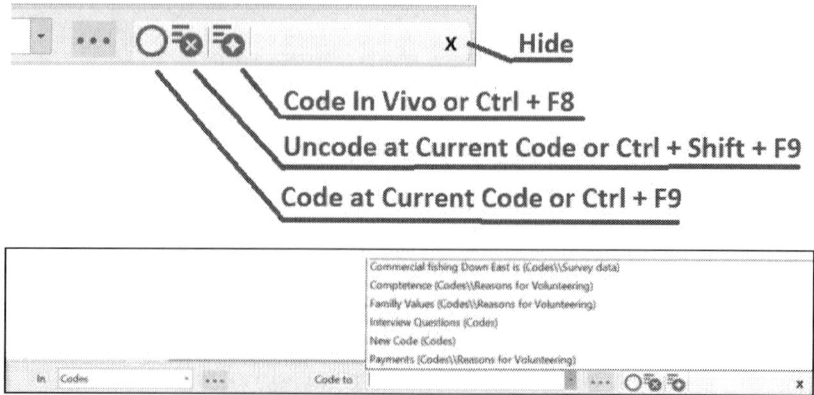

As soon as you type the code name in the text box possible alternatives will show and you can easily select the right code.

Drag-and-Drop Coding

Drag-and-drop coding is probably the fastest and easiest coding method. Using this method and a customized screen is, according to us, the best way to code your data.

1. Select the folder in **Data\\ Files** or its subfolder in the Navigation View with the Source Item that you want to code.
2. Open the Source Item in the List View that you want to code.
3. Select the text or image that you want to code.
4. Select **Coding\\Codes** and the folder with the Codes that you want to code to.
5. With the left mouse button pressed, drag the selection from the Source Item to the Code that you want to code to.

Use Right Detail View and close the Navigation View to fully optimize your screen location. This view allows you to drag source data easily into a Code.

Go to **Home | Workspace → Right**

Go to **Home | Workspace → Dashboard Mode**

(see page 46)

You can apply this technique when you need to create a new Code. You simply drag your selection at a space below the list of Codes or Cases and the field turns blue. As soon as you release the mouse button the **New Code** dialog box appears and you need to decide the Code name, location and possibly a description.

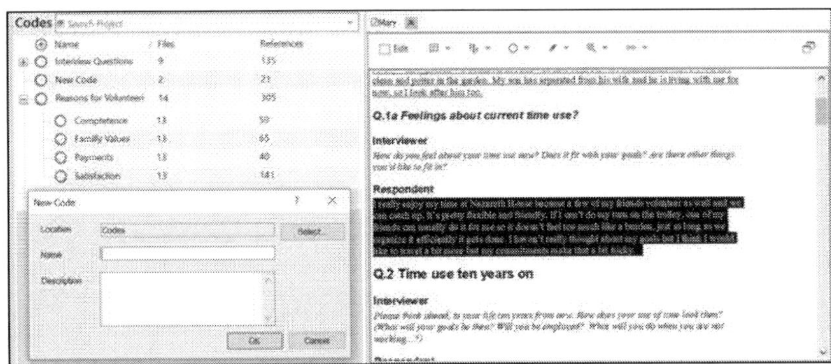

6. Confirm with **[OK]**.

Menus, Right-Click, or Keyboard Commands

While we prefer drag-and-drop coding, you will no doubt find yourselves in situations where you need to code using another method.

Coding a Source Item

1. Select the folder in **Data\\ Files** in in the Navigation View with the Source Item that you want to code.
2. Open the Source Item or Items in the List View that you want to code.
3. Select the text or image that you want to code.
4. Go to **Home | Code → Code Selection**
   or <**Item Type**> **| Code → Code Selection**
   or **[Ctrl]** + **[F2]**
   or **Recent Codes →** <**select**>

alternatively

4. Right-click and select **Code**
   or **[Ctrl]** + **[F2]**
   or **Code to Recent Codes** <**select**>

And this is the new **Select Code Items** dialog box:

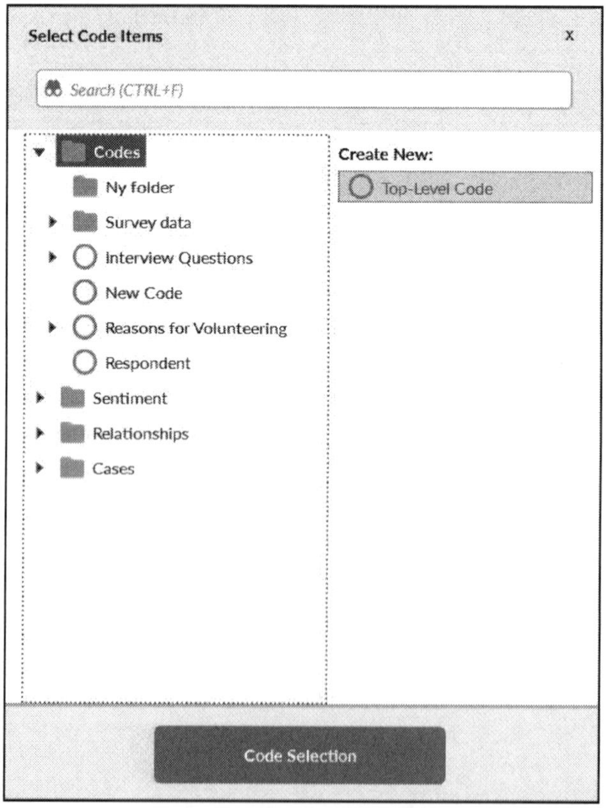

In this dialog box you can select one or several existing codes to code to. Note that the top text box offers a search function and can easiiy be used for searching among existing codes. When you select **[New Code]** the result, depending on what location you highlight, may look like the example at the arrow above.

Finally, type a name in the text box and confirm with **[OK]**. If you want to add a description then select the new Code in the List View, right-click and select **Code Properties** or **[Ctrl]** + **[Shift]** + **[P]**.

An alternative that will give you the same result (New Code) is when you select a source, right-click and select **Create As → Create As Code**.

Coding Source Items to Cases

This function can be used when several Source Items need to be converted to Cases. For example, you can create a list of Cases if you have recently imported a number of interview transcripts.

1. Select the **Data\\Files** folder or its subfolder with the Source Item(s) that you want to code.
2. Select the Source Item(s) or Items in the List View that you want to create as Cases.
3. Right-click and select **Create As → Create As Cases...**

The selected sources will be coded at a new Case or Cases and the **Select Location** dialog box will let you decide in what folder or under what parent Case the new Cases will be located. One Case for each selected source will be created with the same name as the sources. The **Select Location** dialog box also makes it possible that you allocate one of the existing Case Classifications to the new Case or Cases.

Coding a Selection from a Source Item

While Cases will often pertain to entire source files, though not always, Codes often involve selections from a Source Item:

1. Select the **Data\\Files** folder or its subfolder with the Source Item(s) that you want to code.
2. Open the Source Item.
3. Select the text or the section that you want to code.
4. Go to **Home | Code → Code Selection...**
   or **<Item Type> | Code → Code election**
   or **[Ctrl]** + **[F2]**
   or **Recent Codes →** <select>

alternatively

4. Right-click and select
   Code Selection
   or **[Ctrl** + **[F2]**
   or **Code to Recent Codes** <select>
   or **Code In Vivo**
   or **[Ctrl]** + **[F8]**

The new **Select Code Items** dialog box will open and you can choose a new or existing Code or Codes to code to.

Uncoding a Source Item

As qualitative data coding is often an iterative process, sources may need to be uncoded.

1. Select the **Data\\Files** folder or its subfolder with the Source Item(s) that you want to uncode.
2. Select the Source Item(s) in the List View that you want to uncode.
3. Go to **Home | Uncode → Uncode...**
   or <**Item Type**> | **Uncode → Uncode...**
   or **[Ctrl]** + **[Shift]** + **[F2]**

alternatively

3. Right-click and select **Uncode...**
   or **[Ctrl]** + **[Shift]** + **[F2]**
   or **Uncode from Recent Codes** <select>

From the **Select Project Items** dialog box you select the Code or Codes that you want to uncode from.

Uncoding a Selection from a Source Item

1. Select the **Data\\Files** folder or its subfolder with the Source Item(s) that you want to uncode.
2. Open the Source Item in the List View that you want to uncode.
3. Select the text or the section that you want to uncode.
4. Go to **Home | Uncode → Uncode...**
   or <**Item Type**> | **Uncode → Uncode...**
   or **[Ctrl]** + **[Shift]** + **[F2]**.

alternatively

4. Right-click and select
   Uncode...
   or **[Ctrl]** + **[Shift]** + **[F2]**
   or **Uncode from Recent Codes** <select>

With the **Select Project Items** dialog box you can select the code(s) you want to uncode from.

Uncoding a Selection from a Code

1. Select the **Coding\\Codes** folder or its subfolder with the code that you want to uncode.
2. Open the Code in the List View that you want to uncode.
3. Select the text or the section that you want to uncode.
4. Go to **Home | Uncode → Uncode...**
   or <**Item Type**> | **Uncode → Uncode...**
   or **[Ctrl]** + **[Shift]** + **[F2]**
   or <**Item Type**> | **Uncode From this Code**

alternatively

4 Right-click and select
Uncode...
or **[Ctrl]** + **[Shift]** + **[F2]**
or **Uncode From Recent Codes <select>**
or **Uncode From This Code**
or **[Ctrl]** + **[Shift]** + **[F3]**

With the **Select Project Items** dialog box you can select the code(s) you will uncode from.

When you select all, **[Ctrl]** + **[A]**, in an open Code and apply **Uncode From This Code** then the whole Code will be uncoded but not deleted, only remain with zero coding.

Uncoding Intersecting Content

Uncode content in one Code that intersects with content in another Code.

1 Select the **Coding\\Codes** folder or its subfolder with the Code that you want to uncode.
2 Select the code(s) in the List View that you want to uncode.
3 Go to **Home | Uncode → Uncode Intersecting Content** or **<Item Type> | Uncode → Uncode Intersecting Content**.

The **Select Project Items** dialog box appears.

4 Select the Code(s) that you want to uncode from.
5 Click **[OK]**.

The Codebook

A long awaited function is the new Codebook for exporting a list of all Codes (not Cases, Sentiments, or Relationships) in any selected Code folder. The export formats are Word (.DOCX), Excel (.XLSX) or Codebook Exchange Standard (.QDC) and the default location is My Documents.

1 Go to **Share | Export → Export Codebook**.

In case there are no subfolders in the Codes folder then the Codebook opens directly.

If here are subfolders then this dialog box opens and you can select the appropriate folder or folders. Confirm with **[OK]**:

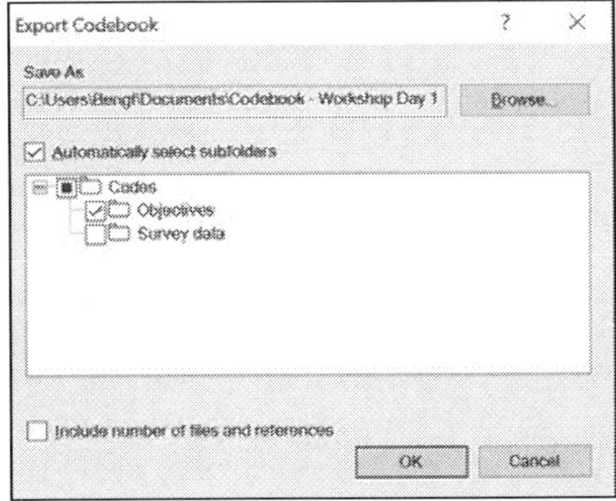

Note, that showing the number of sources and references is an option here.

The Codebook now opens directly and may look like this (.docx):

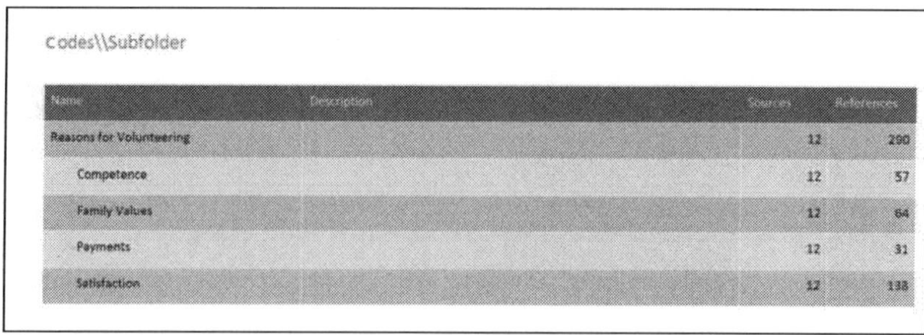

Codes\\Subfolder

Name	Description	Sources	References
Reasons for Volunteering		12	290
Competence		12	57
Family Values		12	64
Payments		12	31
Satisfaction		12	138

The layout allows the Description in the middle column and for future updates many of us are requesting an *Aggregate* mark and an indication of a linked *Memo* when existing.

There is also an option to import a Codebook from another project and create a Code structure in your current project provided that the format is Codebook Exchange Standard (.QDC):

1 Go to **Import | Codebook**.

Autocoding – By Themes

This function is depending on the current text content language that is decided at Project Properties, see page 52.

When Autocoding by theme, NVivo will analyze your source items using an algorithm to find segments of text containing groups of words or phrases and then assigning those segments of text to automatically generated Codes. These “themes” are grouped in Codes and are sorted after occurrence.

1. Select the **Data\\Files** folder or its subfolder with the source item(s) or **Coding\\Codes** with the code(s) that you want to autocode.
2. Select source item(s) or code(s) in the List View that you want to autocode.
3. Go to **Home | Auto Code**
   or right-click and select **Auto Code...**

The **Auto Code Wizard – Step 1** appears:

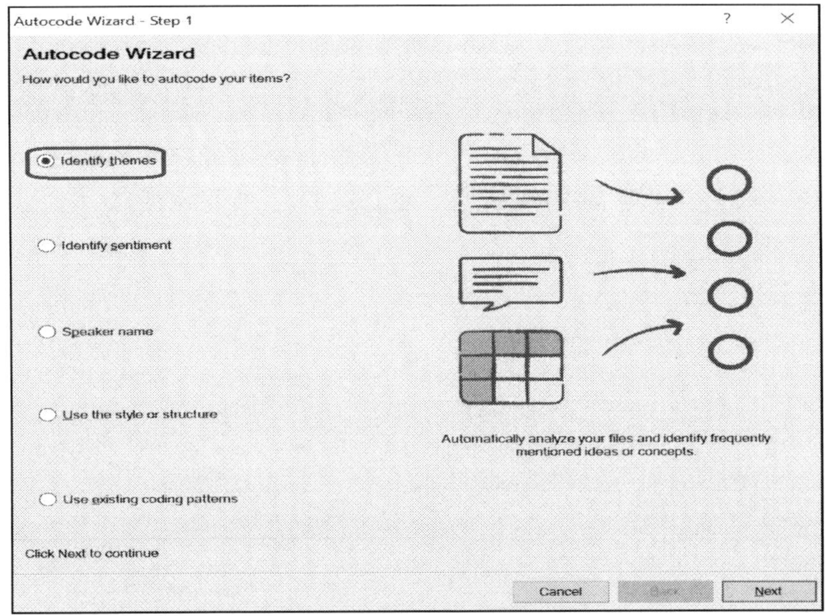

4 Select *Identify themes* and click **[Next]**.

The **Auto Code Wizard – Step 2**[4] appears:

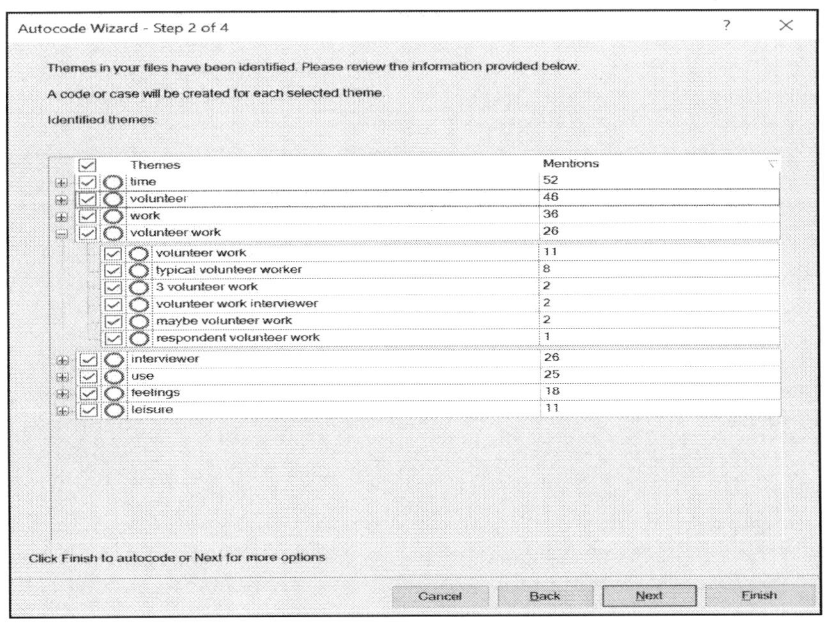

[4] You may be asked to download the current term list for the language of your data.

5 NVivo has found a number of words or phrases with repeated occurrence. By clicking on + a detailed occurrence will show. You can deselect certain results by unchecking. Click [**Next**].

The **Auto Code Wizard – Step 3** appears:

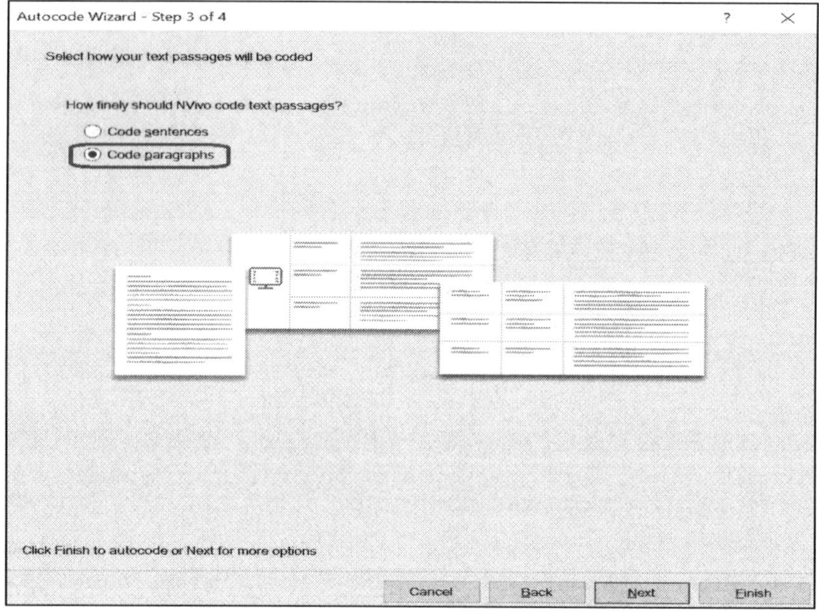

6 We select *Code paragraphs* and click [**Next**].

The **Auto Code Wizard – Step 4** appears:

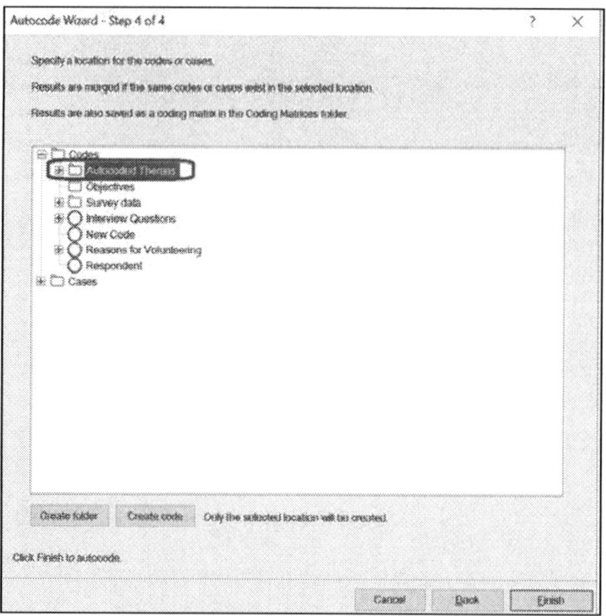

7 NVivo suggests location for the new Codes. You can modify with the **[Create folder]**- and **[Create code]**-buttons. Click **[Finish]**.

The result is twofold: a Coding matrix located at **Queries\\Coding Matrices**:

Autocode Themes Results 2020-07 | Compared by number of coding ref

	A : feelings	B : interviewer	C : leisure	D : time
1 : Files\\Interviews\\Anna	2	5	3	12
2 : Files\\Interviews\\Bernadette	0	1	0	1
3 : Files\\Interviews\\Fredric	2	2	1	6
4 : Files\\Interviews\\Grace	2	2	1	8
5 : Files\\Interviews\\Ken	3	2	1	5
6 : Files\\Interviews\\Mary	2	3	1	5
7 : Files\\Interviews\\Nick	2	3	1	6
8 : Files\\Interviews\\Phoebe	2	6	1	4
9 : Files\\Interviews\\Sunil	3	2	2	5

..and an **Hierarchy Chart** which is described in detail from page 349.

The Codes thus created are located under **Coding\\Codes\\Autocoded Themes** (default)\\:

Autocoded Themes — Search Project

Name	Files	References	Created on	Created by
feelings	8	18	2020-07-08 09:33	NV
interviewer	9	26	2020-07-08 09:33	NV
leisure	8	11	2020-07-08 09:33	NV
time	9	52	2020-07-08 09:33	NV
use	8	25	2020-07-08 09:33	NV
volunteer	9	45	2020-07-08 09:33	NV
volunteer work	9	26	2020-07-08 09:33	NV
work	9	36	2020-07-08 09:33	NV

The difference between a Coding matrix and a Code tree is important: The Coding matrix cannot be edited but the hierarchical code tree can be used for continued coding or other modifications.

Autocoding – By Sentiment

This feature is language dependent and can only work for the language set in Project Properties, Text content language, page 52.

NVivo analyzes your source items or Codes to identify sentiment in words or phrases. The result is Codes named **Positive** or **Negative** with child Codes named **Very** and **Moderately** respectively. These specific sentiment Codes are included in the project template and are therefore permanent and cannot be changed, moved or renamed. They can however be copied to other Code locations for supplementary or manual coding.

Sentiment — Search Project

Name		Files	References	Created on	Created by
Positive		0	0	2018-08-30 15:52	BME
Very positive		0	0	2018-08-30 15:52	BME
Moderately positive		0	0	2018-08-30 15:52	BME
Negative		0	0	2018-08-30 15:52	BME
Moderately negativ		0	0	2018-08-30 15:52	BME
Very negative		0	0	2018-08-30 15:52	BME

1. Select the **Data\\Files** folder or its subfolder with the source item(s) or **Coding\\Codes** with the code(s) that you want to autocode.
2. Select source item(s) or code(s) in the List View that you want to autocode.
3. Go to **Home | Auto Code**
   or right-click and select **Auto Code...**

The **Auto Code Wizard** – **Step 1** appears:

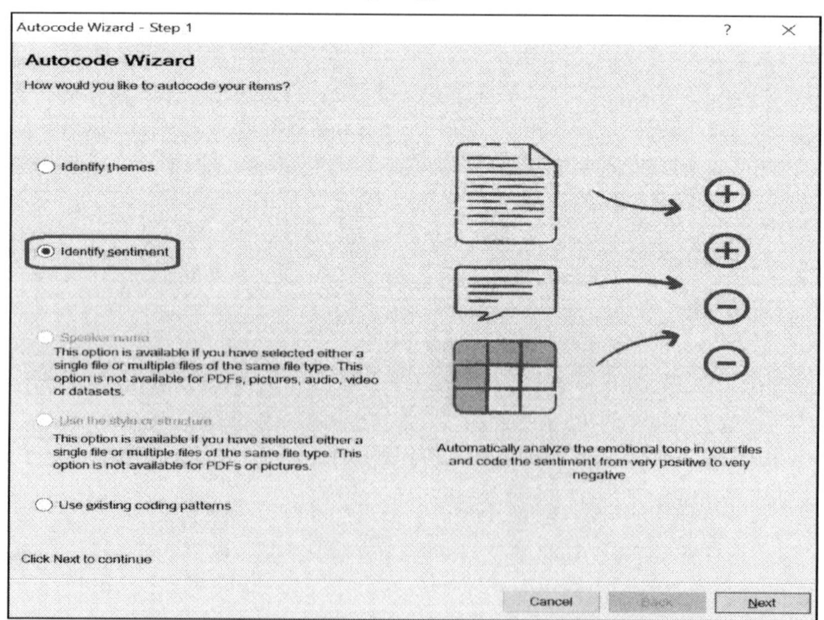

4. Select *Identify sentiment* and click **[Next]**.

The **Auto Code Wizard – Step 2** appears:

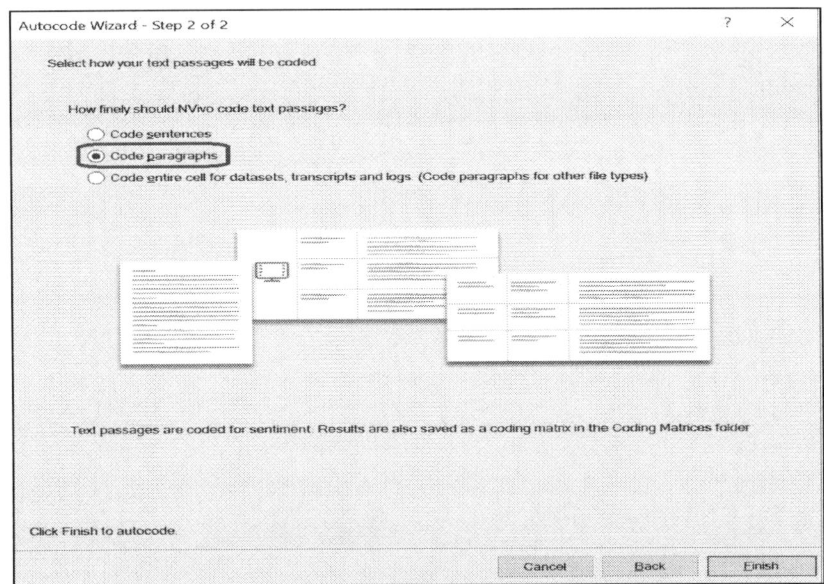

5 We select *Code paragraphs* and click **[Finish]**.

The result is twofold, a Coding matrix located under **Queries\\Code Matrices**:

	A : Very negative	B : Moderately negative	C : Moderately positive	D : Very positive
1 : Files\\Interviews\\IMG_5865	0	0	0	0
2 : Files\\Interviews\\Mary	1	3	5	3
3 : Files\\Interviews\\Nick	1	3	3	3
4 : Files\\Interviews\\Phoebe	1	1	6	4
5 : Files\\Interviews\\Sunil	1	0	4	4

..and an **Hierarchy Chart** which is described in detail from page 349.

The Sentiments thus created are located under **Coding\\Sentiment**:

Sentiment

Name	Files	References	Created on	Created by
Positive	4	32	2018-08-30 15:52	BME
Very positive	4	14	2018-08-30 15:52	BME
Moderately positive	4	18	2018-08-30 15:52	BME
Negative	4	11	2018-08-30 15:52	BME
Moderately negativ	3	7	2018-08-30 15:52	BME
Very negative	4	4	2018-08-30 15:52	BME

The difference between these two results is important: The Coding matrix cannot be edited but the hierarchical code tree can be used for continued coding or other modifications.

A new context dependent Ribbon menu, **Sentiment**, is now available and is opened each time a Sentiment Code is opened.

Autocoding – By Speaker Name

This option is useful in case you need to analyze the text following a heading representing a certain speaker in an interview or a focus group.

1. Select the **Data\\Files** folder or its subfolder with the source item(s) that you want to autocode.
2. Select the source item(s) in the List View that you want to autocode.
3. Go to **Home | Auto Code**
   or right-click and select **Auto Code...**

The **Auto Code Wizard – Step 1** appears:

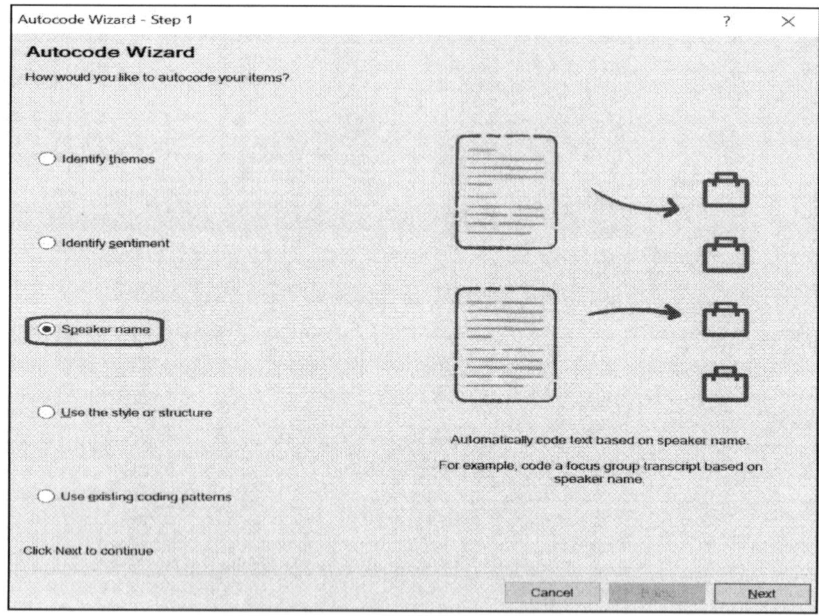

4. Select *Speaker name* and click **[Next]**.

The **Auto Code Wizard – Step 2** appears:

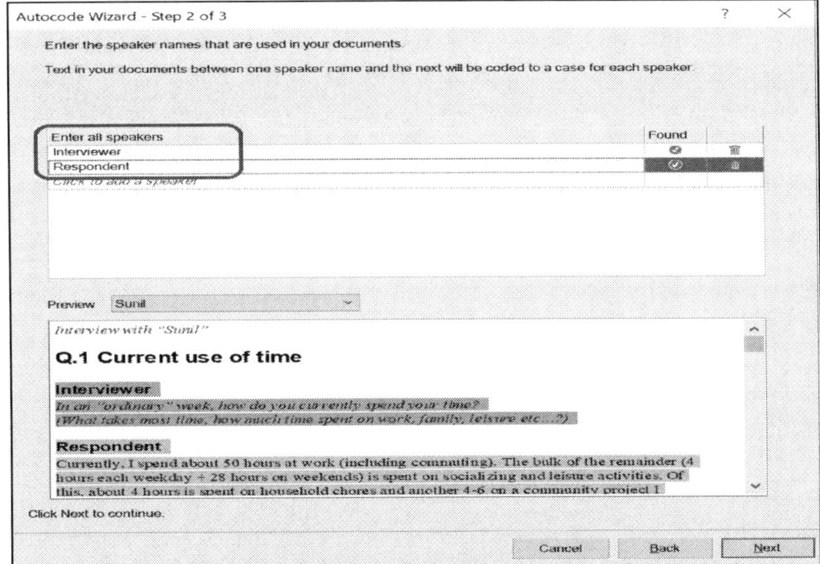

5 Enter the names of the speakers that you can identify in the preview window. When found a mark is displayed in the Found column and the text is highlighted in the preview window.

The **Auto Code Wizard – Step 3** appears:

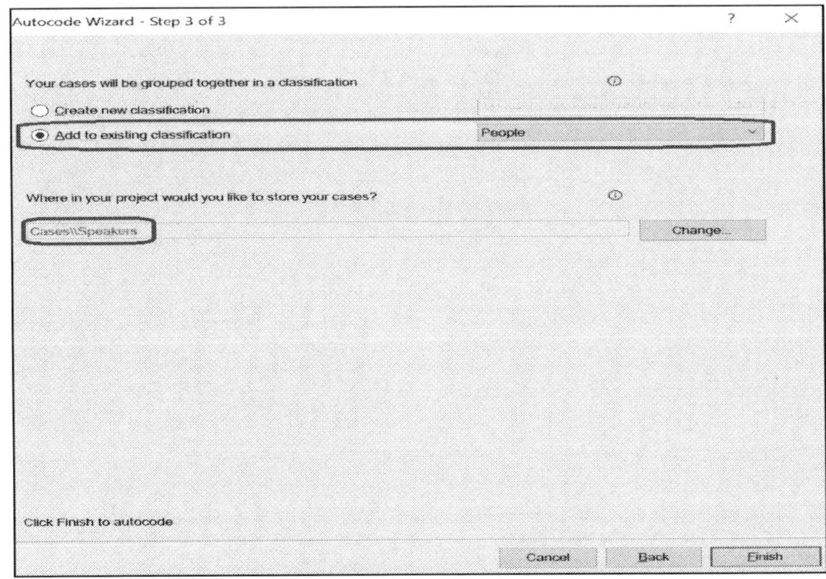

6 Finally, you need to decide upon the Case Classification and the location of the Cases that are the result of this autocoding procedure.

7 Confirm with **[Finish]**.

Autocoding – By Structures

This feature is not language dependent as it is based on the use of paragraph styles (Heading 1, Heading 2, etc.) to create a hierarchical Code structure. The feature is only applicable to source items and not to codes. Autocoding by structures codes the text under each heading under the name of the heading. If several documents are being auto coded at the same time or separately and they have the same structure of styles and headings then common Codes are created automatically. A practical usage of this feature is when you apply a custom Word template with an established style set as a questionnaire for interviews. Autocoding can be applied to properly structured interview transcripts to, for example, code Source Item contents according to Cases upon import:

> **Did you know?** Our website has custom autocoding Word templates to help structure your research data: www.formkunskap.com

1. Select the **Data\\Files** folder or its subfolder with the source item(s) that you want to autocode.
2. Select the source item(s) in the List View that you want to autocode.
3. Go to **Home | Auto Code**
   or right-click and select **Auto Code...**

The **Auto Code Wizard** – **Step 1** appears:

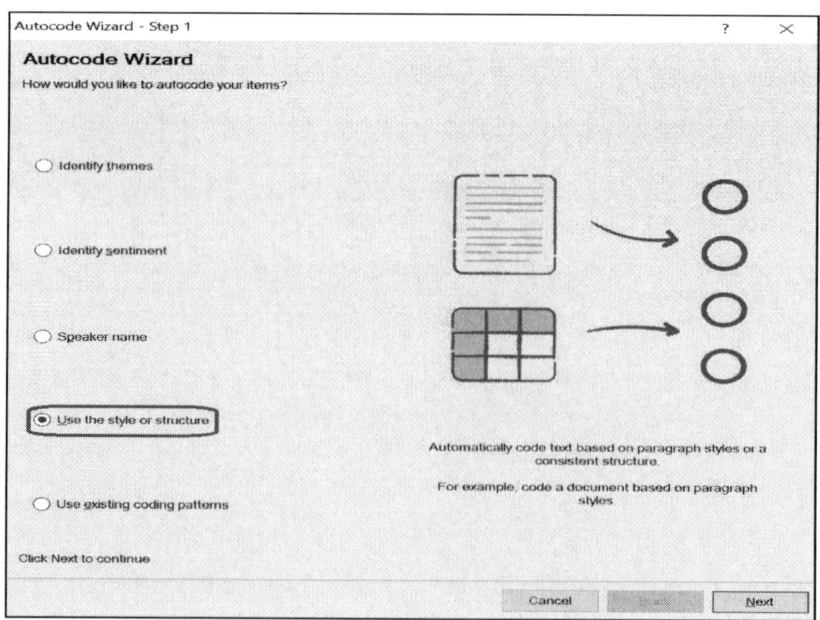

4. Select *Use the style or structure* and click **[Next]**.

The **Auto Code Wizard – Step 2** appears:

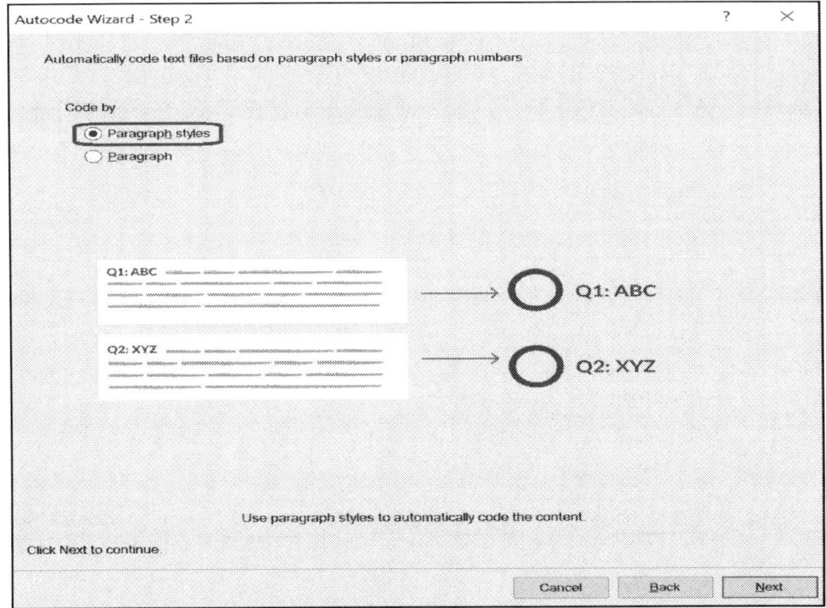

5 First you need to decide if your coding will be according to paragraph styles or paragraph numbers. In this example we decide *Paragraph styles*. Click **[Next]**.

The **Auto Code Wizard – Step 3** appears:

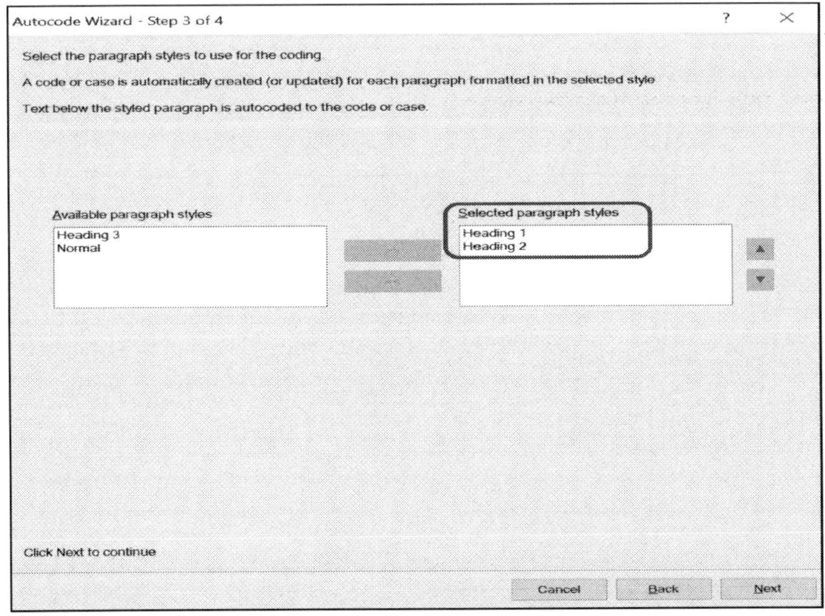

6 First, you need to decide which paragraph styles should become the base for the new Code structure. NVivo will

find all existing paragraph styles in any Word document. The styles are selected with the [>>] button and are then transferred to the right-hand textbox. Click [**Next**].

The **Auto Code Wizard – Step 4** appears:

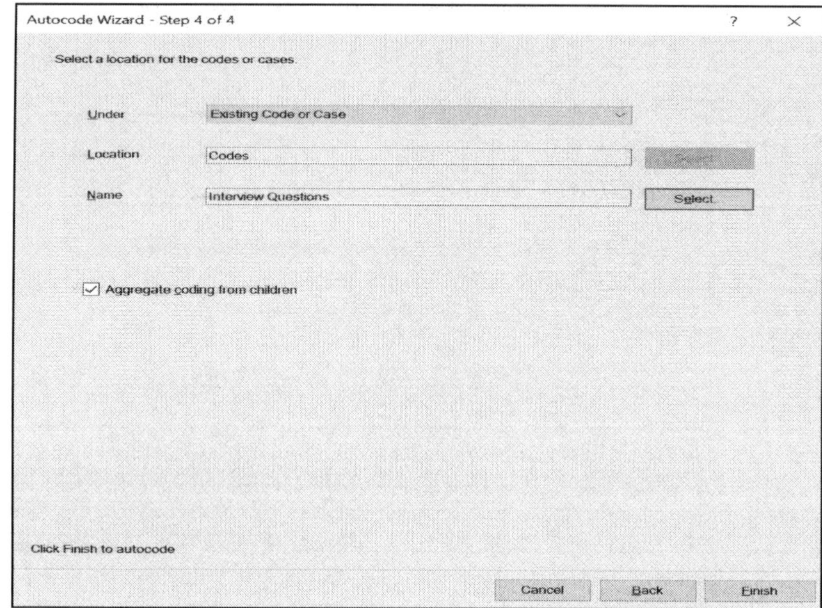

7 The option *Existing Code* allows you to select the parent Code under which the new Codes will be located. If you select *New Code* then you name the new Code and decide its location in a folder or under a parent Code. In either case underlying Codes will be named after the text in respective paragraph style (Heading 1, Heading 2 etcetera). Checking *Aggregate* makes the whole new code tree aggregated. Finally click [**Finish**].

- ♦ -

It is also possible to auto code transcripts of audio- or video-items. Suppose that we have an audio item and a transcript with two optional columns, Speaker and Organization:

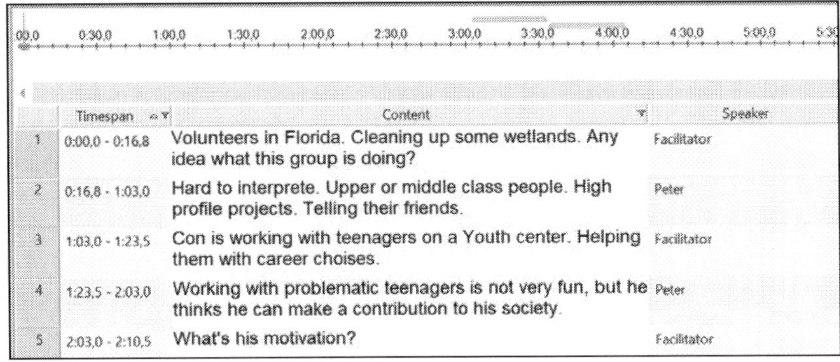

	Timespan	Content	Speaker
1	0:00,0 - 0:16,8	Volunteers in Florida. Cleaning up some wetlands. Any idea what this group is doing?	Facilitator
2	0:16,8 - 1:03,0	Hard to interprete. Upper or middle class people. High profile projects. Telling their friends.	Peter
3	1:03,0 - 1:23,5	Con is working with teenagers on a Youth center. Helping them with career choises.	Facilitator
4	1:23,5 - 2:03,0	Working with problematic teenagers is not very fun, but he thinks he can make a contribution to his society.	Peter
5	2:03,0 - 2:10,5	What's his motivation?	Facilitator

If you select *Use the Style and Structure* and then *Selected Transcript Fields* autocoding will then be based on these optional columns which will create new Codes named after the column contents:

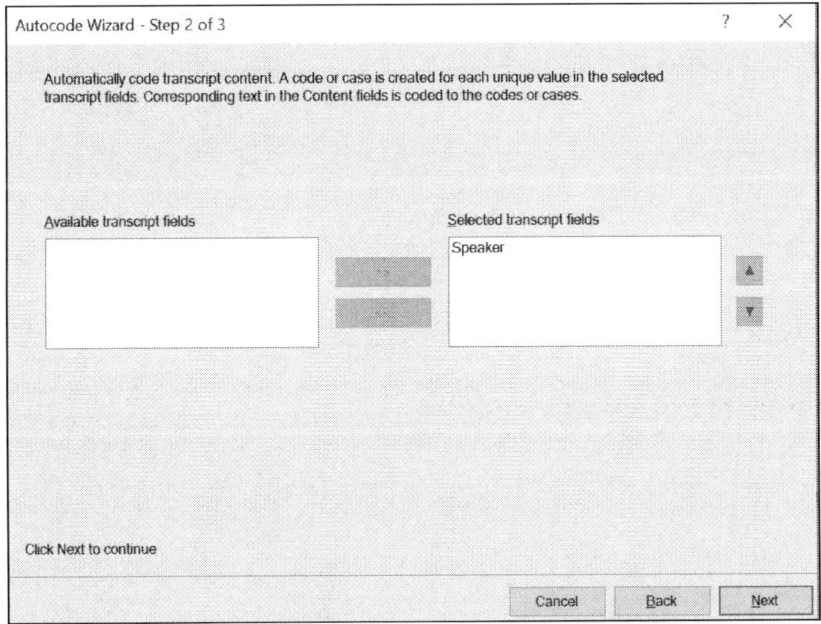

In this example, *Facilitator* and *Peter* will become new Codes and the text in the column Content will then be the coded text.

Autocoding – By Patterns

This feature is not language dependent as it uses its own project data as input for the analysis. This method is based on selected codes which you then use for coding more source items or codes applying frequent words found in the codes that form the pattern.

1. Select the **Data\\Files** folder or its subfolder with the source item(s) or **Coding\\Codes** with the code(s) that you want to autocode.

2 Select source item(s) or code(s) in the List View that you want to autocode.
3 Go to **Home | Auto Code**
or right-click and select **Auto Code...**

The **Auto Code Wizard – Step 1** appears:

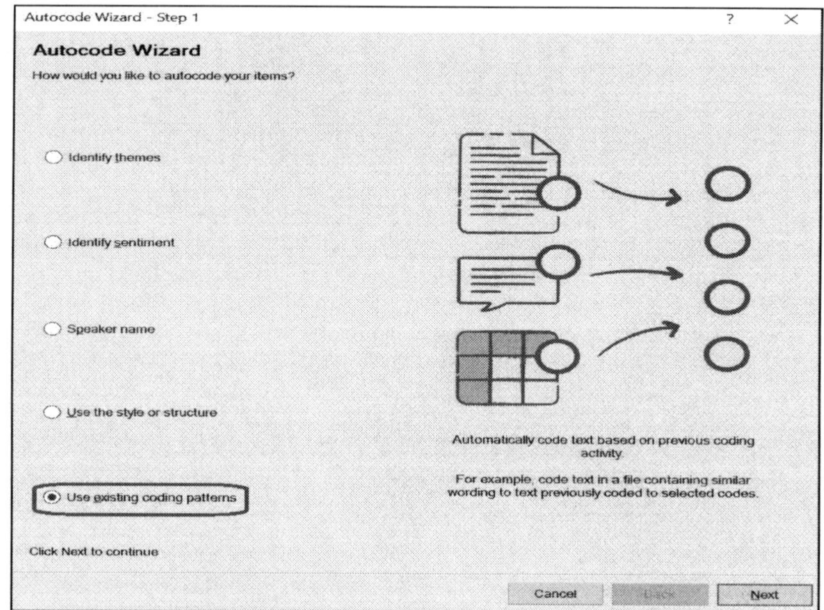

4 Select *Use existing coding patterns* and click **[Next]**.

The **Auto Code Wizard – Step 2** appears:

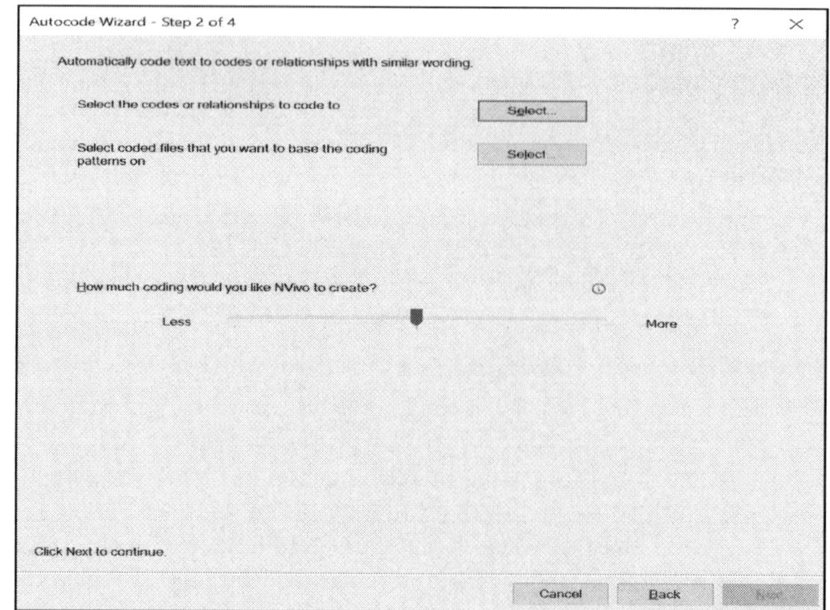

5 With the [**Select...**]-button you select the codes with pattern for your autocoding. The slider **How much...** is used to specify more or less coding based on the occurrence of relevant words in the pattern codes. Click [**Next**].

The **Auto Code Wizard – Step 3** appears:

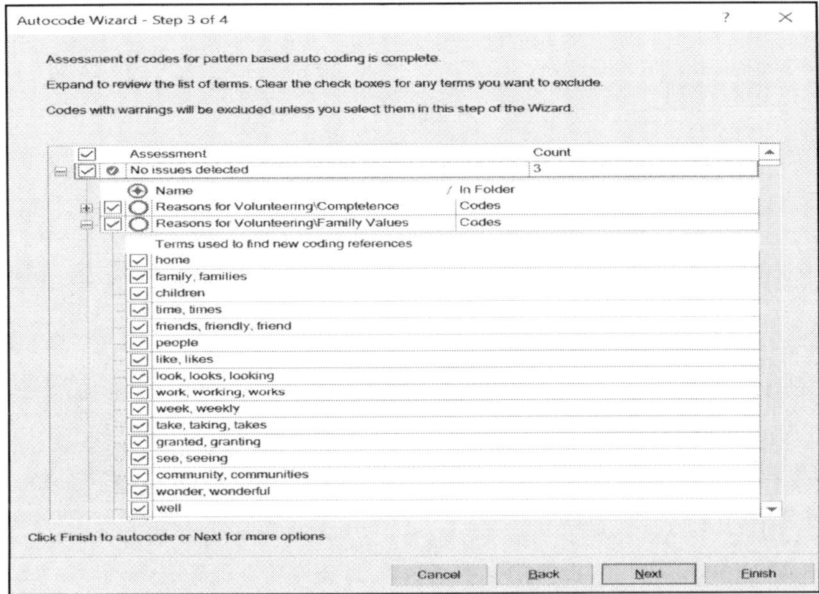

6 This is the result of the autocoding and you can accept or uncheck each separate term. Click [**Next**].

The **Auto Code Wizard – Step 4** appears:

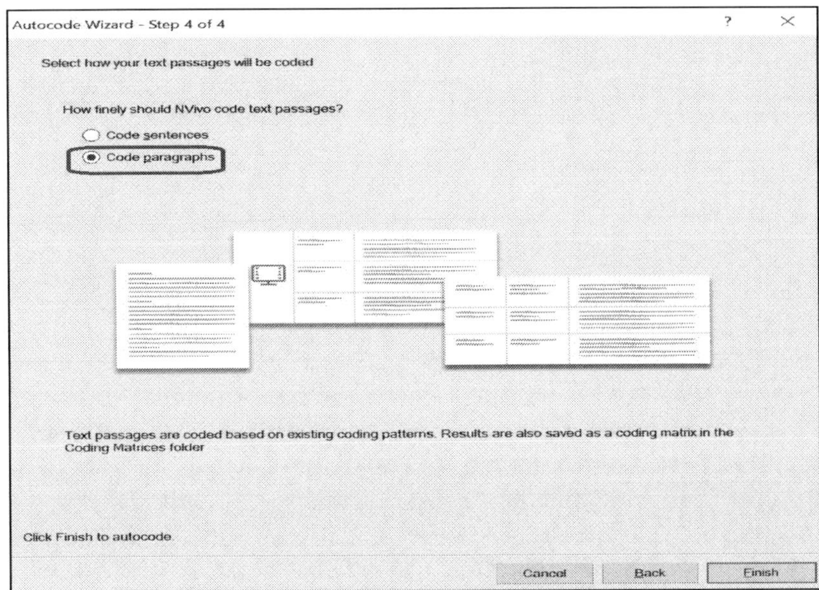

7 We choose *Code paragraphs* and click [**Finish**].

The result is twofold, a new coding matrix located at **Queries\\Coding Matrices**:

Autocode Pattern Results 2020-07-			
	A : Codes\\Reasons for V...	B : Codes\\Reasons for V...	C : Codes\\Reasons for V...
1 : Files\\Interviews\\Phoebe	11	10	5
2 : Files\\Interviews\\Sunil	1	3	1

..and the autocoded source items:

Sunil	13	90	2018-08-30 16:45
Phoebe	13	183	2018-08-30 16:45

The number of codes per source is the total number of codes, its aggregated parent code and the coding matrix.

Range Coding

Range coding is another principle for a rational coding of certain source items. The basis for range coding is the paragraph number in a document, the row number in a transcript or picture log or the timespan in an audio- or video item.

The available options depend on the type of item that has been selected for range coding. The command is **Home | Range Code** and in this case only existing Codes can be used to code to by using the **[Select...]**-button.

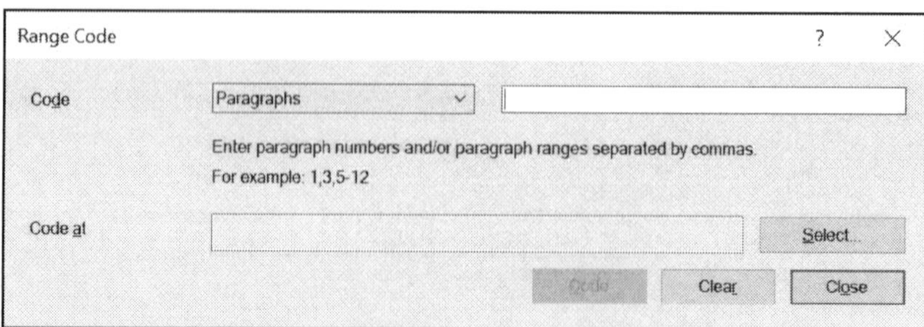

The coding takes place when you click **[Code]**.

In Vivo Coding

In Vivo coding is an established term used within qualitative research long before dedicated software existed. In Vivo coding creates a new Code from the selection of text and then, using the *In Vivo* command, the selected text (max 256 characters) will become the Code name. The new Code's location is

> **Tips**: Use In Vivo Coding like this: Select a Heading in your Source Item with a text that will become the Code name. Apply In Vivo Coding. Continue coding at this Code with the Quick Coding bar.

always in the **Coding\\Codes** folder. Code name and location can be changed later.

1 Select the text you want to NVivo code.
2 Go to **<Item Type> | Code In Vivo**
or right-click and select **Code In Vivo**
or **[Ctrl]** + **[F8]**.

You can also use the Quick Coding bar described earlier in this chapter.

Coding by Queries

Queries can be instructed to save the result. The saved result is a Code, a Case or a Coding matrix and is instantly created when the query is run, see Chapter 14, Queries.

Visualizing your Coding

Opening a Code

1 Select the **Coding\\Codes** or its subfolder.
2 Select the Code in in the List View that you want to open.
3 Go to **Home | Item → 'Open' → Open Code...**
or right-click and select **Open Code...**
or double-click the Code in the List View
or **[Ctrl]** + **[Shift]** + **[O]**.

A new context dependent Ribbon menu, **Code**, is now available and is opened each time a Code is opened. Each open Code is displayed in the Detail View and could therefore be docked or undocked. These windows always have a certain number of view mode tabs on its right side. If the Code has only been used to code text then the view mode tabs are: *Summary*, *Reference* and *Text*.

The *Reference* view mode is the default, automatically selected each time a Code is opened:

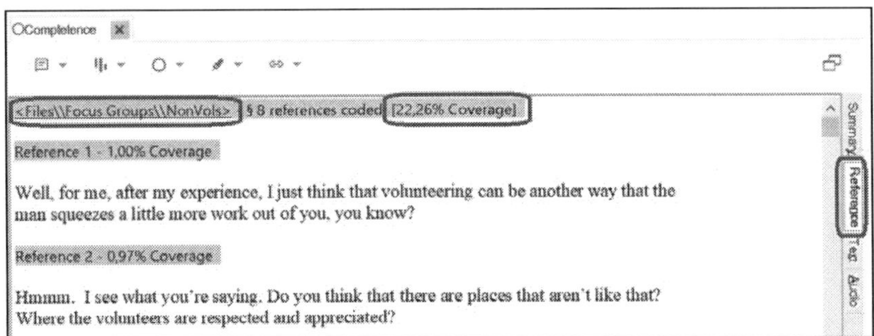

The link with the name of the Source Item opens the Source Item in the Detail View. You can also point at or select a section, right-click and select **Open Referenced Source**. When a Source Item is opened via a Code like this the coding at the current Code is highlighted.

References coded are coded segments (like a text-segment) of a source item.

Coverage means that the Code or a result of a query corresponds to a certain percentage of the whole Source Item that is coded measured in number of characters.

Hiding/Unhiding Reference to Source Items

1. Open a Code.
2. Go to **Code | Content → Coding Information**.
3. Uncheck *Files, References* or *Coverage*.

The option *Files* hides the reference to Source Items, coded sections and its coverage.

The option *References* hides information about each coded section and its coverage.

The option *Coverage* hides information about coverage of the Source Items and its coded sections.

The presentation can be displayed in many ways by going to **Code | Content → Coding Context, Coding By Users, Coding Information, Coding Excerpt**, or **Text**.

The *Summary* view mode displays all coded Source Items as a list of shortcuts. Each such shortcut can be opened with a double-click and the coded section is highlighted:

Competence
Name
In Folder
References
Coverage
Anna
Files\\Interviews
12
39,01%
Bernadette
Files\\Interviews
5
15,39%
Fredric
Files\\Interviews
6
31,43%
Grace
Files\\Interviews
4
13,89%
Ken
Files\\Interviews
3
13,19%
Summary
Reference
Text

The *Text* view mode displays all coded text Source Items as thumbnails in the upper part of List View. Clicking on a thumbnail displays the coded sections of that Source Item. Double-clicking the thumbnail opens the whole Source Item and the coded sections are highlighted:

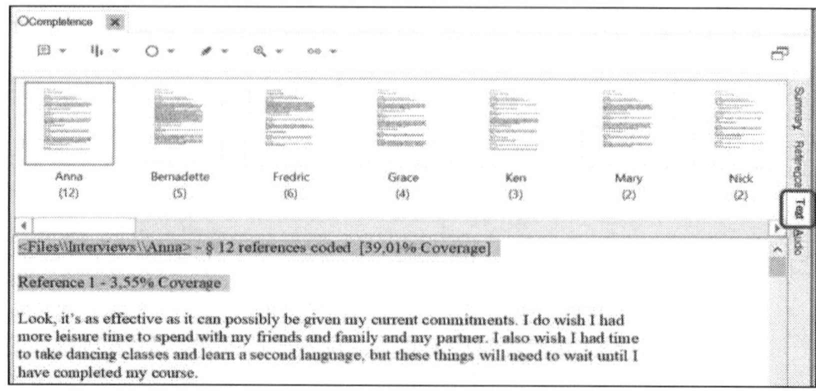

Competence
Anna (12)
Bernadette (5)
Fredric (6)
Grace (4)
Ken (3)
Mary (2)
Nick (2)
Summary
Reference
Text
Audio
<Files\\Interviews\\Anna> - § 12 references coded [39,01% Coverage]
Reference 1 - 3,55% Coverage
Look, it's as effective as it can possibly be given my current commitments. I do wish I had more leisure time to spend with my friends and family and my partner. I also wish I had time to take dancing classes and learn a second language, but these things will need to wait until I have completed my course.

The PDF mode displays all coded PDF items as thumbnails in the upper part of the List View. Clicking on a thumbnail displays the coded sections of that PDF item. Double-clicking the thumbnail opens the whole PDF item and the coded sections are highlighted:

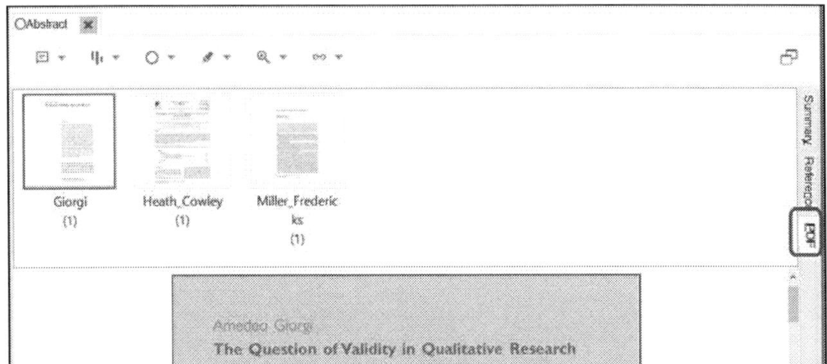

The *Audio* view mode provides a visual interface to easily listen to segments of coded audio:

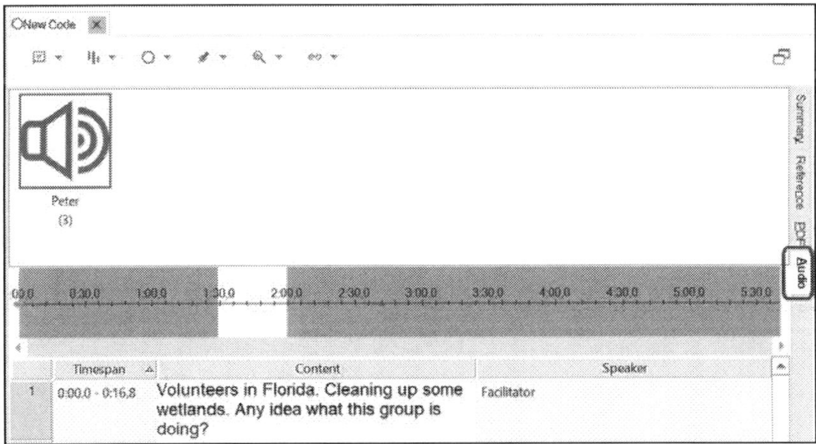

The *Video* view mode provides a visual interface to easily view segments of coded video:

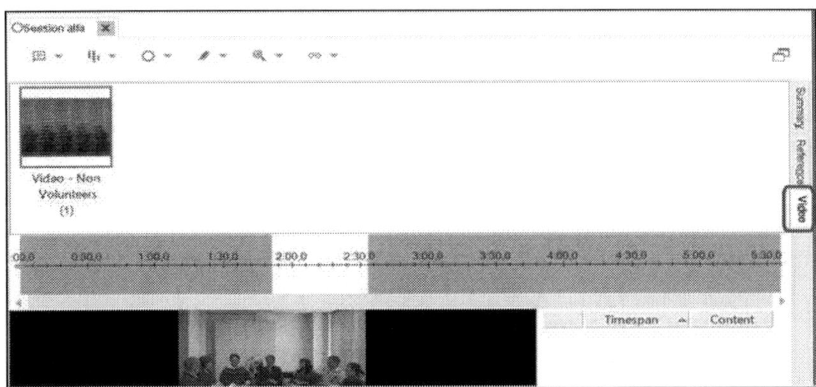

The *Picture* View mode provides an interface to view regions of coded image sources:

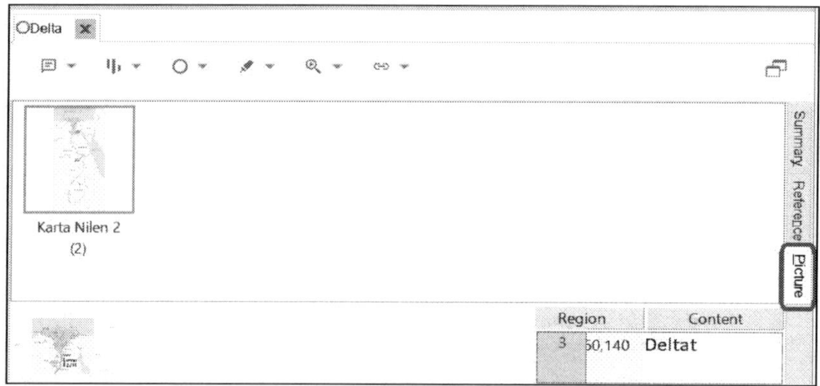

The *Dataset* view mode displays sections of coded dataset sources:

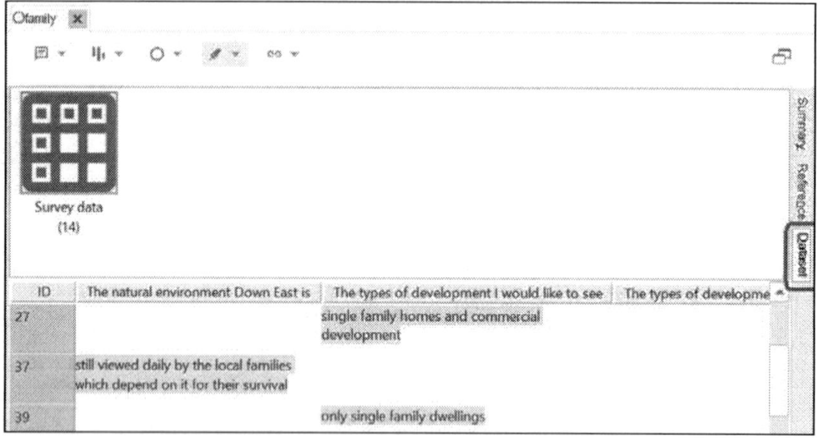

Viewing Coding Excerpt

1 Open a Code.
2 Go to **Code |Content → Coding Excerpt**.
3 Select *None, Start* or *All*.

The option *None*.

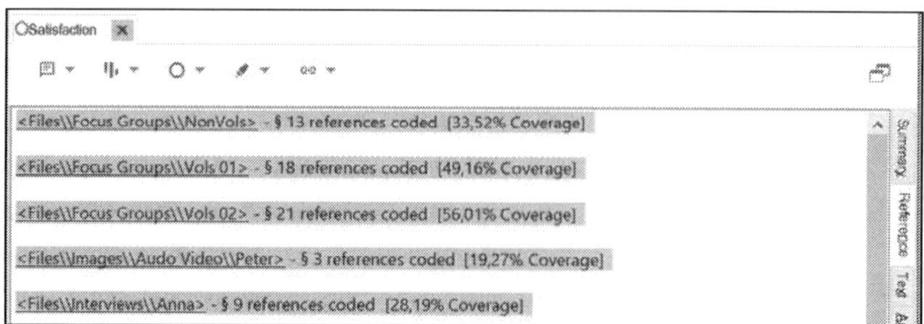

The option *Start*:

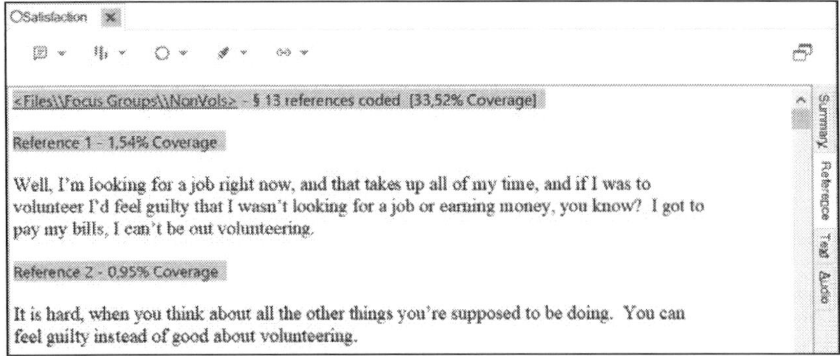

OSatisfaction
Summary
Reference
Text
Audio
<Files\\Focus Groups\\NonVols> - § 13 references coded [33,52% Coverage]
Reference 1 - 1,54% Coverage
Well, I'm looking for a job right now, and that takes up all of my time, and if I was to volunteer I'd feel guilty that I wasn't looking for a job or earning money, you know? I got to pay my bills, I can't be out volunteering.
Reference 2 - 0,95% Coverage
It is hard, when you think about all the other things you're supposed to be doing. You can feel guilty instead of good about volunteering.

The option *All* is the default and has been shown above.

Viewing Coding Context

1. Open a Code.
2. Select the text or section that you want to show in its context.
3. Go to **Code | Content → Coding Context** or right-click and select **Coding Context**.
4. Select *None, Narrow, Broad, Custom...* or *Entire Source.*

Example using the option *Broad* for a code coding a text source item:

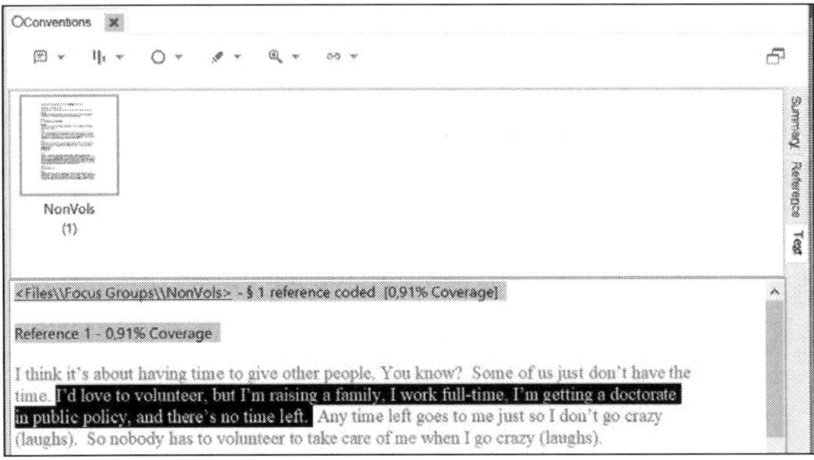

OConventions
Summary
Reference
Text
NonVols
(1)
<Files\\Focus Groups\\NonVols> - § 1 reference coded [0,91% Coverage]
Reference 1 - 0,91% Coverage
I think it's about having time to give other people. You know? Some of us just don't have the time. I'd love to volunteer, but I'm raising a family, I work full-time, I'm getting a doctorate in public policy, and there's no time left. Any time left goes to me just so I don't go crazy (laughs). So nobody has to volunteer to take care of me when I go crazy (laughs).

Example using the option *Broad* for a code coding an Audio source. Playback is possible for the interval including the context.

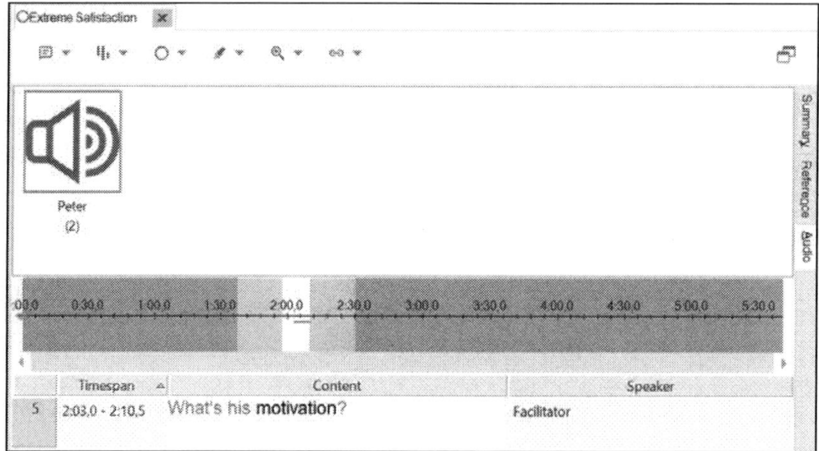

Example using the option *Narrow* for a code coding a Picture source.

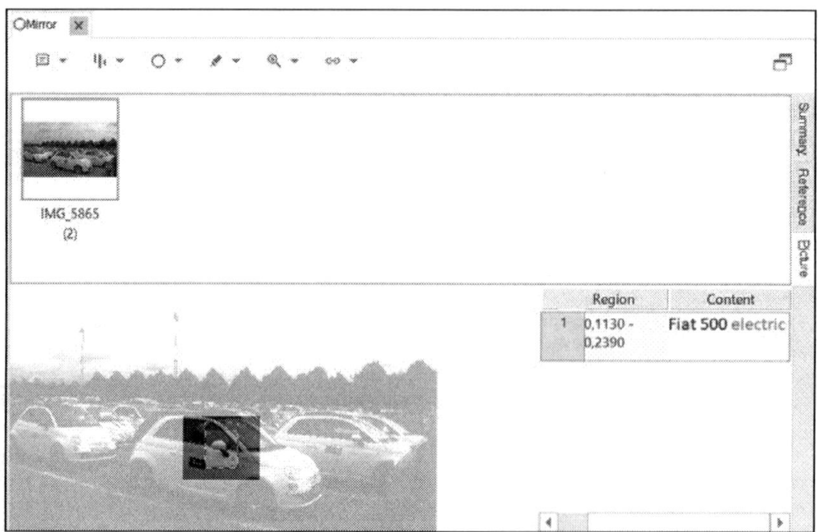

Highlighting Coding

The coded text or section in a Source Item can be highlighted in brownish color. Settings made are individual to Project Items and are temporarily saved during a work session, but are reset to none when a project is closed.

1 Go to <**Item Type**> | **Highlight**.

There are several options:

None	Highlighting is off.
All Coding	Highlights all Codes that the Item is coded at.
Matches for Query	Highlights the words used by Text Search Queries.
Coding for Selected Items	Opens Select Project Items showing current Codes, other Codes are dimmed.

Coding Stripes

The open document, memo, or Code can be made to show the current coding as colored vertical stripes in a separate right-hand window. Coding stripes are shown in Read-Only mode or in Edit mode. Using the **Refresh** on top of the window recovers colors and stripes.

1 Go to <**Item Type**> | **Coding Stripes**

There are several options:

None	Coding Stripes are off.
All	Shows all Codes that the Item is coded at.
Selected Items...	Opens Select Project Items showing current Codes, other Codes are dimmed. Is active when coding stripes have been selected.
Coding Density Only	Shows only the Coding Density Bar and no Codes.
Number of Stripes...	Selects the number of stripes (7 - 200).
Items Last Selected	Shows the Codes that have recently been selected.
Most Coding	Shows the Codes that are most coded at.
Least Coding	Shows the Codes that are least coded at.
Recently Coded	Shows the Codes that have recently been used.

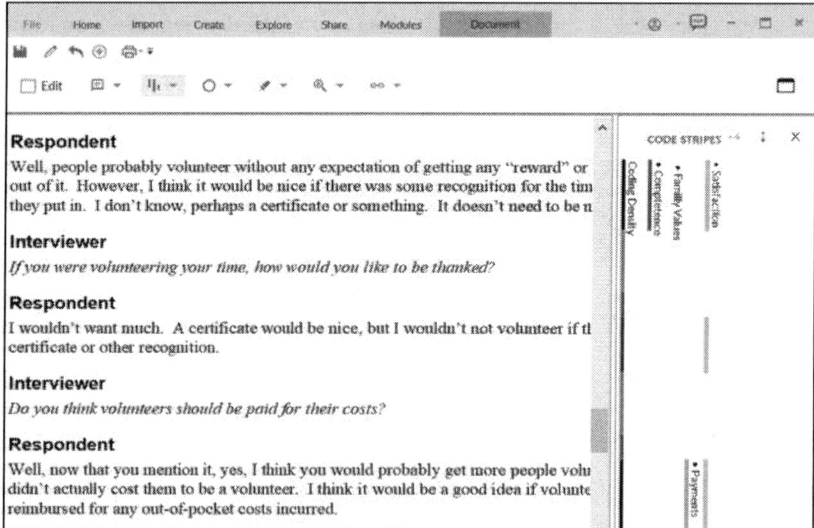

What can you do with Coding Stripes?

When you point and right-click at a certain coding stripe the following options will show: **Highlight Coding, Open Code..., Uncode, Hide Stripe, Show Sub-Stripes, Hide Sub-Stripes** and **Refresh**.

A click on the coding stripe highlights the coded area and double-click opens the Code.

By pointing at a coding stripe the Code name is shown. By pointing at the Coding Density Bar all Code names are shown that are coded at near the pointer.

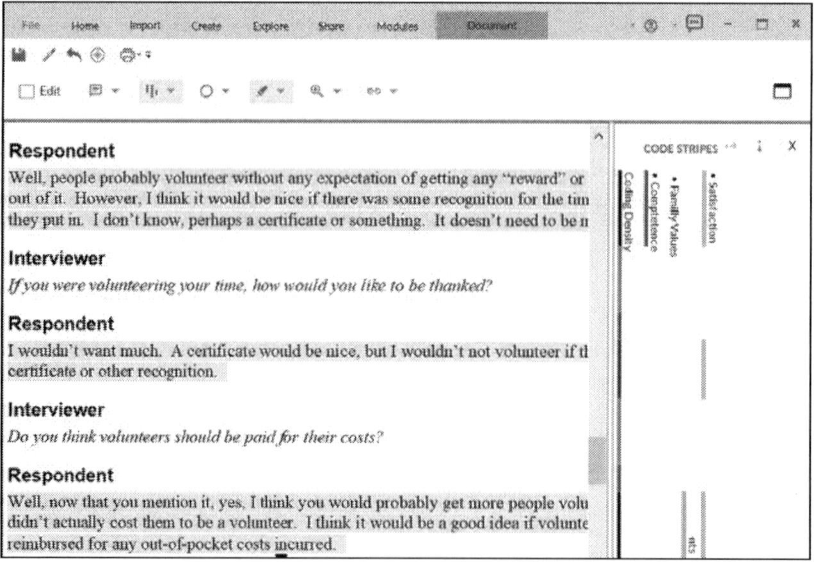

Color Marking of Coding Stripes

The colors of the coding stripes are automatically selected by NVivo. You can also use a custom color scheme, see page 26.

1. Show coding stripes using any of the above options.
2. Go to <Item type> | **Coding Stripes → Select Colors**.

Choosing *Automatic Colors* lets NVivo set the colors randomly and choosing *Item Colors* your individual colors will be applied. Codes without individual colors will be shown white.

Printing with Coding Stripes

See Chapter 5, section Printing with Coding Stripes (page 83).

Viewing a Code that Codes a PDF

The PDF Source

A coded PDF showing coding stripes can for example look like this (the content of bookmark panel depends on the original PDF and can be hidden or unhidden by toggling **PDF | Bookmarks**:

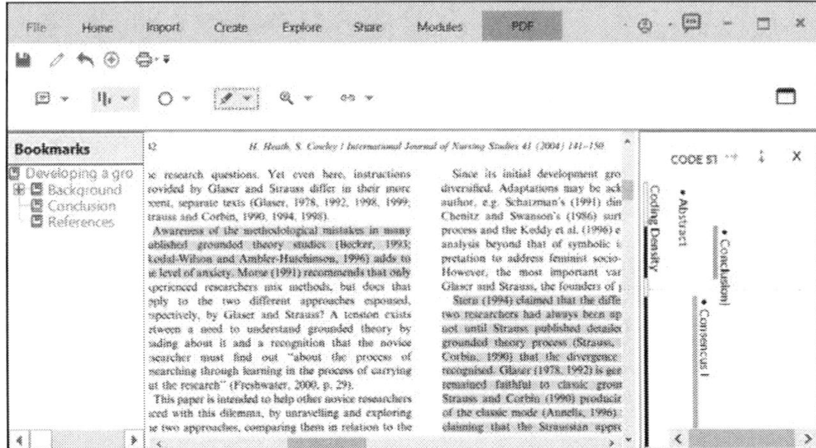

When you need to code a complete PDF document with any of the commands '**Code Sources at <Code>**' or '**Create As Code**' or '**Create As Cases**' the number of references in that Code is calculated like this:

All text is one reference and each page is a region.

Exploring the Code

A Code that codes a PDF item will show the PDF in the Summary tab, in the Reference tab and in the specific PDF tab as follows:

The **Summary** tab will show the PDF as any other shortcut in the list of coded items.

The **Reference** tab will show coded text as plain text and coded region as coordinates:

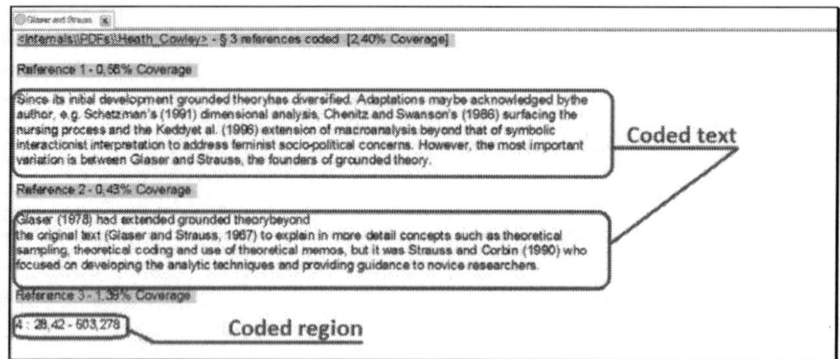

The **PDF** tab will show coded text or region as clear windows in the original PDF layout. Only coded pages with show:

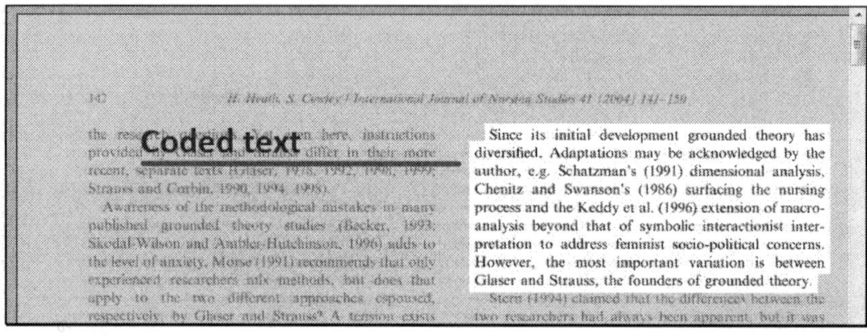

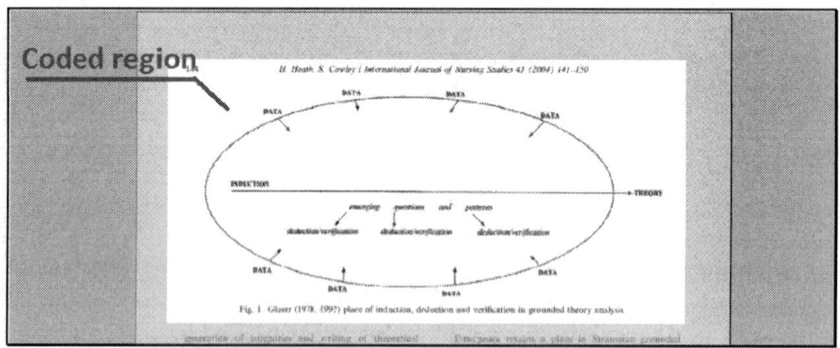

14. QUERIES

The Folder Structure for Queries

The project folder structure for Queries are: Query Criteria, Query Results, and Coding Matrices. The default folders as shown in the Navigator are:

These folders and the names are not possible to delete, move, or rename. The folder names are depending on the user interface language setting, see page 39. However, the user can create subfolders to the default folder **Queries\\Query Criteria**.

This chapter is about how to create and run various kinds of queries. In our experience, new NVivo users are sometimes intimidated by Queries - many types exist and using them effectively can take some practice. Remember, although not every query type will be right for project, every query type requires similar elements of foundational input. You will find queries increasingly simple once you read this chapter and learn the key features of a Query.

NVivo also includes a very useful Query Wizard, **Explore | Query Wizard**. This tool is a well-constructed graphical means for helping researchers find what type of Query to use. For our purposes, we recommend understanding and practicing each Query individually. The Query Wizard provides a false sense of security for new users. But the beauty of Queries will reveal itself when you practice time and again how to use each distinct method.

When you create a query, you first decide whether it will become a new NVivo item within the **Queries\\Query Criteria** folder.

The option *Save Criteria* is available in the dialog boxes **New <Query Type> Query** *Save Criteria* lets you type a name of the query and it will be saved for future use. The saved queries respond the same as other NVivo items - they can be copied, pasted, and moved into folders. Query items open into query dialog boxes where you can adjust the settings of each query. Importantly, you will need to **Run** a query before you will see any search results; queries can be created without being **Run**.

You can construct simple queries that find certain items or text elements. You can also construct complex queries that combine search words and Codes or that combine several Codes. The results of queries based on search words and Codes can generate new Codes, sets or data visualizations like Word Clouds, or both. You can also merge query results with existing Codes.

NVivo offers eight different query types: Text Search Queries, Word Frequency Queries, Coding Queries, Matrix Coding Queries, Crosstab Queries, Coding Comparison Queries, Compound Queries, and Group Queries. We will discuss Coding Comparison Queries further in Chapter 24, Collaborating with NVivo. Saving a query, editing a query, moving a query to another folder, deleting a query and previewing or saving results are dealt with in the next chapter, Common Query Features.

The Query Wizard

For beginners who are not yet experienced of using queries the Query Wizard can be of help to decide which type of query to apply.

1 Go to **Explore | Query Wizard**

The **Query Wizard** dialog box appears and the four options display the clarifying graphs as follows:

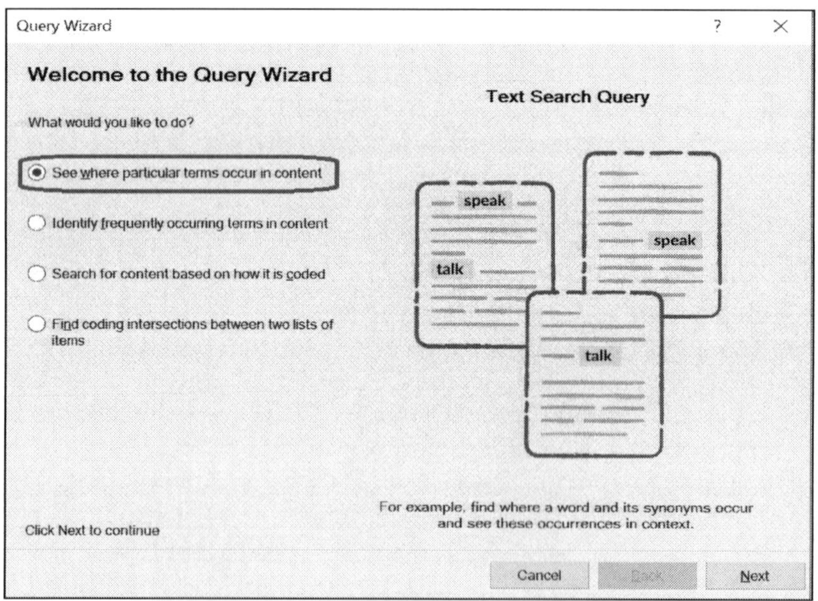

The above option will create a **Text Search Query**.

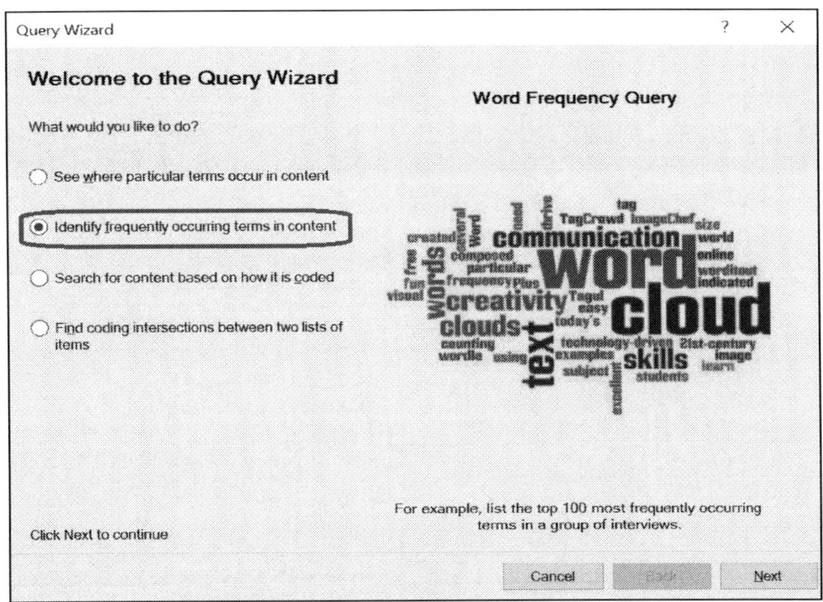

The above option will create a **Word Frequency Query**.

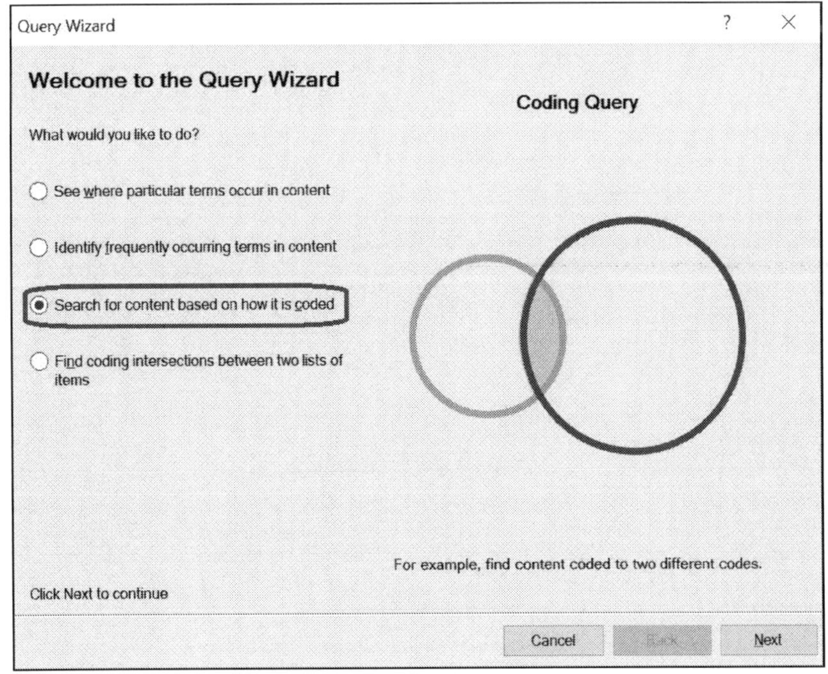

The above option will create a **Coding Query**.

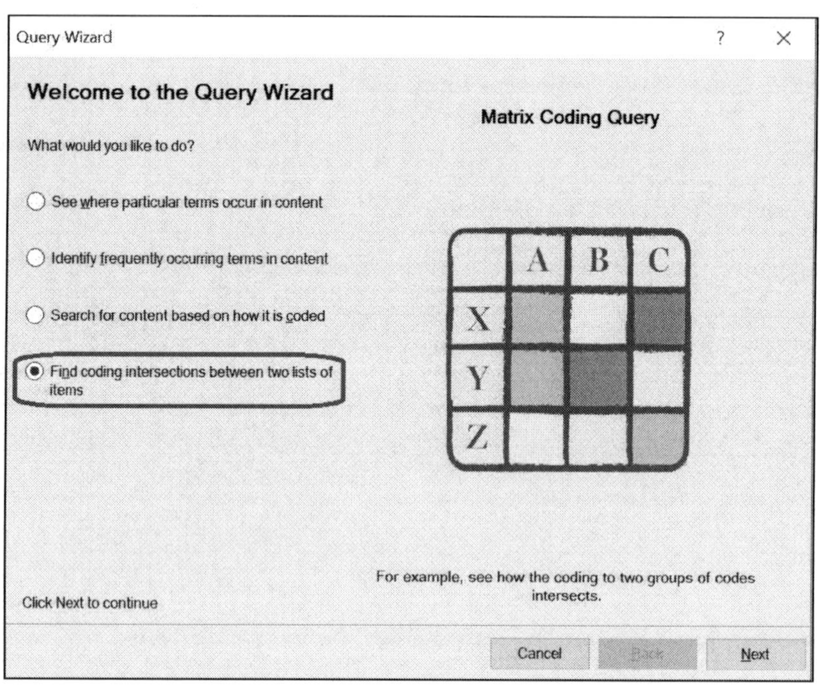

The above option will create a **Matrix Coding Query**.

Text Search Queries

Text Search Queries search for certain words or phrases among items:

1 Go to **Explore | Text Search**.
  Default folder is **Queries\\Query Criteria**.
  Go to 4.

alternatively

1 Select the **Queries\\Query Criteria** folder or its subfolder.
2 Go to **Explore | Text Search**.
  Go to 4.

alternatively

2 Click on an empty space in the List View.
3 Right-click and select **New Query → Text Search**.

A new context dependent Ribbon menu, **Code**, is now available and is opened each time a Text Search Query is opened.

The **Text Search Query – Results Preview** dialog box appears:

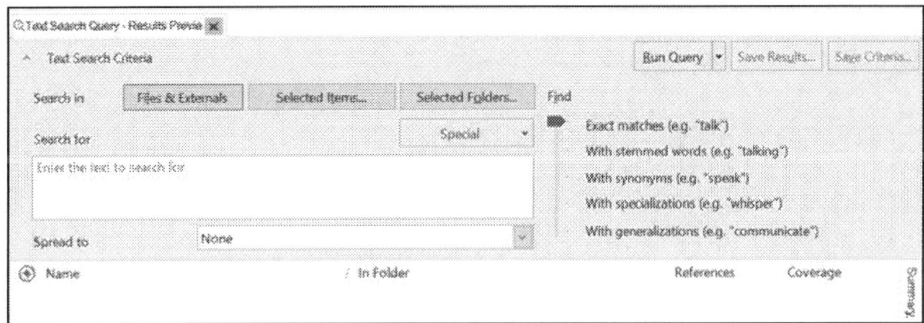

4 Type the search word or the search criteria in the **Search for** text box, for example `'motivation OR reason'`. Move the **Find** slider over the option *Including stemmed words,* this way the query searches words with same stem as the typed search words. (English, French, German, Portuguese and Spanish only).
5 Use the options at **Spread to**: Coding References, Narrow Context, Broad Context, Custom Context or Entire Source.

When several words are typed in a sequence, e.g. `ADAM EVE`, the search is made as an OR-combination and when the words are surrounded by quotes, `"ADAM EVA"`, an exact phrase search is run. In case a phrase search includes a stop word like `"ADAM and EVA"` then the search string is automatically modified to `"ADAM EVA"` and the result will include **ADAM <stop word> EVA**.

The slider **Find** has five options:

Position	**Result**	**Example**
Exact match	Exact matches only	sport
With stemmed words	Exact matches Words with the same stem	sport, sporting
With synonyms	Exact matches Words with same stem Synonyms[5] (words with a very close meaning)	sport, sporting, play, fun
With specializations	Exact matches Words with same stem Synonyms[1] (words with a very close meaning) Specializations (words with a more specialized meaning)	sport, sporting, play, fun, running, basketball
With generalizations	Exact matches Words with same stem Synonyms[3] (words with a very close meaning) Specializations (words with a more specialized meaning—a 'type of') Generalizations (words with a more general meaning)	sport, sporting, play, fun, running, basketball, recreation, business

All settings work for NVivo's text content languages. The text content language options are available when you go to **File → Info → Project Properties,** the **General** tab: *Text Content Language* (see page 51). If this setting is made for *Other* then only 'Exact match' can be used but can be combined with the conventional operators under [**Special**] which offers the following optional search functions:

Option	Example	Comment
Wildcard ?	ADAM?	? represents *one* arbitrary character
Wildcard *	EVA*	* represents *any number* of arbitrary characters
AND	ADAM AND EVA	Both words must be found
OR[6]	ADAM OR EVA	Either word must be found
NOT	ADAM NOT EVA	Adam is found where Eve is not found
Required	+ADAM EVA	Adam is required but Eve is also found
Prohibit	-EVA ADAM	Adam is found where Eve is not found
Fuzzy	ADAM~	Finds words of similar spelling
Near...	"ADAM EVA"~3	Adam and Eve are found within 3 words from each other
Relevance...	ADAM^2EVA	Adam is 2 times as relevant as Eve is

6 Confirm with [**Run Query**].

---

[5] Each content language has its own built-in, non-editable synonym list.

[6] The operator OR can be replaced by space like 'ADAM EVA'.

The format of the result depends on the settings in the dialog box **Text Search Query – Results Preview** (page 231).

After you run a Text Search Query, the ***Summary*** tab displays a list of shortcuts in the List View and can look like this. These shortcuts contain the search results within a given Source Item. The Summary tab is default:

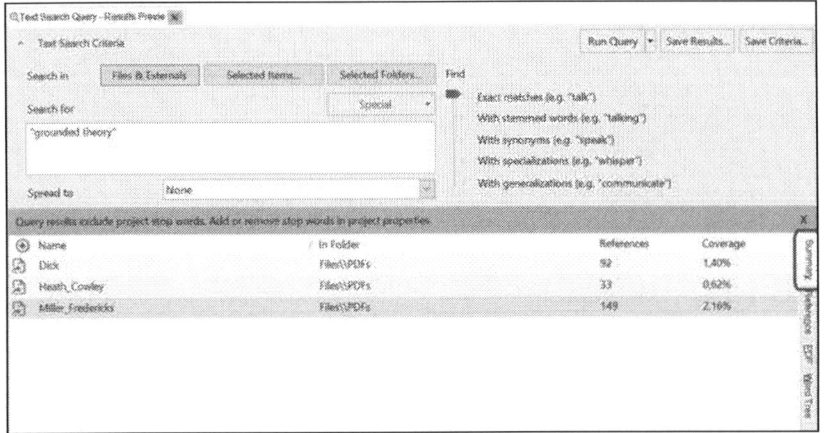

The list of shortcuts can easily be sorted by clicking on the column head. When you double-click on such shortcut the item will open and the search words are highlighted:

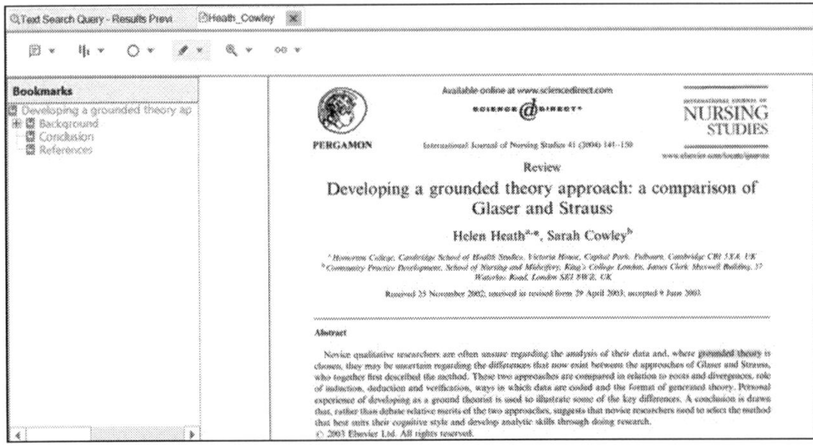

Creating a Set

You might find it useful to combine results from your search into a Set:

1 Select the shortcuts that you want to create as a set.

2 Go to **Create | Static Set → New Static Set...**
or right-click and select **Create As → Create As Static Set...**

3 Type a name of the new set and confirm with **[OK]**.

alternatively, if you already have a set:

1 Select the shortcuts that you want to add to a set.

2 Go to **Create | Static Set → Add to Static Set...** or right-click and select **Add to Static Set...**
3 Select Set in the **Select Set** dialog box.
4 Confirm with **[OK]**.

Creating a Code or Cases

You can also combine results from your search into a new Code or Cases:

1 Select the shortcuts that you want to create as a Code.
2 Right-click and select **Code Whole Files** or **[Ctrl]** + **[F2]** (selected sources will be coded at one existing Code or a new Code)
or **Create As → Create as Code** (selected shortcuts will become *one* new Code)
or **Create As → Create as Cases** (one new Case per item will be created)
3 Type a name for the new Code. When Cases are created, they will inherit the names of the sources. The **Select Location** dialog box makes it optional that you allocate one of the existing Case Classifications to the new Case(s). Confirm with **[OK]**.

Saving Search Results

1 Select the shortcuts that you want to create as a Code.
2 Right-click and select **[Save Results}** (all selected shortcuts will be merged into one new Code) or right-click and select **Store Selected Query Results** (selected shortcuts will be merged into one new Code) or select **Store Query Results** for all shortcuts.

The **Store Query Results** dialog box is shown.

3 Determine the name and location of the new Code.

As al alternative you may also use the **[Run Query]**-button and its optional right arrow allowing you to Run and Save Result for all items in one go:

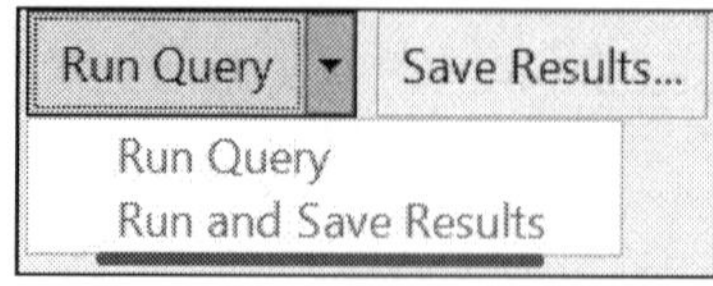

After a query has been run you nay also use the **[Save Results...]**-button.

The *Reference* view mode displays 5 words on each side of the search word (Coding Context) and otherwise the view options are the same as for an open Code (see Chapter 13, section Visualizing your Coding, page 187):

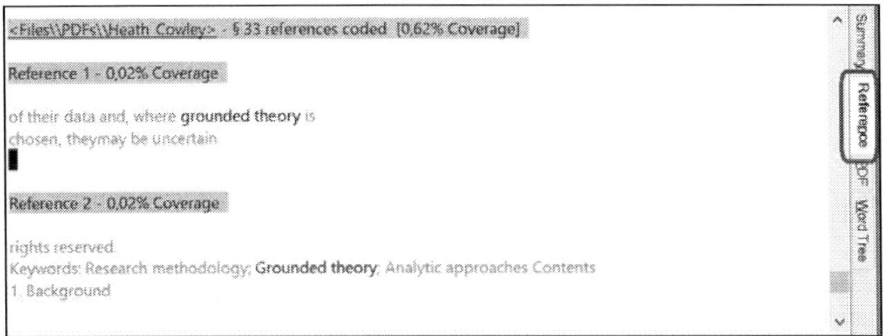

The *Text/PDF* view mode is also identical as for an open Code (see page 188):

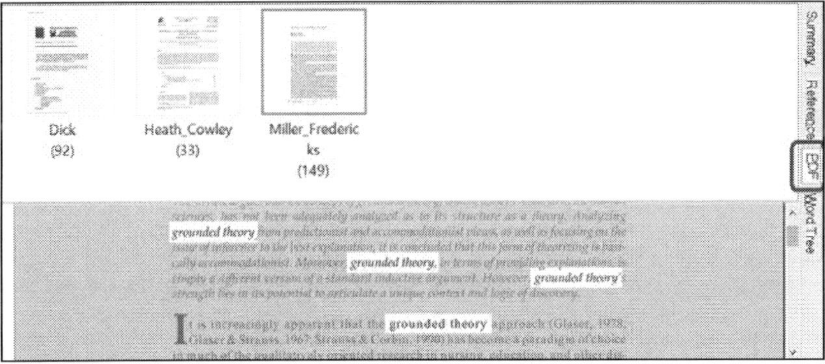

Word Trees

The *Word Tree* view mode is a feature for Text Search Queries that visualizes how a word occurs within a corpus of sentences. This is one of our favorite NVivo visualizations. Remember, to generate a Word Tree you need to ensure query options set for *Preview* and that Spread Coding is off:

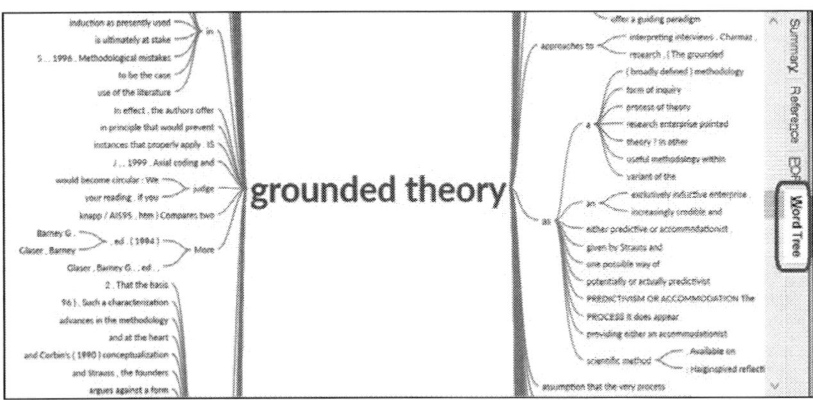

A new context dependent Ribbon menu, **Word Tree**, now appears and there you can find a list called **Root Term**. This list is sorted by frequency, and displays words resulting from the placement of the **Find** slider. Each selected Root Term creates a new Word Tree. You can also decide the number of words (Context Words) that surrounds a Root Term.

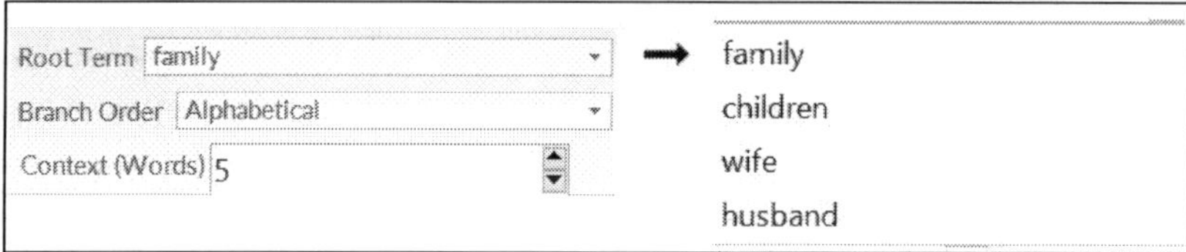

Finally, you can also click any word of the Word Tree and the whole branch will be highlighted. Double-clicking a selected branch opens a Code preview. Clicking the root term will highlight all branches of the Word Tree. You can also select a branch, right-click and the following menu appears: Run Text Search Query (similar to double-clicking the branch), Export Word Tree, Print and Copy. A full Word Tree can also be exported as a low-resolution image. Unfortunately, at present NVivo does not contain functionality for exporting high-resolution images. But we have requested this function and we are hopeful for the future.

Word Frequency Queries

Word Frequency Queries makes it possible to make a list of the most frequent words in selected items: Source Items (Files), Codes etc.

1 Go to **Explore | Word Frequency**.
Default folder is **Queries\\Query Criteria** or its currently open subfolder.
Go to 4.

alternatively

1 Select the **Queries\\Query Criteria** folder or its subfolder.
2 Go to **Explore | Word Frequency**.
Go to 4.

alternatively

2 Click at an empty space in the List View.
3 Right-click and select **New Query → Word Frequency**.

A new context dependent Ribbon menu, **Word Frequency Query**, is now available and is opened each time a Word Frequency Query is opened.

The **Word Frequency Query Results** dialog box appears:

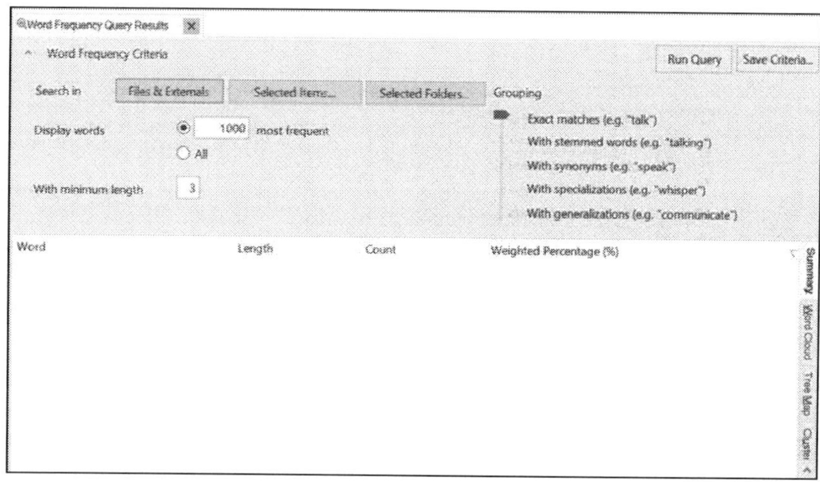

The **Grouping** slider is described under **Text Search Queries** (see page 202) where the corresponding function is called **Find** slider.

4 When choosing **[Selected Items...]** or **[Selected folders...]** from the **Search in** drop-down list and then the **Select Project Items** dialog box appears and is used like a Text Search Query.

5 When items and other options have been decided, then click **[Run Query]** or go to **Word Frequency Query | Run Query**.

The result may look like this, with the *Summary* tab open by default:

Word	Length	Count	Weighted Percentage (%)
theory	6	446	1,40
grounded	8	348	1,10
time	4	325	1,02
work	4	306	0,96
volunteer	9	300	0,94
like	4	239	0,75
research	8	202	0,64
people	6	186	0,59
interviewer	11	183	0,58
respondent	10	175	0,55
one	3	165	0,52
think	5	164	0,52

Select *one* word (it is not possible to select more than one in this instances), right-click and the following options appear:

- *Open Code Preview* (or double-click or key command **[Ctrl]** + **[Shift]** + **[O]**) opens like any Code with search words and synonyms highlighted with Narrow Coding Context (5 words).
- *Run Text Search Query*
  or go to **Word Frequency Query | Run Text Search Query**. The **Text Search Query** dialog box is shown with the search word and synonyms transferred to the search criteria. The options Selected Items are inherited from the **Word Frequency Query**

dialog box. The dialog box can be edited before you run it. See also page 201 on what you can do with Text Search Queries.

- *Export List...*
- *Print List...*
- *Create As Code...*
  Creates a Code with the search word and synonyms and a Narrow Coding Context (5 words). The Context Setting is retained in the **Coding\\Codes** folder or its subfolder during the ongoing work session.
- *Add to Stop Words List*[7]

Word Clouds

The *Word Cloud* tab displays a custom tag cloud based on your query:

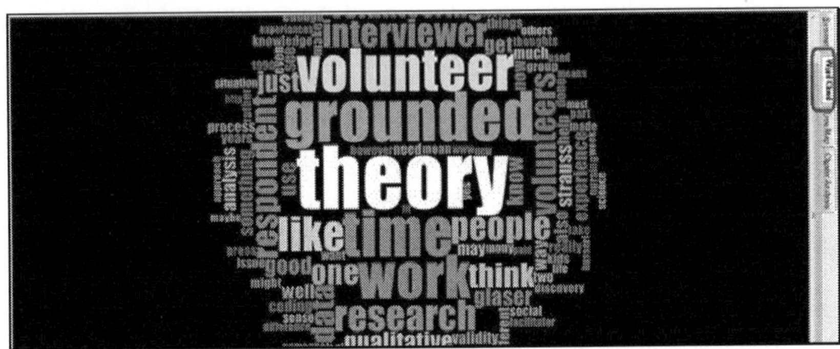

The Word Cloud tab displays up to 100 words. The size of the words reflects their frequency. Words are sorted alphabetically and include stemmed words and synonyms if the Word Frequency Query is set accordingly. Click on a word and a Text Search Query is created and runs with results displayed as a Code preview.

Tree Maps

The *Tree Map* tab displays a custom tree map based on your query:

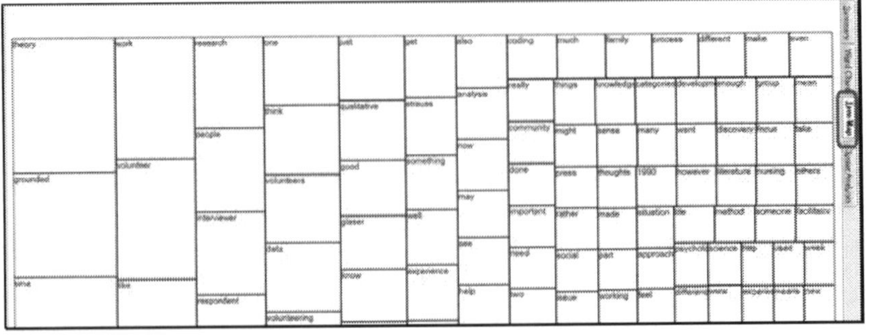

[7] Alternatively: Go to **Word Frequency Query | Add to Stop Words List**.

The Tree Map tab displays up to 100 words. The size of the area of each element reflects the frequency of the word. Click on a word and a Text Search Query is created and run with the results displayed as a Code preview. For more on Hierarchy Charts and Tree Maps, see page 349.

Cluster Analysis

The *Cluster Analysis* tab displays a custom cluster analysis based on your query:

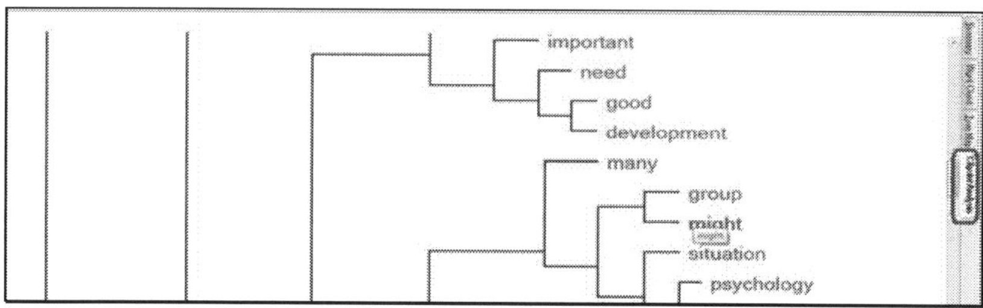

The Cluster Analysis tab displays up to 100 words. Words that co-occur are clustered together. When this tab has been selected the new options ubder the context dependent Ribbon menu **Word Frequency Query** is shown and you can choose between 2D Cluster Map, 3D Cluster Map, Horizontal Dendrogram, Vertical Dendrogram or Circle Graph. With **Word Frequenct Query | Select Data** you can choose the metric coefficient. Selecting **Word Frequency Query → Cluster Maps** when viewing 2D or 3D lets you present the size of symbols reflecting its occurrence. The Cluster map applies a certain color for each cluster in each type of cluster diagram. In order to study the clustering structure you can vary the number of clusters as any number between 1 and 20 (10 is default) in each type of cluster diagram by going to **Word Frequency Query | Clusters**.

Tag Clouds, Tree Maps, and Cluster Analysis can also be used like this: Select a word in the graph, right-click and the menu is similar to the one explained on page 207. Only the Cluster Analysis has two unique alternatives: Copy (the whole graph) and Select Data (Pearson, Jaccard's or Sørensen's coefficients).

For more on Cluster Analysis, see page 356.

Coding Queries

Coding Queries are advantageous when you have advanced your project's structure in such a way that you can acquire project insights via complex queries.

1 Go to **Explore | Queries → Coding**.
Default folder is **Queries\\Query Criteria** or its currently open subfolder.
Go to 4.

alternatively

1 Select the **Queries\\Query Criteria** folder or its subfolder.
2 Go to **Explore | Queries → Coding**.
Go to 4.

alternatively

2 Click at an empty space in the List View.
3 Right-click and select **New Query → Coding**.

A new context dependent Ribbon menu, **Code**, is now available and is opened each time a Coding Query is opened.

The **Coding Query – Results Preview** dialog box appears:

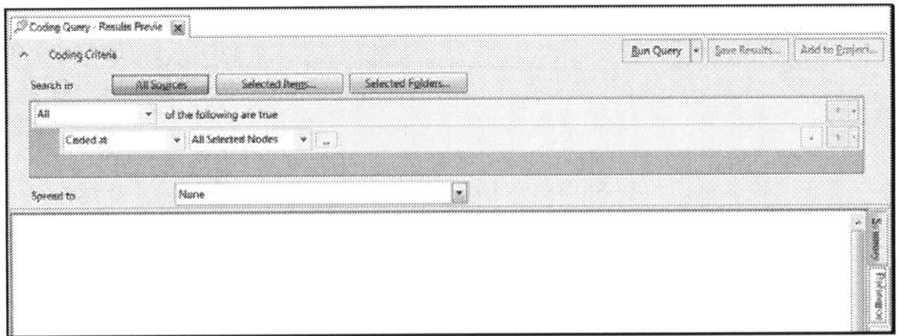

4 Each criteria row allows you to select *Coded at* or *Not Coded at* and *All Selected Codes* or *Any Selected Code* or *Any Case Where* and then specify at the [...]-button.

To the right in the dialog box there is an option to add or delete rows and other options to modify the criterions:

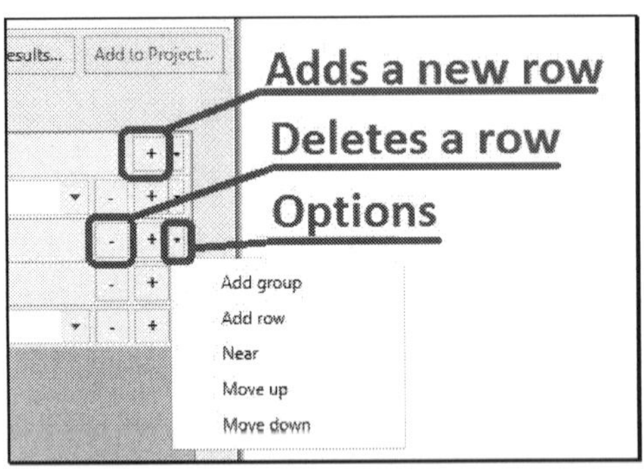

or

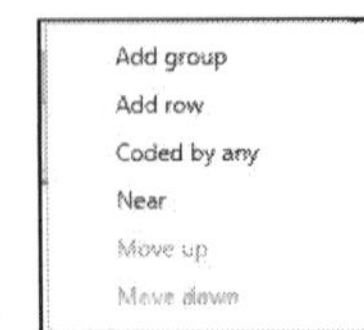

An example of a Coding Query. Observe, the operators All and Any corresponds to the well-known AND and OR.

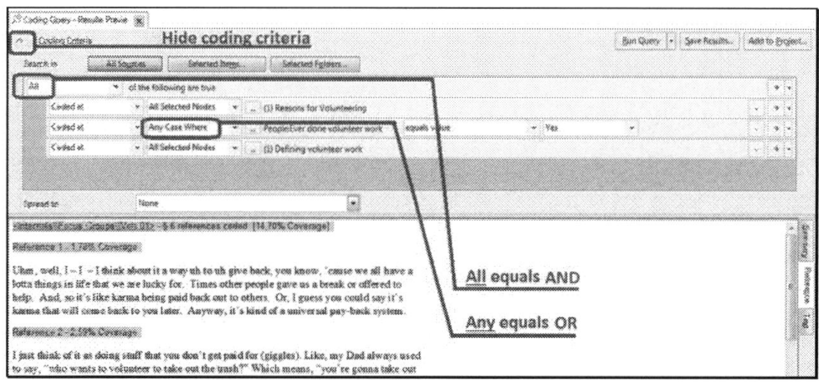

The **[Save Results...]**-button decides name and location of the Code that is a result of the query. The **Store Query Results** dialog box is shown.

The [**Run Query**]-button runs the query as a preview unless you choose **Run Query → Run and Save Results** and the query is run followed by the **Store Query Results** dialog box. Observe that the default location in this box is the **Queries\\Query Results** folder each time the query is re-run.

Matrix Coding Queries

Matrix Coding Queries have been introduced to display how a set of Codes relates to another set of Cases. The results are presented in the form of a matrix or table.

Example: We want to explore how different age groups relate to certain selected themes represented by Codes.

1 Go to **Explore | Query | Matrix Coding Query**.
Default folder is **Queries\\Query Criteria** or its currently open subfolder.
Go to 4.

alternatively

1 Select the **Queries\\Query Criteria** folder or its subfolder
2 Go to **Explore | Query | Matrix Coding Query**.
Go to 4.

alternatively

2 Click on an empty space in the List View.
3 Right-click and select **New Query → Matrix Coding Query**.

A new context dependent Ribbon menu, **Matrix**, is now available and is opened each time a Matrix Coding Query is opened.

The **Matrix Coding Query** - **Results Preview** dialog box appears:

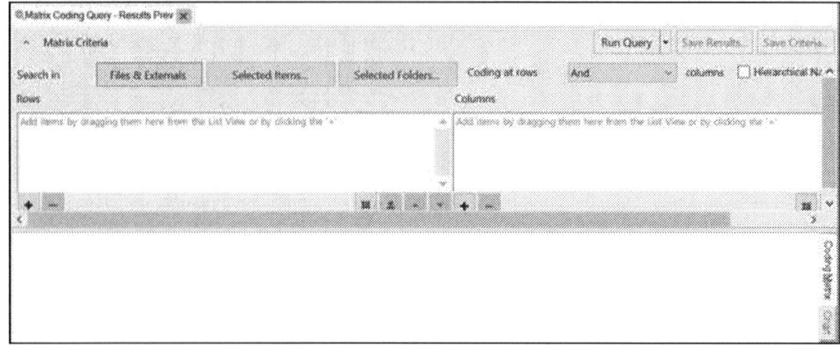

4 Start by adding items to the left list box be either dragging item from the List View or using the [+]-button which offers *Select Items...* or *Select Attribute Values...* We apply ***Select Items*** and all values of the Attribute Age Groups:

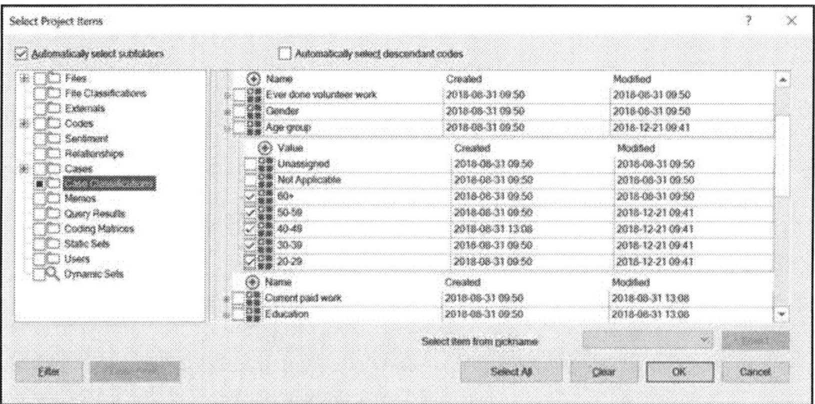

5 Repeat this action for the right list box.

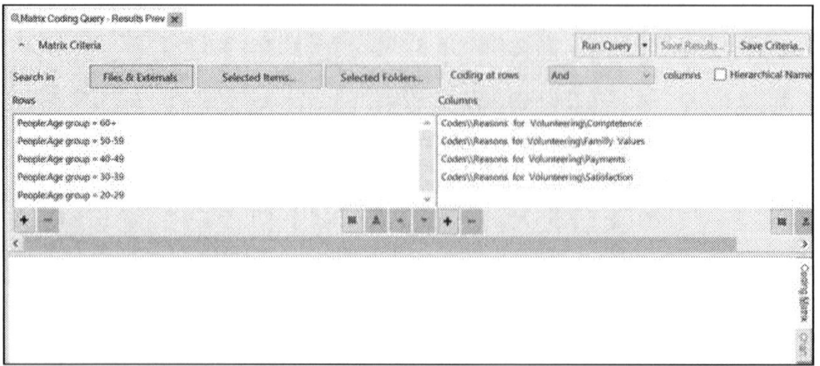

This button makes it possible to display collections as a single rows or members separately.

This button makes it possible to select items from named user(s).

This button makes it possible to move selected row(s) up.

This button makes it possible to move selected row(s) down.

This button makes it possible to add items.

This button makes it possible to delete selected row(s).

6 Click [**Save Criteria...**] to save the query in the **Queries\\Query Criteria** folder.

7 Click [**Run Query**] and the result shows like this, which is a preview mode:

	A : Competence	B : Family Values	C : Payments	D : Satisfaction
1 : People:Age group = 60+	23	26	11	43
2 : People:Age group = 50...	3	3	2	11
3 : People:Age group = 40...	5	3	3	11
4 : People:Age group = 30...	41	28	18	41
5 : People:Age group = 20...	30	37	15	60

8 Click [**Save Results...**] and the result is a **Coding Matrix** and you need to give the matrix a name and possibly a description and the locations are either the folders **Queries\\Query Results** or **Queries\\Coding Matrices**.

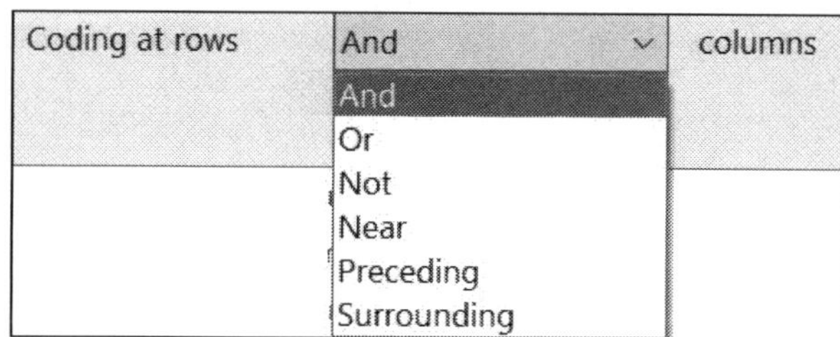

9 Please note, that the default operator between rows and columns is AND. In the drop-down list of the dialog box there are other options depending on your research situation.

You can also show a Chart of this matrix. Click the *Chart* tab on the right side of the window:

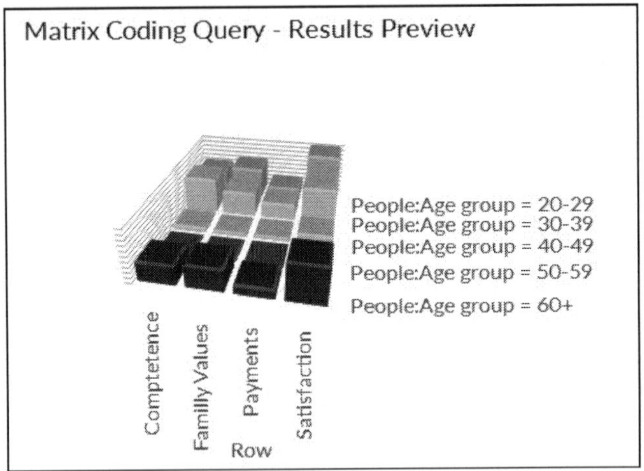

The context dependent ribbon menu **Chart** opens when the matrix is showing as a Chart. The Chart options allow adjusting formatting, zooming and rotating. By going to **Chart | Type** the following drop-down menu appears:

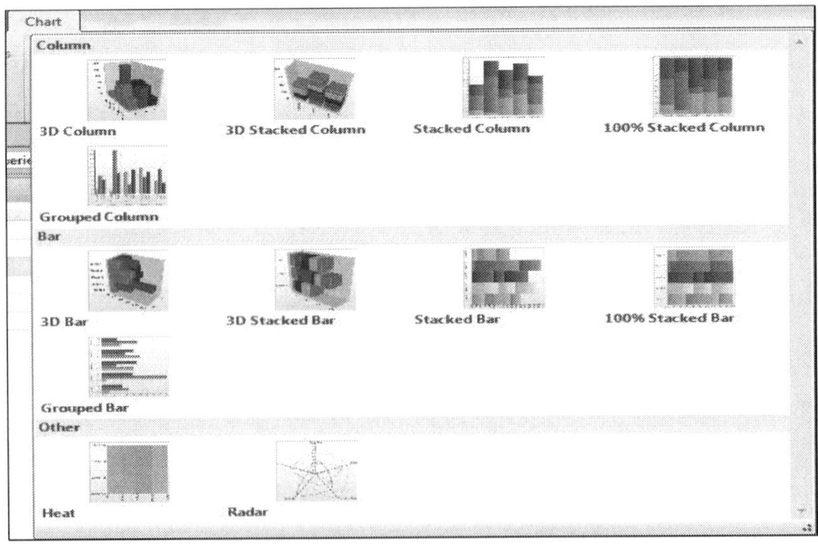

Here you can choose from various types of diagrams.

Opening a Cell

A matrix is a collection of cells. Each cell is a Code. You may need therefore to study each cell separately.

1. Open the matrix.
2. Select the cell you want to open.
3. Right-click and select **Open Coding Matrix Cell** or double-click the cell.

The cell opens and can be analyzed as any other kode. This Code is an integral part of the matrix and if you want to save it as a new Code then select the whole Code in the *Reference* view mode and go to **Home | Code → Code Selection...** or right-click and select **Code Selection...** or **[Ctrl]** + **[F2]**.

Viewing Cell Content

There are several options to view cell content when cells are not opened.

1 Open the matrix.
2 Go to **Matrix | Cell Content →** <select>
or right-click and select **Cell Content →** <select> any of the following options:

- Coding References
- Files Coded → Select Classification
- Cases Coded → Select Classification
- Row Percentage
- Column Percentage
- Worda Coded
- Coding Presence
- Duration Coded

Hiding/Unhiding Row Numbers

1 Open the matrix.
2 Go to **Matrix | Hide & Unhide → Row IDs**
or right-click and select **Row → Row Ids**.

Hiding Rows

1 Open the matrix.
2 Select one or more rows that you want to hide.
3 Go to **Matrix | Hide & Unhide → Hide Row**
or right-click and select **Row → Hide Row**.

Hiding/Unhiding Rows with Filters

1 Open the matrix.
2 Click the 'funnel' in a certain column head
or select a column and go to **Matrix | Sort & Filter → Filter Column**.

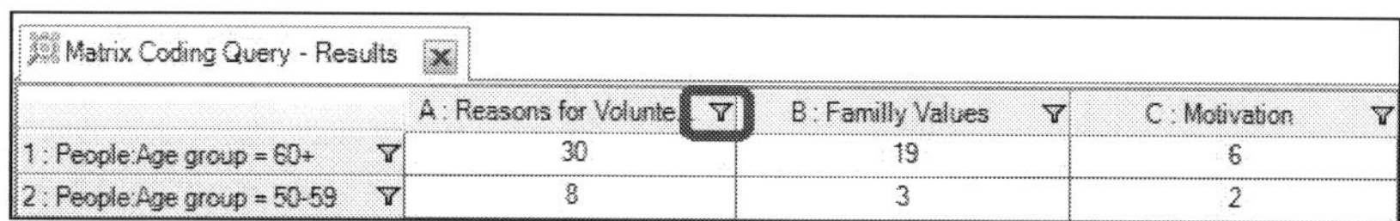

Matrix Coding Query - Results

	A : Reasons for Volunte	B : Familly Values	C : Motivation
1 : People:Age group = 60+	30	19	6
2 : People:Age group = 50-59	8	3	2

The **Coding Matrix Filter Options** dialog box appears:

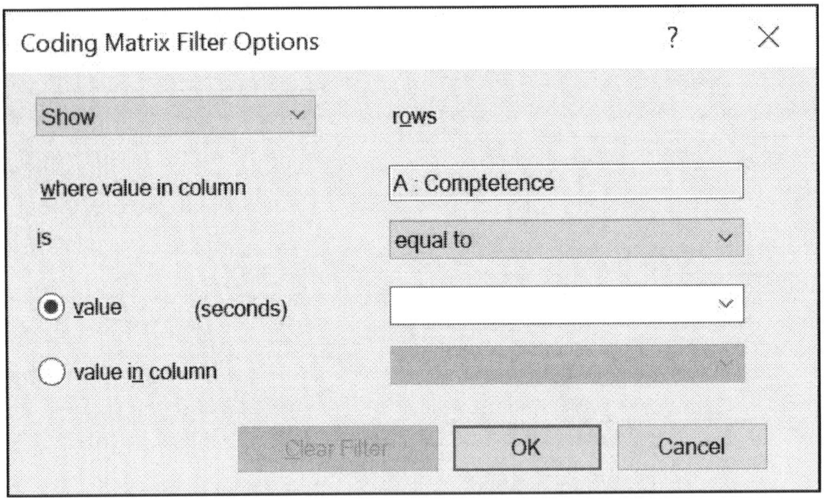

3 Select value and operator for hiding or unhiding. Confirm with **[OK]**. When a filter is applied the funnel turns *red*.

To clear a filter use **[Clear Filter]** in the **Coding Matrix Filter Options** dialog box.

Unhiding Rows

1 Open the matrix.
2 Select one row on each side of the hidden row that you want to unhide.
3 Go to **Matrix | Hide & Unhide → Unhide Row** or right-click and select **Row → Unhide Row**.

Unhiding All Rows

1 Open the matrix.
2 Go to **Matrix | Sort & Filter → Clear All Column Filters** or right-click and select **Column → Clear All Column Filters**.

Hiding/Unhiding Column Letters

1 Open the matrix.
2 Go to **Matrix | Hide & Unhide → Column IDs** or right-click and select **Column → Column IDs**.

Hiding Columns

1 Open the matrix.
2 Select one or more columns that you want to hide.
3 Go to **Matrix | Hide & Unhide → Hide Column** or right-click and select **Column → Hide Column**.

Unhiding Columns

1 Open the matrix.
2 Select one column on each side of the hidden column.
3 Go to **Matrix | Hide & Unhide → Unhide Column** or right-click and select **Column → Unhide Column**.

Unhiding All Columns

1 Open the matrix.
2 Go to **Matrix | Sort & Filter → Clear All Row Filters** or right-click and select **Column → Clear All Row Filters**.

Transposing the Matrix

Transposing means that rows and columns are changing places.

1 Open the matrix.
2 Go to **Matrix | Transpose** or right-click and select **Transpose.**

Moving a Column Left or Right

1 Open the matrix.
2 Select the column or columns that you want to move. If you want to move more than one column, they need to be adjacent.
3 Go to **Matrix → Move Column Left/Move Column Right**.

Resetting the Whole Matrix

1 Open the matrix.
2 Go to **Matrix | Reset Settings** or right-click and select **Reset Settings**.

Viewing the Cells Shaded or Colored

1 Open the matrix.

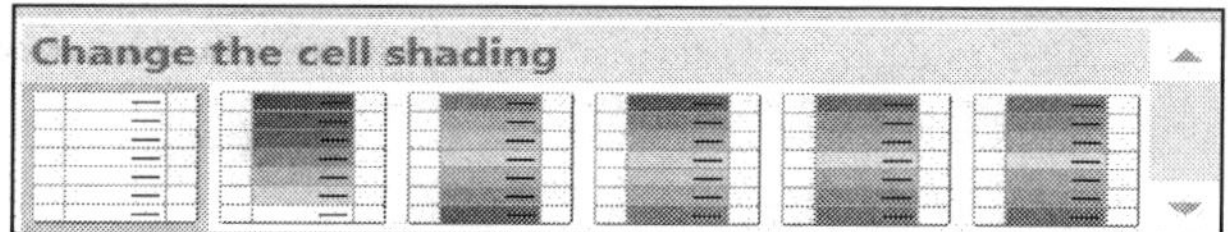

2 Go to **Change the cell shading** in the Matrix ribbon **→ <select>** or right-click and select **Cell Shading → <select>**.

Exporting a Matrix

1 Open or select the matrix.
2 Go to **Share | Export → Export** or right-click and select **Export Coding Matrix...** or **[Ctrl]** + **[Shift]** + **[E]**.

The **Save As** dialog box is shown and you can decide file name, location, and file type: .XLSX, .XLS, .TXT, or .SAV. Confirm with **[Save]**.

When you view a Chart you can export the image in the following file types: .PNG, .JPG, .BMP, .GIF, .SVG, or .PDF.

Converting a Matrix to Codes

There are situations when you need to convert cells in a matrix to Codes.

1. Open or select the matrix.
2. Copy by going to **Home | Clipboard → Copy**
   or right-click and select **Copy**
   or **[Ctrl]** + **[C]**.
3. Click **Coding\\Codes** or its subfolder.
4. Go to **Home | Clipboard → Paste**
   or right-click and select **Paste**
   or **[Ctrl]** + **[V]**.

The **Paste** dialog box appears:

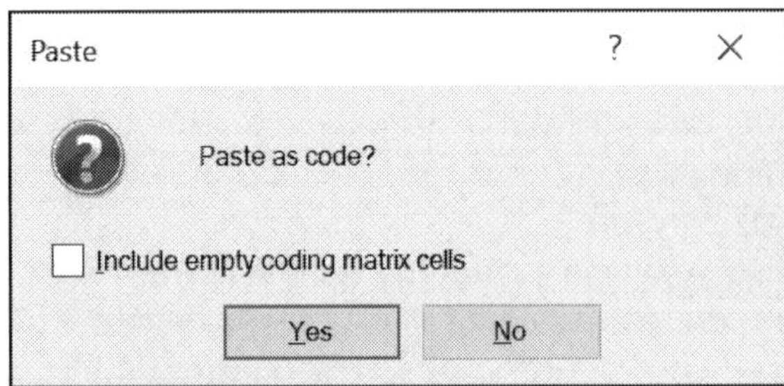

5. Confirm with **[Yes]**.

The result is a hierarchical Code[8] where the Parent Code inherits the name of the matrix, called 'Matrix Parent'. The first generation Child Codes are the rows, called 'Row Parents' and the grandchildren Codes have contents from each cell. These Codes can then be used for Cluster Analysis (see page 356).

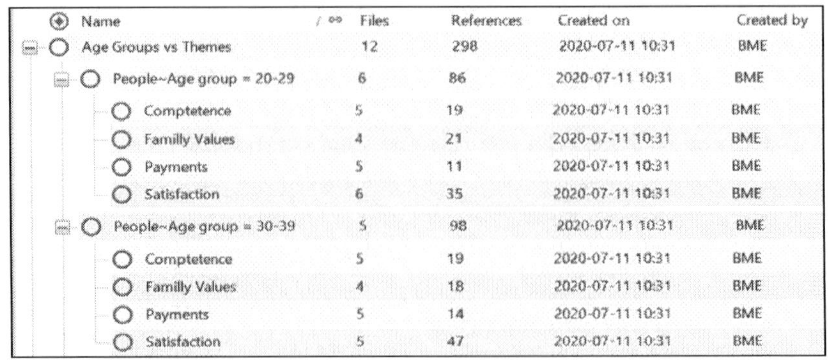

Name	Files	References	Created on	Created by
Age Groups vs Themes	12	298	2020-07-11 10:31	BME
People~Age group = 20-29	6	86	2020-07-11 10:31	BME
Comptetence	5	19	2020-07-11 10:31	BME
Familly Values	4	21	2020-07-11 10:31	BME
Payments	5	11	2020-07-11 10:31	BME
Satisfaction	6	35	2020-07-11 10:31	BME
People~Age group = 30-39	5	98	2020-07-11 10:31	BME
Comptetence	5	19	2020-07-11 10:31	BME
Familly Values	4	18	2020-07-11 10:31	BME
Payments	5	14	2020-07-11 10:31	BME
Satisfaction	5	47	2020-07-11 10:31	BME

[8] When *converting a Coding Matrix* to Codes then the "Matrix Parent" and the "Row Parents" are set with the *Aggregate* function. This method is giving the correct number of Sources but the number of references is suffering from the imperfection we mentioned on page 140.

Crosstab Queries

This query option gives you a quick way to check the spread of coding across cases and demographic variables. For example, you could use a Crosstab query to: Check how often interview respondents refer to a particular topic or issue or Compare what different demographic groups have said about a certain theme.

1 Go to **Explore | Queries → Crosstab**.
Default folder is **Queries\\Query Criteria** or its currently open subfolder.
Go to 4a or 4b.

alternatively

1 Select the **Queries\\Query Criteria** folder or its subfolder.
2 Go to **Explore | Queries → Crosstab**.
Go to 4a or 4b.

alternatively

2 Click on an empty space in the List View.
3 Right-click and select **New Query → Crosstab**.

A new context dependent Ribbon menu, **Crosstab**, has now opened and is opened each time a Crosstab Query is opened. The dialog box **Crosstab Query - Results Preview** appears.

4a Selecting **Crosstab codes against** *Attributes:*

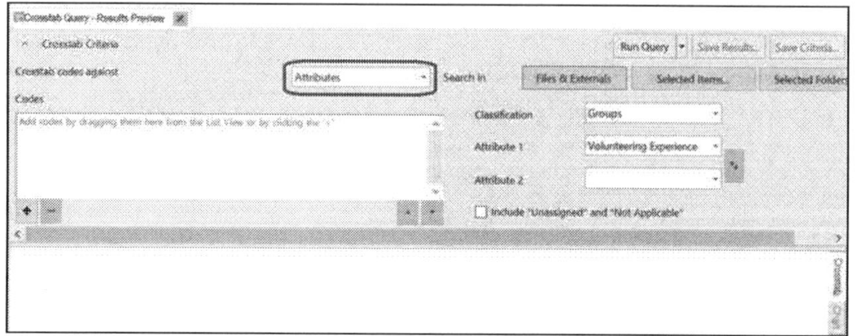

5a Select *Attributes* on the Crosstab codes against dropdown list.
6a The [+] button brings up the **Select Project Items** dialog box. Select your codes and click **[OK]**.
7a In the drop-down list **Classification** we have selected *People* and for **Attribute 1** we have selected *Ever done volunteer work.*
8a Click **[Run Query]**
or go to **Crosstab | Run Query**.

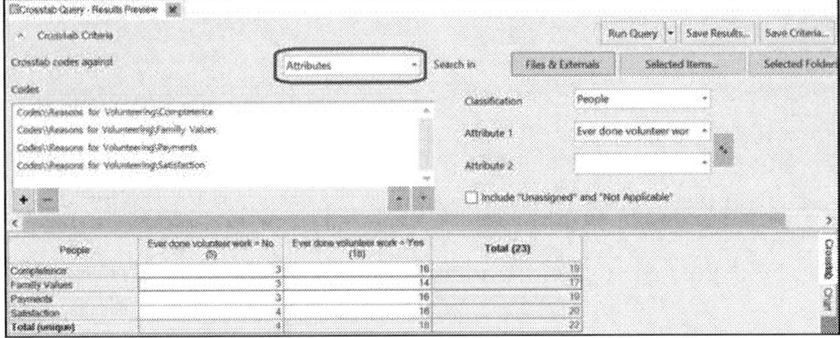

4b Selecting **Crosstab codes against** *Cases:*

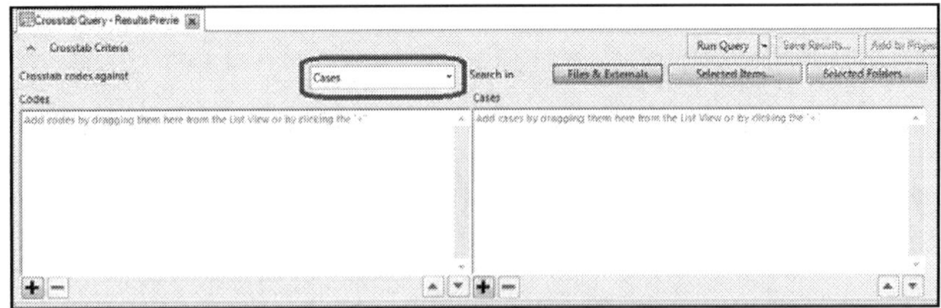

5b Select *Cases* on the **Crosstab codes against** dropdown list.

6b The [+] button brings up the **Select Project Items** dialog box. Select your codes and click **[OK]**.

7b In the drop-down list **Cases** we have used the right [+] button that brings up the **Select Project Items** dialog box. Select your Cases and click **[OK]**.

8b Click **[Run Query]**
or go to **Crosstab | Run Query**.

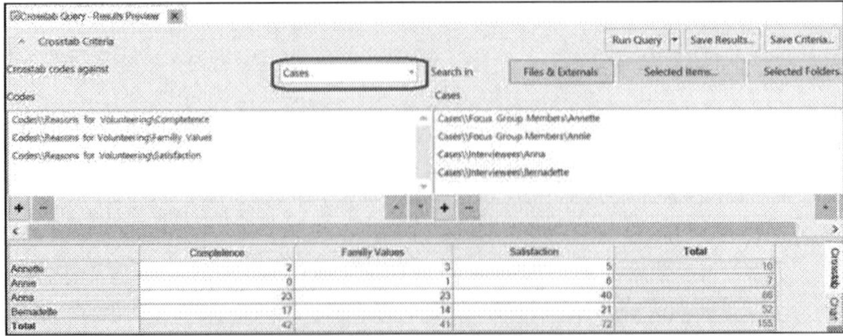

Notes on Saving the Result of a Crosstab Query. Using the [**Save**} or [**Run and Save Results**] buttons allows you to save the result in the **Queries\\Query Results** folder. From here you cannot move or copy this item.

Click the **Chart** tab on the right of the query results to display the results in a chart. See also above what is said about Coding Matrices.

Exporting a Crosstab Result

1 Open or select the Crosstab result.

2 Go to **Share | Export → Export**
or right-click and select **Export Crosstab Results...**
or **[Ctrl]** + **[Shift]** + **[E]**.

The **Save As** dialog box is shown and you can decide the file name, location, and file type: .XLSX, .XLS, .TXT, or .SAV.

When you view a Chart you can export the image in the following file types: .PNG, .JPG, .BMP, .GIF, .SVG, or .PDF.

Compound Queries

Compound Queries make it possible to create complex queries that can combine Code searches with text searches.

1 Go to **Explore | Queries → Compound**.
Default folder is **Queries\\Query Criteria** or its currently open subfolder.
Go to 4.

alternatively

1 Select the **Queries\\Query Criteria** folder or its subfolder.

2 Go to **Explore | Queries → Compound**.
Go to 4.

alternatively

2 Click at an empty space in the List View.

3 Right-click and select **New Query → Compound**.

The **Compound Query** dialog box is shown. The query is divided into *Subquery 1* and *Subquery 2*. The operator[9] between them can be chosen among several options.

---

[9] See page 236 onward for explanations of the other operators on this drop-down list.

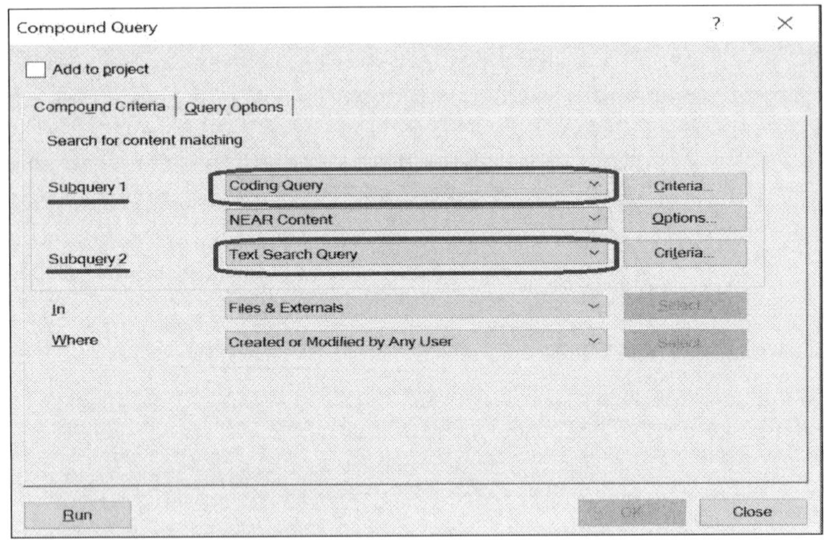

4 Choose *Coding Query* at **Subquery 1**.
5 The **[Criteria...]** button opens the **Subquery Properties** dialog box with an **Advanced** tab that is similar to the **Coding Query** dialog box.

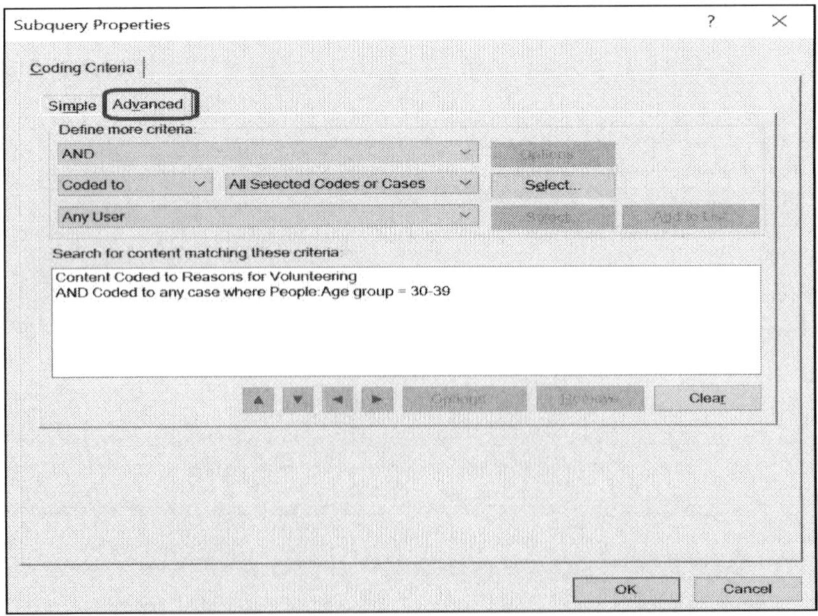

6 We use the **Advanced** tab and use the following criteria: The Code *Reasons for Volunteering* AND the *Age Group 30–39*. Click **[Add to List]** for each criterion. See the section about Coding Queries, page 209.
7 Click **[OK]**.

8 In the **Compound Query** dialog box select the operator *NEAR Content* and with the **[Options...]** button you select *Overlapping*.

9 Choose *Text Search Query* at **Subquery 2**.

10 The **[Criteria...]** button opens the **Subquery Properties** dialog box, which is similar to the **Text Search Query** dialog box.

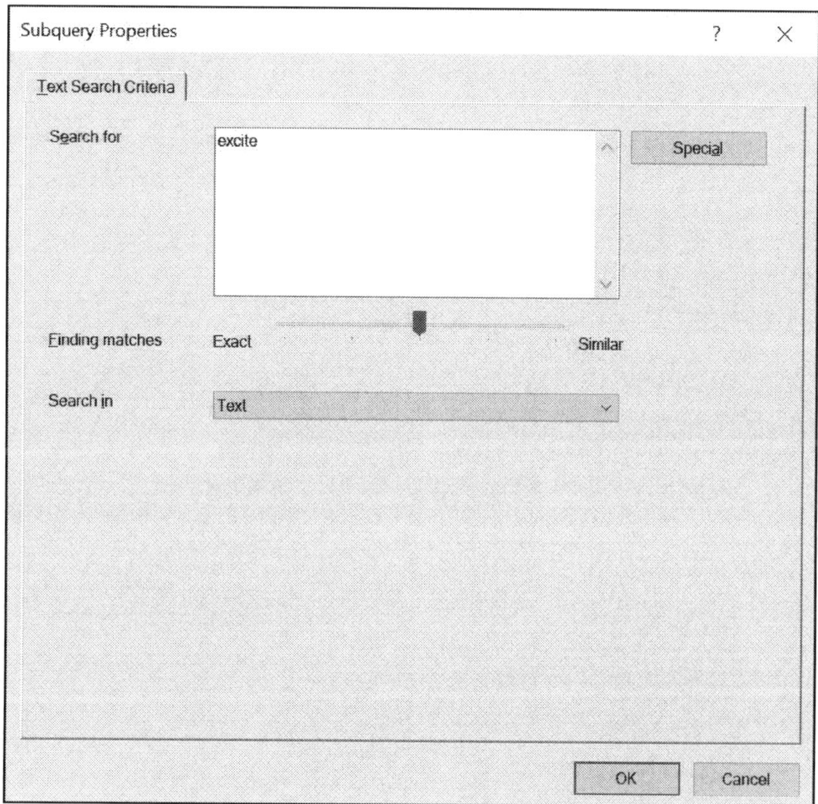

11 Type `excite` in the text box **Search for**, and pull the slider below two steps to the right which includes *Stemmed search* and synonyms.

The **Finding matches** slider is the same as described under **Text Search Queries** (see page 202).

12 Use the **Add to Project** checkbox to save the criterion under the **Queries\\Query Criteria** folder. Click **[OK]**.

13 Click **[Run]** in the **Compound Query** dialog box.

The format of the results depends on the settings made under the **Query Options** tab in the dialog box **Compound Query** or **Compound Query Properties** (see page 231).

A new context dependent Ribbon menu, **Code**, is now available and is opened each time a Compound Query is opened. When you have run a Compound Query with *Preview Only* the result looks like under Text Search Queries, page 203 and onwards, with two exceptions: The Word Tree tab is not included and the option **Store Selected Query Results** for selected shortcuts in Summary view is also not included.

Group Queries

Use Group Queries to find items that are associated in a particular way with other items in your project. You could for example explore the difference in coding between sources (scope items) with a Group query. When you run the query, the results are displayed in Detail View with the coded Codes grouped under each scope item.

1 Go to **Explore | Queries → Group**.
Default folder is **Queries\\Query Criteria** or its currently open subfolder.
Go to 4.

alternatively

1 Select the **Queries\\Query Criteria** folder or its subfolder.
2 Go to **Explore | Queries → Group**.
Go to 4.

alternatively

2 Click on any empty space in the List View.
3 Right-click and select **New Query → Group**.

In each case, the **Group Query** dialog box appears:

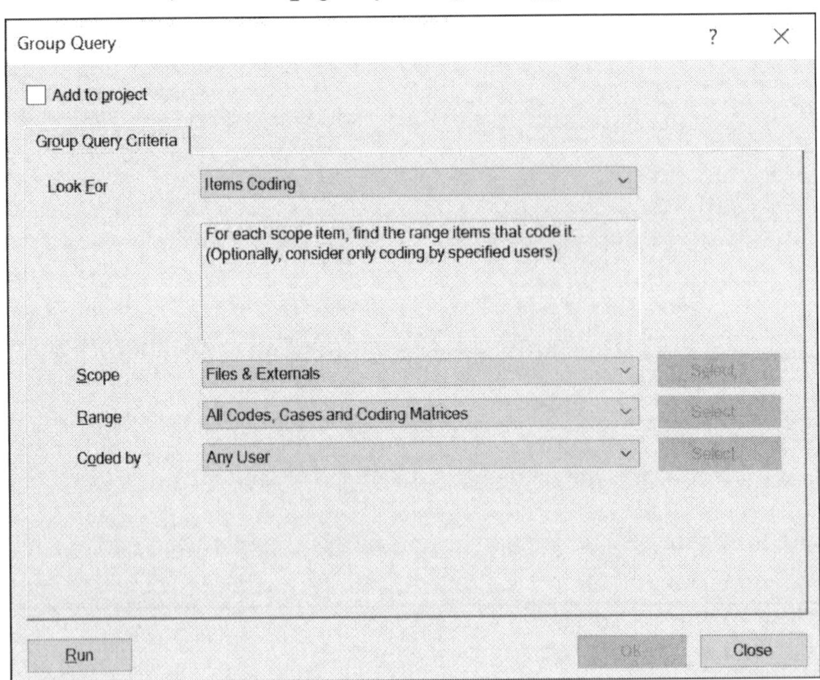

The **Look For:** drop-down list has the following options:

Items Coding	For each scope item, find the range items that code it. (Optionally, consider only coding by specific users)
Items Coded to	For each scope item, find the range items that it codes. (Optionally, consider only coding by specific users)
Items by Attribute Value	For each attribute value in the scope, find the items in the range that have that value assigned.
Relationships	For each scope item, find the items that it has a relationship of the selected direction/type with.
See Also Links	For each scope item, find the range items that it has s See Also link with.
Map Items	For each map in the scope, find the range items that appear in the map.
Maps	For each scope item, find the maps in the range that it appears in.

Depending on what options you select the **Scope** and **Range** drop-down lists offers corresponding alternatives.

Let's assume that you need to explore what Codes two selected sources items are coded to.

4 Select *Items Coding* from the **Look For** drop-down list.
5 Select *Selected Items* from the **Scope** drop-down list.
6 Click the **[Select]** button and from the **Select Project Items** dialog box select for example two Source Items (two interviews). Click **[OK]**.
7 Select *Selected Items* from the **Range** drop-down list.
8 Click the **[Select]** button and from the **Select Projects** dialog box select for example the **Child Codes** under **Reasons for Volunteering**. Click **[OK]**.
9 Finally click **[Run]** in the **Group Query** dialog box.

Group Query Results are displayed as an expandable list in the Detail View. This list cannot be saved. The query, however, can be saved with the **Add to Project** button, see Chapter 16, Common Query Features. When the saved query is run the expandable list appears again.

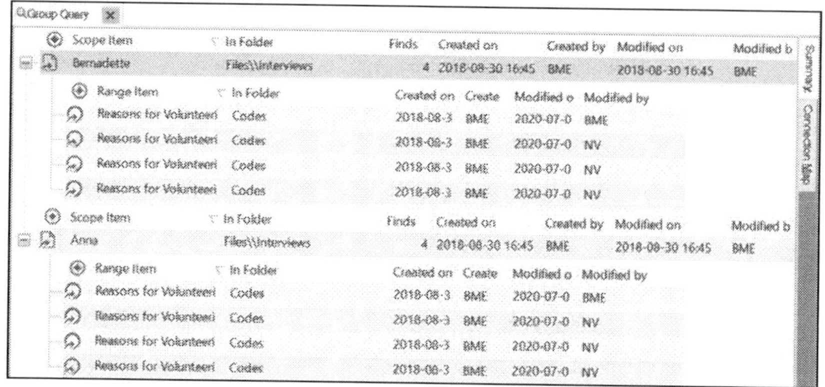

Selecting the **Connection Map** tab to the right the following graph is shown:

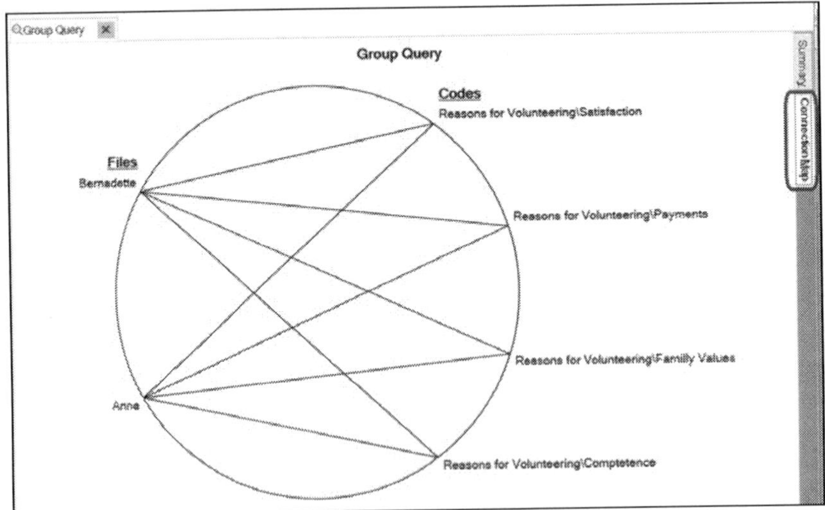

In a corresponding way you can select any scope item like Code(s), map(s), and then the range of its related items.

Exporting and copying this map is also an option.

.

.

15. COMMON QUERY FEATURES

This chapter deals with the functions and features common to several types of queries. The Filter function which is described here is an example of a common query feature. One way to benefit from the filter function is letting the filter eliminate unwanted items. For example, you can use the filter to eliminate Codes that were created later than last week.

The Filter Function

The [**Select Items...**] button is available in many dialog boxes when queries are created. This button always opens the **Select Project Items** dialog box:

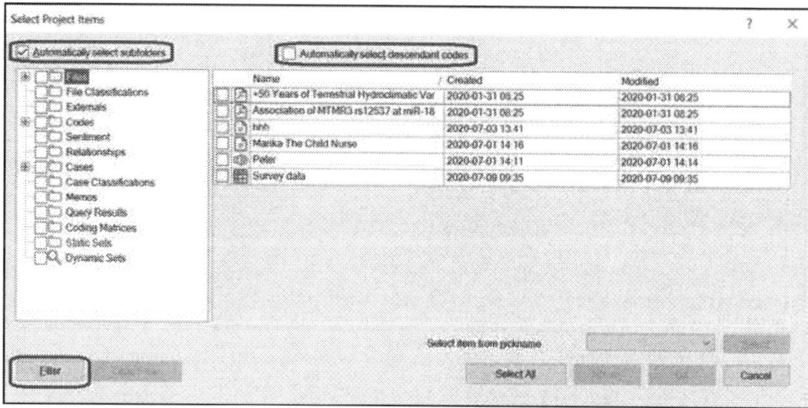

Automatically select subfolders means that when a folder is selected in the left hand window all the underlying subfolders and items will be selected. Folders which cannot have subfolders (Codes, Sets, and Results) will select all of the items therein.

Automatically select descendant codes means that when a certain item in the right-hand window has been selected all underlying items are also selected.

The **[Filter]** button is always available at the bottom left corner of the **Select Project Items** dialog box and this button opens the **Advanced Find** dialog box:

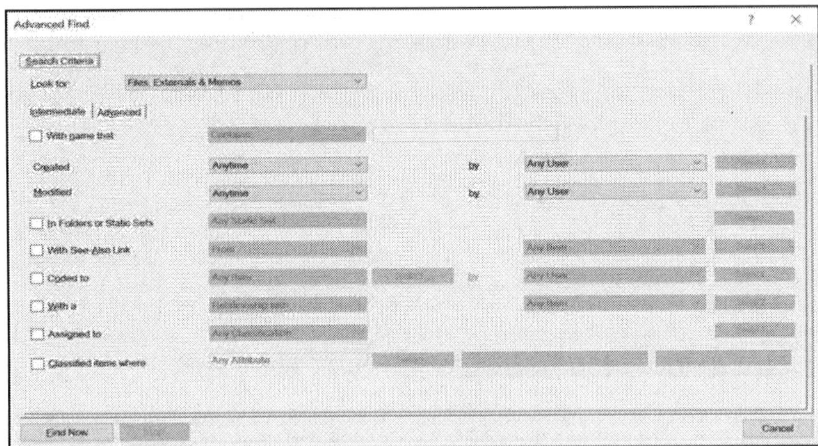

These are the same as the Advanced Find search functions (see page 311).

Saving a Query

As mentioned at the beginning of previous chapter, Queries made can be saved so that they can be run again at a later stage or be copied and edited for future needs.

The region from the upper right corner of the dialog for Text Search, Word Frequency, Coding, Matrix Coding, and Crosstab is:

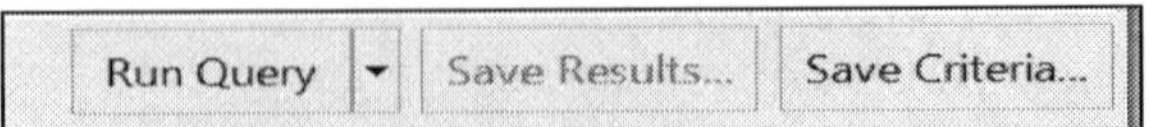

1 Click **[Save Criteria...]** and this dialog opens:

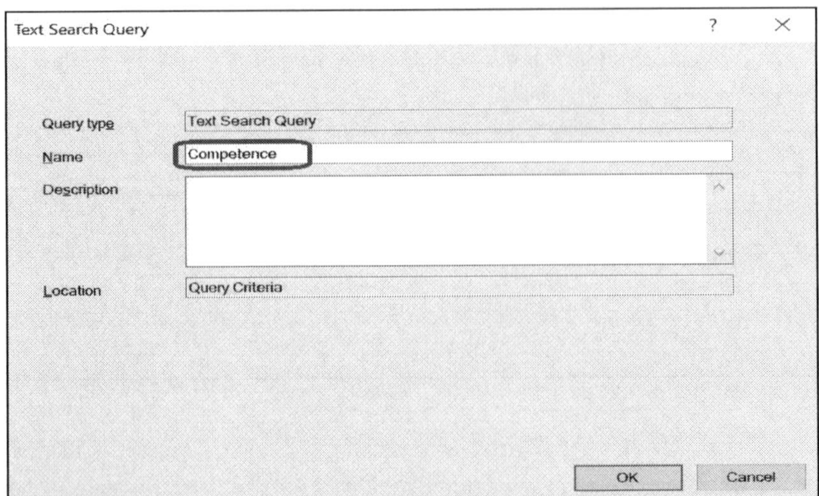

2 Type a name (compulsory) and a description (optional), then click [**OK**].

The dialogs for Compound Coding, Coding Comparison and Group Queries are different:

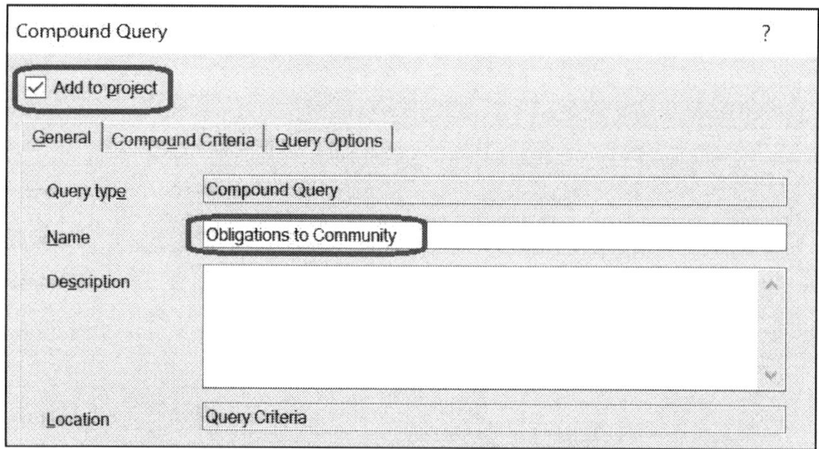

1 Check **Add to project** and a new general tab will show.
2 Type a name (compulsory) and a description (optional), then click [**Run**] or [**OK**].

Saving a Result

The result of a query can be displayed on the screen using the option *Preview Only*. The result is shown but not saved.

Preview Only for Text Search Queries opens the Summary tab (see page 188).

Preview Only for Coding Queries and Compound Queries opens the Reference tab (see page 187).

Preview Only for Matrix Search Queries opens the Coding Matrix tab (see page 213).

If you want to save the result as a Code there are a few options to choose from, for example *Create Results as New Code* or *Merge Result into Existing Code*.

The region from the upper right corner of the dialog for Text Search and Coding Queries is:

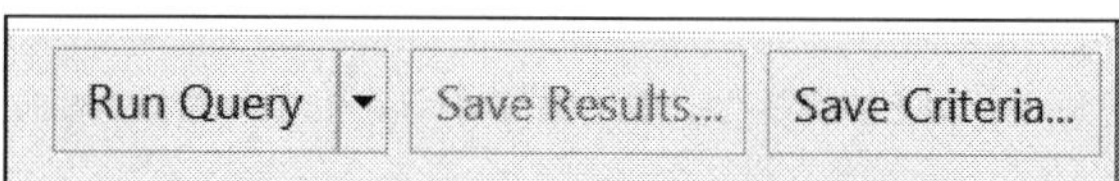

In order to save a result you must first both run and view the result as a preview using [**Run Query**] and then use [**Save Results...**] or using the **Run and Save Results** option under the [**Run Query**] button:

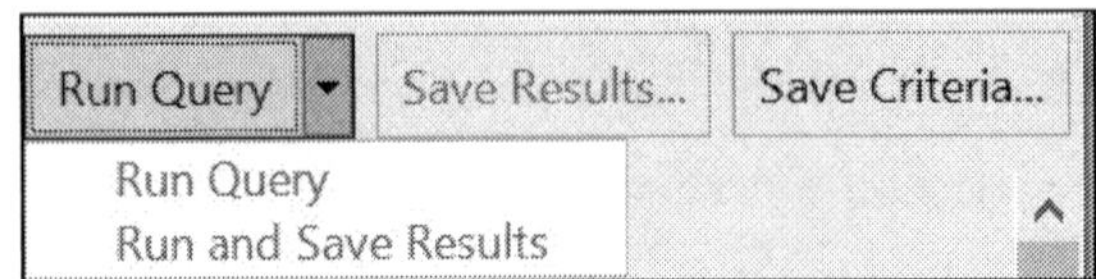

Next the **Store Query Results** dialog box appears:

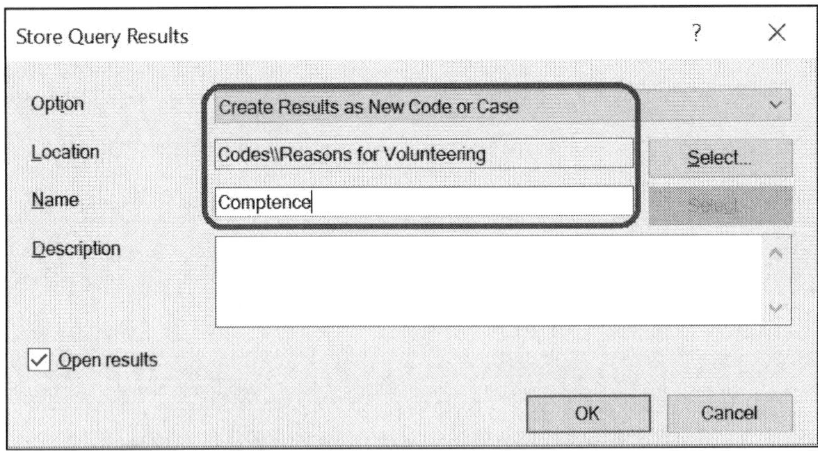

1. Choose *Create Results as New Code* from the **Options** drop-down list. Check *Open results* when you want open the Code when the query is run.
2. Accept default **Location** *Results*[10] or use **[Select]** and choose another location, for example the *Codes* folder when you want to use this Code for future coding or else future editing.
3. Type a name (compulsory) and a description (optional), then **[OK]**.

[10] Storing results in the *Results* folder means that the Code cannot be edited nor can it be used for further coding or uncoding.

For Compound Coding, Coding Comparison and Group Queries the dialog is:

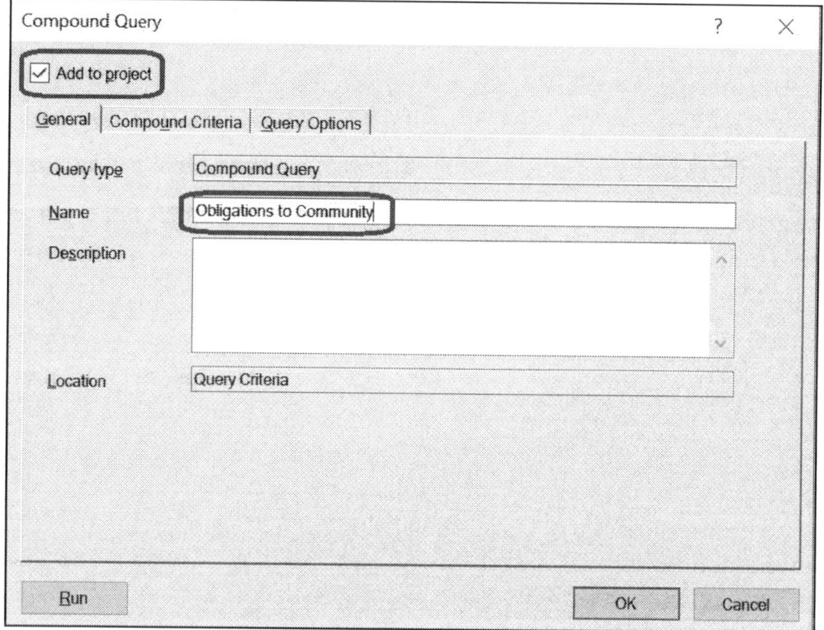

1. In the **Compound Coding Query** dialog box select the **Query Options** tab.
2. Choose *Create Results as New Code or Case* from the **Options** drop-down list. Check *Open results* when you want to open the Code when the query is run. Check *Create results if empty* if you want to create an 'empty' Code when zero result.
3. Accept location **Queries\\Query Results**[11] or choose another location, **Coding\\Codes**, with the [**Select**] button.
4. Type a name (compulsory) and a description (optional), then click [**Run**] or [**OK**].

- ♦ -

Results from Word Frequency Queries, Coding Comparison Queries and Group Queries cannot be saved - only preview is possible. However, such results can always be displayed by running a saved query anew.

[11] Storing results in the **Queries\\Query Results** folder means that the Code cannot be edited nor can it be used for further coding or uncoding.

Spread Coding

Spread Coding is a function that is used to widen the coding from a given result of a query. For instance, a Text Search Query finds words and by spreading the coding the result can be set to code each surrounding paragraph where the words are found.

The **Spread Coding** drop-down list allows you to decide options for coding surround sections of data nearby your coded query result. The following options[12] are available for Text Search, Coding and Compound Queries:

- None
- Coding Reference (applicable when searching in Codes)
- Narrow Context
- Broad Context
- Custom Context
- Entire File

The dialog box for a Text Search Query or a Coding Query is:

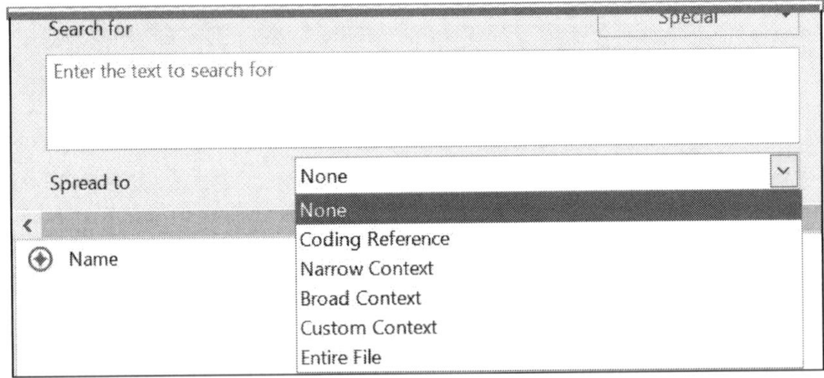

[12] As alternatives to *Narrow* and *Broad* you may use *Custom* which can override these settings for any specific task.

The dialog box for a **Compound Query** is:

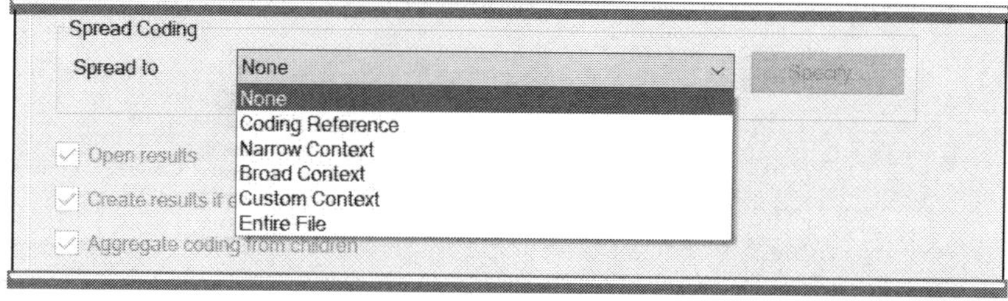

- ♦ -

Using **Explore | Last Run Query** the last run query is opened again and you may modify or edit the query. Each time a query is run it is also saved provided such option has been selected. When editing a query, you can for example apply *Surrounding Paragraphs* under *Custom Context* at the **Spread Coding** drop-down list. Saving the result, however, requires a separate action as described earlier.

About the Query Results Folder

The **Queries\\Query Results** folder is the default folder where a result of query is saved. You can however modify **Query Properties** so that query results will be saved in any Code location. But there are some advantages in using the **Queries \\Query Results** folder.

First, it is practical to see if the result is reasonable (before it is saved in its final location or made into a Code) or if the query needs immediate modification. Sometimes, you need to verify if the criterion is saved, and not only the result, go to the command **Home | Item → 'Properties' → Linked Query Properties...**, or right-click and select **Linked Query Properties...** If the Query Criterion has been saved its name is now in the dialog box **Properties** and if not, the name is replaced by for example *Text Search Query.*

Codes in the Results folder cannot be edited or used for further coding or uncoding and commands like **Uncode from this Code** and **Spread Coding** are unavailable. After verifying your Code in the Results folder, you should move the result to a location under Codes, where it can be more fully analyzed.

When you run a Text Search Query that is saved in the Results folder Coding Context Narrow (5 words) is activated, but the Coding Context is reset as soon as the Code is moved to a location under Codes. If you then should need Coding Context this feature can be activated with a separate command (see page 191).

Editing a Query

A saved query can be run anytime:

1 Select the **Queries\\Query Criteria** folder or its subfolder.
2 Select the query in the List View that you want to run.
3 Go to **Home | Item → 'Open' → Run Query**
or right-click and select **Run Query...**

You can always optimize a saved query so that it fulfils your changing needs. Or you may wish to copy a query before editing:

1 Select the **Queries\\Query Criteria** folder or its subfolder.
2 Select the query in the List View that you want to edit.
3 Go to **Home | Item → 'Open' → Open Query**
or right-click and select **Open Query...**
or **[Ctrl]** + **[Shift]** + **[O]**.

The **<select> Query Properties** dialog box allows you to modify the name and the description of the query.

1 Select the **Queries\\Query Criteria** folder or its subfolder.
2 Select the query in the List View that you want to rename.
3 Go to **Home | Item → 'Properties' → Query Properties...**
or right-click and select **Query Properties...**
or **[Ctrl]** + **[Shift]** + **[P]**.

One of the following dialog boxes is shown:

- **Text Search Query Properties**
- **Word Frequency Query Properties**
- **Coding Query Properties**
- **Matrix Coding Query Properties**
- **Crosstab Query Properties**
- **Compound Query Properties**
- **Coding Comparison Query Properties**
- **Group Query Properties**

The **Text Search Query Properties** dialog box is:

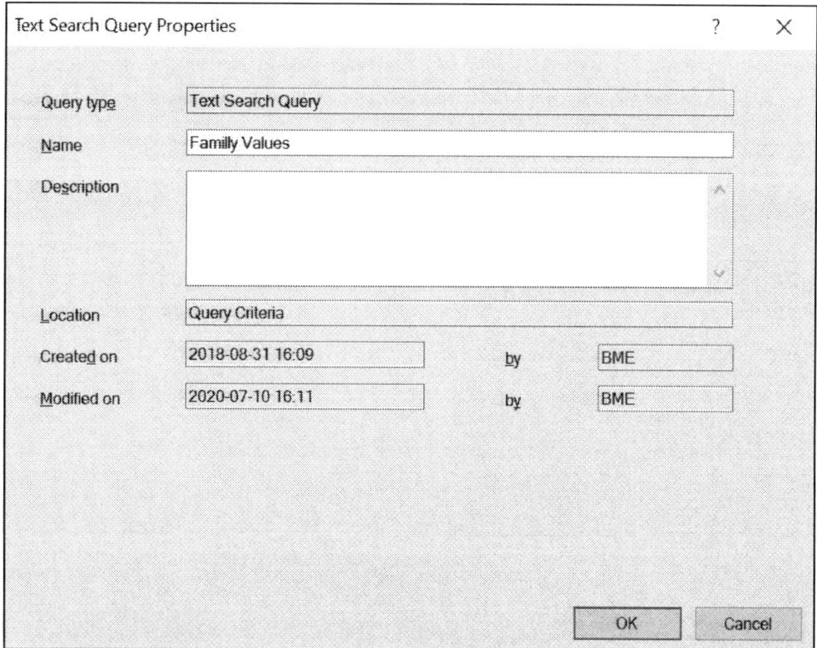

In this dialog box you cannot modify anything but the name and the description of the query. Other modifications and editing requires that you need to open the query as described above.

The Operators

In the **Matrix Coding Query** and **Compound Query** dialog boxes there are drop-down lists with various operators: AND, OR, NOT, AND NOT, NEAR, PRECEDING and SURROUNDING. The following charts explain the results when these operators are applied.

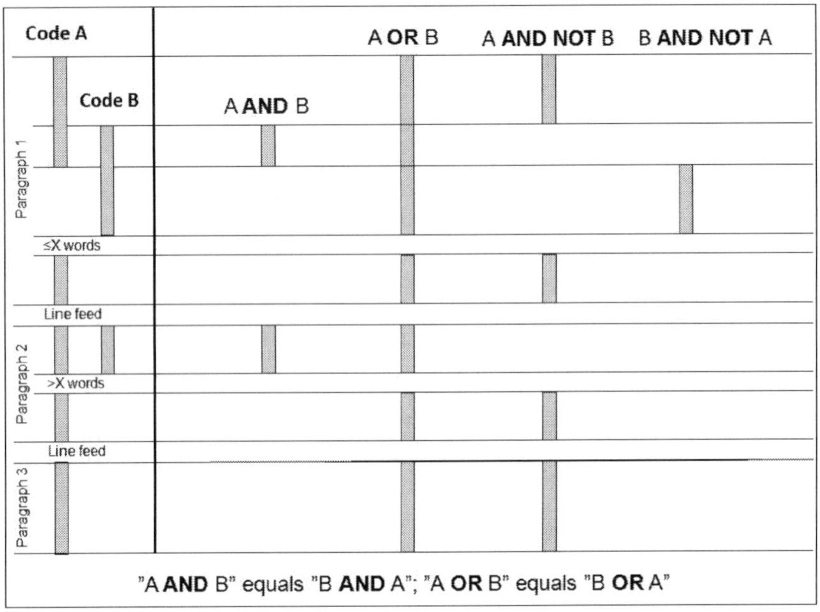

Code A
Code B
A **AND** B
A **OR** B
A **AND NOT** B
B **AND NOT** A
Paragraph 1
≤X words
Line feed
Paragraph 2
>X words
Line feed
Paragraph 3

"A **AND** B" equals "B **AND** A"; "A **OR** B" equals "B **OR** A"

AND displays the elements of a document where both A and B have been coded.

OR displays the elements of a document where either A or B or both A and B have been coded.

AND NOT displays the elements of a document where A but not B have been coded.

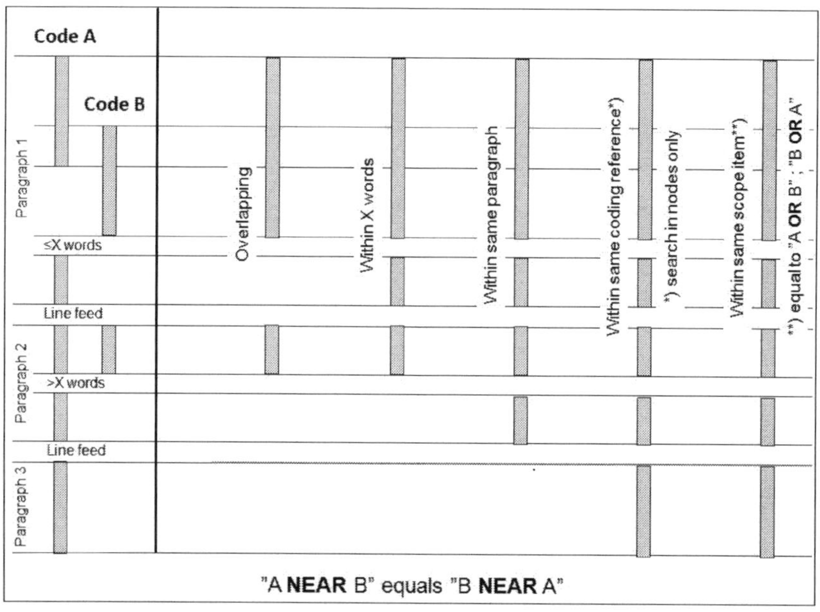

NEAR Content Overlapping displays the elements of a document where A and B are overlapping.

NEAR Content In Custom Context[13]. The [**Specify**] button allows you to select between Broad Context, Narrow Context or Custom Context.

For example:

- **NEAR Context Within X words** displays the elements of a document where A and B are within X words from each other.
- **NEAR Context In Surrounding Paragraph** displays the elements of a document where A and B are within same paragraph delimited by line feed.

NEAR Content In Same Scope Item displays the elements of a document where A and B are within the same document.

NEAR Content In Same Coding Reference displays the elements of a document where A and B are within the same Code.

[13] As alternatives to *Narrow* and *Broad* you may use *Custom* which can override these settings for any specific task.

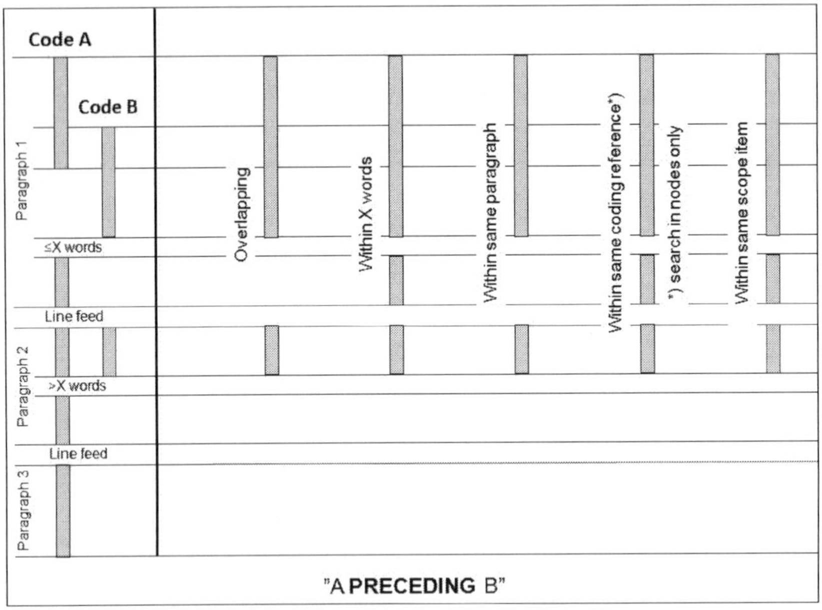

"A PRECEDING B"

PRECEDING Content Overlapping displays the elements of a document where A and B overlap as long as A is coded earlier or from the same starting point as B.

PRECEDING Content In Custom Context[14]**.** The **[Specify]** button allows you to select between Broad Context, Narrow Context or Custom Context.

For Example:

- **PRECEDING Context Within X words** displays the elements of a document where A and B are within X words as long as A is coded earlier or from the same starting point as B.
- **PRECEDING Context In Surrounding Paragraph** displays the elements of a document where A and B are within the same paragraph delimited by line feed as long as A is coded earlier or from the same starting point as B.

PRECEDING Content In Same Scope Item displays the elements of a document where A and B are within same document as long as A is coded earlier or from the same starting point as B.

PRECEDING Content In Same Coding Reference displays the elements of a document where A and B are within same Code as long as A is coded earlier or from the same starting point as B.

[14] As alternatives to *Narrow* and *Broad* you may use *Custom* which can override these settings for any specific task.

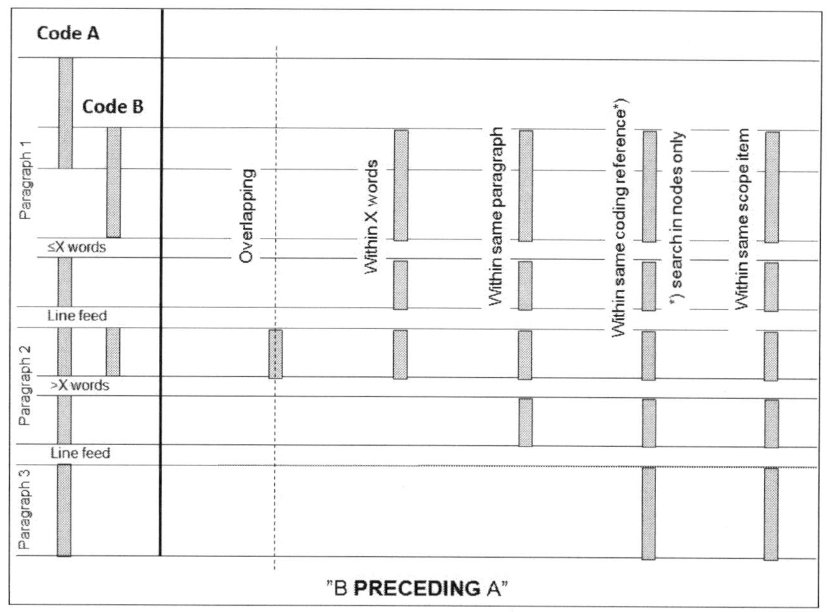

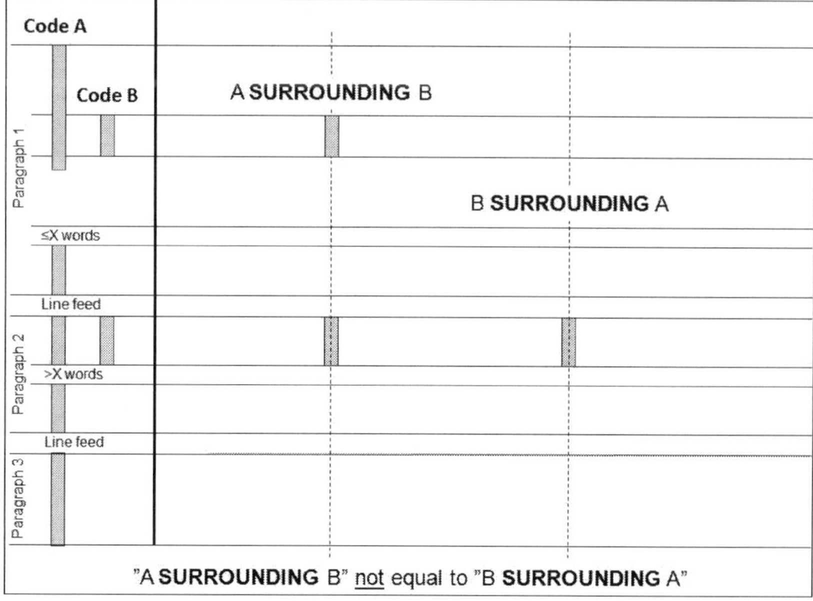

SURROUNDING Content displays the elements of a document where A overlaps B as long as A is coded earlier or from the same starting point as B and terminates later than or at the same point as B.

Shortcut Queries on many Ribbon Menus

To facilitate analysis of many project items the context dependent ribbons will offers shortcuts to the most powerful queries, charts, and diagrams.

The mentioned functions are available for the following ribbon menus:

- **Document**
- **PDF**
- **Audio**
- **Video**
- **Picture**
- **Memo**
- **Code**
- **Case**
- **Query Results**

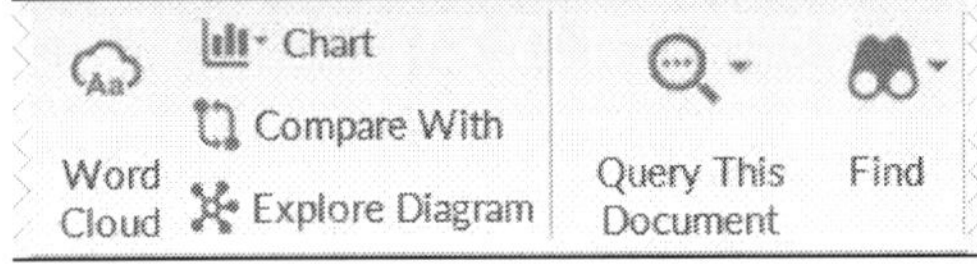

As soon as a project item is opened in the Detail View these shortcuts are available in the right section of respective ribbon menu.

That means for example, that as soon as you open a document, a PDF, or a Code you can immediately with one click reach its Word Cloud.

16. HANDLING BIBLIOGRAPHIC DATA

Along with source material that is gathered as project evidence, reference material (e.g., peer-reviewed academic research papers) often play a crucial role in grounding a qualitative research project. NVivo also allows users to import reference material, including full-text documents, from common reference handling software like EndNote, RefWorks and Zotero. When imported, reference materials become Source Items and as a result they can be coded and analyzed the same way as other sources. For advanced analysis, we offer a method of using the Framework Matrices (see Chapter 17, About the Framework Method) to efficiently work with academic reference material, such as Literature Reviews. This chapter is about importing bibliographic data stored in certain selected reference handling software. The file types that can be imported to NVivo are: .XML for EndNote and .RIS for RefWorks and Zotero .

In this chapter, we will use as an example importing data into NVivo from EndNote (the top reference handling software, in our opinion). The following two reference records will be exported from Endnote:

🖇	Author	Year	Title	Journal	Ref Type	URL	Last Updated
🖇	Cafazzo, J. ...	2009	Patient-perceived barriers to the ado...	Clinical jour...	Journal Arti...	http://www.ncbi.nlm...	2011-08-24
	Ritchie, L.; P...	2011	An exploration of nurses' perceptions ...	Applied nur...	Journal Arti...	http://www.ncbi.nlm...	2011-08-24

The clip symbol indicates that one reference has a file attachment (typically a PDF full text article) and the other not.

On the next page, you will see a shot of a typical reference from EndNote. As you can see, each reference listing contains a wealth of meta-data about a single reference:

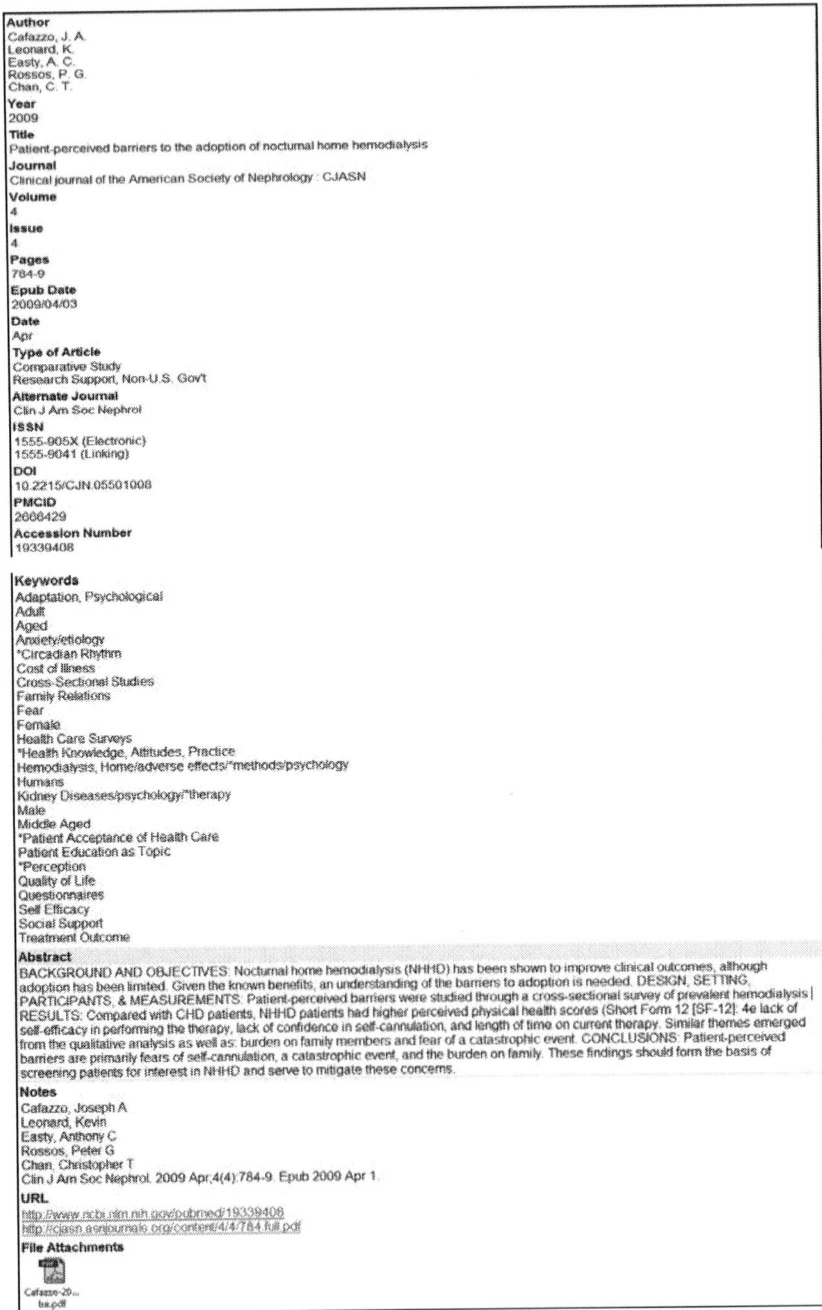

Author
Cafazzo, J. A.
Leonard, K.
Easty, A. C.
Rossos, P. G.
Chan, C. T.

Year
2009

Title
Patient-perceived barriers to the adoption of nocturnal home hemodialysis

Journal
Clinical journal of the American Society of Nephrology : CJASN

Volume
4

Issue
4

Pages
784-9

Epub Date
2009/04/03

Date
Apr

Type of Article
Comparative Study
Research Support, Non-U.S. Gov't

Alternate Journal
Clin J Am Soc Nephrol

ISSN
1555-905X (Electronic)
1555-9041 (Linking)

DOI
10.2215/CJN.05501008

PMCID
2666429

Accession Number
19339408

Keywords
Adaptation, Psychological
Adult
Aged
Anxiety/etiology
*Circadian Rhythm
Cost of Illness
Cross-Sectional Studies
Family Relations
Fear
Female
Health Care Surveys
*Health Knowledge, Attitudes, Practice
Hemodialysis, Home/adverse effects/*methods/psychology
Humans
Kidney Diseases/psychology/*therapy
Male
Middle Aged
*Patient Acceptance of Health Care
Patient Education as Topic
*Perception
Quality of Life
Questionnaires
Self Efficacy
Social Support
Treatment Outcome

Abstract
BACKGROUND AND OBJECTIVES: Nocturnal home hemodialysis (NHHD) has been shown to improve clinical outcomes, although adoption has been limited. Given the known benefits, an understanding of the barriers to adoption is needed. DESIGN, SETTING, PARTICIPANTS, & MEASUREMENTS: Patient-perceived barriers were studied through a cross-sectional survey of prevalent hemodialysis | RESULTS: Compared with CHD patients, NHHD patients had higher perceived physical health scores (Short Form 12 [SF-12]: 4e lack of self-efficacy in performing the therapy, lack of confidence in self-cannulation, and length of time on current therapy. Similar themes emerged from the qualitative analysis as well as: burden on family members and fear of a catastrophic event. CONCLUSIONS: Patient-perceived barriers are primarily fears of self-cannulation, a catastrophic event, and the burden on family. These findings should form the basis of screening patients for interest in NHHD and serve to mitigate these concerns.

Notes
Cafazzo, Joseph A
Leonard, Kevin
Easty, Anthony C
Rossos, Peter G
Chan, Christopher T
Clin J Am Soc Nephrol. 2009 Apr;4(4):784-9. Epub 2009 Apr 1.

URL
http://www.ncbi.nlm.nih.gov/pubmed/19339408
http://cjasn.asnjournals.org/content/4/4/784.full.pdf

File Attachments
Cafazzo-20...

The communication between reference handling software and NVivo is in the form of an XML structured file. Reference handling software typically allows you to export a collection of citations. The export command from for example EndNote is **File → Export** and the file type must be set as XML. This creates you a file with all the above information including a file path to the PDF.

Importing Bibliographic Data

In NVivo go to **Import | Bibliography → EndNote**. With the file browser you will find the XML-file you exported from your reference handling software. Click **[Open]**.

The **Import from EndNote** dialog box appears:

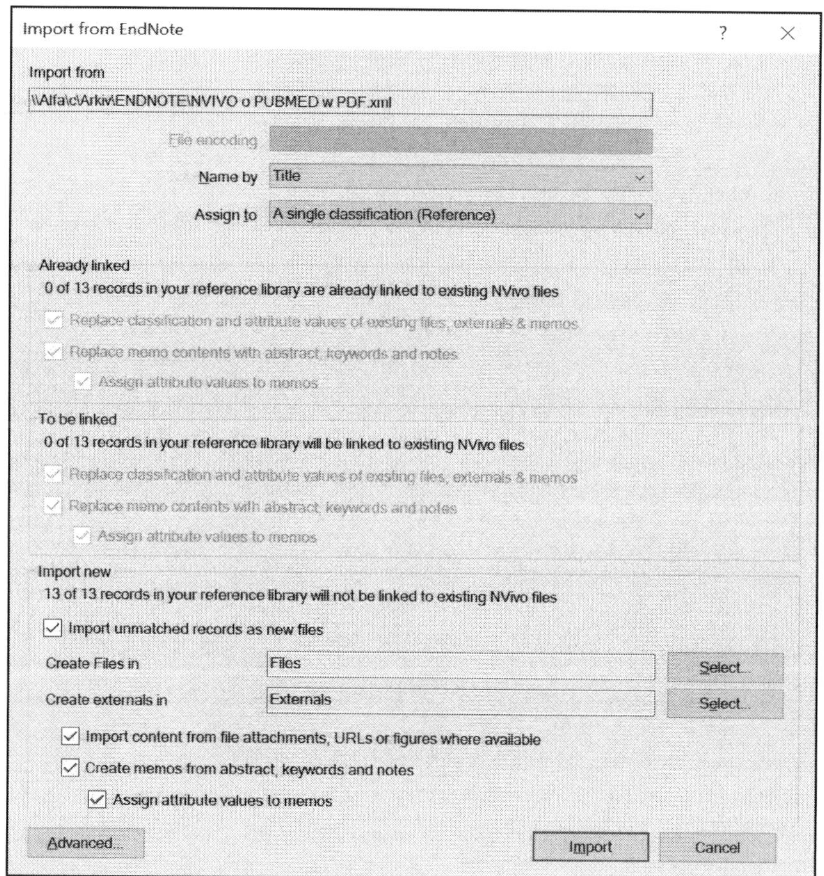

The first option is under **Name by** and the alternatives are: Title and Author and year.

The second option is to decide if you want one File Classification for all your bibliographic data, Reference. Then there will be one attribute called Reference Type and the values will be Journal Article, Book, Conference Proceedings etc. If this is your preference then select **Assign to:** ***A single classification (Reference).***

If you instead prefer one File Classification for each reference type then select

Assign to: ***Different classifications based on record type.***

The next option is under the section **Import new** at the bottom of the screen. The first example is a reference with a linked PDF and the second example without PDF. The principle is that PDFs will be imported as Internal Source Items and other references will be imported as External Source Items.

Under the section **Import unmatched records as new files** you need to define one location for Internal sources and one location for External sources. In our example we have created these two folders:

Data\\Files\\Bibliographic Data and

Data\\Externals\\Bibliographic Data.

The option *Import source content from file attachments, URLs or figures where available* is necessary when you want to import a PDF or any other resource. If you uncheck this option then the record will be imported as an External item.

The option *Create memos from abstract, keywords and notes* is selected when each bibliographic item will have a linked memo with the mentioned content.

The option *Assign attribute values to memos* assigns same classification and same attribute values to the linked memo as the linked item.

The [**Advanced**] button makes it possible for some individual settings for the items that is about to be imported. This is useful when you need to import bibliographic data as an update to previously imported data.

The PDF Source Item

The internal PDF Source Item has the same look and layout as the original article and can now be coded, linked, searched and queried:

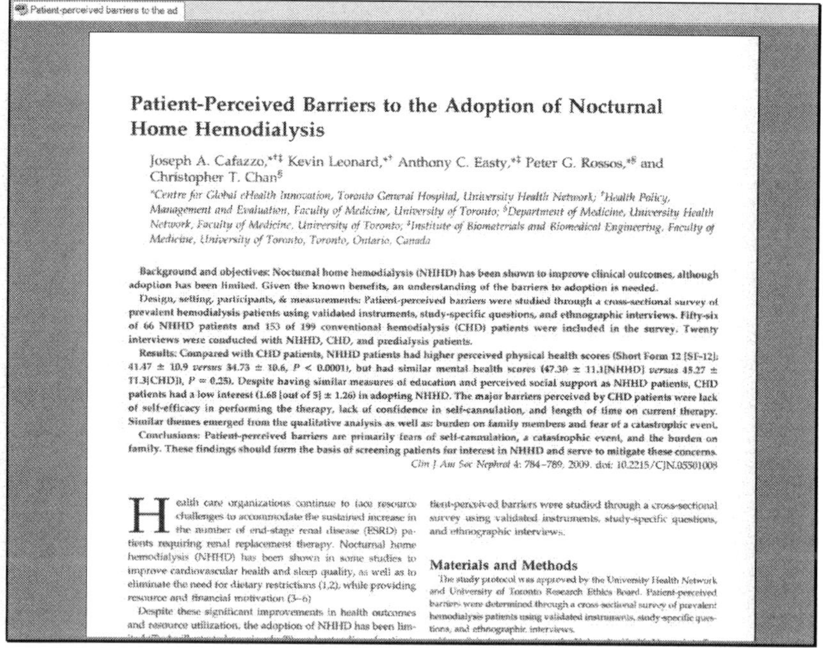

Patient-perceived barriers to the ad

Patient-Perceived Barriers to the Adoption of Nocturnal Home Hemodialysis

Joseph A. Cafazzo,[*†‡] Kevin Leonard,[*†] Anthony C. Easty,[*‡] Peter G. Rossos,[*§] and Christopher T. Chan[§]

[*]Centre for Global eHealth Innovation, Toronto General Hospital, University Health Network; [†]Health Policy, Management and Evaluation, Faculty of Medicine, University of Toronto; [§]Department of Medicine, University Health Network, Faculty of Medicine, University of Toronto; [‡]Institute of Biomaterials and Biomedical Engineering, Faculty of Medicine, University of Toronto, Toronto, Ontario, Canada

Background and objectives: Nocturnal home hemodialysis (NHHD) has been shown to improve clinical outcomes, although adoption has been limited. Given the known benefits, an understanding of the barriers to adoption is needed.

Design, setting, participants, & measurements: Patient-perceived barriers were studied through a cross-sectional survey of prevalent hemodialysis patients using validated instruments, study-specific questions, and ethnographic interviews. Fifty-six of 66 NHHD patients and 153 of 199 conventional hemodialysis (CHD) patients were included in the survey. Twenty interviews were conducted with NHHD, CHD, and predialysis patients.

Results: Compared with CHD patients, NHHD patients had higher perceived physical health scores (Short Form 12 [SF-12]: 41.47 ± 10.9 *versus* 34.73 ± 10.6, $P < 0.0001$), but had similar mental health scores (47.30 ± 11.1[NHHD] *versus* 45.27 ± 11.3[CHD]), $P = 0.25$). Despite having similar measures of education and perceived social support as NHHD patients, CHD patients had a low interest (1.68 [out of 5] ± 1.26) in adopting NHHD. The major barriers perceived by CHD patients were lack of self-efficacy in performing the therapy, lack of confidence in self-cannulation, and length of time on current therapy. Similar themes emerged from the qualitative analysis as well as: burden on family members and fear of a catastrophic event.

Conclusions: Patient-perceived barriers are primarily fears of self-cannulation, a catastrophic event, and the burden on family. These findings should form the basis of screening patients for interest in NHHD and serve to mitigate these concerns.

Clin J Am Soc Nephrol 4: 784–789, 2009. doi: 10.2215/CJN.05501008

Health care organizations continue to face resource challenges to accommodate the sustained increase in the number of end-stage renal disease (ESRD) patients requiring renal replacement therapy. Nocturnal home hemodialysis (NHHD) has been shown in some studies to improve cardiovascular health and sleep quality, as well as to eliminate the need for dietary restrictions (1,2), while providing resource and financial motivation (3–6)

Despite these significant improvements in health outcomes and resource utilization, the adoption of NHHD has been lim-

tient-perceived barriers were studied through a cross-sectional survey using validated instruments, study-specific questions, and ethnographic interviews.

Materials and Methods

The study protocol was approved by the University Health Network and University of Toronto Research Ethics Board. Patient-perceived barriers were determined through a cross-sectional survey of prevalent hemodialysis patients using validated instruments, study-specific questions, and ethnographic interviews.

The **PDF Properties**, **General** tab, has now the following content imported through the XML file. The name of the PDF-item is the name of the EndNote file attachment, which can be set in EndNote to correspond to the title of the article. As you can see below, the abstract has been copied into the Description field of the PDF source:

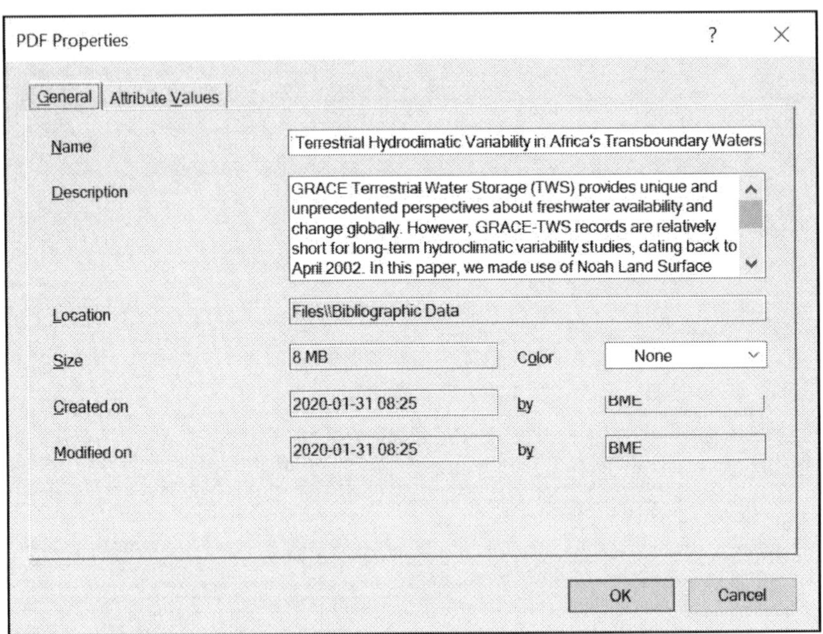

The **PDF Properties**, **Attribute Values** tab, has now the following content:

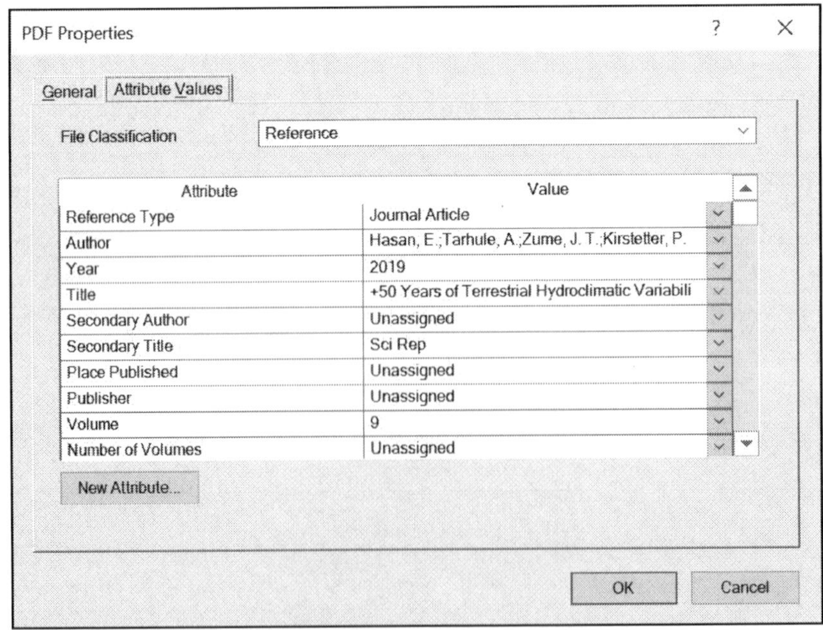

Author is one of the Attributes and the values are the list of author names for each Source Item.

Keywords is also an Attribute (not shown here) and its values are the whole list of keywords originating from this Source Item (see page 242).

The Linked Memo

If you elect to create a linked memo it will have the same name as the linked item. The memo is a normal text document and can be edited and otherwise handled as any Source Item. The content in our example is from the Abstract, Keywords and Notes fields of the original reference record. This is a useful feature because it allows you to search and code the abstract, which is not possible when the abstract is only located in the source description field.

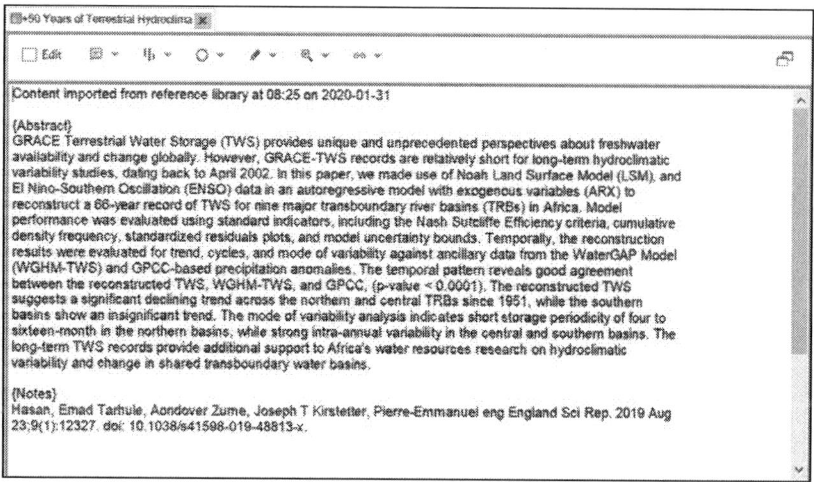

The **Memo Properties**, **General** tab, has now the following content:

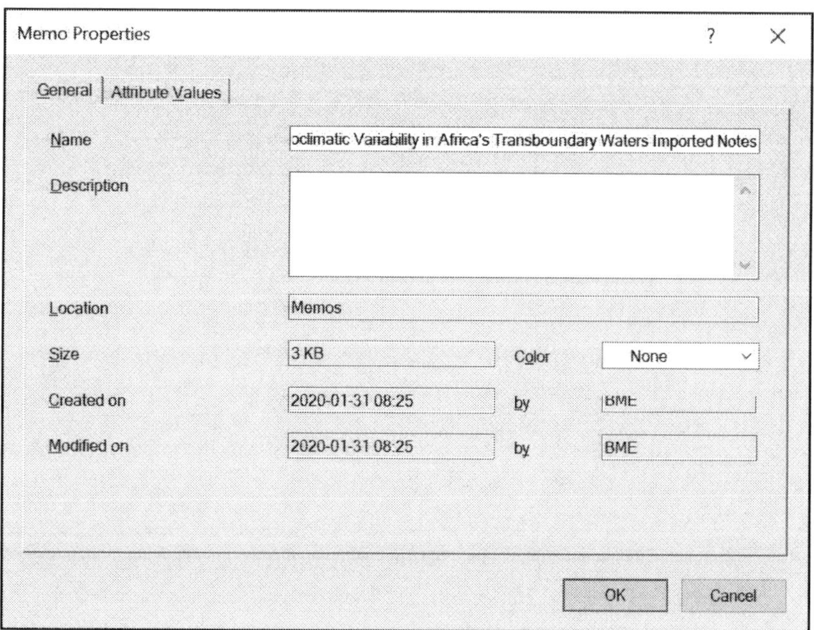

The **Memo Properties**, **Attribute Values** tab, has now the following content in a case where *Assign attribute values to memos* in the **Import from EndNote** dialog box has been checked:

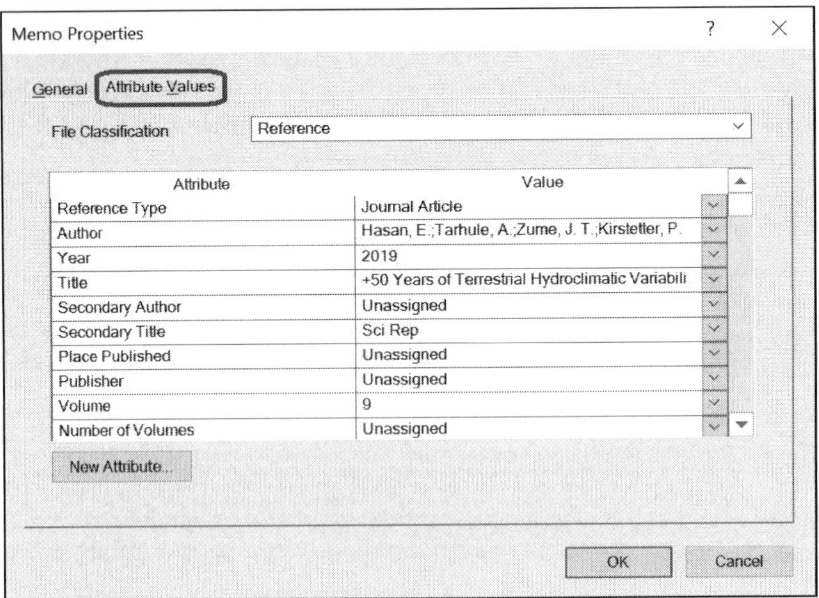

The Classification and Attribute values are identical with those of the linked item.

Exporting Bibliographic Data

You can export bibliograhic data either from source files or from the File Classification created with a Bibliographic ID, normally when importing from a reference handling software.

Exporting from a PDF item

1. Select one or more PDF items from the List View.
2. Go to **Share | Export → Export**
   or **[Ctrl]** + **[Shift]** + **[E]**
   or right-click and select **Export → Export PDF...**
   for exporting individual PDFs.

alternatively

2. Go to **Share | Export → Export Bibliography → <select>**
   or right-click and select **Export → Export to <select>**
   for exporting bibliographic data to a reference handling software.

Exporting from a File Classification

1. Select one File Classification from the List View.
2. Go to **Share | Export → Export Bibliography → <select>**
   or right-click and select **Export → Export to <select>**
   for exporting bibliographic data to a reference handling software.

The External Source Item

Bibliographic records without file attachments (like PDFs) are imported as External source items. These items have a link leading to the external source from where the records were captured. External items have also a linked Memo with similar properties as explained above. Exploring the External Properties, you will find that the description field has a copy of the abstract like the Internals have. The Externals are also classified along with the Internals.

External Properties dialog box, the *General* tab:

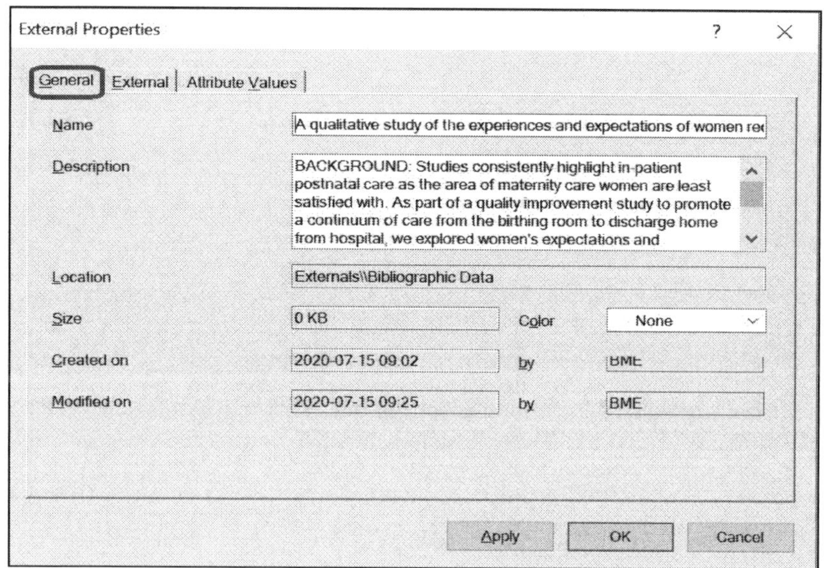

External Properties dialog box, the *External* tab:

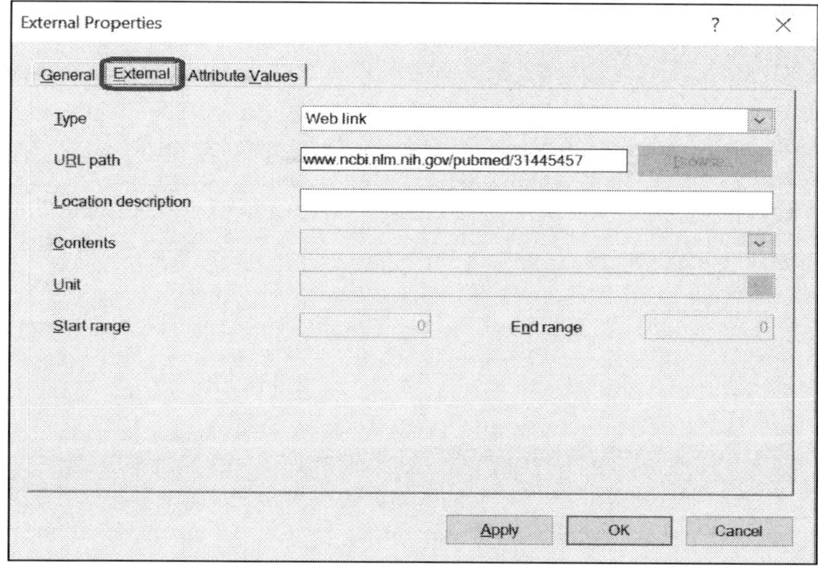

External Properties dialog box, the *Attribute Values* tab:

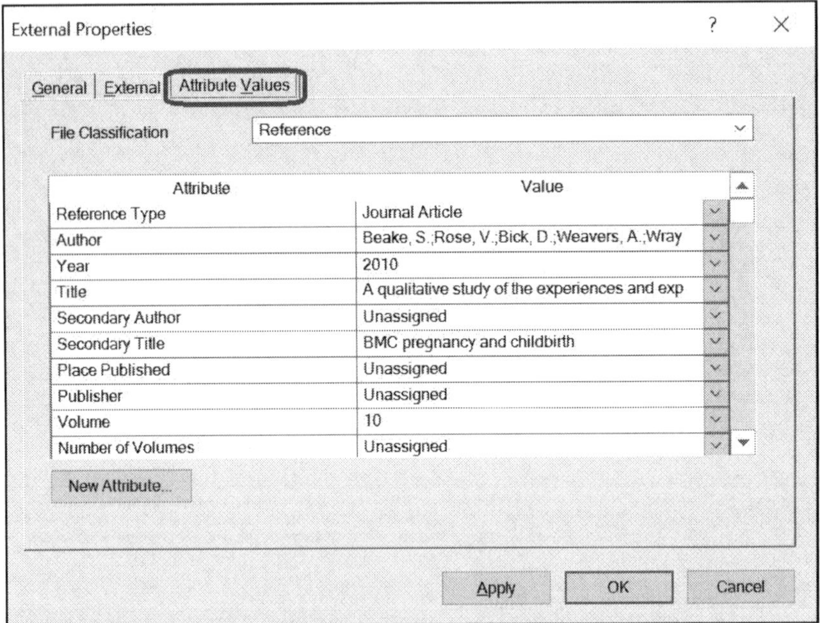

You open the external file by selecting from the List View, right-click and select **Open External File**. Mostly this message will show.

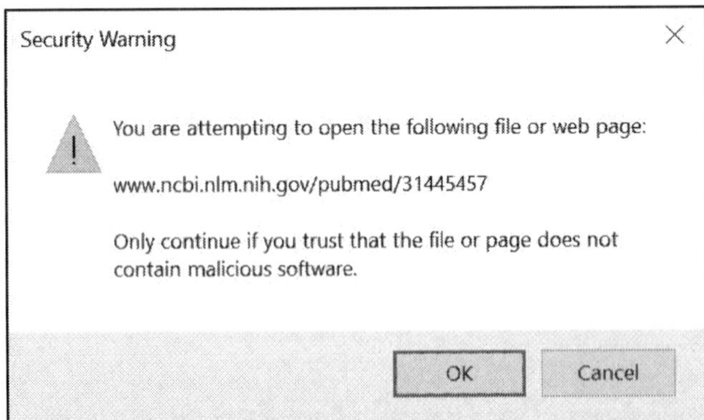

Security Warning
You are attempting to open the following file or web page:
www.ncbi.nlm.nih.gov/pubmed/31445457
Only continue if you trust that the file or page does not contain malicious software.
OK
Cancel

After confirming with **[OK]** your web-browser opens and you reach the target site or file.

17. ABOUT THE FRAMEWORK METHOD

Framework is a qualitative data analysis method developed by the UK's largest, independent not-for-profit research institute, the National Centre for Social Research (NatCen) in the 1980's.

The Framework method is used to organize and manage research through the process of summarization, resulting in a robust and flexible matrix output which allows the researcher to analyze data both by case and theme. It's used by hundreds of researchers in areas such as health research, policy development and program evaluation.

NatCen developed specialty software called FrameWork to support this method. This software is no longer developed, but through a partnership between NatCen and QSR, NVivo now provides new functionality to support the Framework method.

Accordingly, the Framework approach will provide you with exciting opportunities to apply this method to textual and non-textual data (audio-visual or images) and adopt other approaches that NVivo also supports such as discourse analysis.

Framework differs from traditional qualitative approaches to analysis as it does not rely on coding and indexing alone.

Introducing the Framework Matrix

Like any matrix, the Framework Matrix consists of rows and columns. Therefore, for those of you who are familiar with Coding Matrices (as a result of a Matrix Coding Query) this approach seems familiar. Thus, rows are Codes, columns are Codes, and the cell content is the intersection (or cross coding) between two Codes also understood as the result of an AND operator. The important difference between a Framework Matrix and a Coding Matrix is that the cells of a Framework Matrix can display data, or they can display any text you enter along with any links you create.

More than a tool for displaying your data, a Framework Matrix is a Source Item that allows you to quickly and easily view your data and write notes and insights about it. One particularly useful function of a Framework Matrix is viewing your data in the Associated View while recording your insights in cells. A second useful function is the ability to easily view a certain Code in a grid that allows you to quickly compare data to other Codes or Cases. A third useful function is the ability to create links between cell content and your source material using summary links.

This is the default view of a Framework Matrix:

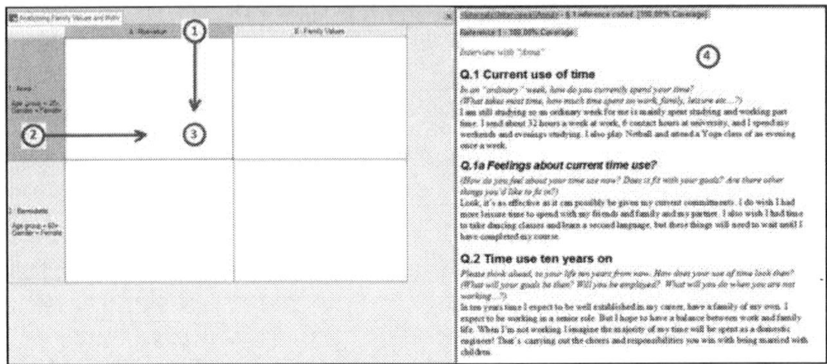

① Rows are defined as Cases. This could be a person or a place or an organization. It could also be literature of any kind for example a set of articles in PDF format. In the latter case PDF Source Items must be created as Cases before they can be used as rows in a Framework Matrix.
Select source items (Files), right-click and select **Create → Create As Cases**.

② Columns are defined as Codes, typically topic or theme Codes. It could also be Codes representing interview questions from structured interviews.

③ The content of a cell is always blank (default) when the first Framework Matrix in a project is created. Several options are now at hand for the user:
You can type any text.
You can let the cell contain the whole or part of the coded content in the intersection between a row and a column. See Auto Summary, see page 255.
You can create Summary links to any content in the Associated view. See Summary Links, see page 256.

④ The Associated View is a separate window to the right of the Framework Matrix showing the whole or parts of the Case of the selected cell or row. There are several options for the Associated View: The whole Code (Row coding), the intersection between a row and a column (Cell coding) or Summary links.

Creating a Framework Matrix

1 Go to **Create | Framework Matrix**.
Default folder is **Notes\\Framework Matrices** or its currently open subfolder.
Go to 4.

alternatively

1 Select the **Notes\\Framework Matrices** folder or its subfolder.

2 Go to **Create | Framework Matrix**.
Go to 4.

alternatively

2 Click on any empty space in the List View.

3 Right-click and select **New Framework Matrix...**
or **[Ctrl]** + **[Shift]** + **[N]**.

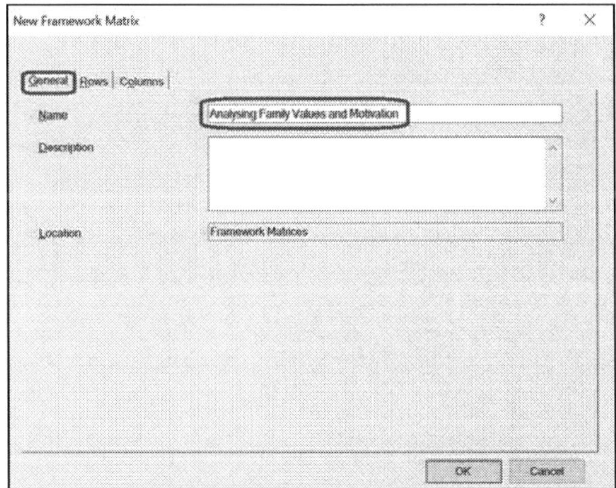

4 In **New Framework Matrix** dialog box type a name (compulsory) and a description (optionally).

5 Click on the **Rows** tab.

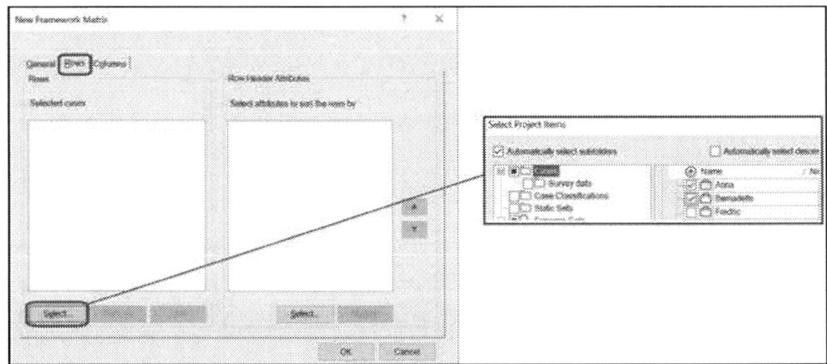

6 Click on the left **[Select]** button and in the **Select Project Items** dialog box select the Cases that you want to become rows in the Framework Matrix, then confirm with **[OK]**.

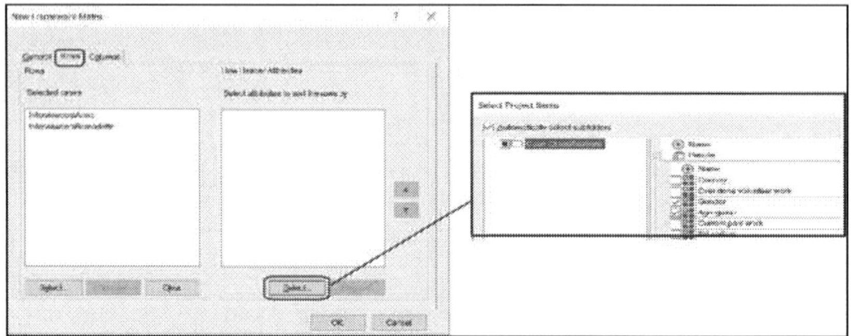

7 Click on the right **[Select]** button and in the **Select Project Items** dialog box select the attributes that you want to become Row Header Attributes in the Framework Matrix, then confirm with **[OK]**.

8 Click on the **Columns** tab.

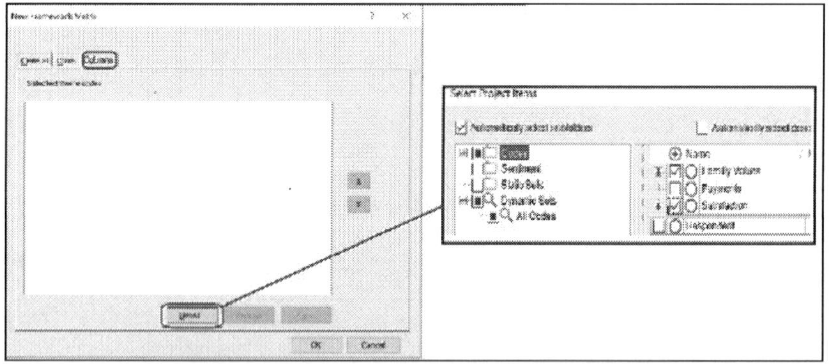

9 Click on the **[Select]** button and in the **Select Project Items** dialog box select the Codes that you want to become columns in the Framework Matrix, then confirm with **[OK]**.

10 When you are finished choosing your Rows and Columns, click **[OK]**.

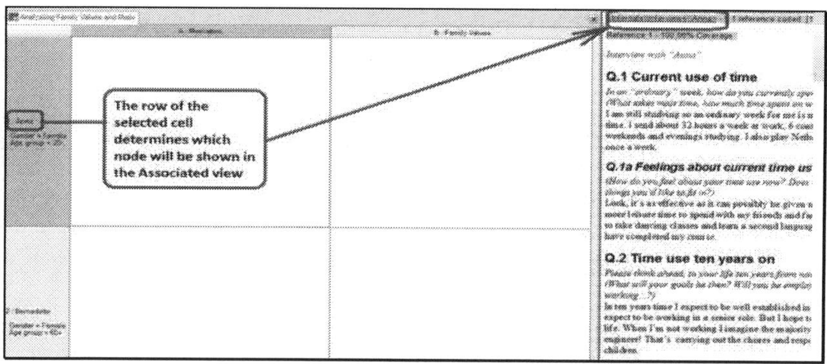

When your Framework Matrix is finished, you will see a screen resembling the above image. The default cell content is blank. A new context dependent Ribbon menu, **Framework Matrix**, has now opened and is opened each time a Framework Matrix is edited.

Remember, a Framework Matrix is a Source Item, so you can create memo-like insights and their attendant links as a way of writing up your insights or generating qualitative data.

Populating Cell Content

With your new Framework Matrix created, you have three options for populating content in the cells:

- Auto-populating the cell with all or part of the content at the 'intersection' between a row and a column. (See Auto Summary below)
- Creating Summary links to any content in the Associated view. (See Summary Links, page 256)
- Typing in any text you wish

Auto Summary

1 Go to **Framework Matrix | Auto Summarize**.

Using Auto Summarize, all cells (irrespective of which cell is selected) will be automatically filled with the content corresponding to the intersection between a row and a column.

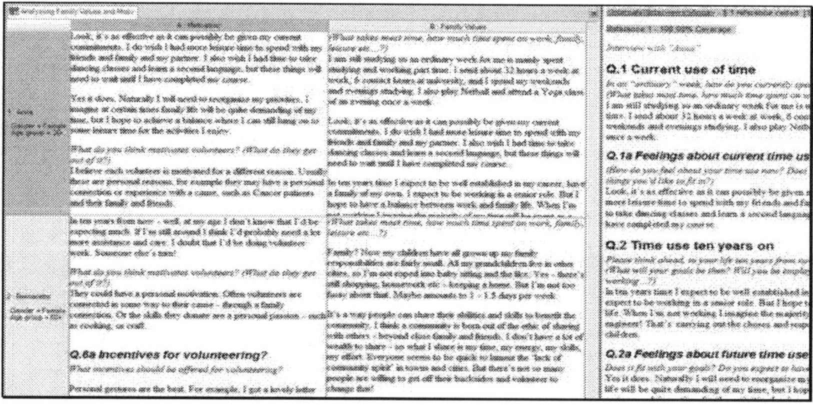

If there is any text in a cell before Auto Summary is applied, then the new content will be pasted after that text. Using Auto Summary will not overwrite extant cell content. Using Auto Summary repeatedly will create repeated content in all cells.

After an Auto Summary, you can modify text in any way you see fit. One best practice we recommend is populating cells with Auto-Summary and then writing your own summary overtop of the content. In this way, you can easily record your insights.

Summary Links

Summary links are connection points between Framework Matrix content and content from your data sources. Like See Also Links, Summary Links allow for shortcutting across your project and moving seamlessly between summary content and your data.

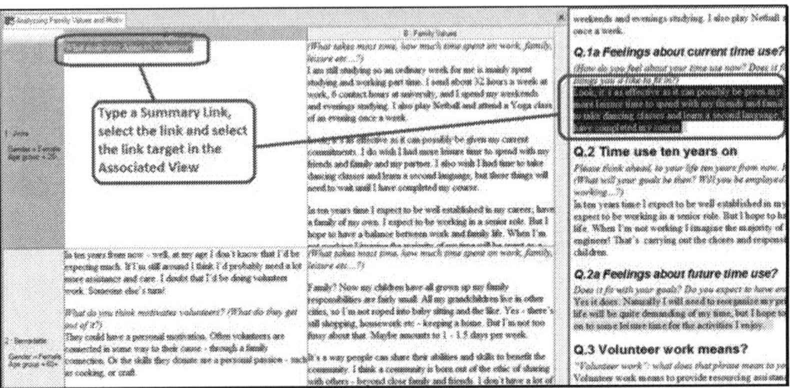

1 If required blank out the current cell content with **[Ctrl]** + **[A]** then the **[Del]** key.
2 Type the text of the new Summary Link.
3 Select this link.
4 Select the linked content in the Associated View.
5 Go to **Framework Matrix | New Summary Link**.

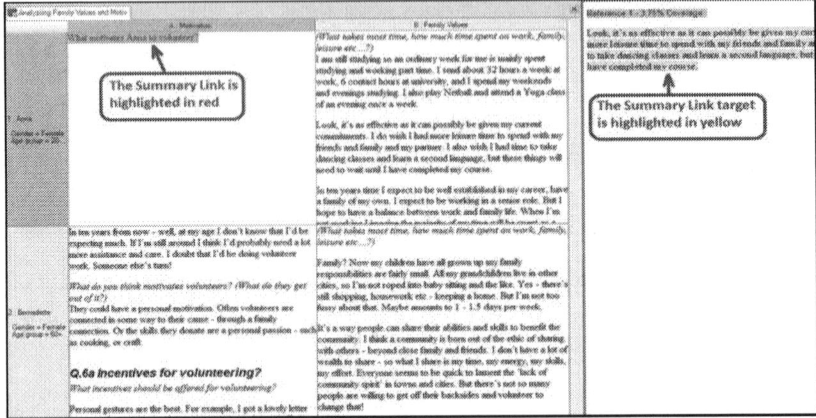

To get the above view you need the following settings:

Go to **Framework Matrix | Associated View | 'Content'**
→ **Cell Coding**
→ **Summary Links.**

Go to **Framework Matrix | Highlight | 'Associated View'**
→ **Summary Links.**

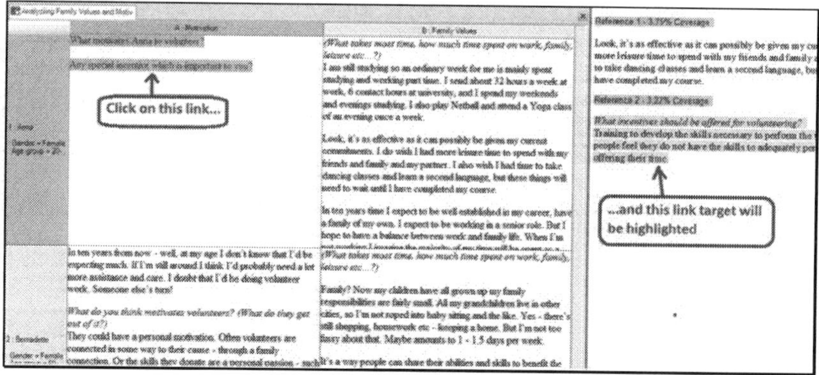

If you need more than one Summary Link in a cell then it is very handy to use the setting:

Go to **Framework Matrix | Highlight | 'Associated View'**
→ **Summary Links from Position.**

Go to **Framework Matrix | Associated View | 'Content'**
→ **Cell Coding.**

More on Associated View

The default settings for the ribbon **Framework Matrix | Associated View | 'Content', Framework Matrix | Highlight,** and **Framework Matrix | Layout/Display** are determined in the **Application Options** dialog box. Go to **File → Options → Display** tab, section **Framework Matrix Associated View Defaults:**

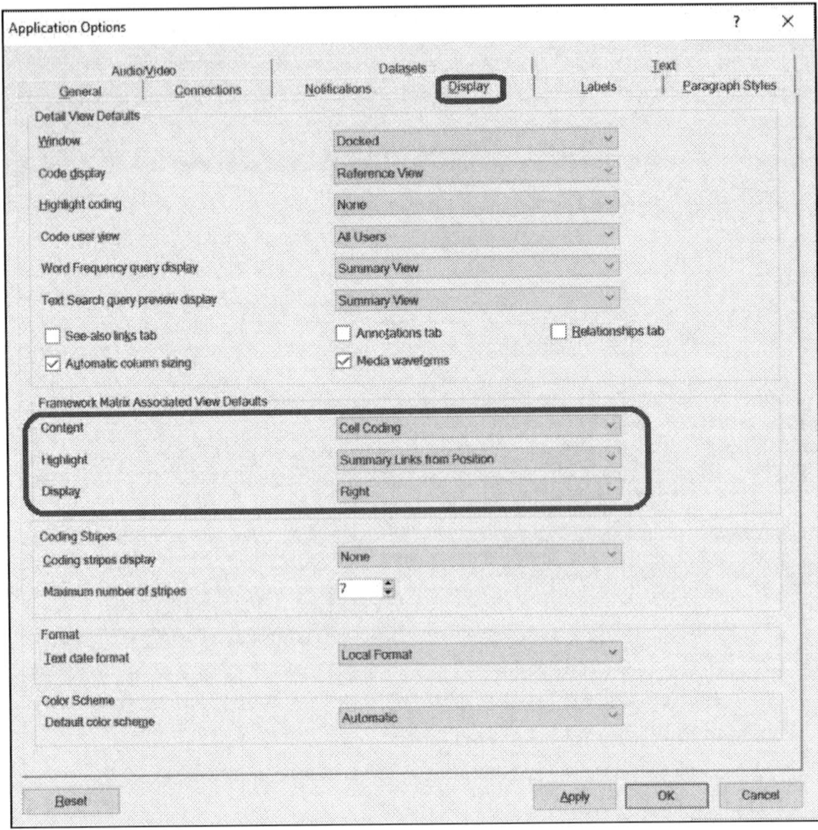

These default settings are restored each time a project is opened and any changes made are kept intact during the current work session.

An alternative setting is:

1 Go to **Framework Matrix | Associated View | 'Content' → Cell Coding**.
2 Go to **Framework Matrix | Highlight | 'Associated View' → Column Coding**.

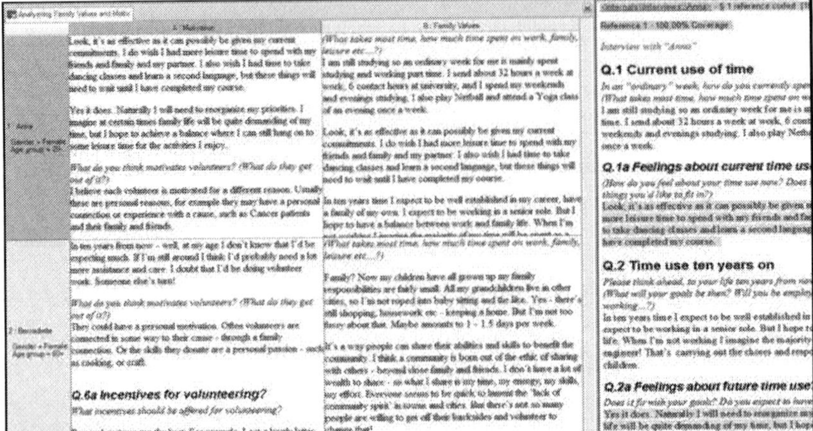

The coded sections are now highlighted depending on which cell has been selected.

- ♦ -

The Associated View can be displayed to the right of or below the Framework Matrix, or be hidden:

1 Go to **File → Options → Display tab**, section **Framework Matrix Associated View Defaults, Display** options:
→ Right
→ Bottom
→ Hide

Working with Framework Matrices

Auto Scroll

1 Go to **Framework Matrix | Highlight | 'Associated View' → Auto Scroll.**

Auto Scroll scrolls the Associated View as follows. When you click on a Summary link in a cell then the Associated View displays the currently highlighted section. If Highlight Column Coding is chosen then the first highlighted section is the coded section and if Highlight Summary Links is chosen then the first highlighted section is the Summary Link. The option Summary Links from Position is useful when you have created more than one Summary Link in a cell.

Where is the Cell Summary stored?

The cell Summary is stored in the intersection between two Codes, one from a row and one from a column in a Framework Matrix. Once created the Summary is stored even if the Framework is deleted. If same combination of two Codes occurs in another Framework the Summary is identical. Changing the Summary in one Framework is therefore instantly mirrored in the other Framework.

Opening a Framework Matrix

1 Select the **Notes\\Framework Matrices** folder or its subfolder.
2 Select the Framework Matrix in the List View that you want to open.
3 Go to **Home | Item → 'Open' → Open Framework Matrix...**
or right-click and select **Open Framework Matrix...**
or double-click on the Framework Matrix in the List View
or **[Ctrl]** + **[Shift]** + **[O]**.

Please note, you can only open one Framework Matrix at a time, but several matrices can stay open simultaneously.

Editing a Framework Matrix

1 Select a Framework Matrix.
2 Go to **Home | Item → 'Properties' → Framework Matrix Properties...**
or right-click and select **Framework Matrix Properties...**
or **[Ctrl]** + **[Shift]** + **[P]**

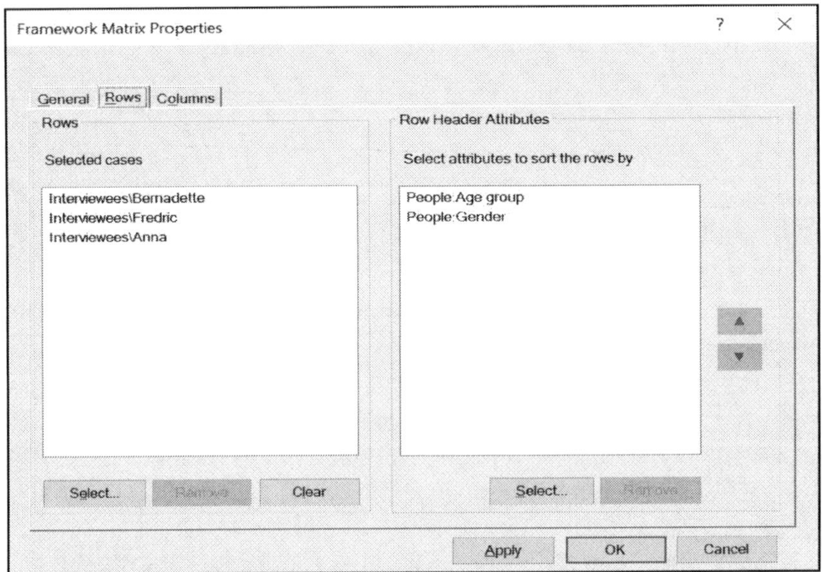

You can add or delete rows and columns.

Importing Framework Matrices

Framework Matrices can be imported along with another project that you import. All Codes which constitute the Framework Matrix must either exist in the open project or must be imported with the Framework Matrix. The Framework Matrix will be updated with the updated Codes.

Exporting Framework Matrices

1 Select the **Notes\\Framework Matrices** folder or its subfolder.
2 Select the Framework Matrix or Matrices in the List View that you want to export.
3 Go to **Share | Export → Export**
or right-click and select **Export → Export Framework Matrix...**
or **[Ctrl]** + **[Shift]** + **[E]**.
4 Decide file name, location, and file type: .TXT, .XLS, or XLSX. Confirm with **[Save]**.

Deleting a Framework Matrix

1 Select the **Notes\\Framework Matrices** folder or its subfolder.
2 Select the Framework Matrix or Matrices in the List View that you want to delete.
3 Right-click and select **Delete**
or **[Del]**.
4 Confirm with **[Yes]**.

Please note that according to what was said about storing Framework Matrices the content of a matrix is not deleted even when the matrix is. The content is saved as the intersection between two Codes. When one of those Codes is deleted the content will be deleted.

Printing Framework Matrices

1 Open a **Framework Matrix**.
2 Go to **File → Print → Print...**
or right-click and select **Print...**
or **[Ctrl]** + **[P]**.

Undocking the Framework Matrix

Undocking a Framework Matrix not possible. However, the Associated View window cab be hidden. One way to use more screen space and still keep the Associated view is closing the Navigation View by going to **Home | Workspace → Dashboard Mode**. Resetting is made with **Home | Workspace → Open**.

Fonts, Font Styles, Size, and Color

The default text style in the Cell Summary is determined by **Project Properties** dialog box, the **Framework Matrices** tab, see page 57:

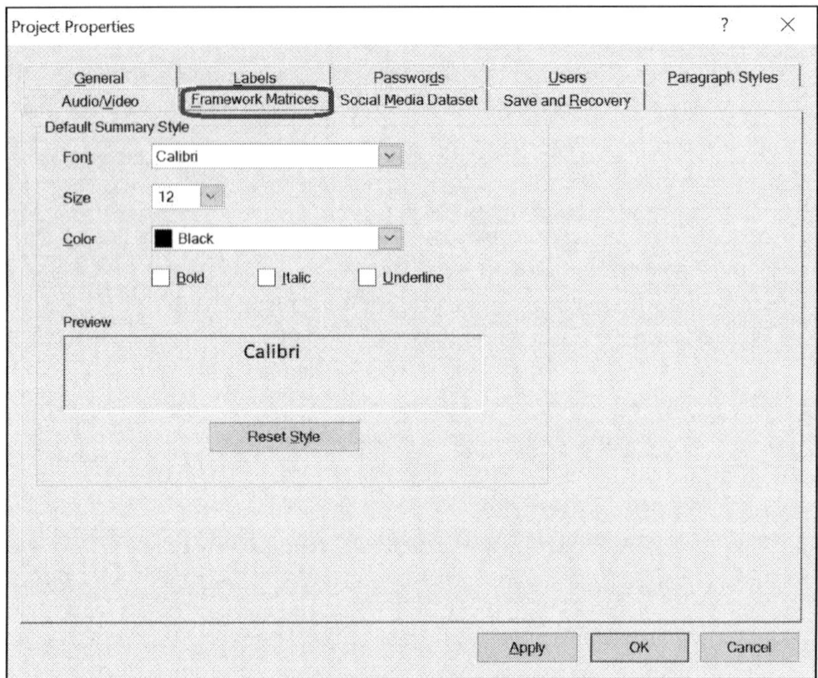

You can add text styles and attributes as an overlay to these default settings:

1 Select the text in a cell.
2 Go to **Framework Matrix | 'Format'** and select font, size, color or attribute.

,

Setting paragraph styles, paragraph alignment, indentation, bulleted or numbered lists is not available for Framework matrices.

Searching and Replacing Words

This feature is the same as when editing Source Items that are documents.

Framework Matrix | Find & Select → Find...
or **[Ctrl]** + **[F]**
Framework Matrix | Find & Select →Replace...
or **[Ctrl]** + **[G]**

However, **Framework Matrix | Find & Select → Go to...** is not available for Framework Matrices.

Spell Checking

NVivo's native spell checking can be used for Framework Matrices, see page 78.

Inserting Date and Time and Symbols

This feature is the same as when editing Source Items that are documents.

Framework Matrix | Insert → Insert Date/Time
or **[Ctrl]** + **[T]**
Framework Matrix | Insert → Insert Symbol...
or **[Ctrl]** + **[Y]**

Organizing Framework Matrices

About Sorting Rows in a Framework Matrix

Rows in a Framework Matrix are sorted according to the selected Attributes and attribute values that are displayed under the name of each row. If no Attributes have been chosen for display the Code names of the rows are sorted alphabetically.

About Sorting Columns in a Framework Matrix

Columns in a Framework Matrix are sorted according the setting in the **Framework Matrix Properties** dialog box where you can change the sort order. You can also select a column, right-click and select **Framework Matrix | Rows & Columns → Move Column Left** (**[Ctrl]** + **[Shift]** + **[L]**) or **Move Column Right** (**[Ctrl]** + **[Shift]** + **[R]**).

Hiding and Filtering Rows and Columns

Hiding and filtering rows and columns in a Framework Matrix (like you could for a Coding Matrix) is not possible in a Framework Matrix.

Adjusting Row Height and Column Width

1 Select a row or a column.
2 Right-click and select **Framework Matrix | Rows & Columns → Row Height (Column Width)**.
3 Enter the row height (column width) in pixels.
4 Confirm with **[OK]**.

The row height and column width can also be adjusted by pointing at the border between rows or between columns and drag with the mouse pointer.

Row heights can also be set to automatically adjust to the amount of text, however maximum value for autofit is 482 pixels:

1. Select a row or rows.
2. Right-click and select **Framework Matrix | Rows & Columns → AutoFit Row Height**.

If you need more row height, then use **Framework Matrix | Rows & Columns → Row Height** instead.

Row heights and Column widths can be reset to default values (values applied when you create a new Framework Matrix).

1. Select any row, column or cell in the Framework Matrix.
2. Go to **Framework Matrix | Rows & Columns → Reset Settings**
   or right-click and select **Reset Settings**.

18. ABOUT SURVEYS AND DATASETS

This section deals with data that originates from both multiple-choice questions and open-ended questions. In NVivo a dataset is a Source Item created when structured data is imported. Structured data is organized in records (rows) and fields (columns). The structured data formats that NVivo can import are Excel spreadsheets, tab-delimited text files and database-tables compatible with Microsoft's Access. A dataset in NVivo is presented in a built-in reader that can display data both as table and as a form. The reader makes it much easier to work on the computer and read and analyze data.

A dataset has two types of fields (columns), namely Classifying and Codable.

Classifying is a field with demographic content of a quantitative nature, often the result of multiple choice questions. The data in these fields is expected to correspond to attributes and values.

Codable is a field with 'open ended content' like qualitative data, typically subject of theme coding.

Datasets can only be created when data is imported. Data is arranged in the form of a matrix where rows are records and columns are fields. Typically, respondents are rows, columns are questions and cells are answers.

Importing Surveys

Our instruction below demonstrates in detail how to apply the Excel format when importing data from a survey. As mentioned above also text file types (.TXT or .CSV) can be imported following same instructions by using **Import | Survey | Text File** instead.

1 Go to **Import | Survey → Excel**
Default folder is **Data\\Files** or its currently open subfolder.
Go to 4.

alternatively

1 Select the **Data\\ Files** or its subfolder.
2 Go to **Import | Survey → Excel**
Go to 4.

alternatively

2 Click on any empty space in the List View.
3 Right-click and select **Import Survey → From Microsoft Excel File...**
4 Select the appropriate Excel-file and click **[Open]**.

> **Tip:** An easy way to convert an Excel-file to text is:
> 1 Select the whole Excel worksheet.
> 2 Copy.
> 3 Open Notepad.
> 4 Paste into Notepad.
> 5 Save with a new name.

The **Survey Import Wizard – Step 1** appears:

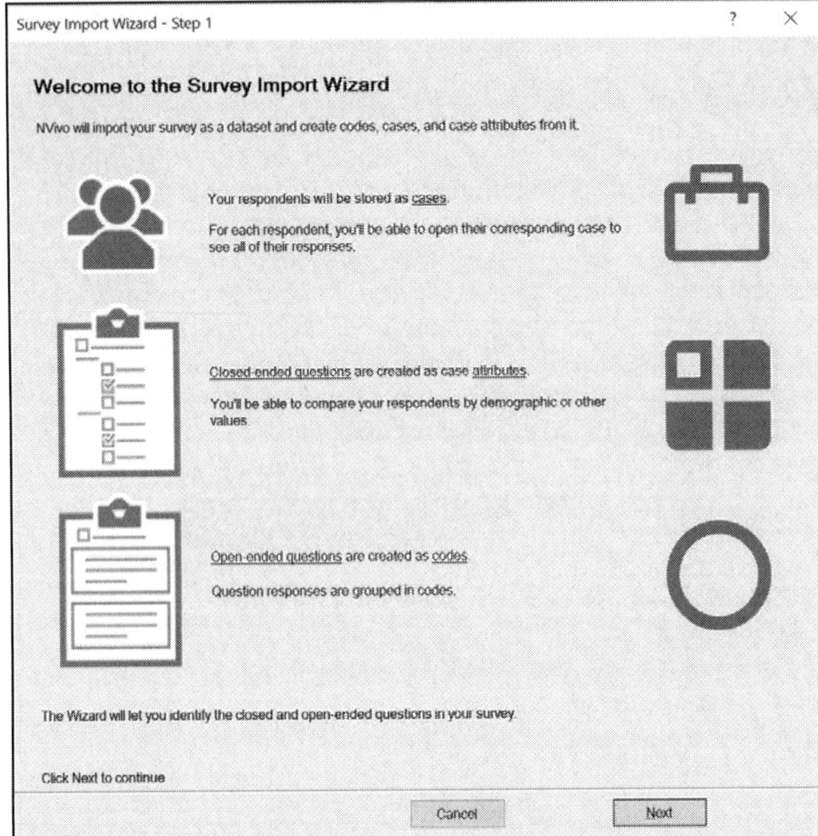

This box informs you how NVivo will handle the data of your imported data.

5 Click [**Next**].

The **Survey Import Wizard** – **Step 2** appears:

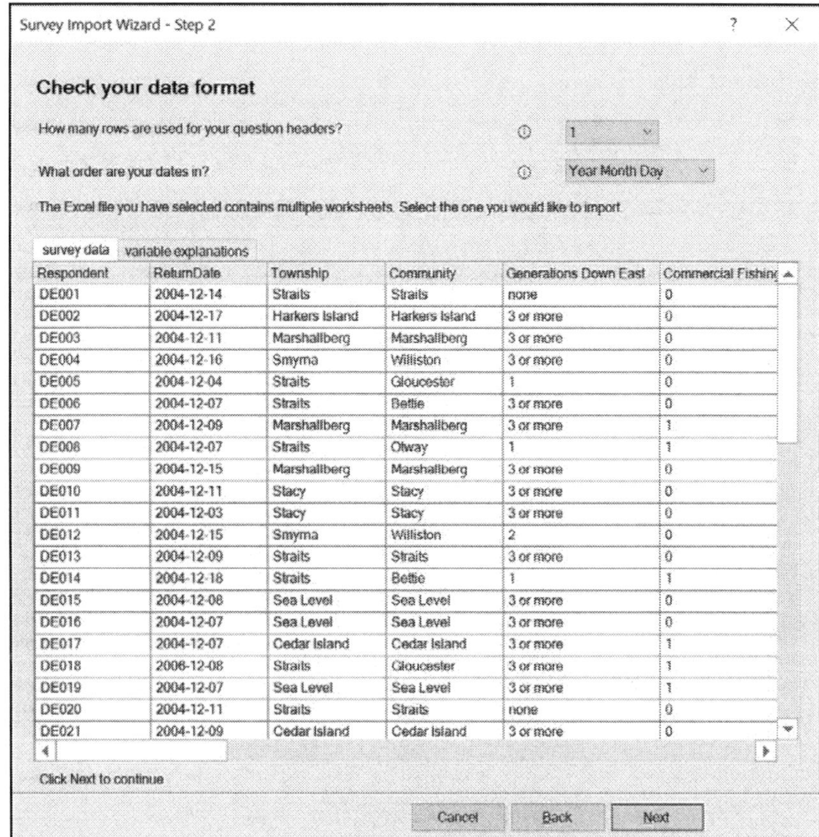

The upper section of the dialog box, SheetName, displays the two sheets of the Excel workbook: survey data and variable explanations. Select a sheet and its contents are displayed under Data Preview. The first 25 records of each are displayed. We select the sheet *survey data*.

You can verify the Time and Date formats and the Decimal symbol against the information displayed in the Data Preview.

It is important that the field names of imported data are only in the first row. Certain datasheets have field names in two rows and if so then the two rows must be merged. If you uncheck the option *First row contains field names* the row instead will contain column numbers.

6 Click **[Next]**.

The **Survey Import Wizard – Step 3** appears:

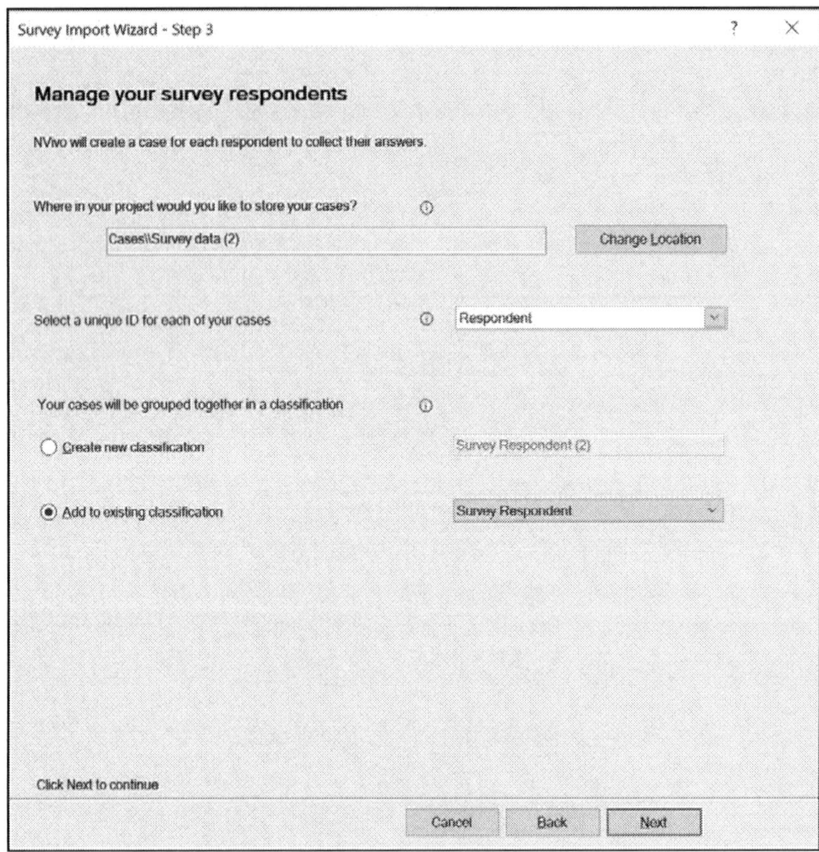

7 Click **[Next]**.

The **Survey Import Wizard – Step 4** appears:

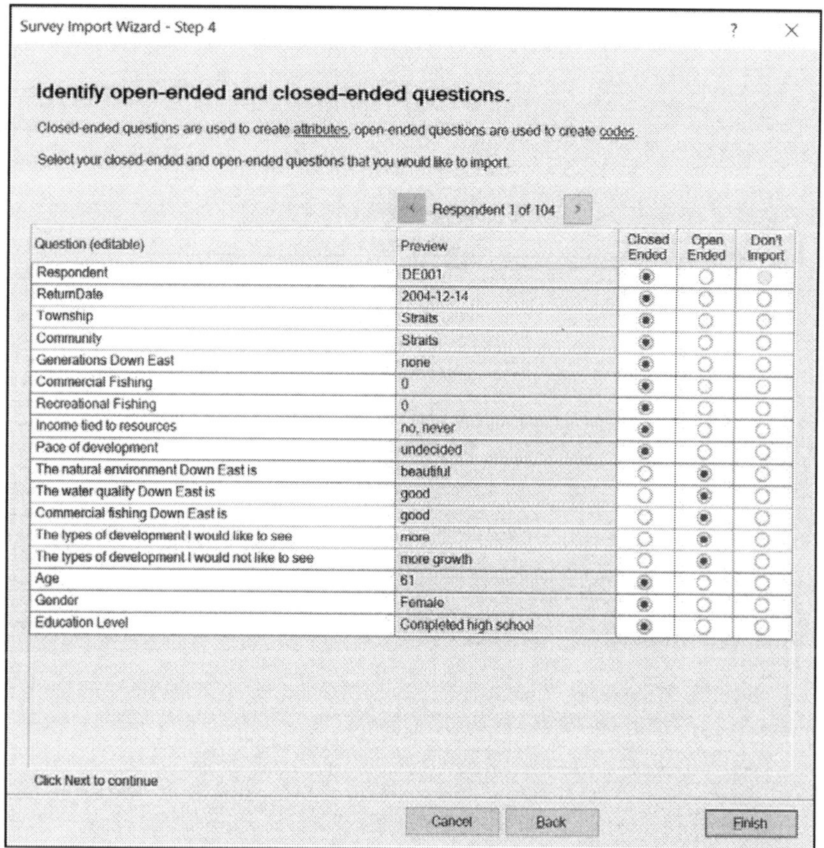

In this dialog box you can change NVivo's interpretation of Closed Ended (Classifying) and Open Ended (Codable) columns. You can also exclude any column from being imported using the *Don't Import* marking.

8 Click **[Finish]**.

The **Survey Import Wizard – Processing survey** appears:

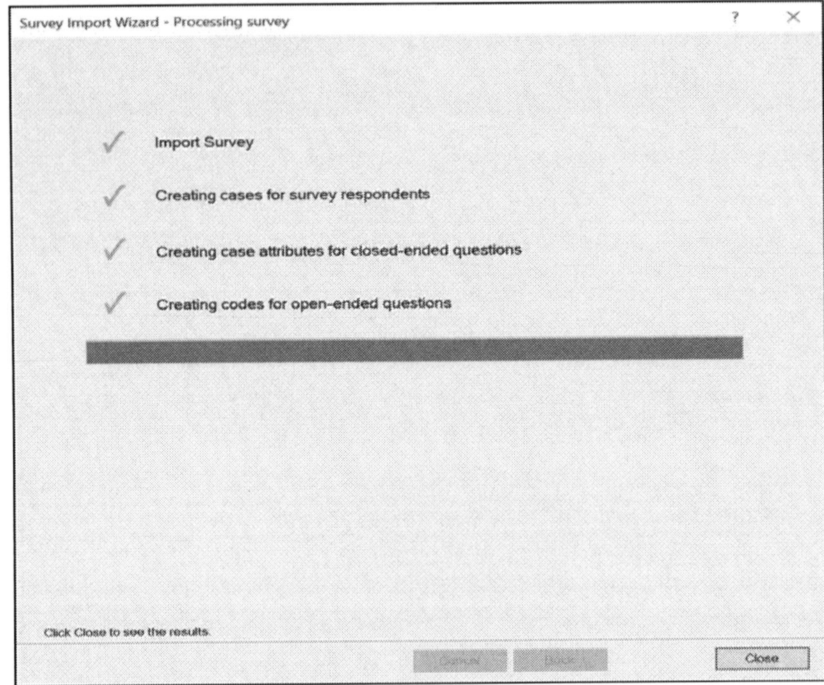

9 When finished then click [**Close**].

A successful import creates a Dataset with the same name as the Excel-file and when it opens in the Detail View and view mode *Table* it appears like this with Classifying fields having a grey background and Codable fields a white background:

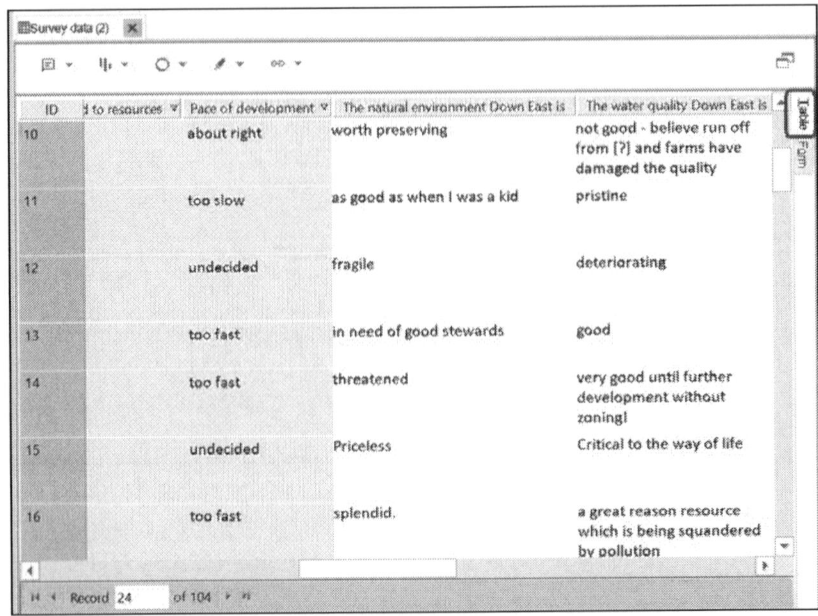

NVivo has created a new leftmost column, ID. A Dataset cannot be edited nor can you create or delete rows or columns. The buttons down left are for browse buttons between records.

View mode *Form* displays one record at a time:

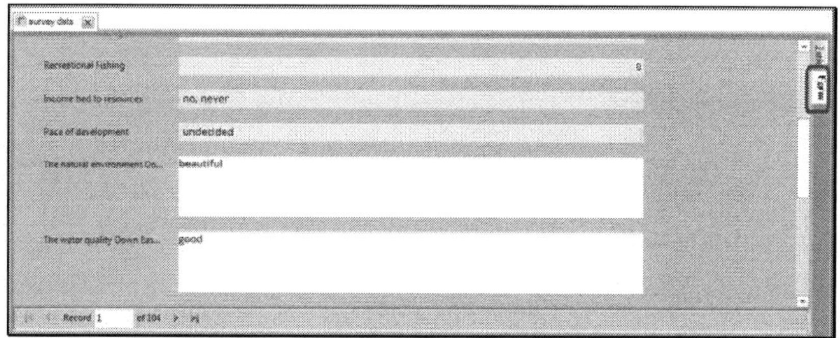

In the **Dataset Properties** dialog box, the **Dataset** tab, you can do certain modifications to a Dataset's presentation:

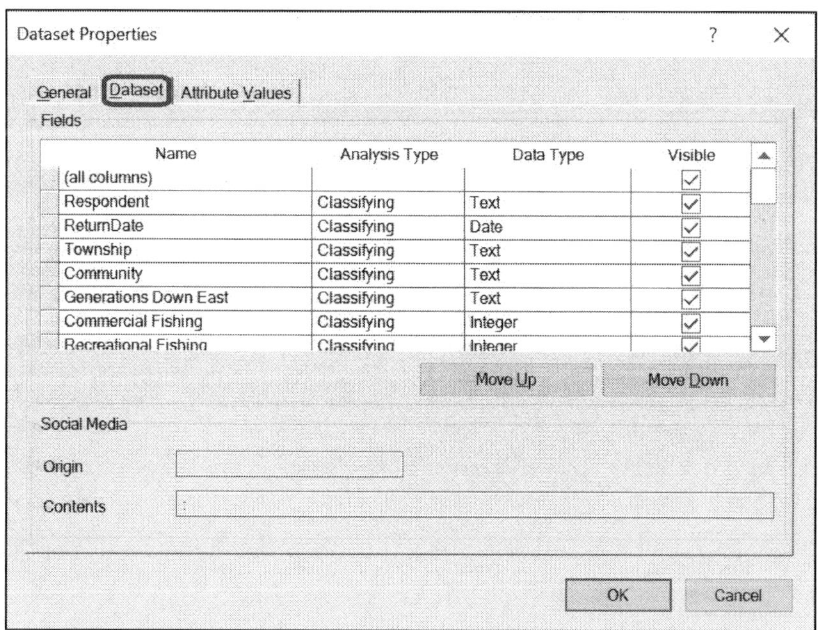

You can change names of a field, hide a field or move a field, but you cannot change Analysis Type or Data Type.

Alternatively, such modifications can also be made directly in a Dataset, view mode *Table*. All rules are as described for a Classification Sheet (Chapter 12, Classifications), and for Matrices (see page 215 and onwards), including the use of filters apply to Datasets.

Exporting Datasets

Datasets can be exported like other Project Items:

1 Select the **Data\\Files** folder or its subfolder.

2 Select the Dataset in in the List View that you want to export.

3 Go to **Share | Export → Export** or right-click and select **Export → Export Dataset...** or **[Ctrl]** + **[Shift]** + **[E]**.

The **Export Options** dialog box now appears.

4 Select applicable options and click **[OK]**. Then a file browser opens and you can decide file name, location, and file type: .XLS, .XLSX, .TXT and HTML.

5 Confirm with **[Save]**.

Coding Datasets

Coding Datasets applies all the common rules: select text in codable fields, right-click and select **Code**.

All coding in a Dataset can be explored like in other Project Items including coding stripes and highlighting.

Autocoding Datasets

Autocoding Datasets is the opportunity to create Cases and Codes to provide a structure to your Dataset content. Autocoding Datasets is fully described related to Autocoding Social Media Datasets (Chapter 19, see page 288).

The earlier described highly automated import procedure of an Excel worksheet includes autocoding of Cases and Codes and a classification of Cases why further instructions will be redundant.

Classifying Datasets

From a Dataset you can create and classify Cases based on the Classifying fields. In certain instances, there could be reasons to update data and especially when you need to apply the Mapping and Grouping feature described later on. We will consider updating the existing Case Classification created when we imported the survey.

1 Select the Dataset in the List View with the data that you want to use for updating the Case Classification or click on the open Dataset in the Detail View.

2 Go to **Home | Case Classification → Classify Cases from Dataset** or right-click and select **Classify Cases from Dataset**.

The **Classify Cases from Dataset Wizard – Step 1** appears:

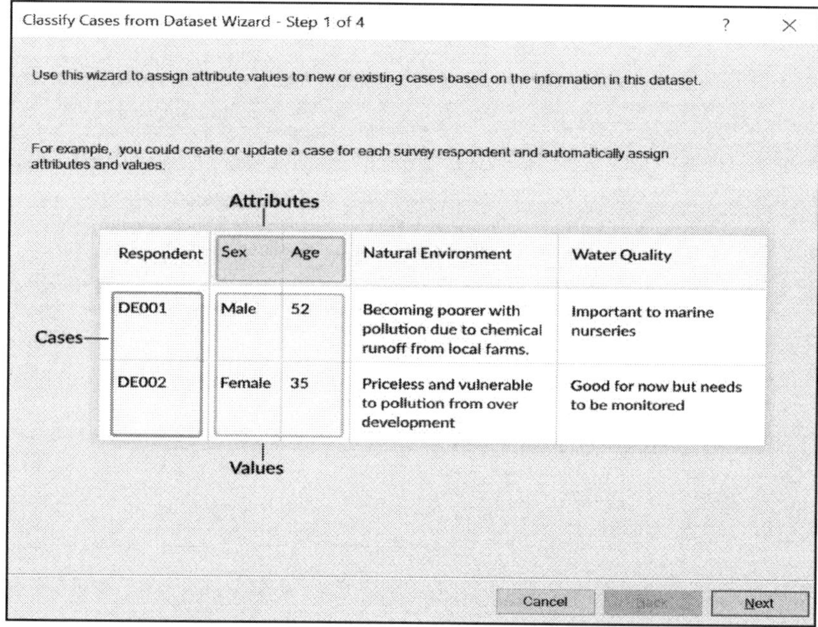

3 Click **[Next]**.

The **Classify Cases from Dataset Wizard – Step 2** appears:

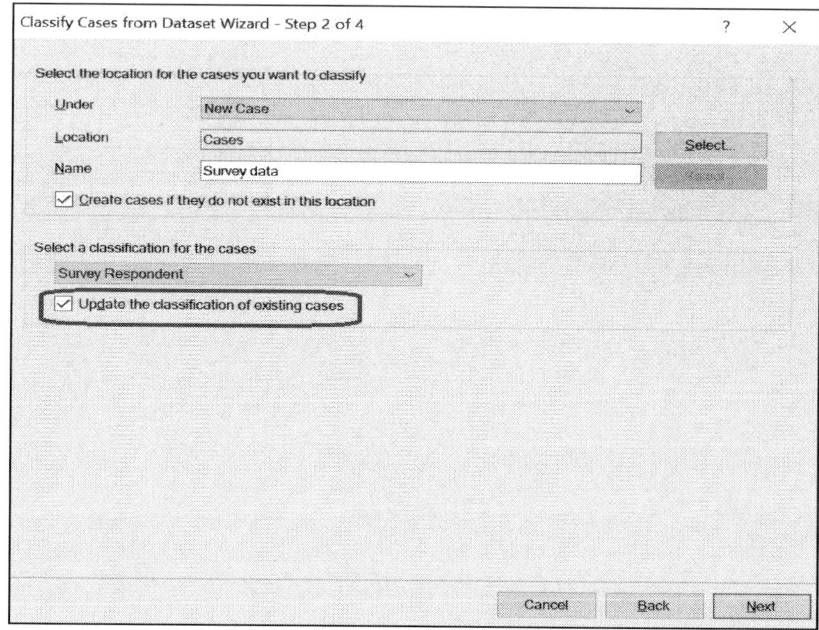

In our example we will update the Classification created during the import. Therefore, it is important to check *Update the classification of existing cases.*

4 Click **[Next]**.

The **Classify Cases from Dataset Wizard – Step 3** appears:

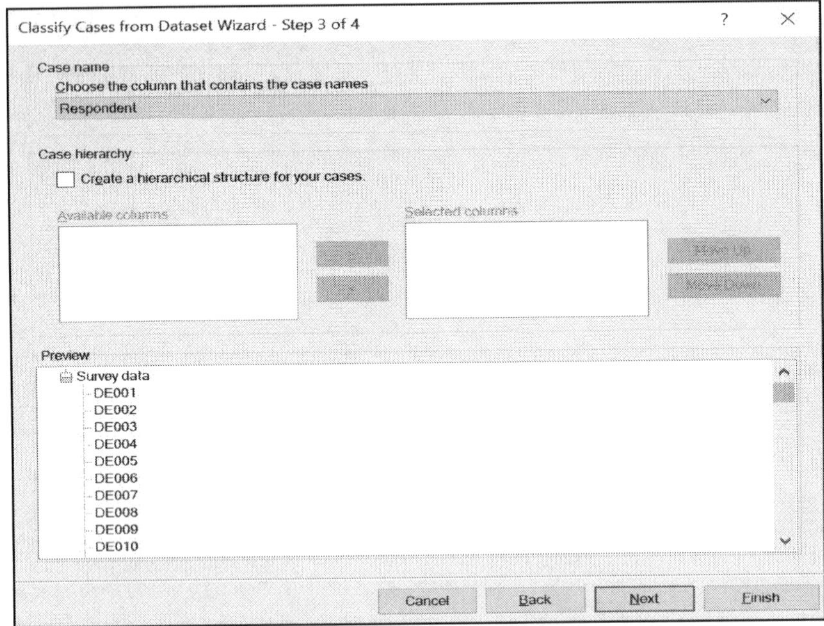

5 We select the column *Respondent* to correspond to the Cases. Click **[Next]**.

The **Classify Cases from Dataset Wizard – Step 4** appears:

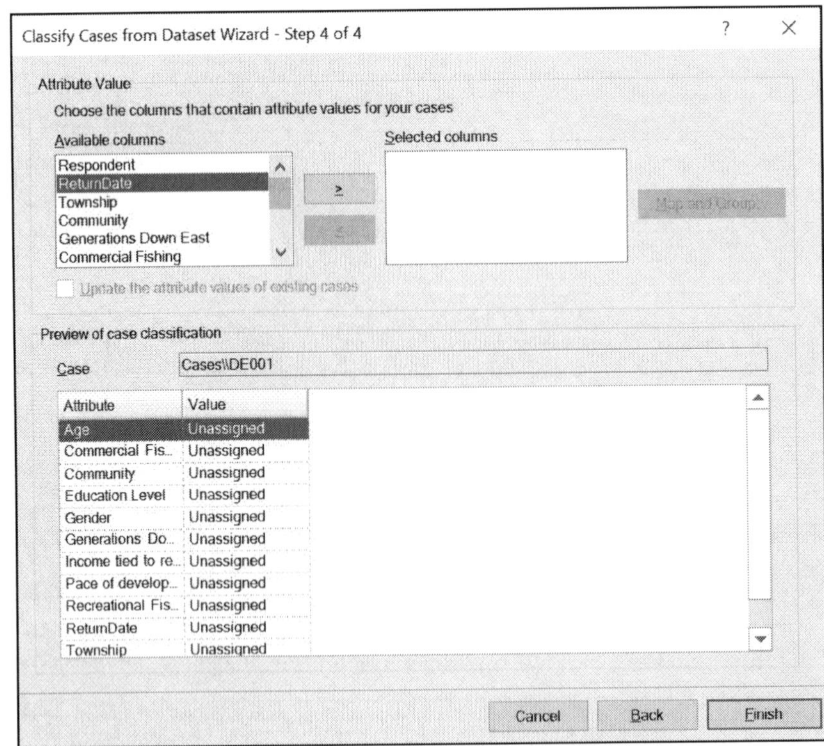

All Classifying fields are listed in the left box, *Available columns*. Use [>] to bring over the fields to the *Selected columns* box. In the section Preview the result from the topmost Code is displayed.

6 Click **[Finish]**.

Mapping and Grouping

We return to the **Classify Codes from Dataset Wizard - Step 4** above. The **[Map and Group]** button can be used to move (or map) the content from one column to another. There is also an option to group discrete numerical values as intervals, typically discrete ages of people to age groups:

1 In **Classify Cases from Dataset Wizard - Step 4** the field *Age* has been moved to the right box, Selected columns.

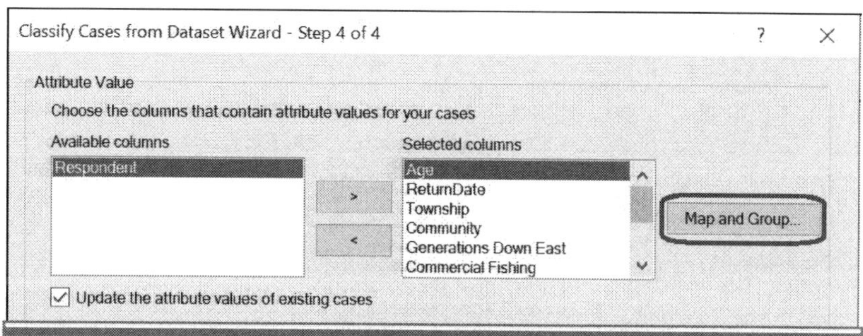

2 Highlight *Age* and click **[Map and Group...]**.

The **Mapping and Grouping Options** dialog box appears:

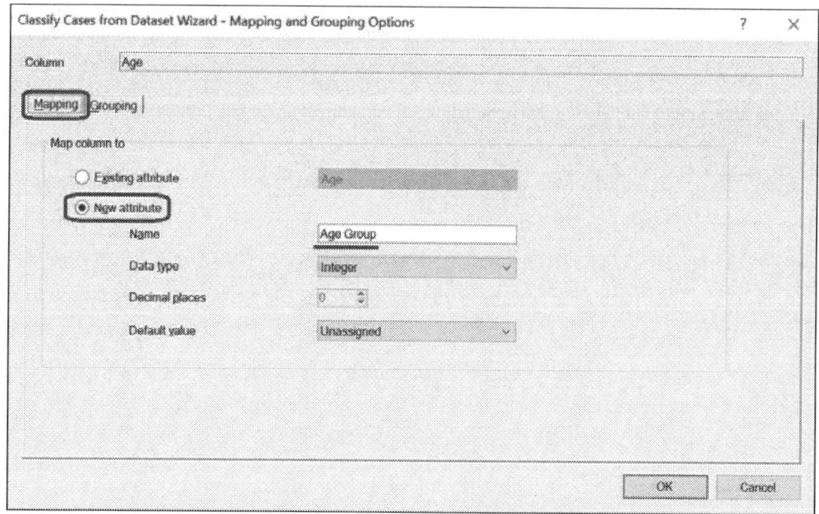

3 Select *New Attribute* which we call *Age Group*. Click on the **Grouping** tab.

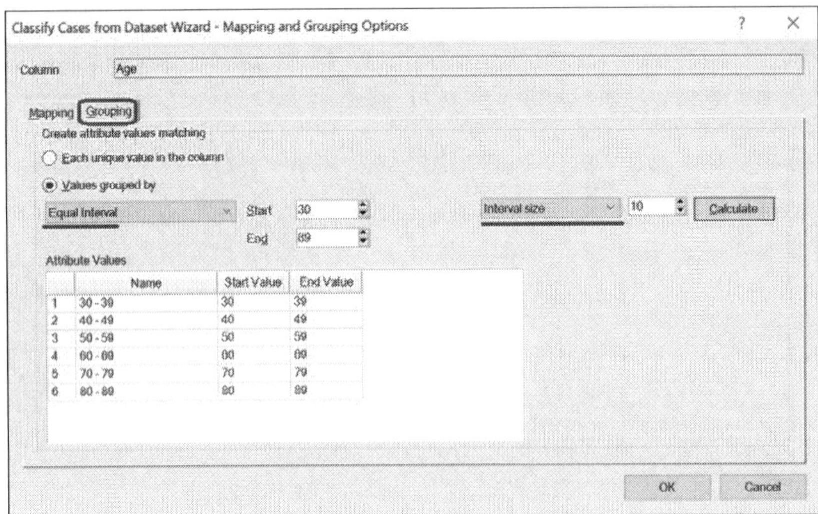

4. You can now decide the size of the interval. You can choose between *Equal Interval, Standard Deviation* or *User-defined Interval.* Confirm with **[OK]** and you will return to **Classify Cases from Dataset Wizard – Step 4**.

Importing from SurveyMonkey

If you use SurveyMonkey to collect survey responses, you can import the completed responses directly into your NVivo project. The imported data becomes a dataset source that you can sort, filter or auto code. You can exclude particular questions from being imported—for example, if they are not relevant to your analysis or if they contain confidential information. You can also change the field names (column headings).

Importing data from SurveyMonkey:

1. Go to **Import | Survey → SurveyMonkey**.
   Default folder is **Data\\Files** or its currently open subfolder.
2. In the **SurveyMonkey Authenticator** dialog box enter your SurveyMonkey Username and Password, and then click **[Login]**.

Follow the instructions in the **Import from SurveyMonkey Wizard**.

Importing from Qualtrics

If you use Qualtrics to collect survey responses, you can import the completed responses directly into your NVivo project. The imported data becomes a dataset source that you can sort, filter or auto code. You can exclude particular questions from being imported—for example, if they are not relevant to your analysis or if they contain confidential information. You can also change the field names (column headings).

Importing data from Qualtrics:

1. Go to **Import | Survey → Qualtrics**.
   Default folder is **Data\\Files** or its currently open subfolder.
2. In the **Qualtrics Authenticator** dialog box enter your Qualtrics Username and Password. Type also your API Token if applicable. Finally click [**Allow Access**].

Follow the instructions in the **Import from Qualtrics Wizard**.

19. INTERNET AND SOCIAL MEDIA

NVivo can import and handle data from internet web pages and social media sites like LinkedIn, Facebook, Twitter, and YouTube. NVivo also features full integration with Evernote and OneNote, the popular cloud-based notetaking/archiving services that will also be discussed in the next chapters.

Introducing NCapture

NCapture is a browser plugin that is delivered and installed with NVivo. NCapture exports web content into files called *web data packages* (a .VCX file) that you will import into NVivo. NCapture allows you to export any website including the website's text, images and hyperlinks. Websites import into NVivo as PDF sources. NCapture also allows you to export data from LinkedIn, Facebook and Twitter. Social media data can also import into NVivo as a PDF source, but more importantly social media data can also be imported as an NVivo Dataset. Presently, NCapture is available as Addins with Internet Explorer and Google Chrome.

Exporting Websites with NCapture

Like most software commands, capturing web data with NCapture in a web-browser can happen in three ways:

1. Select the **Extensions** from the toolbar of the web browser (Google Chrome) and then **NCapture**. If NCapture is installed but not activated then go to **Manage Extension**:

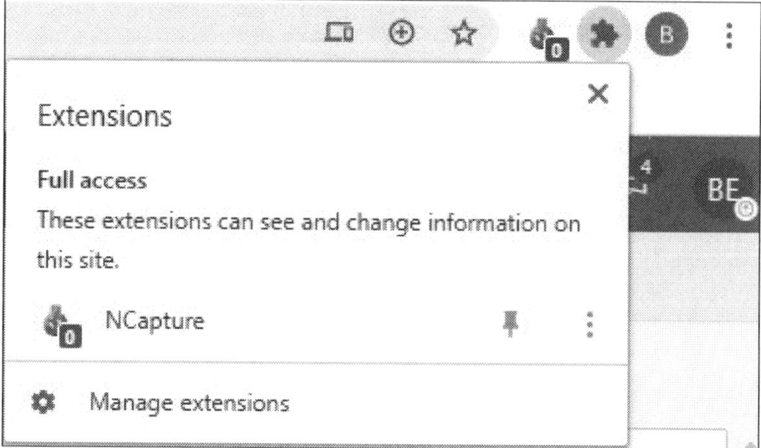

Importantly, you can export numerous *web data packages* during your online research. NVivo does not require you to import your web data until you're ready. When you select to import a website to NVivo, the **Capture for NVivo** dialog box appears in the web-browser:

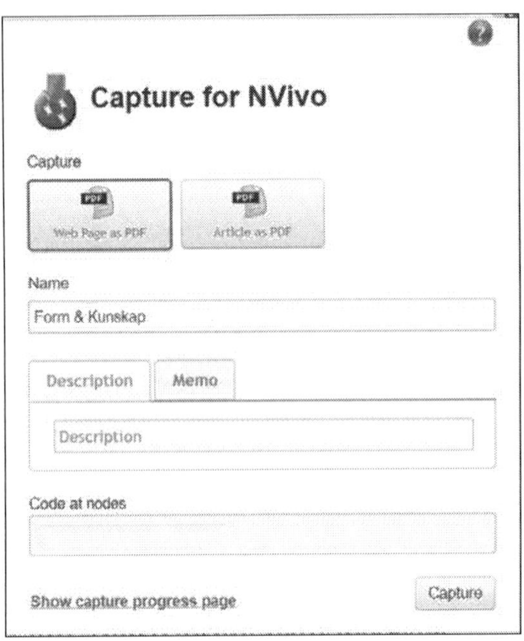

For websites, your Source Type will be Web Page as PDF by default as NVivo can currently only create website data packages that will be imported as PDF sources. But a variety of useful options are available for you to customize how your web data package can be imported into NVivo:

Source name will be the name of your new PDF source –the website's name will be the default here.

The *Description/Memo* tab allows you to type custom text that you want to add into *description field* of the PDF Source Item or a newly created *linked memo* with the same name as the Source Item. Which of these options works best for you will depend on your project - remember, linked memo content can be searched and coded; the description field text cannot.

Code at codes: You can type the names of any number of new or existing Codes here. NCapture only has the ability to code web content at Codes located in the **Coding\\Codes** folder. The imported PDF Source Item will be 100% coded at Codes that you specify.

Importing Websites with NCapture

After NCapture exports your data, you will need to retrieve and import the newly created web data package (.VCX) file(s). When you have returned to NVivo:

1 Go to **Import | NCapture**
Default folder is **Data\\Files** or its currently open subfolder.
Go to 4.

alternatively

1 Select the **Data\\Files** folder or its subfolder.
2 Go to **Import | NCapture**
Go to 4.

alternatively

2 Click on any empty space in the List View.
3 Right-click and select **Import from → Import from NCapture...**

The **Import From NCapture** dialog box appears:

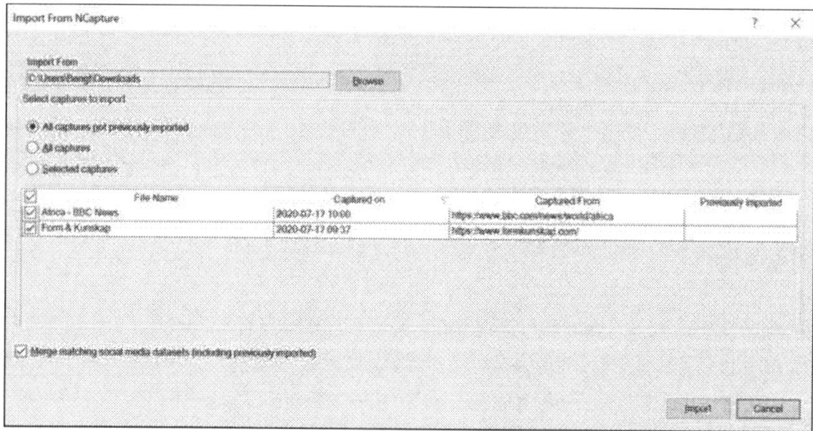

At the bottom of this dialog box, all recently imported items from NCapture are listed. NVivo will detect if there are web data packages that you have already imported, and so the default selection is *All captures not previously imported.* You can also select to import *All captures* or *Selected captures.*

4 Click **[Import]** and the result will be as follows:

The sample PDF Source item below is an export from the website '*Africa - BBC News*'. You'll notice that the webpage title is the same as the name of the PDF source file. Imported NCapture websites are classified with the File Classification 'Reference'. Values are inserted by default for the following Attributes: Reference Type, Title, keywords, URL and Access Date. As you'll recall from our sample export image above, this entire PDF source will be coded at two

Codes, *Africa - BBC News* and a linked memo will have been created sharing the PDF source's name, *Africa - BBC News*.

Now you can open the source and hyperlinks are clickable like in any PDF item by using **[Ctrl]** + click

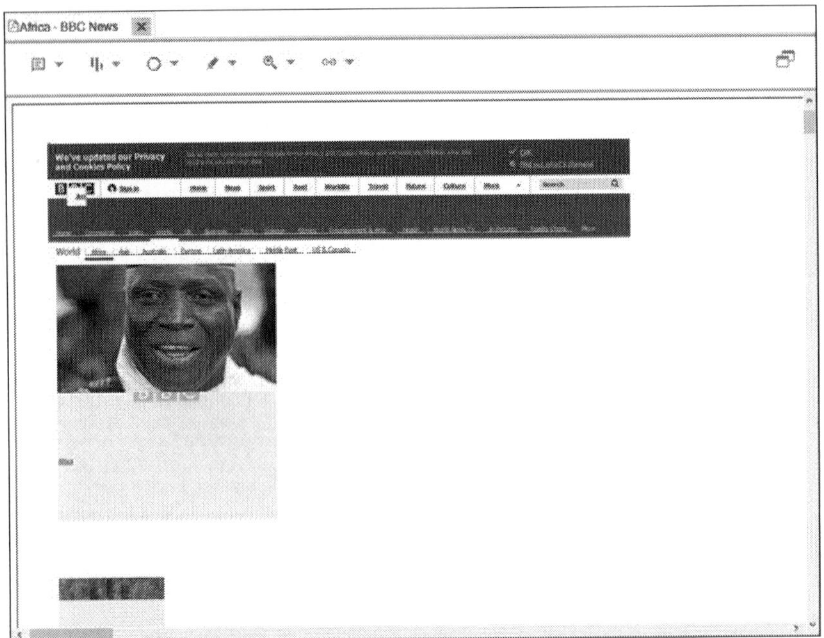

Social Media Data and NCapture

NCapture can also be used to capture data from Facebook, Twitter, and LinkedIn. Social media web data packages can be created as PDF sources or Datasets, which will be the focus of our description below.

Due to each social media site's unique structure, NCapture captures different types of data from each site. While a summary of the complete functionality of Facebook, Twitter, and LinkedIn is beyond our purposes here, we will provide an explanation of the types of data you can capture from each site. Importantly, your ability to capture social media data is contingent on the privacy settings of the individual or group whose data you are interested in capturing (e.g., some Twitter users may require you to be their Follower before you can capture their Twitter data).

Importantly, you can use NCapture to gather social media data over a period of time and then easily update the data later. When you import web data packages containing social media data, by default, new data will be merged with old data so long as the original social media properties (e.g., hashtags, usernames, etc.) remains the same.

NCapture for Facebook Data

NCapture allows you to capture Facebook wall posts and data about their authors. Whether from an individual's Facebook wall (e.g., Allan McDougall), a Group wall (e.g., the Stockholm Sailing Club), or a Page wall (e.g., QSR International), NCapture can export wall posts, tags, photos, hyperlinks, link captions, link descriptions, number of 'likes', comments, comment 'likes', dates and times of posts and comments. Further, NCapture can export authors' names, genders, birthdays, locations, relationship statuses, bios, religions, and hometowns.

NCapture for Twitter Data

NCapture allows you to capture Twitter tweets and data about their authors. Unlike Facebook, which is largely based on users being connected as 'friends' or as fans who 'like' a specific page, Twitter profiles and their attendant tweets are (typically) publicly available. As a result, along with individual user streams, full Twitter searches can also be exported with NCapture. Whether for user streams or search results, NCapture can export tweets along with their attendant usernames, mentions (usernames within tweets), hashtags (user-driven keywords), timestamps, locations, hyperlinks (if any), retweets (reposts by other users), and usernames of any 'retweeters'. Unlike NCapture's ability to export demographic data from Facebook, NCapture for Twitter captures data associated with a user's influence level (or klout), such as number of tweets, number of followers, and the number of users they are following.

NCapture for LinkedIn Data

Capturing social media data from LinkedIn is more similar to Facebook than Twitter. NCapture allows you to capture discussions and comments from LinkedIn groups, rather than individual user's LinkedIn profile pages. LinkedIn recently limited access to their web service (API), restricting the information available to apps like NCapture. As a result, you can no longer capture a LinkedIn group discussion as a dataset using NCapture. You can still capture a group discussion, and any other page in LinkedIn, as a PDF.

> **Tip:** Although you can't export LinkedIn users' profile data as a dataset with NCapture, you can still export user profiles as a PDF source. While unstructured, these PDF source can still be searched and coded after you import them into NVivo.

NCapture for YouTube

You can capture video clippings from YouTube as a Video item with or without comments or as a PDF.

When importing a video clipping to NVivo it behaves like other video items. However, the video clipping is always external (Not embedded) why Internet must be connected. In all other respects everything is working normally, that is you can create transcript rows and you can code.

When importing comments as a Dataset NCapture will create a number of columns (typical for Video) and will decide that the columns Comment and Reply are the only Codable columns.

The video item and the dataset (but not the PDF) are classified as a File Classification named YouTube with 13 attributes.

Exporting Social Media Data with NCapture

Once you have found social media data that you need then activate NCapture from Internet Explorer or Google Chrome as described above. For social media web data packages, you can usually select between a Dataset and a PDF-page:

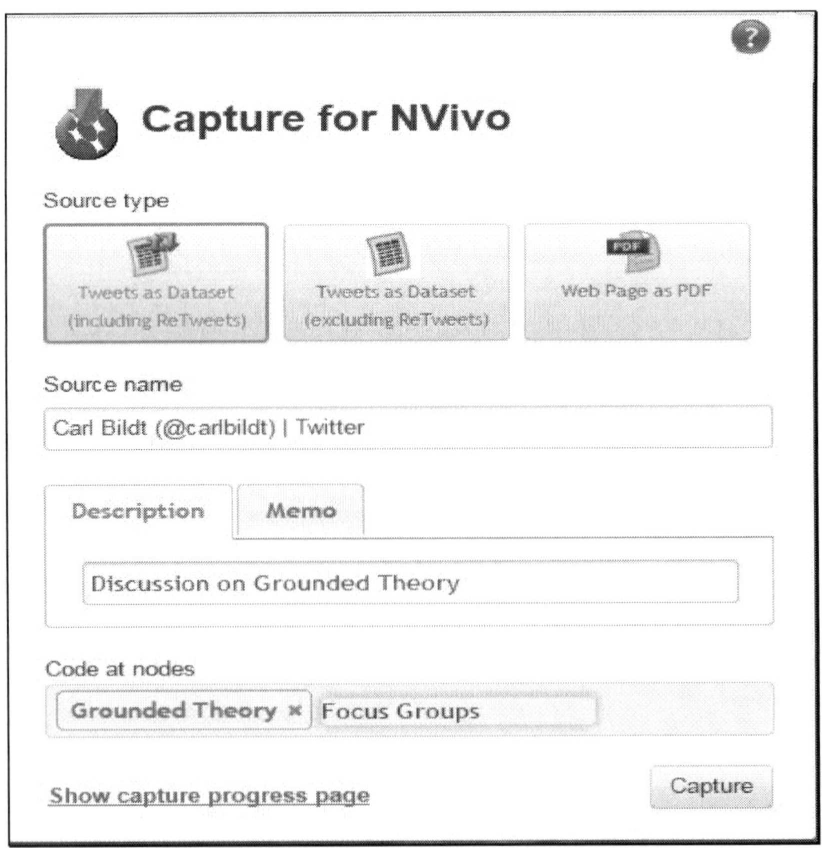

Like exporting websites with NCapture, when you export social media data you can create an item description, linked memo, and Codes. After completed the **NCapture** dialog box, click [**Capture**].

Importing Social Media Data with NCapture

Now that you've exported your social media data to a web data package, it's time to import:

1 Go to **Import | NCapture**.
  Default folder is **Data\\Files** or its currently open subfolder.
  Go to 4.

alternatively

1 Select the **Data\\Files** folder or its subfolder
2 Go to **Import | NCapture**.
  Go to 4.

alternatively

2 Click on any empty space in the List View.
3 Right-click and select **Import from → Import from NCapture...**

The **Import From NCapture** dialog box appears:

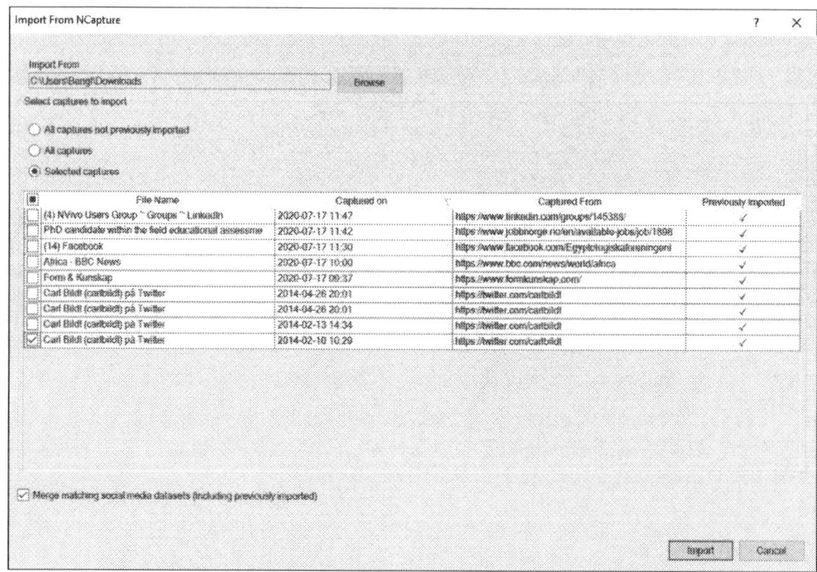

4 Like website data, at the bottom of this dialog box all recently imported items from NCapture are listed. NVivo will detect if there are web data packages that you have already imported, and so the default selection is *All captures not previously imported.*
5 Click [**Import**] and the result will be as follows:

When NCapture exports a photo from Facebook, the photos are stored as separate picture source file in the same folder as the Facebook dataset when imported. The icon shown is a *source shortcut* and a placeholder that allows you to easily navigate between your dataset and the photos.

The sample Dataset Source Item below is an export from the 'NVivo Users Group on LinkedIn'. You'll notice the Dataset Source Item contains the LinkedIn group name. Imported NCapture social media data is classified with the File Classification 'Reference'. Values are inserted by default for the following Attributes: Reference Type, Title, keywords, URL and Access Date. As you'll recall from our sample export image above, this entire Dataset source will be coded at two Codes, *Grounded Theory* and *Focus Groups*, and a linked memo has been created sharing the Dataset source's name, *NVivo Users Group on LinkedIn*.

Now you can open the Source and view it in several modes: Table (default), Form, or as a Cluster Analysis. The latter mode is unique for Datasets from Social Media and usually clusters Usernames.

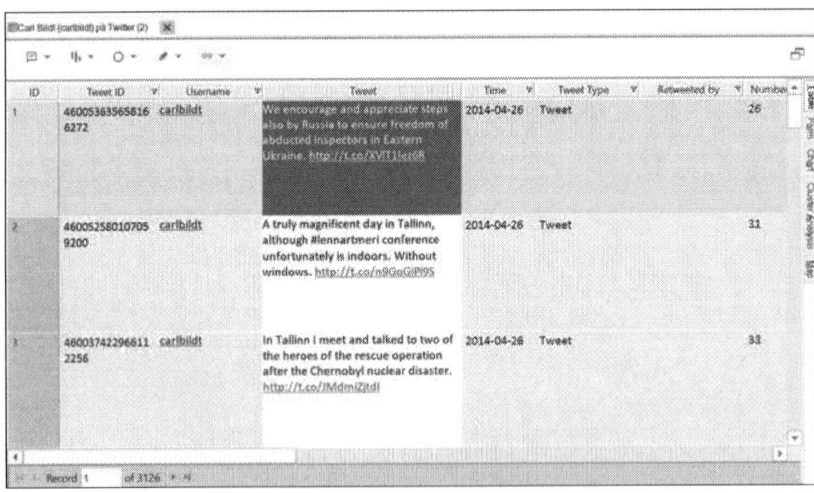

Working with Social Media Datasets

What makes working with social media Dataset sources so exciting, like working with any Dataset source, is your ability to easily edit, customize, and survey your structured data through Dataset Properties:

1 Select the **Data\\Files** folder or its subfolder.
2 Select the dataset that you want to edit.
3 Go to **Home | Item → 'Properties' → Dataset Properties...** or right-click and select **Dataset Properties...** or **[Ctrl}** + **[Shift]** + **[P]**.

Within the **General** tab you can change the name and description of your social media Dataset.

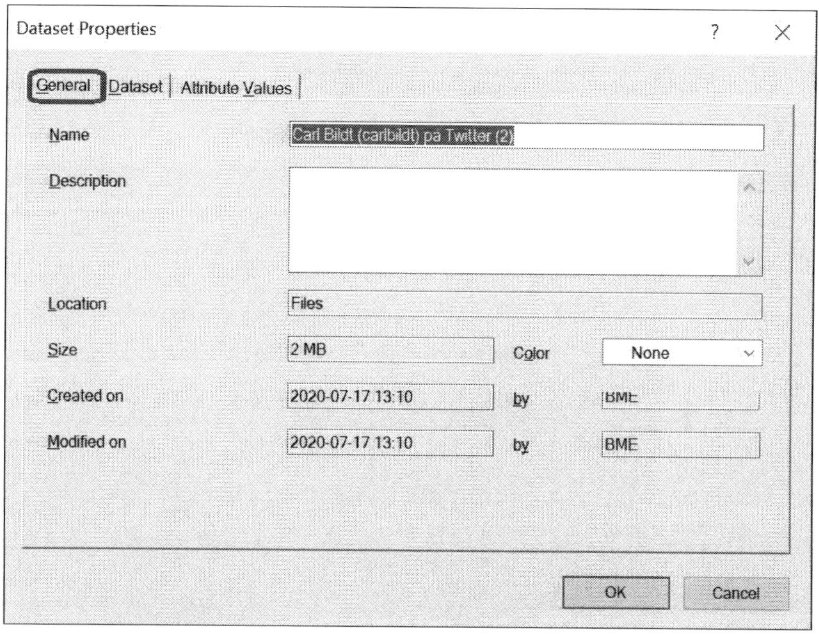

The **Dataset** tab allows you to view your Dataset fields and move some fields up or down. Upon importing your social media web data package, NVivo has already decided which columns are Classifying (a limited set of options) and which columns are Codable (editable text) respectively. Within this tab you can uncheck Visible on any row with data you deem unnecessary.

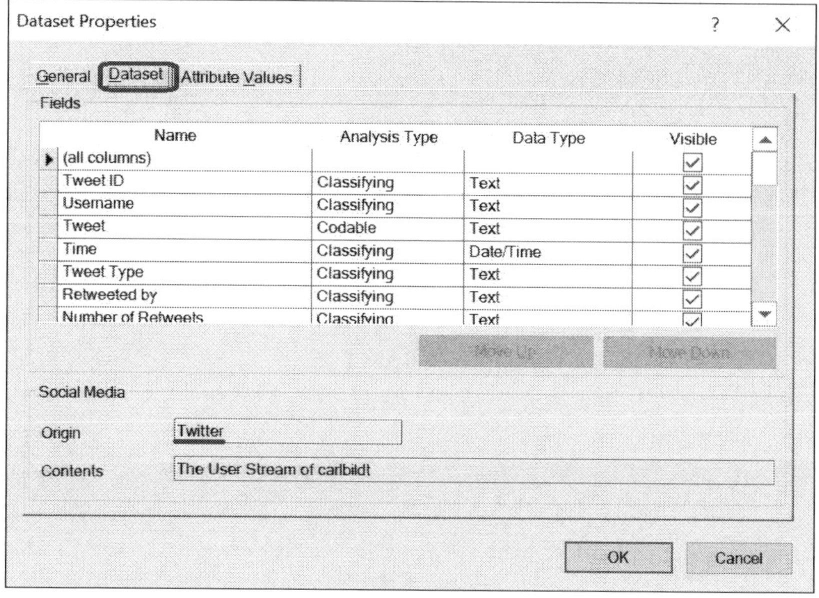

The **Attribute Values** tab allows you to view default Attribute Value information. You can select a custom Classification if that is useful for your project:

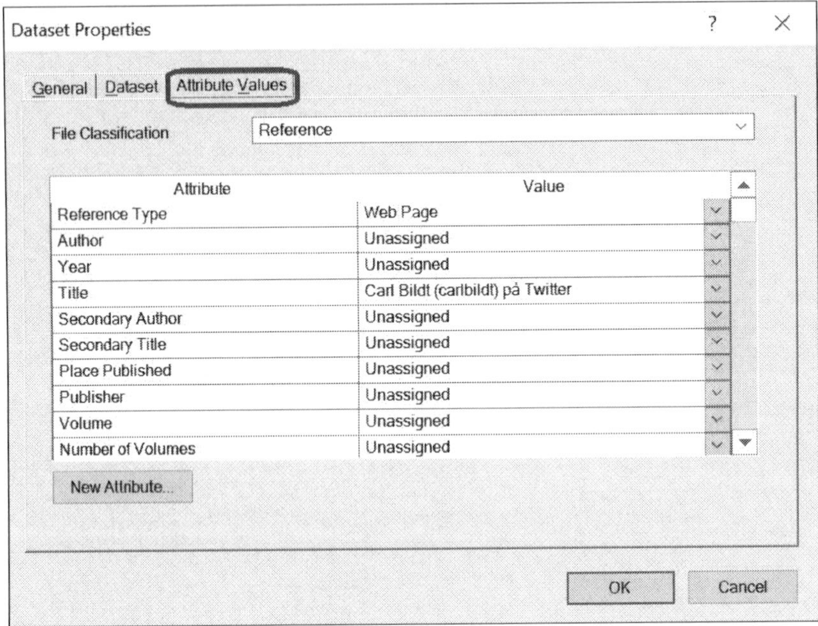

Analyzing Social Media Datasets

Several methods for analyzing social media Datasets exist in NVivo. Like any open Dataset source, you can search for patterns in your data by hiding, sorting, or filtering rows and columns. More advanced analysis functions such as Word Frequency Queries and Text Search Queries can offer insight into some themes in your data as well. Further, visualizations of social media data can be achieved using chart functions (see page 343).

Autocoding a Dataset from Social Media

Perhaps the most useful tool for social media web data is autocoding.

1. Select a Dataset in the List View that you want to auto code.
2. Go to **Home | Auto Code**
   or right-click and select **Auto Code...**

The **Autocode Wizard - Step 1** appears:

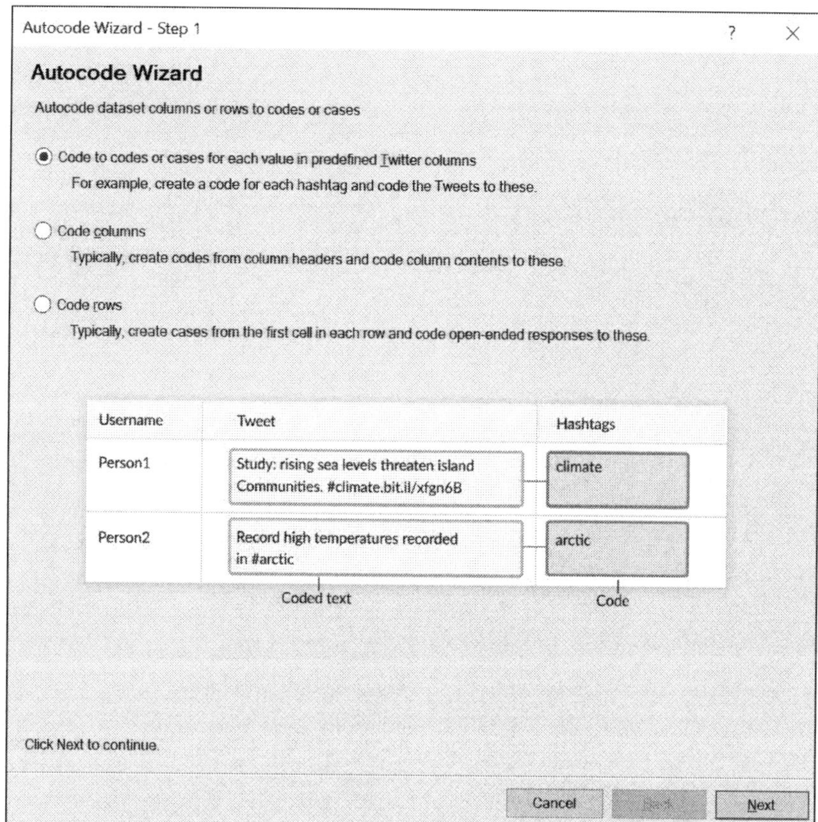

The first option, ***Code to Codes or Cases for each value in predefined LinkedIn (or Facebook or Twitter) columns*** is unique for importing social media compared to other types of Datasets. For example, using the Auto Code Dataset Wizard we can create Codes containing all of the content generated by one user, or all of the comments generated during a group discussion.

3 Click **[Next]**.

The **Autocode Wizard** - **Step 2** appears:

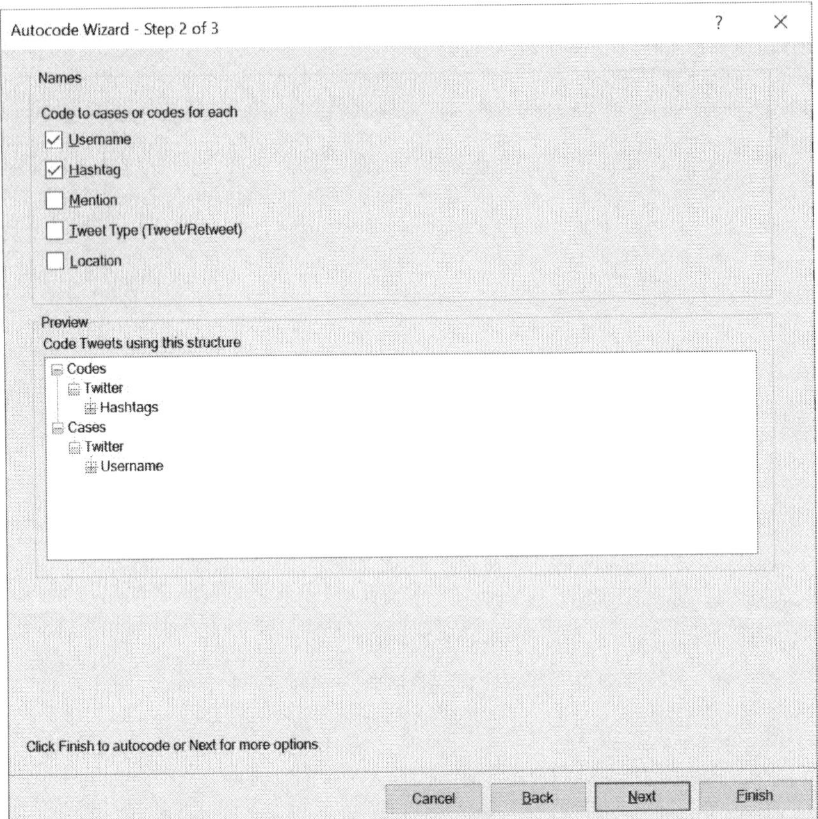

The **Auto Code Dataset Wizard** provides a preview of the resulting Code structure that your autocoding will generate. As you can see in the above image, by selecting to code data at Username and Discussion, Code hierarchies will be created where all of the data generated by each user will be coded into a Code named after that user.

4 Click [**Next**].

The **Autocode Wizard** - **Step 3** appears:

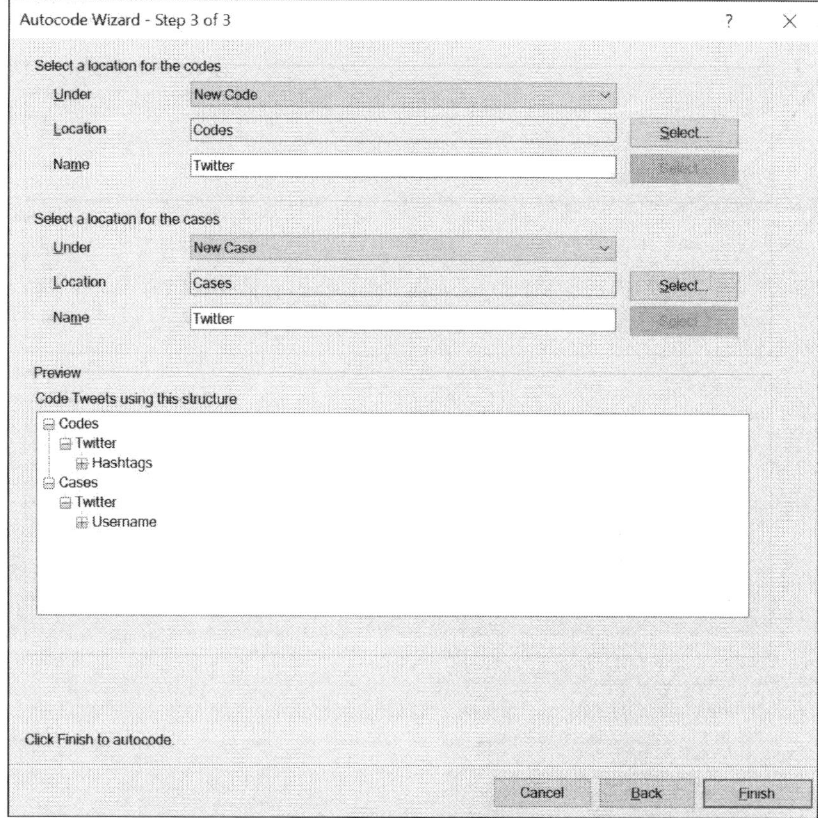

Default settings will create Codes and apply a Case Classification named LinkedIn User, Facebook User or Twitter User which classifies the users under respective parent Code LinkedIn/Username, Facebook/Username or Twitter/Username. Also, other Codes have been created under the parent Codes LinkedIn (Discussion), Facebook (Conversation) or Twitter (Hashtags).

Like other NVivo Datasets, the auto code wizard can also allow you to create Codes based on the columns (e.g., all hashtags would become Codes within a parent Code called hashtags) and cell values of the Dataset (e.g., all unique hashtags become their own Codes with each occurrence auto coded).

Privacy levels can vary using social media so contact QSR Support if you have any problems with importing social media data.

5 Finally click [**Finish**].

The result from these operations is not only an easy-to-handle dataset, a set of Cades (Usernames) and a set of Codes (Comment text, Post, Title) but also a File Classification and a Case Classification.

The File Classification **Reference** was created when data from NCapture was imported as a dataset:

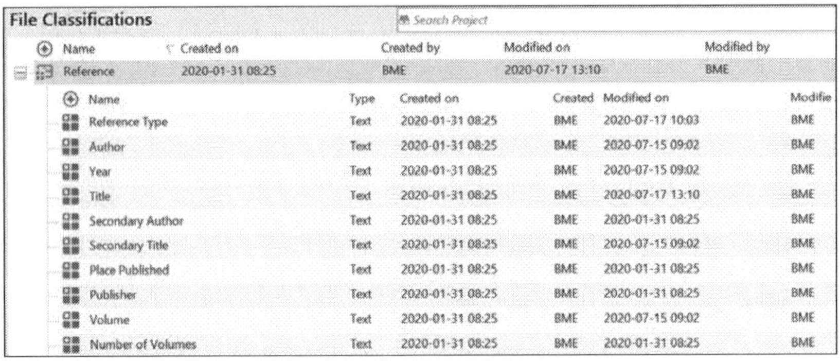

File Classifications

Search Project

Name	Created on	Created by	Modified on	Modified by
Reference	2020-01-31 08:25	BME	2020-07-17 13:10	BME

Name	Type	Created on	Created	Modified on	Modifie
Reference Type	Text	2020-01-31 08:25	BME	2020-07-17 10:03	BME
Author	Text	2020-01-31 08:25	BME	2020-07-15 09:02	BME
Year	Text	2020-01-31 08:25	BME	2020-07-15 09:02	BME
Title	Text	2020-01-31 08:25	BME	2020-07-17 13:10	BME
Secondary Author	Text	2020-01-31 08:25	BME	2020-01-31 08:25	BME
Secondary Title	Text	2020-01-31 08:25	BME	2020-07-15 09:02	BME
Place Published	Text	2020-01-31 08:25	BME	2020-01-31 08:25	BME
Publisher	Text	2020-01-31 08:25	BME	2020-01-31 08:25	BME
Volume	Text	2020-01-31 08:25	BME	2020-07-15 09:02	BME
Number of Volumes	Text	2020-01-31 08:25	BME	2020-01-31 08:25	BME

Installing NCapture

For Internet Explorer:

1. Download NCapture.IE.exe from QSR's web page.
2. Close Internet Explorer.
3. Launch NCapture.IE.exe and follow the prompts to complete the installation.

For Google Chrome:

1. Run Google Chrome.
2. Find the link with the installation guide on QSR's web page.
3. Follow the prompts to complete the installation.

Check your Version of NCapture

For Internet Explorer:
Go to **Tools → Manage Add-ons**
View the version number for **NCapture for NVivo** in the list.

For Google Chrome:
Go to **Tools → Extensions**
View the version number for **NCapture for NVivo** in the list.

20. SOCIAL NETWORK ANALYSIS

The ability for researchers to build sociograms for social network analysis (SNA) is one of NVivo's powerful new features. Social network analysis is an interdisciplinary process for investigating—often by way of visualization—the composition and consistency of social phenomena. Examples of social phenomena studied with social network analysis can include but are not limited to social media communities, networks of friends and families, or more conceptual topics like mapping idea dissemination.

The SNA methodology fits well with NVivo insofar as Codes form the primary units for analysis. SNA defines a Case as a person or thing, which matches NVivo's definition of a Case. Sociograms are a mapping tool for visualizing the ways that Cases relate to one another. Sociograms allow researchers to answer questions that involve how elements of a social phenomenon interact and connect. They are analytic tool with a variety of applications, such as identifying where ideas have originated, revealing people or individuals with access to too few resources, or observing how students use a classroom computer. In short, NVivo now allows researchers using SNA to beautifully visualize and dynamically interact with the links between Cases as sociograms.

Making Sociograms

Prior to building sociograms, you will have had to code relationships between your Cases. For more on Relationships see page 138. You can build three types of sociograms in NVivo. First, *egocentric sociograms*, which highlight one particular Case—the "ego"—and display how other Cases connect to it. Second, ***network sociograms***, which display the relationships between a group of your Cases. Third, *Twitter sociograms*, which ostensibly are the same as network sociograms but are accessed as a tab within an open Twitter Dataset detail view.

Creating an Egocentric Sociogram

1 Select any Case.
2 Go to **Explore | Social Network Analysis → 'Egocentric Sociogram' → Egocentric Sociogram** (this button will be grey if a Case is not selected).
3 The sociogram will appear in the Detail View with the egocentric Case appearing as a star shape.

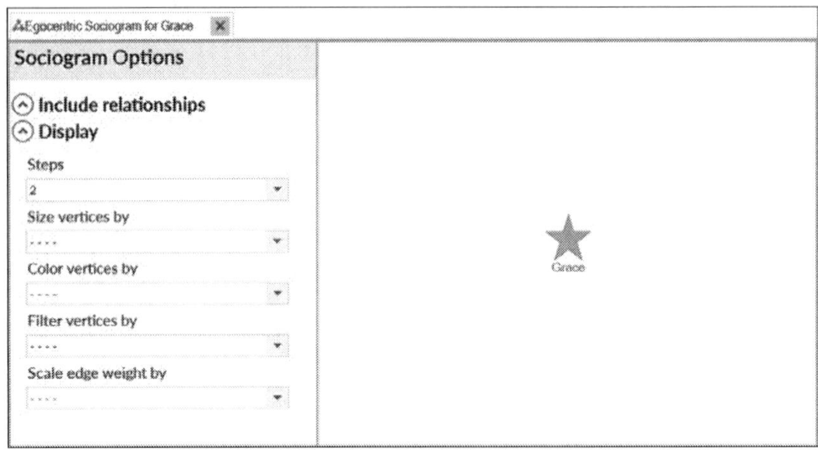

Creating a Network Sociogram

1 Go to **Explore | Social Network Analysis → 'Network Sociogram' → Network Sociogram...**
2 The **Select Project Items** dialog box will open.
3 Select the Cases you wish to visualize.
4 The Network Sociogram with the **Sociogram Options** panel will appear in the detail view.

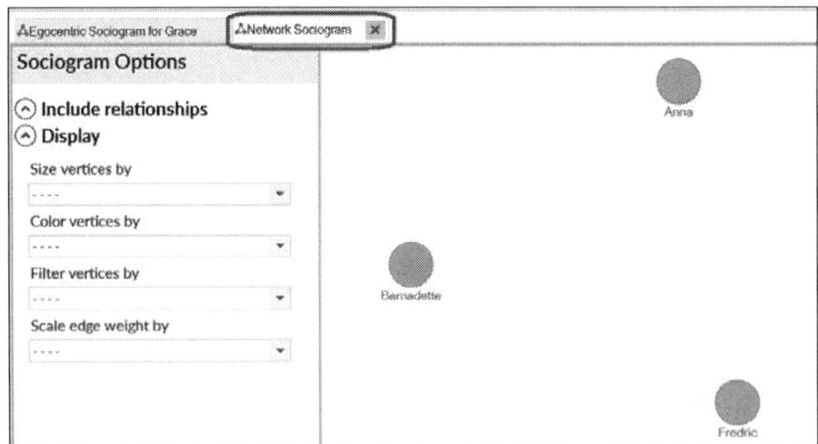

Directly under the heading **Sociogram Options**, a set of filters allow you to adjust the types of relationships between your Cases. For egocentric sociograms and network sociograms, these filters appear under the heading **Include relationships**. Simply check or uncheck a relationship type to include or omit it from your sociogram. Once an adjustment is made, you will need to select **Click to redraw** in order to recreate your sociogram.

Creating a Twitter Sociogram

1. Open any Twitter Dataset.
2. Select the **Twitter Sociogram** tab in detail view.
3. The Twitter sociogram will appear.

Adjusting Sociograms

When a sociogram opens, you will see Vertices and Edges—the terms used for Cases (Vertices) and the lines that represent the relationships connecting the Cases (Edges).

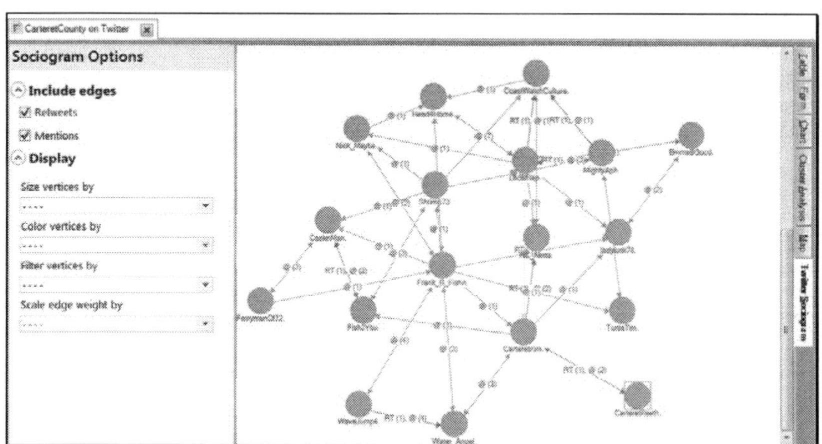

Once you have opened a sociogram, a diverse array of Sociogram Options for filtering this visual data are available. While these filters may adjust which Cases and Edges appear, they do not omit their presence in the overall project—this may seem like a minor point, but the positioning of Cases and Edges directly impacts how NVivo quantifies and calculates sociogram metrics, called *Centrality measures*. More on this below.

Displaying Relationships on your Sociogram

Directly under the heading **Sociogram Options**, a set of filters allow you to hide or unhide certain properties.

For Twitter sociograms, you will have access to only two filters, under the heading **Include edges**: *Retweets* and *Mentions*.

> **Did you know?** On the NVivo help website, the article "Understand sociogram centrality measures" outlines several important things to know for researchers using centrality measures. In summary, it warns researchers intending to use centrality measures from their sociograms to ensure they carefully consider how and whether to integrate certain Cases into their sociograms. For example, intermingling, say, Cases for people and organizations can cause the meaningless saturation or dilution of some centrality measures.

Displaying Degrees of Connection on your Sociogram (Egocentric Sociograms only)

As the title indicates, this Sociogram Option filters the number of connective steps between the egocentric Case and its connected Cases. For example, 1 step will only display Cases that directly connect to the egocentric Cases, whereas selecting 2 steps, etc. show additional degrees of connectivity.

Using Size, Color and Line Weight to distinguish Sociogram Cases and Relationships

The **Display** heading under **Sociogram Options** allows you to adjust how Edges and Cases appear based on three types of *Centrality measures*, the background calculations run by NVivo to quantify how Cases relate with each other. Cases' appearance can be adjusted according to size and color.

When adjusting **Size vertices by** and **Color vertices by**, know that *degree* centrality counts the number of Cases that are connected, *betweenness* counts how often a Case lies on the shortest path between two other Cases, and *closeness* is a measure of 'reach' insofar as the speed of information transfer is considered to represent the sum of the shortest distances from a Case to all of the other Cases in the sociogram. Cases will be sized and colored depending on *Centrality measures*.

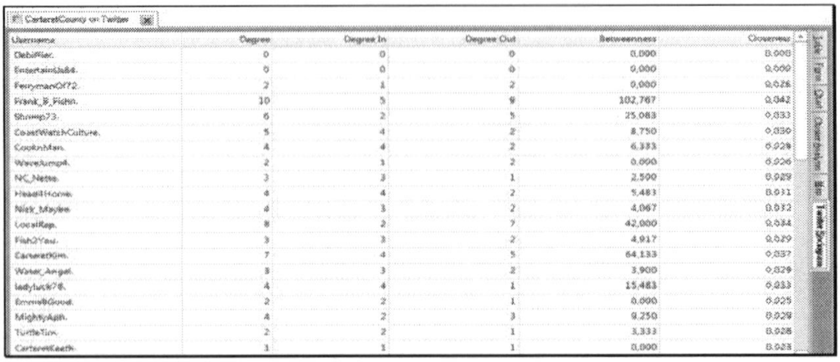

CarteretCounty on Twitter

Username	Degree	Degree In	Degree Out	Betweenness	Closeness
DebiFier.	0	0	0	0,000	0,000
EntertainUs84.	0	0	0	0,000	0,000
FerrymanOf72.	2	1	2	0,000	0,026
Frank_B_Fishn.	10	5	9	102,767	0,042
Shrimp73.	6	2	5	25,083	0,033
CoastWatchCulture.	5	4	2	8,750	0,030
CookinMan.	4	4	2	6,333	0,028
WaveJump4.	2	1	2	0,000	0,026
NC_Netse.	3	3	1	2,500	0,029
HeadHome.	4	4	2	5,483	0,031
Nick_Maybe.	4	3	2	4,067	0,032
LocalRep.	8	2	7	42,000	0,034
Fish2You.	3	3	2	4,917	0,029
CarteretKim.	7	4	5	64,133	0,037
Water_Angel.	3	3	2	3,900	0,029
ladyluck78.	4	4	1	15,483	0,033
EmmaBGood.	2	2	1	0,000	0,025
MightyApp.	4	2	3	9,250	0,029
TurtleTim.	2	2	1	3,333	0,028
CarteretKeath.	1	1	1	0,000	0,023

As you might expect, codes with higher values will be the largest or colored the darkest. Lower values will be the opposite.

The thickness of Edges (edge weight) can also be adjusted. Select **Scale edge weight by** to make lines more distinct based on the number of relationships associated with a given Case.

Filter Cases by Centrality Measure

Cases can also be filtered by *Centrality measure*. Under **Filter vertices by**, you can quantitatively filter Cases based on the extent to which they represent a certain measure. For example, you filter Cases according to a betweenness measure of between 0.05 and 0.1.

Reviewing your Sociogram's Centrality Measures

Selecting Centrality Measures under the contextual Sociogram or Twitter Sociogram tab allows you to view how Edges and Vertices appear based on the three primary types *Centrality measures* described above: degree, betweenness and closeness.

Two more Centrality Measures: Density and Reciprocity

Sociograms use five types of *Centrality measures* as a metric for calculating the influence of Cases in relation to one another, not just the three outlined above. However, density and reciprocity are measurements that reflect an entire sociogram, so they do not feature in the sociogram interface. You can find both shown in the NVivo **Status Bar** when an entire sociogram is selected:

Density is a ratio based on a count of Case pairs that are connected in a sociogram divided by the total number of connections possible. The density score is purported to display the level of *connectedness* in a sociogram.

Reciprocity shows the percentage of relationships in a sociogram that are reciprocated. The reciprocity score is purported to represent the level of reciprocal relations within a sociogram.

21. USING EVERNOTE WITH NVIVO

NVivo can also import data from Evernote. If you aren't already an Evernote user, it is a software suite designed for note taking and archiving. Evernote is cloud-based, which means that your notes are stored on an online server rather than on a local hard drive on a computer. The name Evernote implies that your notes will be archived 'forever' on the Evernote server. Do you have privacy concerns about uploading data to a cloud-based service like Evernote? Check with your institution's IT group or ethics office to find out what kind of data you are allowed to capture on Evernote and other popular cloud-based resources like Dropbox, SkyDrive, and Google Drive.

Evernote for Data Collection

Evernote has gained popularity because of its functionality for smart phone users. As a note taking program that is available on Blackberry, iPhone, iPad, and Android smart phones.

For qualitative researchers, a smart phone with Evernote installed offers a range of new possibilities for data collection. From the same device, researchers can record audio and video, take photos, capture web data, and easily upload all of these multimedia resources into NVivo.

Exporting Notes from Evernote

Evernote notes must be exported as an .ENEX file from the Evernote client, which is basically an XML format, for further import to NVivo. While a tutorial on how to use Evernote is beyond our purposes here, we have included a screen shot below displaying the File menu in Evernote. In order to export this picture note, simply go to **File → Export → Export as a file in ENEX format**:

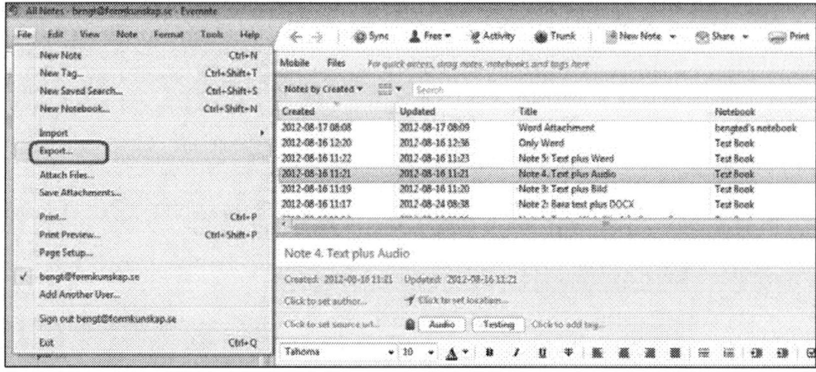

Importing Evernote Notes into NVivo

Remember you can batch import a set of notes or an entire Evernote notebook to an .ENEX file. Once you save your .ENEX file you can easily import its content into NVivo:

1 Go to **Import | Notes & Email → Evernote.**
Default folder is **Data\\Files** or its currently open subfolder.
Go to 4.

alternatively

1 Select the **Data\\Files** folder or its subfolder

2 Go to **Import | Notes & Email → Evernote.**
Go to 4.

alternatively

2 Click on any empty space in the List View.

3 Right-click and select **Import From → Import from Evernote...**

The **Import from Evernote** dialog box appears:

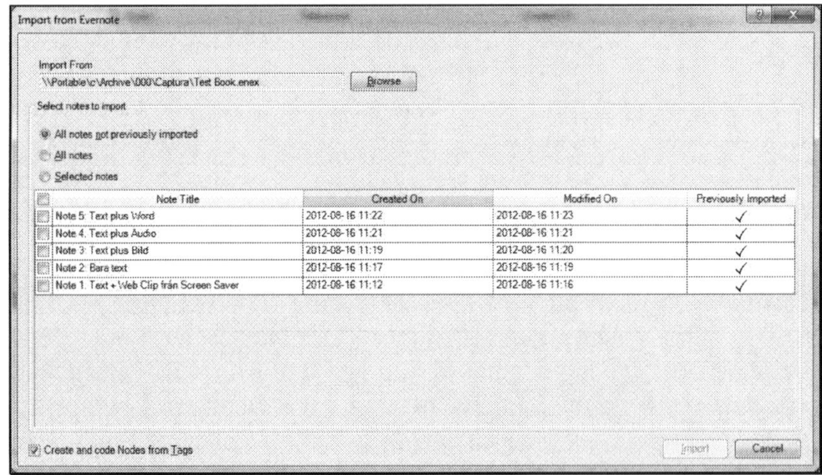

This example shows the import dialog when a notebook has been exported. The bottom of the dialog box contains a list of each individual note included in the .ENEX file. NVivo will detect if there are notes in the .ENEX that you have already imported, and so the default selection is to import *All notes not previously imported.* Alternatively, you can select import *All notes* or import *Selected notes.* Select the notes that you want to import.

4 Click **[Import]**.

Evernote Note Formats in NVivo

Not all Evernote data will be imported as internal sources, so it is a good idea to familiarize yourself with the following list of Evernote types of data and their attendant locations in NVivo:

- Evernote text notes will become a document Source in the **Data/Files** folder or its sub-folder
- Evernote notes with file attachments (e.g., PDFs, photos, images, audio files, or video files) will retain their file types. Any text that accompanies these notes will become a linked memo associated with the newly imported Source Item.
- Evernote web clippings (i.e., web page which has been saved to Evernote via an Evernote Web Clipper) will be imported as PDF Source Item.

Autocoding your Evernote Tags

Some Evernote users using note tagging as a way of linking notes together with broad categories for later reference and searching. Evernote tags in this sense are similar to NVivo Codes. A nice feature for importing your tagged Evernote notes allows you to convert your tags to Codes when you import the Evernote note. These Codes are created in the **Coding\\Codes** folder (if they do not already exist). The Code will code the entire imported source. If you do not want to create Codes when your notes are imported, clear the *Create and code Codes from Tags* check box in the **Import from Evernote** dialog box.

22. USING ONENOTE WITH NVIVO

NVivo contain native capacity for importing data from OneNote 2010 or OneNote Online. If you aren't already a OneNote user, it is a software suite designed for note taking and archiving. OneNote is cloud-based, which means that your notes are stored on an online server rather than on a local hard drive on a computer.

Exporting Notes from OneNote

Export to NVivo is made by an Addin component normally installed when NVivo is installed. OneNote pages must be exported as a .NVOZ file from the OneNote client, which is basically an XML format, for further import to NVivo. While a tutorial on how to use OneNote is beyond our purposes here, we have included a screen shot below displaying the **Share** ribbon in OneNote. In order to export these pages, simply go to **Share | NVivo | Export:**

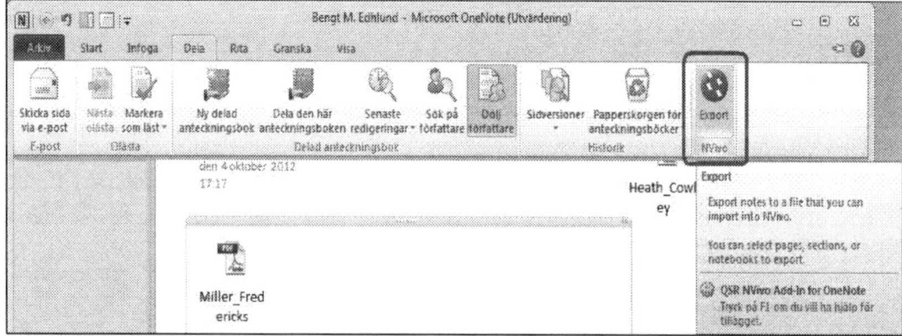

Then the **Export for NVivo** dialog box appears.

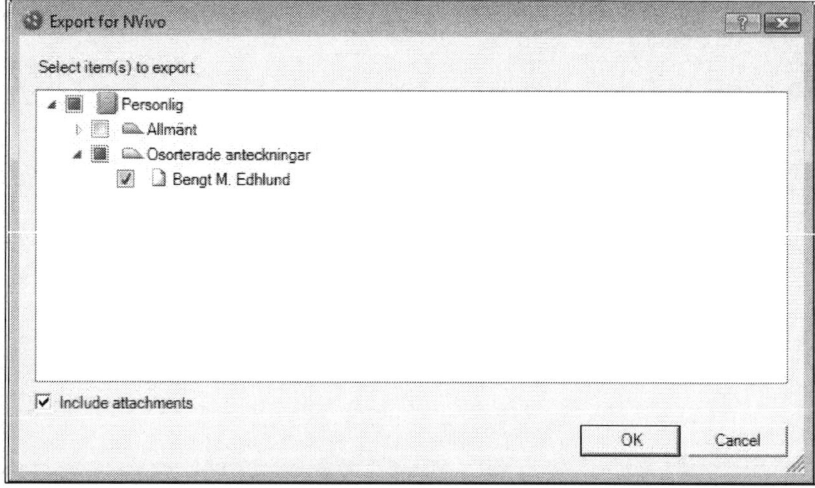

Importing OneNote Notes into NVivo

Once you save your .NVOZ file you can easily import its content into NVivo:

1 Go to **Import | Notes & Email → OneNote**.
Default folder is **Data\\Files** or its currently open subfolder.
Go to 4.

alternatively

1 Select the **Data\\Files** folder or its subfolder
2 Go to **Import | Notes & Email → OneNote**.
Go to 4.

alternatively

2 Click on any empty space in the List View.
3 Right-click and select **Import from → Import from OneNote...**

The **Import From OneNote** dialog box appears:

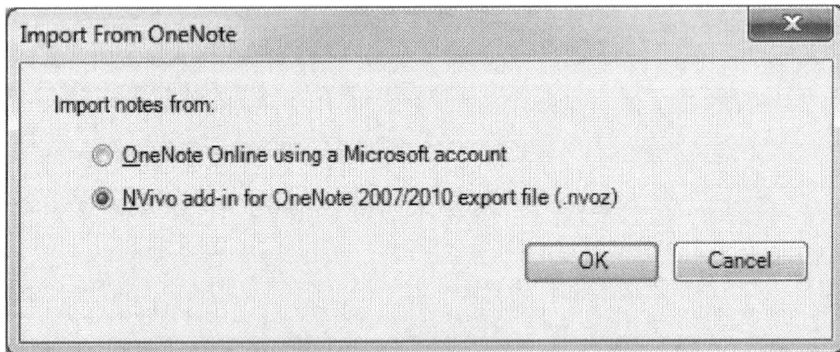

4 Select **NVivo add-in for OneNote**. Click **[OK]**. Then find and select the .NVOZ file you want to import.

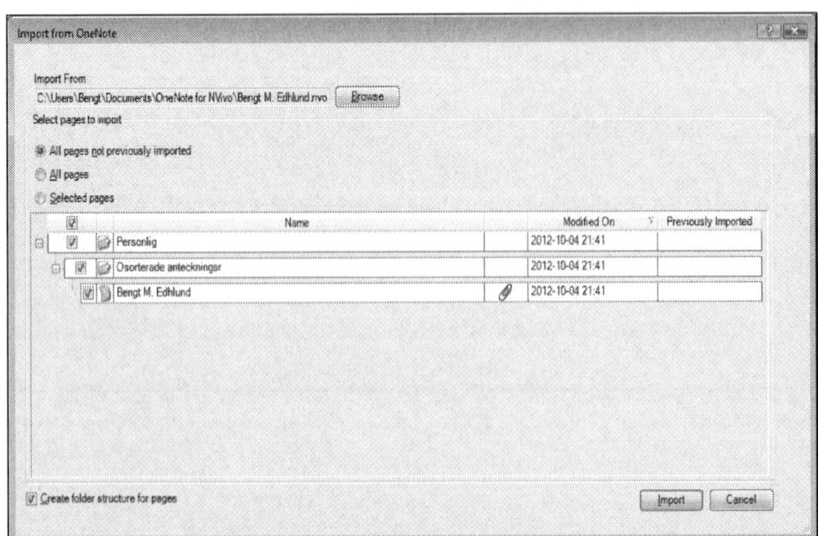

This example shows the import dialog when a notebook has been exported. The bottom of the dialog box contains a list of each individual note included in the .NVOZ file. NVivo will detect if there are notes in the . NVOZ that you have already imported, and so the default selection is to import *All pages not previously imported.* Alternatively, you can select import *All pages* or import *Selected pages.* Select the pages that you want to import.

5 Click [**Import**].

Importing from OneNote Online

Referring to point 5 above. Alternatively select **OneNote Online using a Microsoft account**. Then click [**OK**].

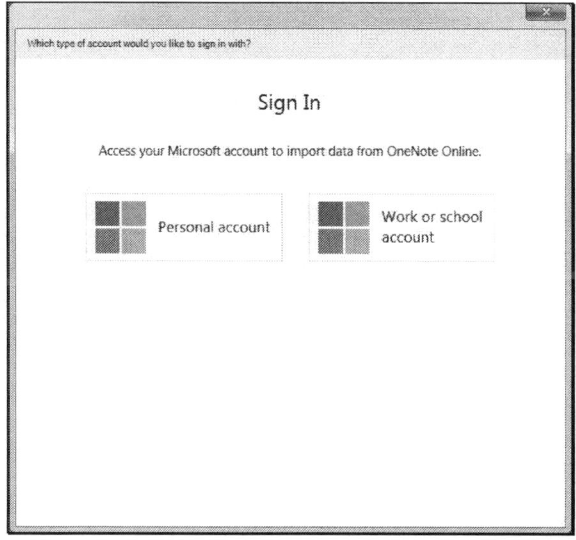

Choose to log in with a Personal account or Work or school account. Enter your user name and password, then sign into OneNote and authorize NVivo to access your notes.

Select the notebooks, sections or pages that you want to import. You can expand each notebook and section to select individual pages.

NOTE: If you want to import all of the pages that have not been previously imported, click **All pages not previously imported**.

Choose whether you want to import your pages as PDFs or documents.

OneNote Note Formats in NVivo

Not all OneNote data will be imported as internal sources, so it is a good idea to familiarize yourself with the following list of OneNote note types and their attendant locations in NVivo:

- OneNote text notes will become a document Source in the **Data\\Files** folder or its subfolder.
- OneNote notes with file attachments (e.g., PDFs, photos, images, audio files, or video files) will retain their file types.

Installing NVivo Addin for OneNote

1 Download NVivoAddIn.OneNote.exe from QSR's website.
2 Make sure that OneNote is not running.
3 Click **Run**.

Check whether NVivo AddIn for OneNote is Installed

For OneNote 2010:

1 Go to **File → Options → Add-Ins**
2 Check if Export for NVivo is on the list.

For OneNote 2007:

1 Go to **Tools → Options → Add-Ins**
2 Check if Export for NVivo is on the list.

23. FINDING AND SORTING PROJECT ITEMS

This chapter is about how to find Project Items. The finding tools in NVivo are *Find* and *Advanced Find*. Using Sets in this context will prove very productive. Another useful function for finding relations between items is *Group Queries*, which is dealt with on page 224. The results of these functions are lists of shortcuts to the found items.

The Folder Structure for Sets

The project folder structure for Sets are: Static Sets and Dynamic Sets. The default folders as shown in the Navigator are:

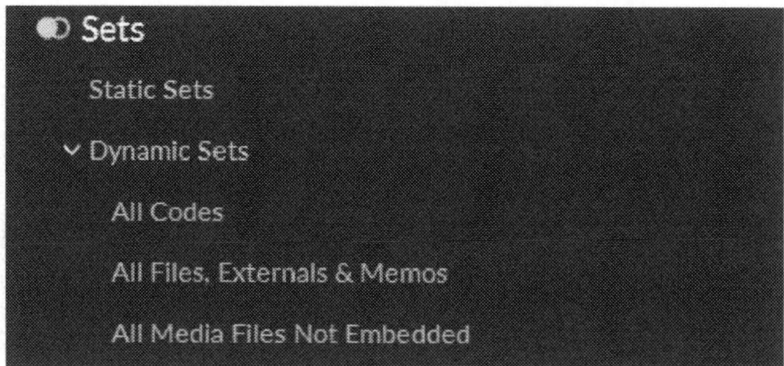

These folders and the names are not possible to delete, move, or rename. The folder names are depending on the user interface language setting, see page 39. However, the user can create items shown the Navigator as items in the folders **Sets\\Static Sets** and **Sets\\Dynamic Sets**.

Three Dynamic Sets (All Codes, All Files, and All Media Files Not Embedded) are defined as default and are kept automatically refreshed.

Creating a Static Set

Static Sets are created by the user and are stored in the folder **Sets\\Static Sets.** These are customized groups of shortcuts to various Project Items or groups of Project Items. A Set is considered a subset or collection of Project Items that allow you to access organized groups of items without moving or copying those items.

1 Go to **Create | Static Set → New Static Set...**
or go to **Sets\\Static Sets** in the Navigation View, right-click and select **New Static Set...**
or **[Ctrl]** + **[Shift]** + **[N]**.

The **New Static Set** dialog box appears:

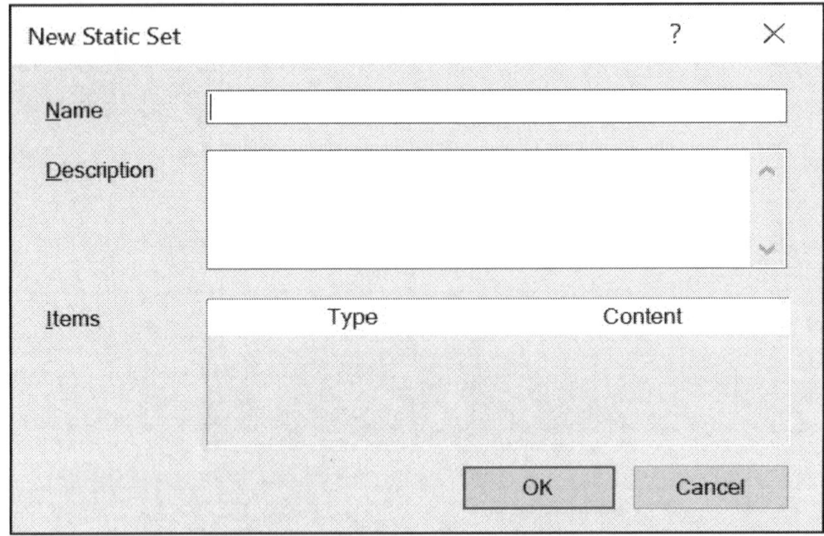

4 Type a name (compulsory) and a description (optional), then **[OK]**.

Next, you need to define the members of your Set:

1 Select the item or items that will form a set.
2 Go to **Create | Static Set → Add To Static Set...**
(or **Create | Static Set → Create as Static Set...** and the **New Static Set** dialog box appears)
or right-click any Project Item and select **Add To Static Set...**
(or right-click and select **Create As → Create as Static Set...** and the **New Static Set** dialog box appears)

The **Select Static Set** dialog box appears:

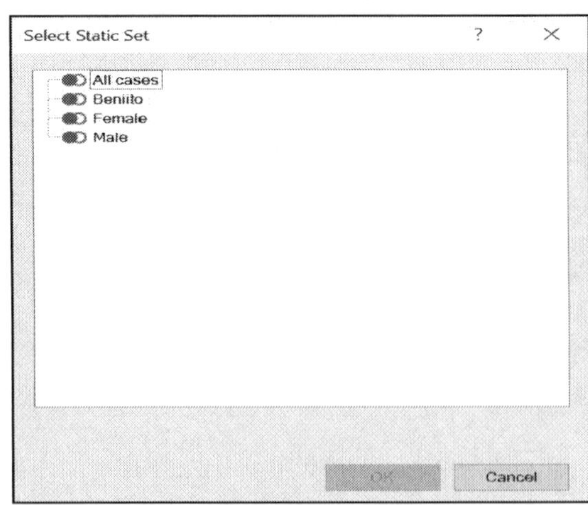

3 Select a set and confirm with **[OK]**.

You can also select items or shortcuts from any folder and paste them into a Static Set. When using **Find**, **Advanced Find**, or **Grouped Find** the result can easily be added to a Static Set.:

1 Select an item (shortcut) or items (shortcuts) that will form a new set.

2 Go to **Create | Static Set... → New Static Set...**

The **New Set** dialog box is shown.

3 Type a name of the new set.

4 Confirm with **[OK]**.

Editing Sets involves Copying, Cutting, Pasting, Sorting, Moving, Deleting Set members as with other project items.

> **Static Sets** are a powerful organizational tool in NVivo, but beginning and intermediate users are sometimes confused by their functionality. The main function of Sets is to allow users the flexibility of organizing project items into temporary or permanent groups.
>
> For example, we are involved in a project involving interview data, focus group data, writing samples, and social media data for a group of 20 undergraduate social science students. As a team, we could organize these data sources according to type of data source (e.g., an interview folder, a focus group folder, etc.) or we could organize these data sources according to student (e.g., a folder for Student 1, a folder for Student 2, etc.). While each method of organization has its merits, Sets allows us to organize project items according to type of data source AND create a Set organizing data sources according to student. As alternative methods of organizing text items present themselves, more and more sets can be generated.

Creating a Dynamic Set

The result of an **Advanced Find** execution can be saved as a Dynamic Set. In fact, this is the only way to create a Dynamic Set. From the Dynamic Set the Advanced Find can be modified and run again thereby refreshing the result.

Some default Dynamic Sets are available for all NVivo projects. Thes Dynamic Sets are kept automatically refreshed. See Folder Structure on page 307.

Find

The bar **Find** is always just above the List View heading. This bar can be hidden or unhidden with **Home | Workspace → Find** which is a toggling function. The easy function is used for finding names of documents (Files), Memos or Codes, not their contents.

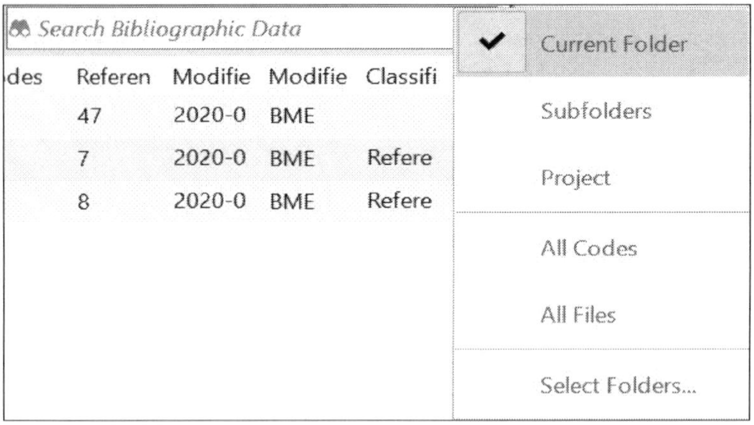

The result is a list of shortcuts in the List View. A shortcut is indicated by a small arrow in the bottom-right corner of the icon. The list cannot be saved but you can create a **Static Set** from selected items from the list (see page 307).

Advanced Find

Advanced Find gives increased specificity to any given search.

1. Go to **Explore | Advanced Find**
   or key command **[Ctrl]** + **[Shift]** + **[F]**.

The **Advanced Find** dialog box is shown.

The drop-down list **Look For** has the following options:

- Files, Externals & Memos
- Documents
- Audios
- Videos
- Pictures
- Datasets
- PDFs
- File Classifications
- Attributes
- Externals
- Static Sets
- Codes
- Codes & Cases
- Relationships
- Relationship Types
- Case Classifications
- Memos
- Framework Matrices
- Queries
- Query Results
- Coding Matrices
- Maps
- Formatted Reports
- Text Reports
- All

As an example of Advanced Find options, you can limit a text search to just the Description box of a certain type of Project Item.

The Intermediate Tab

The **Intermediate** and **Advanced** tabs are independent of each other.

Below is the **Intermediate** tab of the **Advanced Find** dialog box:

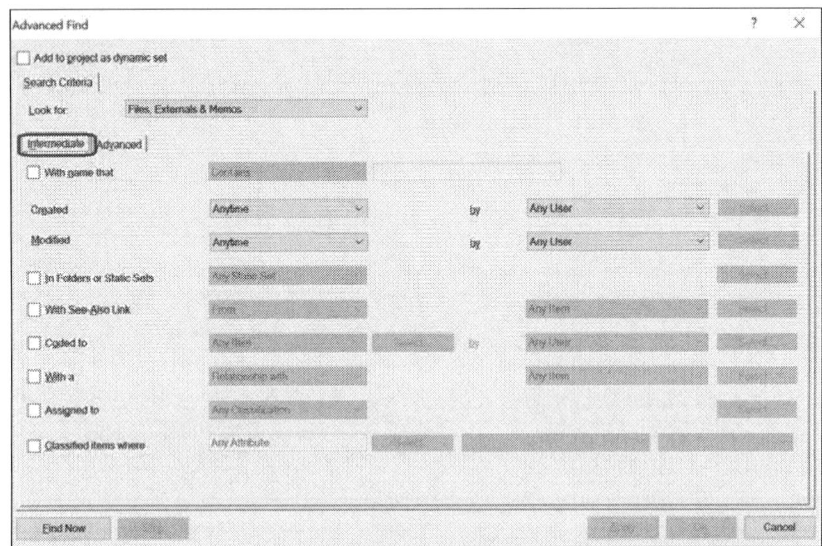

As soon as any option in the Intermediate tab has been chosen the corresponding [**Select...**] button is activated and opens the **Select Project Items** dialog box. The exact shape of this dialog box is determined by the selected option.

This function can be used to create a list with items matching certain criteria, like:

- Codes created *last week*
- Cases that are *Male*
- Memos with a 'See Also Link' from the Code *Adventure*
- Documents that are coded at the Code *Passionate*
- Codes that code the document *Volunteers Group 1*
- Sets containing *Codes*

The Advanced Tab

The **Advanced** tab offers other types of criteria:

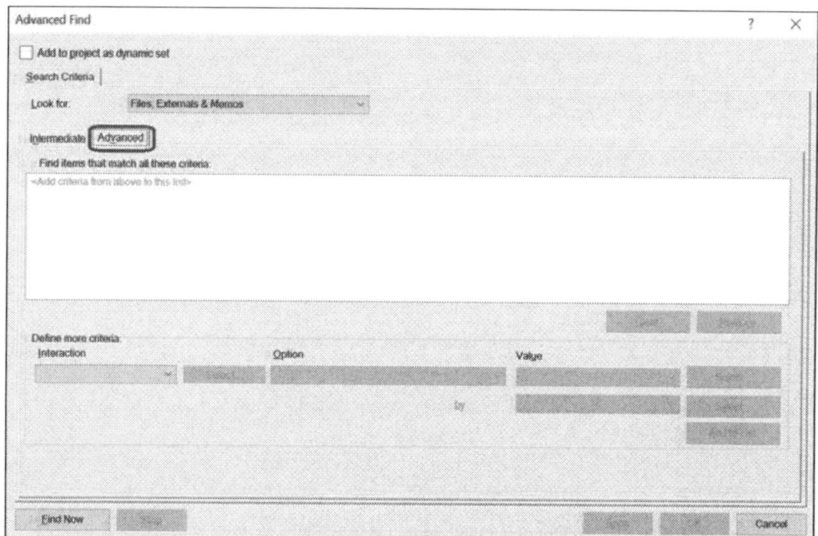

The **Interaction** drop-down list depends on the type of item that you have selected at **Look for**. For example, if *Documents* is selected the drop-down list *Define more criteria, Interaction* has the following options:

- Document
- Name
- Description
- Created
- Modified
- Size (MB)
- Attribute

> The contents of a Description can be searched with this tool, but not the contents in an Annotation.

1 Select *Codes* from the **Look for:** drop-down list. In the section *Define more criteria, Interaction* the drop-down list now has options specifically for Codes.
In this case, select *Attribute* and then:
Age Group / equals value / 30-39 and the dialog box looks like this:

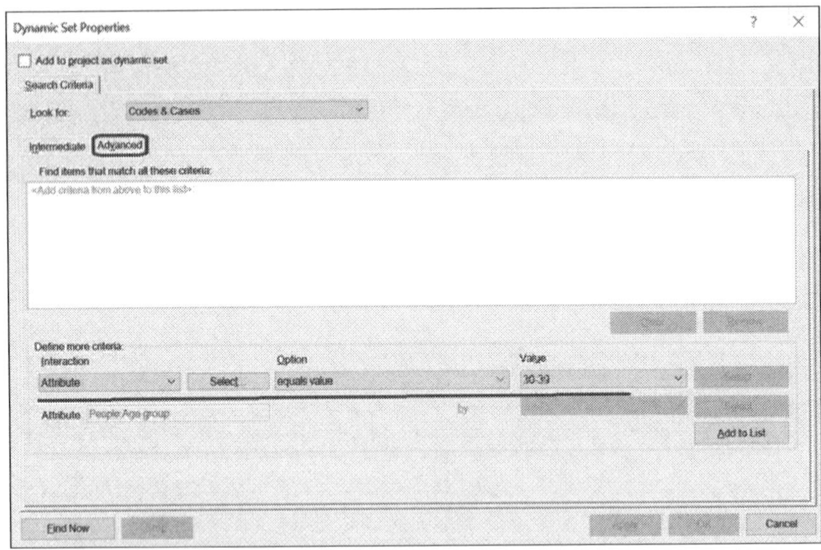

2 Click [**Add to List**] and the search criteria moves to the box **Find items that match all these criteria**.

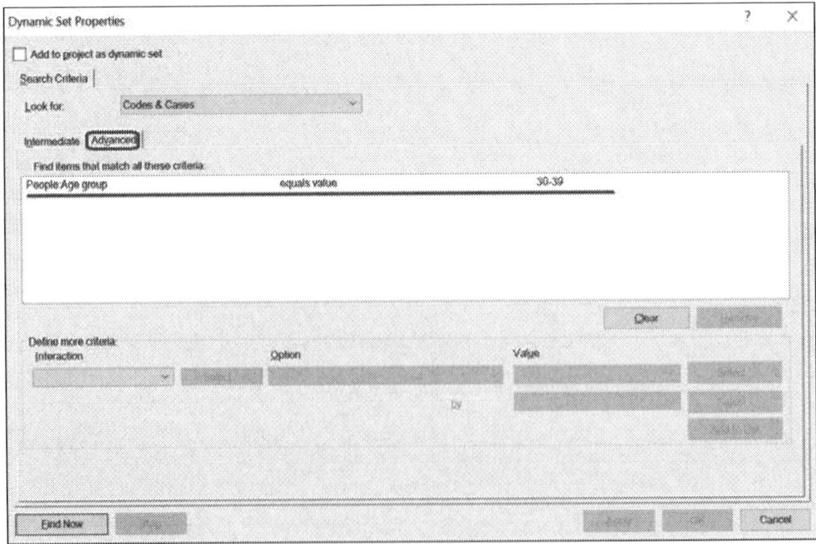

3 You can now add another criterion for example a limitation to women. Then again click [**Add to List**].

4 Finally, the search is done with [**Find Now**] and the result looks like this:

Find Results

Name	In Folder	Created on	Created by	Modified on	Modified by
Focus Group Members\Elaine	Cases	2018-08-30 17:0	BME	2018-08-31 13:08	BME
Focus Group Members\Marie	Cases	2018-08-30 17:0	BME	2018-08-31 13:08	BME
Focus Group Members\Roberta	Cases	2018-08-30 17:0	BME	2018-08-31 13:08	BME
Interviewees\Phoebe	Cases	2018-08-30 16:4	BME	2018-08-31 09:50	BME

The result is a list of shortcuts that match the search criteria. This list can be stored as a Dynamic Set provided that *Add to project as dynamic set* has been marked in the upper left corner of the **Advanced Find** dialog box and a name (compulsory) and a description (optional) of the New Dynamic Set has been given.

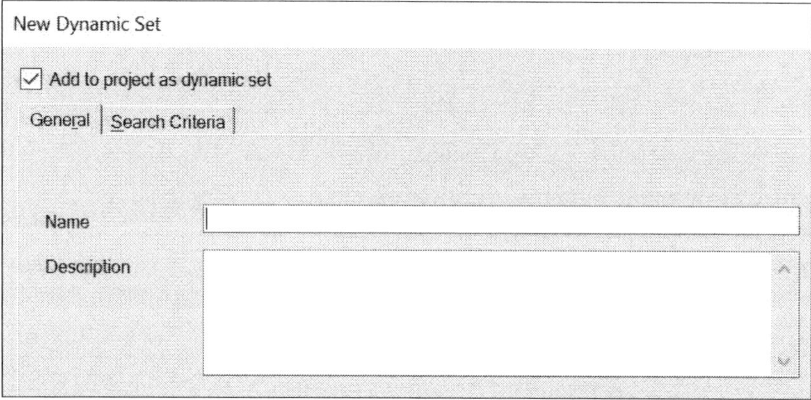

In case you need to recall or modify the Advanced Search, go to the the saved Dynamic Set, rightclick and select **Dynamic Set Properties...** or [**Ctrl**] + [**Shift**] +[**P**]. Then the **Advanced Find** dialog box appears now named **Dynamic Set Properties.**

You may modify the search criteria and run again but then the previous result will be replaced by the new result. The Dynamic set is revised accordingly.

In case you prefer to keep the previously saved Dynamic set, then we recommend that you use copy and paste and revise one of the sets.

It is also possible to create a new Static Set of your previous result.

Sorting Items

This section applies to all items that can be viewed in a list usually in the List View, but sometimes also in the Detail View. For example, when a Code is opened in view mode Summary, a list is shown in the Detail View.

1 Display a list of items in the List View.
2 Go to **Home | Workspace → Sort By → <select>**.

The options offered depend on of the type of items in the list. Codes, for example, can be arranged hierarchically, so for Codes there is a special sorting option, *Custom.*

1 Display a list with Codes in the List View.
2 Select the Code or Codes that you want to move. If you want to move more than one Code, they must be adjacent.
3 Go to **Home | Workspace → 'Sort by' → Move Up/ Move Down**
or right-click and select **Move Up/Move Down**
or **[Ctrl]** + **[Shift]** + **[U]**/**[Ctrl]** + **[Shift]** + **[D]**.
(this function does not exist for Dynamic Sets)

This sorting is automatically saved even if you temporarily change the sorting. You can always return to your Custom sorting:

1 Display a list of items in the List View.
2 Go to **Home | Workspace → 'Sort by' → Custom**.

This command is a toggling function. When you use the command again it sorts in the opposite order.

You can also use the column heads for sorting. Sorting by commands or sorting with column heads always adds a small triangle to the column head in question. Clicking again on this column head turns the sorting in the opposite order.

Codes

Search All Files, Externals & Mem

Name	Files	References	Created on	Created by
Respondent	1	1	2020-07-07 11:12	BME
Reasons for Volunteering	14	296	2018-08-31 16:18	BME
Satisfaction	11	120	2018-08-31 16:17	BME
Payments	13	39	2018-08-31 16:15	BME
Familly Values	13	68	2018-08-31 16:10	BME
Comptetence	13	69	2018-08-31 16:13	BME

24. COLLABORATING WITH NVIVO

As technology and interdisciplinarity facilitate more complex qualitative and mixed methods studies, teamwork has become increasingly important for researchers. The focus of this chapter focuses on how a team can operate using a single project file. The first half of this chapter explains some collaboration tools features in NVivo. The second half explains some general insights on collaborating with NVivo.

NVivo project files are not locked to a specific license, though they can be password-protected. This means that although NVivo projects are designed to be used by one person at a time, several users can, say, send a project file back and forth via a USB stick or even email.

Collaborating on the same NVivo project can be organized in a number of ways:

- Team members can use the same data but each individual creates his/her Codes and codes accordingly – perhaps importing to a master project later.
- Team members use different data but use a common Code structure.
- Team members use both the same data and a common Code structure.

One collaborative option we have used involves each team member using their own project file and then merging their discrete project files into a master file. In cases where individual team members plan to merge their analytic progress into a master project file, merging projects is described on page 59. Review the options of the **Import Project** dialog box to find out how it can suite your needs. If Codes with same names need to merge you can select Merge into existing item. Remember that Codes and other items must have the same name and must be located on the same level of the folder structure before they can be merged successfully. Further, the contents of the Source Items must be identical.

NVivo includes several useful tools for collaborative data analysis:

- View Coding Stripes by Selected Users.
- View Coding by Users in an open Code (using sub-stripes).
- *Coding Comparison Queries* for comparing two coders working with the same sources and Codes. This is an important option that improves a project's validity and quantifies inter-rate reliability.

Current User

An important concept for teamwork in NVivo is the **Current User**. In **File → Options** and the **Application Options** dialog box, the **General** tab identifies the current user. When a project is open you can change the current user. However, it is not possible to leave the Name and Initial boxes empty.

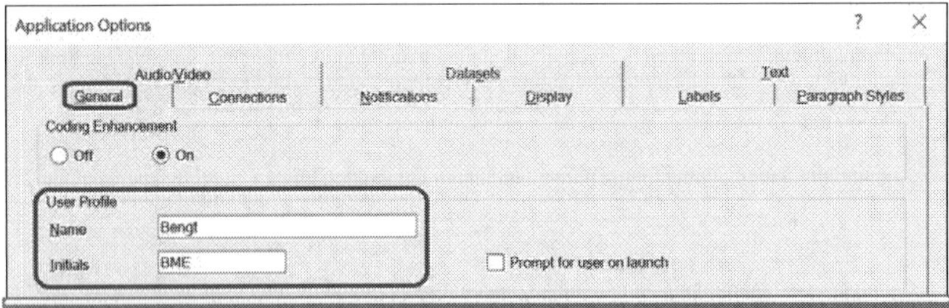

If you select the option *Prompt for user on launch* then the **NVivo Setup - User Profile** dialog box is prompted each time NVivo is started:

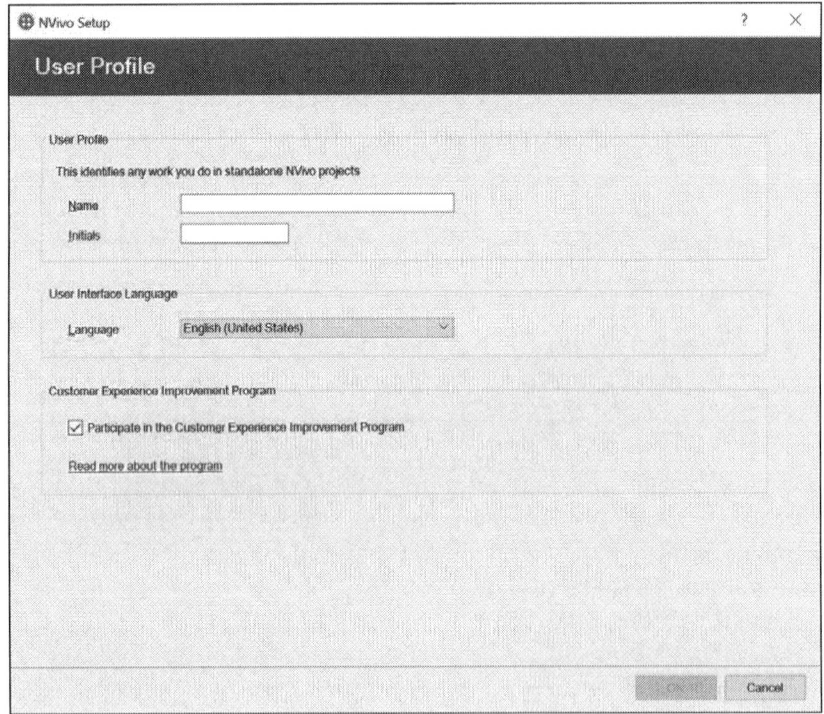

All users who have worked on the project are listed in **File → Info → Project Properties...** and in the **Project Properties** dialog box, under the **Users** tab:

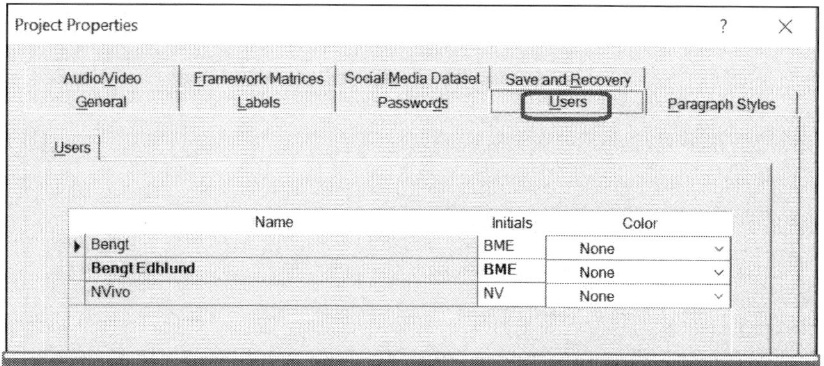

The current user is written in bold. The small triangle in the left column indicates the user who created the current project. In this box you cannot change the names but the initials. You can replace one user with another. Select a user and click **[Remove}**. NVivo will ask you who will replace the deleted user.

To the left in the status bar the current user is shown:

The initials are used so you can trace who created or modified each project item.

Viewing Coding Stripes

Coding stripes and sub-stripes can be used to display the coding that individual team-members have made (see page 193):

1 Open the Source Item (File) or Code you wish to review.
2 Go to **<Item Type> | Coding Stripes → *Show Coding Stripes' → Selected Items...**

The **Select Project Items** dialog box is shown. Codes that code the current item have names in **Bold**. When you select **Users** (and select individual users) one coding stripe per user is shown. When you point at one such stripe the names of the Codes at which each user has coded will show.

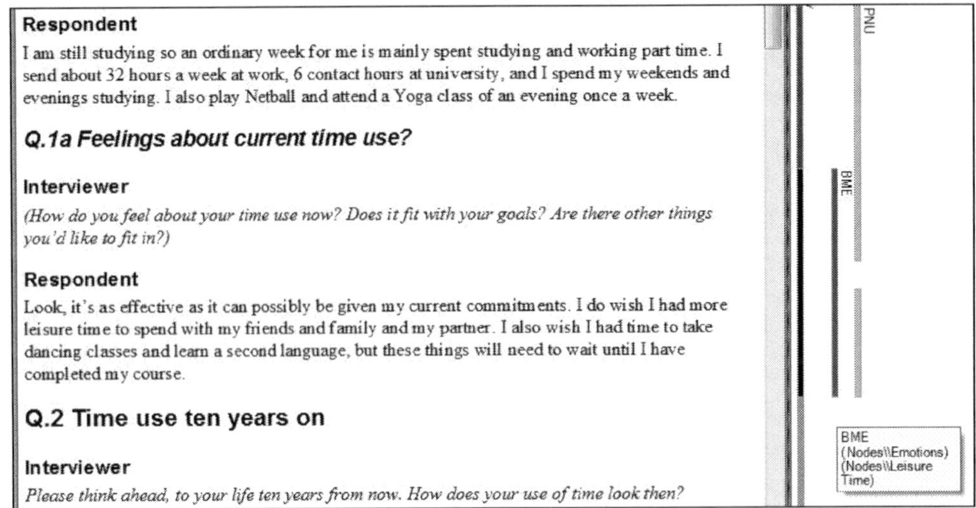
Respondent
I am still studying so an ordinary week for me is mainly spent studying and working part time. I send about 32 hours a week at work, 6 contact hours at university, and I spend my weekends and evenings studying. I also play Netball and attend a Yoga class of an evening once a week.
Q.1a Feelings about current time use?
Interviewer
(How do you feel about your time use now? Does it fit with your goals? Are there other things you'd like to fit in?)
Respondent
Look, it's as effective as it can possibly be given my current commitments. I do wish I had more leisure time to spend with my friends and family and my partner. I also wish I had time to take dancing classes and learn a second language, but these things will need to wait until I have completed my course.
Q.2 Time use ten years on
Interviewer
Please think ahead, to your life ten years from now. How does your use of time look then?
PNU
BME
BME
(Nodes\\Emotions)
(Nodes\\Leisure Time)

When you instead select **Codes** (and select some individual codes) one coding stripe per Code is shown. When you point at one such stripe the names of the users who has coded at those Codes will show. The sub-stripes are Users.

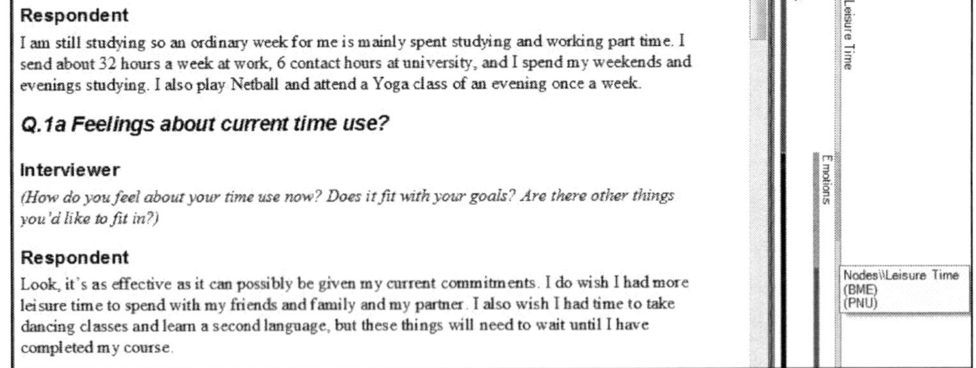
Respondent
I am still studying so an ordinary week for me is mainly spent studying and working part time. I send about 32 hours a week at work, 6 contact hours at university, and I spend my weekends and evenings studying. I also play Netball and attend a Yoga class of an evening once a week.
Q.1a Feelings about current time use?
Interviewer
(How do you feel about your time use now? Does it fit with your goals? Are there other things you'd like to fit in?)
Respondent
Look, it's as effective as it can possibly be given my current commitments. I do wish I had more leisure time to spend with my friends and family and my partner. I also wish I had time to take dancing classes and learn a second language, but these things will need to wait until I have completed my course.
Leisure Time
Emotions
Nodes\\Leisure Time
(BME)
(PNU)

You can also display sub-stripes at the same time as the normal coding stipes by pointing at a coding stripe, right-click and select **Show Sub-Stripes → More Sub-Stripes...** and select one or more sub-stripes that you want to show. Here are some sub-stripes for Users:

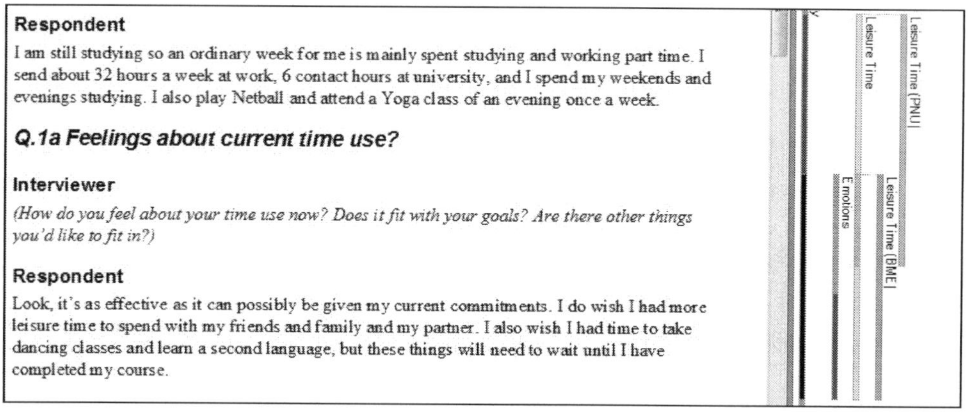

Respondent

I am still studying so an ordinary week for me is mainly spent studying and working part time. I send about 32 hours a week at work, 6 contact hours at university, and I spend my weekends and evenings studying. I also play Netball and attend a Yoga class of an evening once a week.

Q.1a Feelings about current time use?

Interviewer

(How do you feel about your time use now? Does it fit with your goals? Are there other things you'd like to fit in?)

Respondent

Look, it's as effective as it can possibly be given my current commitments. I do wish I had more leisure time to spend with my friends and family and my partner. I also wish I had time to take dancing classes and learn a second language, but these things will need to wait until I have completed my course.

Leisure Time (PNU)
Leisure Time
Leisure Time (BME)
Emotions

Assessing inter-rater reliability

For projects interested in studying inter-rater reliability it is possible to compare how two people or two groups of people have coded the same material. This is possible provided that the same source material and the same Code structure have been used:

1 Go to **Explore | Query → Coding Comparison**.
Default folder is **Queries\\Query Criteria** or its currently open subfolder.
Go to 4.

alternatively

1 Select the **Queries\\Query Criteria** folder or its subfolder.
2 Go to **Explore | Query → Coding Comparison**.
Go to 4.

alternatively

2 Click on any empty space in the List View.
3 Right-click and select **New Query → Coding Comparison**.

The **Coding Comparison Query** dialog box appears:

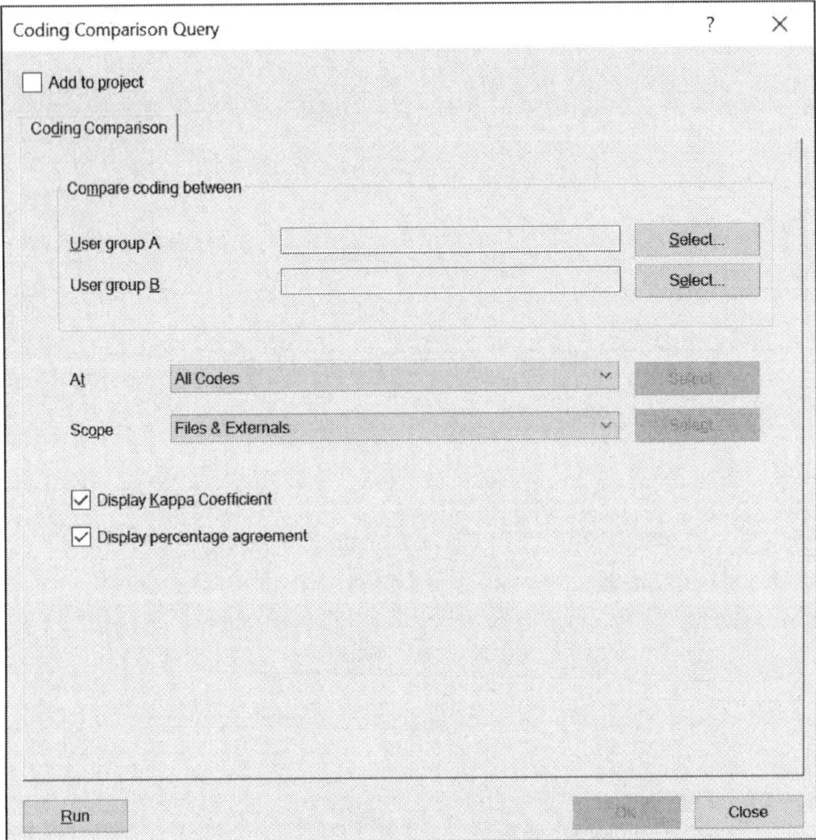

4 Define User group A and B with the **[Select...]** buttons which give access to all users that have been working in the project.
5 The **At** drop-down list determines the Code or Codes that will be compared.
6 The **Scope** drop-down list determines the Source Item or items that will be compared.
7 Select at least one of the options *Display Kappa Coefficient* or *Display percentage agreement*.
8 You can save the query by checking *Add To Project*.
9 Run the query with **[Run]**.

The result can look like this:

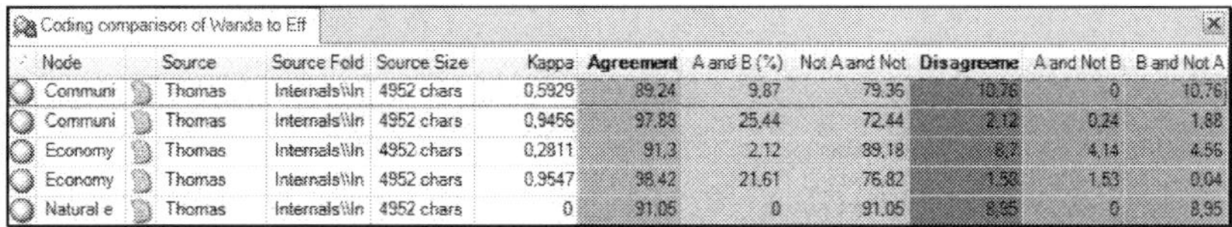

Coding comparison of Wanda to Eff

Node	Source	Source Fold	Source Size	Kappa	Agreement	A and B (%)	Not A and Not	Disagreeme	A and Not B	B and Not A
Communi	Thomas	Internals\\In	4952 chars	0,5929	89,24	9,87	79,36	10,76	0	10,76
Communi	Thomas	Internals\\In	4952 chars	0,9456	97,88	25,44	72,44	2,12	0,24	1,88
Economy	Thomas	Internals\\In	4952 chars	0,2811	91,3	2,12	89,18	8,7	4,14	4,56
Economy	Thomas	Internals\\In	4952 chars	0,9547	98,42	21,61	76,82	1,58	1,53	0,04
Natural e	Thomas	Internals\\In	4952 chars	0	91,05	0	91,05	8,95	0	8,95

The percentage agreement columns indicate the following values:

- **Agreement Column** = sum of columns **A and B** and **Not A and Not B.**
- **A and B** = the percentage of data item content coded to the selected Code by both Project User Group A and Project User Group B.
- **Not A and Not B** = the percentage of data item content coded by neither Project User Group A and Project User Group B.
- Disagreement Column = sums of columns A and Not B and B and Not A.
- **A and Not B** = the percentage of data item content coded by Project User Group A and not coded by Project User Group B.
- **B and Not A** = the percentage of data item content coded by Project User Group B and not coded by Project User Group A.

From each row of the result from a Coding Comparison Query any *Code* can be analyzed like this:

1 Select a row from the list of results.
2 Go to **Home | Item → 'Open' → Open Code...**
 or right-click and select **Open Code...**
 or **[Ctrl]** + **[Shift]** + **[O]**.

Any Code that is opened from such list is showing the coding stripes and sub-stripes that belong to the users who are compared.

From each row of the result from a Coding Comparison Query any *Source Item* can be analyzed like this:

1 Select a row from the list of results.
2 Go to **Home | Item → 'Open' → Open <Item Type>**.
or right-click and select **Open <Item Type>**
or **[Ctrl]** + **[Shift]** + **[O]**
or double-click on the row.

Any Source Item that is opened from such a list shows the coding stripes and sub-stripes that belong to the users who are compared:

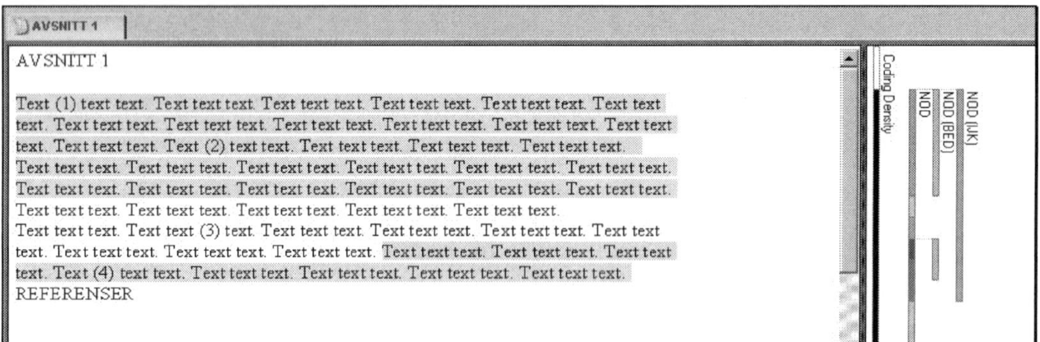

Coding stripes can always display the coding made by an individual user. This is made by pointing at a certain coding stripe, right-clicking and selecting **Show Sub-Stripes** and then selecting one or several users. Hiding sub-stripes is made using **Hide Sub-Stripes**.

Maps and Reports

During team project meetings, mapping can be illustrative and useful. Any Code structure can easily be made understandable using NVivo Maps (see the next chapter).

Reports are created by going to **Share | New <select> Report**. These reports can be used to study Codes and coding made by the different team-members, see Chapter 28, Reports.

Tips for Teamwork

Based on our years of experience working with hundreds of qualitative researchers using NVivo, we offer our colleagues the following tips for collaborating with NVivo:

- Appoint **an NVivo coordinator** for the research project.
- Set up **file name protocols**, read-only, storage locations, backup locations, file distribution and archiving.
- Set up **rules for audio and video files** like file types and file distribution. For example, should you use embedded items or external files?
- Set up a **Coding strategy**. Such a strategy can be communicated in a number of ways. It is easy to make a Code template in the form of a project without Source Items. Each Code should have 'instructions' written in the Code's Description field (max 512 characters) or in the form of a linked Memo, which is easier to write, read, print and code. The Code template can be distributed to team-members, saved with a new name and developed into a project in its own right. Importantly, the Code template's structure must not be modified by users. When new ideas are evolved, users should instead create new Codes in addition to the Code template and create Memo Links.
- Determine how **Case Classifications** and **File Classifications** will be applied. Such Codes can be interviewees or other research items like places, professions, products, organizations, phenomena. In some situations, it is useful to work with different classifications.
- Set up **rules for the master project** including protocols for merging and updating. Define a new project with a new name that clearly indicates that it is a merged project. Possibly a new set of user names will be defined for this purpose. Import one partial project at a time with **Import Project** and the option 'Merge into existing item'. Items with same name and same location will be merged.
- Hold periodic **team meetings** for the project. Such meetings should compare and analyze data (as described in this chapter), summarize discussions, and make decisions. Distribute minutes from each meeting.
- Assuming that the work has come to a stage where different members have submitted contributions to the project, make sure that the team has the standardized **usernames** when they work with their respective parts.

Continuing to Work on a Merged Project

After exploring a merged project you have two options to proceed:

- Each user continues with the original individual projects and at a certain point of time you make a completely new merger – perhaps archiving the original merger.
- Each user continues to work on the merged project and archives the original individual portions.

We recommend continuing with the first option up to a certain point and then, if the team agrees, deciding to focus on the merged project later.

Using NVivo with Dropbox, OneDrive, or Google Drive

Some researchers we have worked with use cloud-based file sharing services like Dropbox, OneDrive and Google Drive as a working solution for collaborating on an NVivo Project. These services allow changes to the NVivo project file to be made across several computers using the 'cloud'. We recommend you turn off the live syncing features of these programs while you are running NVivo. We have been contacted by a number of colleagues and clients who have lost data while simultaneously using NVivo and syncing its attendant (.NVP) file. Again, cloud-based utilities can be useful for team collaboration, but taking the proper precautions can avoid costly loss of analysis time due to software crashes.

When you need to access a project file stored on any cloud service either copy the file to your local drive or create a new project and import the project file. Never open a project file from a USB memory or any cloud service.

NVivo Collaboration Cloud

Collaboration Cloud is an NVivo add-on module designed to allow teams located at different sites to collaborate. It allows you to upload projects to the cloud to share. Collaborators download the projects, work on them, upload their modified copies, then you can download these and merge them into the original version.

Collaboration Cloud is a yearly subscription service, purchased from the myNVivo-portal. The basic pack allows five people to collaborate, and you can buy further seats singly to add to this. Enterprise organizations should contact QSR Sales.

Collaboration Cloud is compatible with both NVivo for Windows and NVivo for Mac, but it is not possible to work cross-platform on a project.

Go to **Modules | Collaboration Cloud**

A Note on NVivo Collaboration Server

NVivo manufacturer QSR International has developed a collaborative software solution called NVivo Collaboration Server (earlier named NVivo for Teams). Projects that are stored in NVivo Collaboration Server can be considerably larger, up to 100 GB or more provided storage space is available. NVivo Collaboration Server allows multiple users to work on the same project from different computers simultaneously. While useful, in our experience the logistical challenges associated with working on a server have kept our colleagues and clients from using this tool. While we support NVivo Collaboration Server, it is beyond the purposes of this book to describe it. Feel free to follow contact us directly if you and your team have any interest in NVivo Collaboration Server.

Presently all versions of NVivo 10 and later for Windows can be connected to NVivo Collaboration Server as user or client software but NVivo for Mac cannot.

25. MAPS

The Folder Structure for Maps

The project folder structure for Visualization is: Maps. The default folder as shown in the Navigator is:

This folder and the name is not possible to delete, move, or rename. The folder name is depending on the user interface language setting, see page 39. However, the user can create subfolders to the default folder **Visualizations\\Maps**.

Maps are useful tools when a project is developing or when a project is ready to begin reporting findings. Maps present ideas and theories visually. In a research team, maps are also useful for team meetings. NVivo offers three types of maps, Mind Maps, Project Maps, and Concept Maps.

Creating a New Mind Map

A Mind Map reflects what you think about a single topic and is usually created quickly or spontaneously.

At the beginning of your project you might use a mind map to explore your expectations or initial theories. Later on, mind maps can help to confirm the structure of your Codes.

1 Go to **Explore | Maps → Mind Map**.
Default folder is **Visualizations\\Maps** or its currently open subfolder.
Go to 4.

alternatively

1 Select the **Visualizations\\Maps** folder or its subfolder.
2 Go to **Explore | Maps → Mind Map**.
Go to 4.

alternatively

2 Click on an empty space in the List View.
3 Right-click and select **New Mind Map...**

The **New Mind Map** dialog box appears:

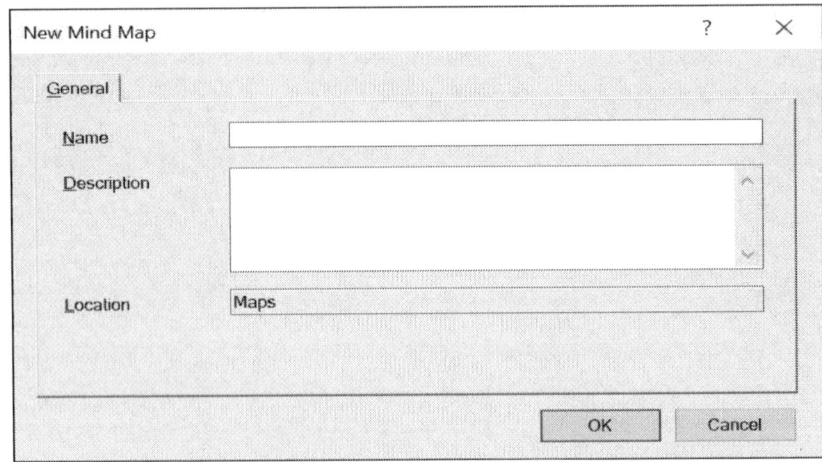

4 Type a name (compulsory) and a description (optional), then **[OK]**.

A new window appears in the Detail View with the Main Idea and it is a good idea to undock with **Home | Workspace → Undock** or click Undock on the Detail View top panel to give you more space on the screen:

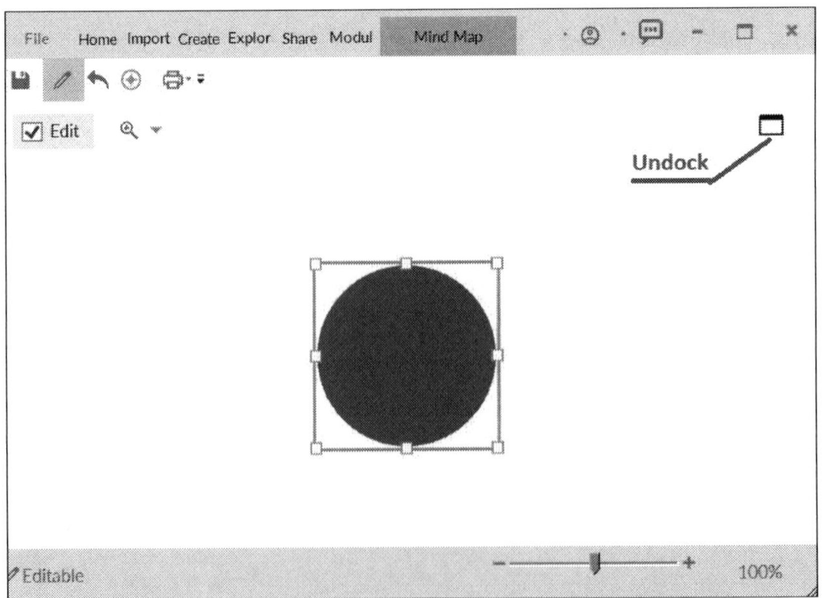

A new context dependent Ribbon menu, **Mind Map**, has now opened and the new Mind Map with the new Main Idea is shown.

5 Select the Main Idea,
go to **Mind Map | Sibling Idea**
or right-click and select **Insert Sibling Idea**
or **[Enter]**.

This image shows one added Sibling Idea:

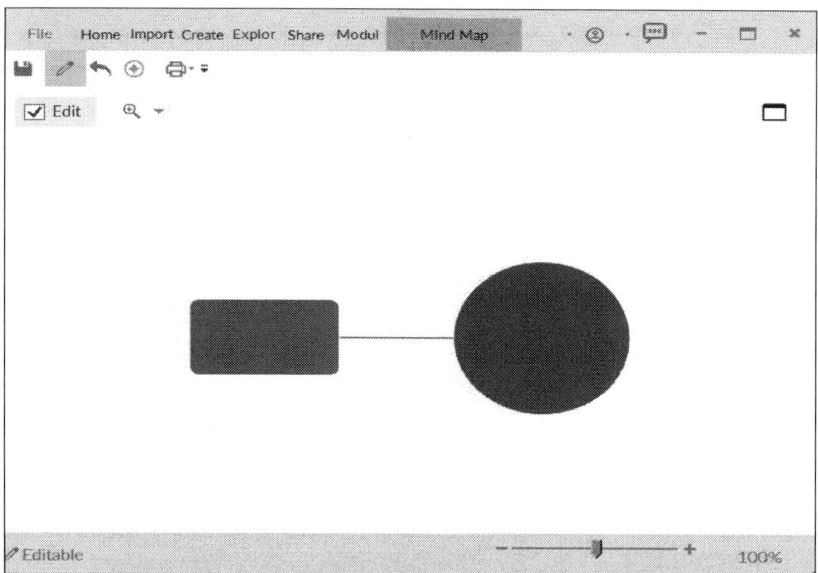

6 Select the new sibling idea,
go to **Mind Map | Child Idea**
or right-click and select **Insert Child Idea**
or **[Ins]**.

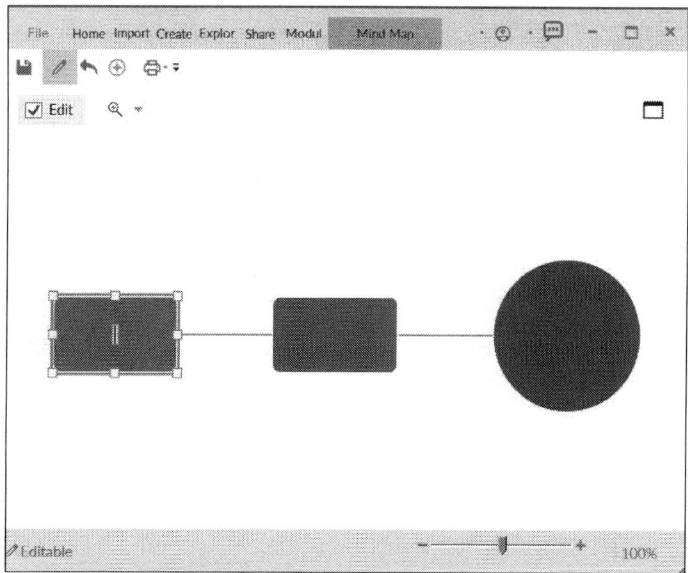

You can insert text in the symbols by selecting, right-click and select **Edit Label** or **[F2]**. Changing fonts, font attribute, color and size you need to select text and to go to **Mind Map | 'Format' → <select>**:

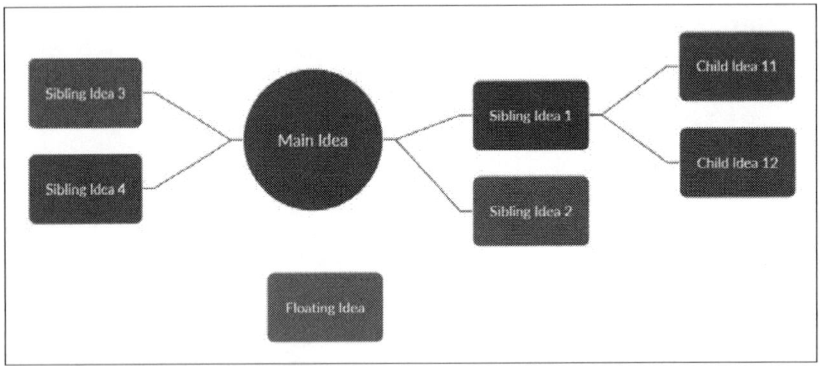

A Floating Idea is inserted by going to **Mind Map | Floating Idea** or right-click and select **Insert Floating Idea**.

Ideas can also be moved around in the map by using normal **Cut** (or **Copy**) and **Paste** commands.

If you want to create Codes based on your Mind Map you need to go to **Mind Map | Create as Codes or Cases** or right-click and select **Create as Codes or Cases**,

Now you select the folder or the Code or Case which will be the location for the new Codes or Cases based on your current Mind Map. Confirm with **[OK]**.

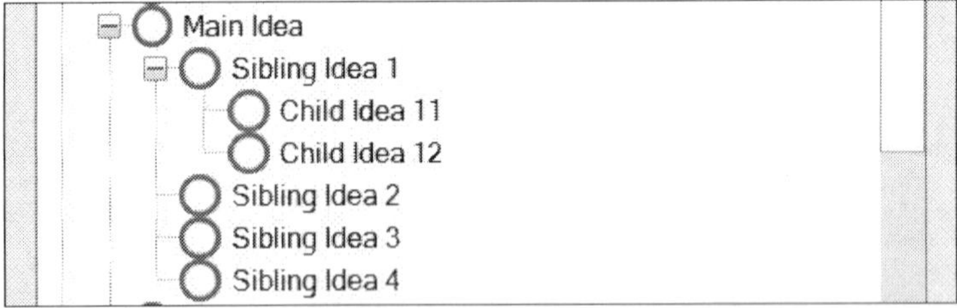

We have chosen to place the new Code tree directly under **Coding\\Codes**.

Layout

You can modify the layout of a map manually by moving any item with the mouse or drag in a corner of a selection to change the size or the proportions between height and width. The connectors between items will adopt as were they elastic.

There are a few layout templates available in NVivo and they can be applied by going to **Mind Map | Layout** or by right-clicking and select **Layout** and the options are: *Mind Map*, *Top Down* or *Left Right*.

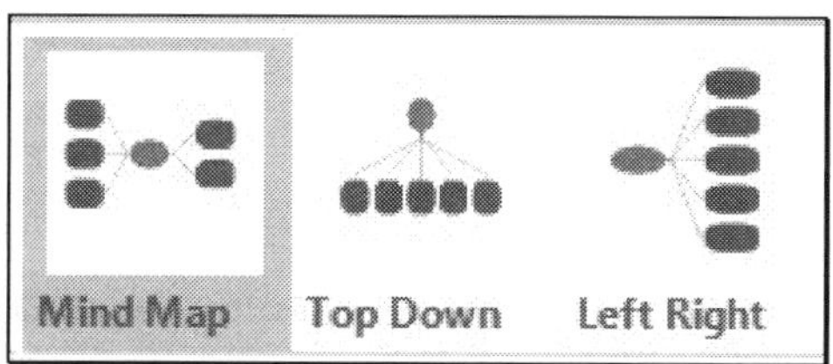

You can also make the items equal in size according to some alternatives from **Mind Map | Resize** after you have selected the items to be resized:

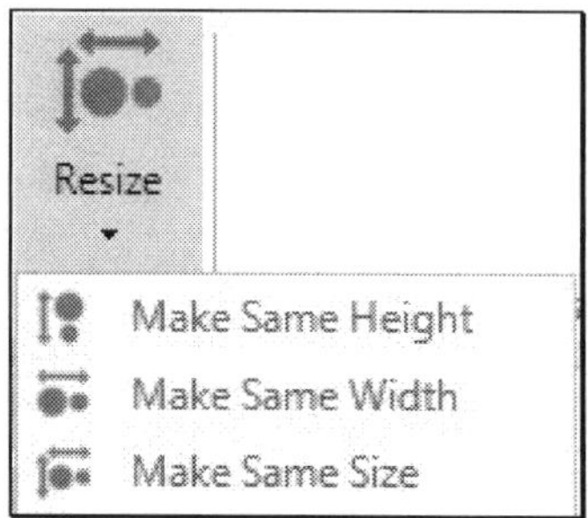

The first selected item becomes the model for the then selected items.

More Formatting Tools

There are several tools for formatting shapes under **Mind Map | Fill, Border Color**, and **Border Width**. Text settings like Fonts, Font Size, and text attributes are available in the **Mind Map** ribbon.

Exporting Mind Maps

Open a Map, go to **Share | Export → Export** or right-click and select **Export → Export Map...** or **[Ctrl]** + **[Shift]** + **[E]**.

Maps can be exported in the following file types: .JPG, .BMP, .GIF, TIF, or .PNG.

You can also copy the whole map or selected items and then go to **Home | Clipboard → Copy** or **[Ctrl]** + **[C]**.

Creating a New Project Map

A Project Map is a way of visually exploring or presenting the data in your project. Project maps are made of shapes that represent the different items in your project and connectors which show links between them.

1 Go to **Explore | Maps → Project Map**.
Default folder is **Visualizations\\Maps** or its currently open subfolder.
Go to 4.

alternatively

1 Select the **Visualizations\\Maps** folder or its subfolder.

2 Go to **Explore | Maps → Project Map**.
Go to 4.

alternatively

2 Click on an empty space in the List View.
3 Right-click and select **New Project Map...**

The **New Project Map** dialog box appears:

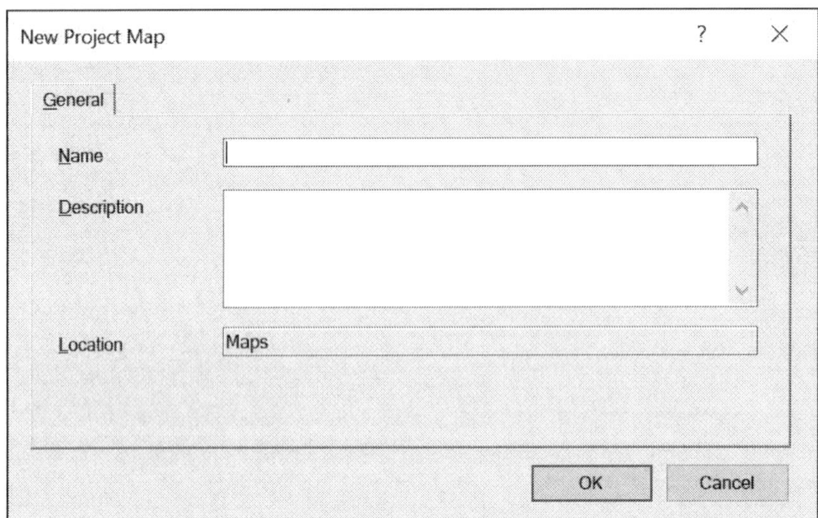

4 Type a name (compulsory) and a description (optional), then **[OK]**.

A new window appears in the Detail View and it is a good idea to undock with **Home | Workspace → Undock** or click Undock on the Detail View top panel to give you more space on the screen:

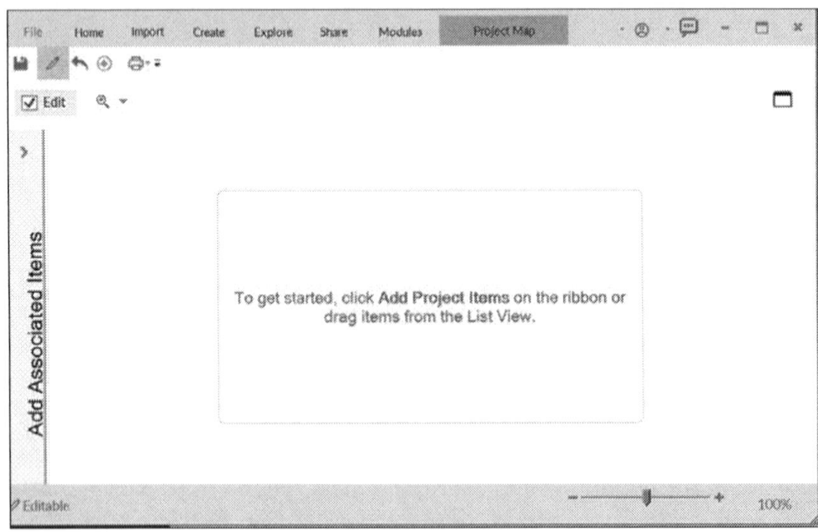

A new context dependent Ribbon menu, **Project Map**, has now opened.

5 Enter **Edit** mode,
go to **Project Map | Add Project Items**
or right-click and select **Add Project Items...**

The **Select Project Items** dialog box appears:

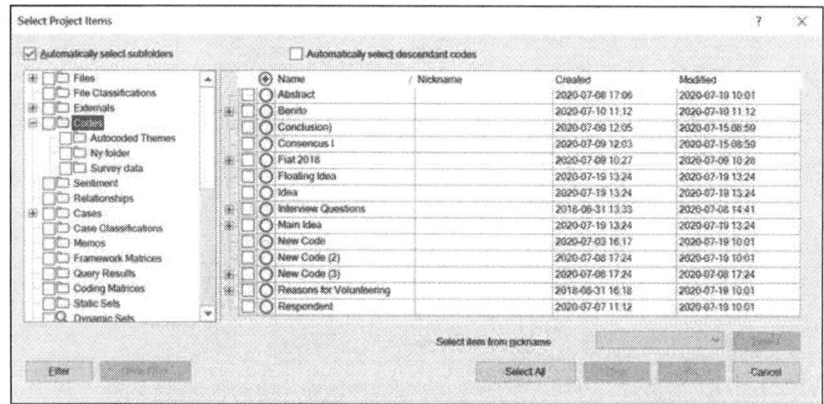

6 Select the **Coding\\Codes** folder and the Code *Family Values*,
then **[OK]**.

Select the item or items now showing and go to **Project Map | Show Associated Items**. Then the left-hand panel Add Associated Items opens in the Detail View.

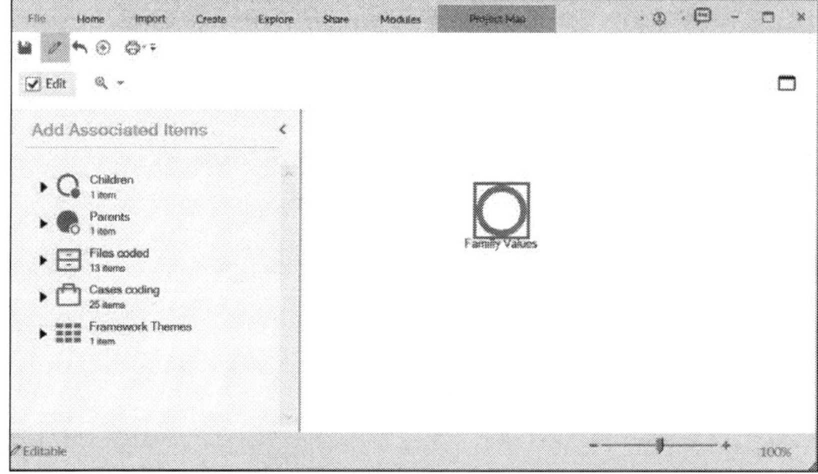

7 Choose some project items (Files coded) in the Add Associated Items panel and drag them to the Project Map:

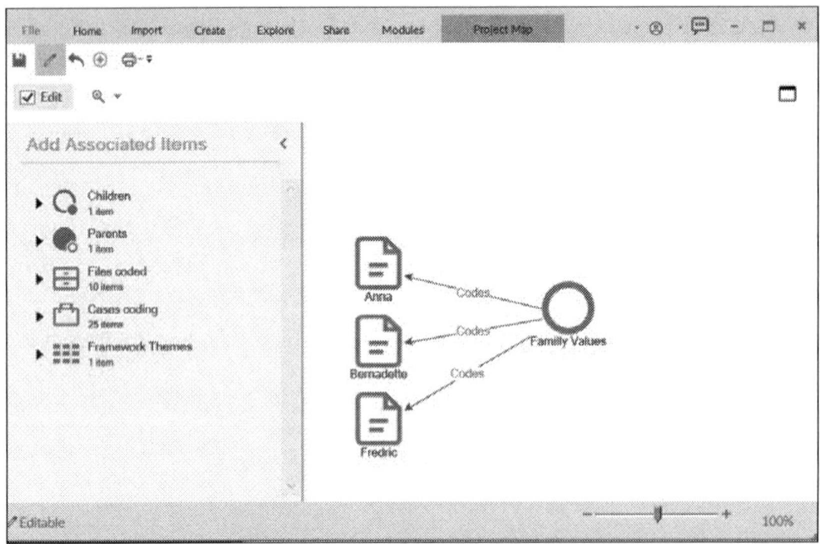

Connections between Items

By default, connections are not shown between items. You can, however, decide which type of connectors you want to hide or show by going to **Project Map | Connectors,** presenting the following options:

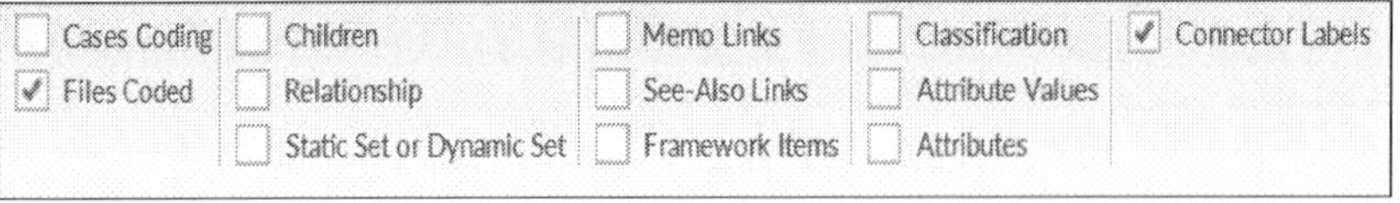

Layout

You can modify the layout of a map manually by moving any item with the mouse. The connectors between items will adopt as were they elastic.

There are a few layout templates available in NVivo and they can be applied by going to **Project Map | Layout** or by right-clicking and select **Layout** and the options are: *Layered Directed Graph, Hierarchical, Circular* or *Directed*:

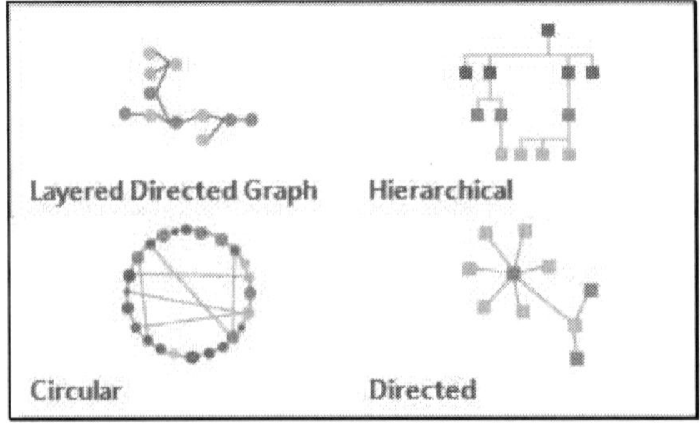

You can also align the items by going to **Project Map | Align** offering the following options:

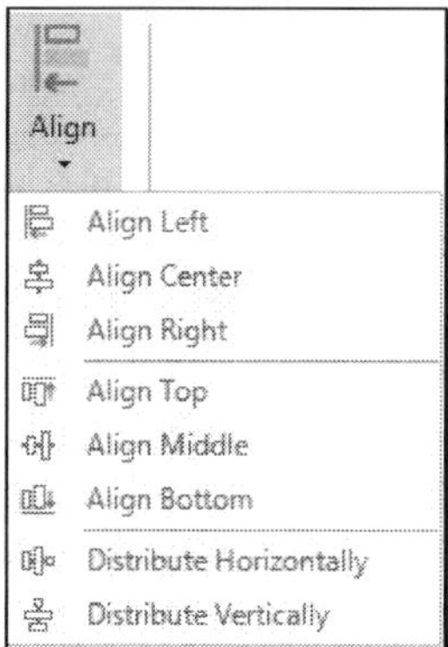

The first item you select is the reference for the items then being selected.

Exporting Project Maps

Open a Map, go to **Share | Export → Export** or right-click and select **Export → Export Map...** or **[Ctrl]** + **[Shift]** + **[E]**.

Maps can be exported in the following file types: .JPG, .BMP, .GIF, TIF, or .PNG.

You can also copy the whole map or selected items and then go to **Home | Clipboard → Copy** or **[Ctrl]** + **[C]**.

Creating a New Concept Map

A Concept Map is a free-form visualization made up of different shapes and connectors. Shapes represent concepts (ideas, people, or data). The connectors between the shapes articulate links such as *this causes...*, *this requires...* or *this contributes to...*

1 Go to **Explore | Maps → Concept Map**.
  Default folder is **Visualizations\\Maps** or its currently open subfolder.
  Go to 4.

alternatively

1 Select the **Visualizations \\Maps** folder or its subfolder.
2 Go to **Explore | Maps → Concept Map**.
  Go to 4.

alternatively

2 Click on an empty space in the List View.
3 Right-click and select **New Concept Map...**

The **New Concept Map** dialog box appears:

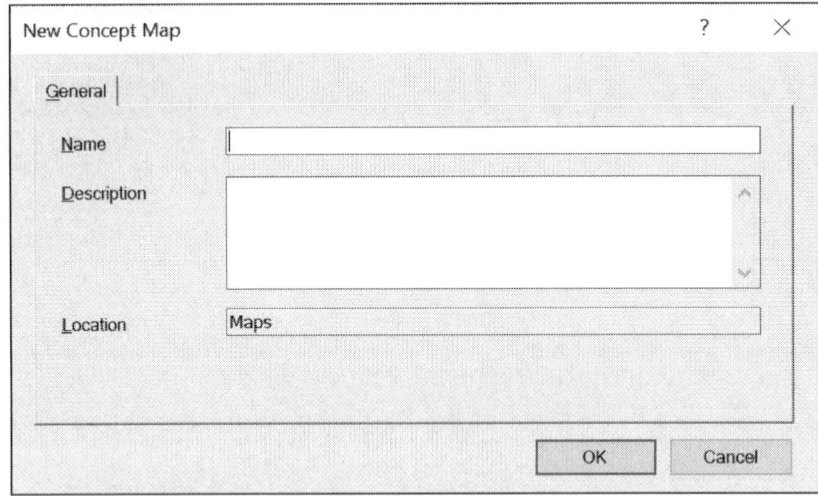

4 Type a name (compulsory) and a description (optional), then **[OK]**.

A new window appears in the Detail View and it is a good idea to undock with **Home | Workspace → Undock** or click Undock on the Detail View top panel to give you more space on the screen:

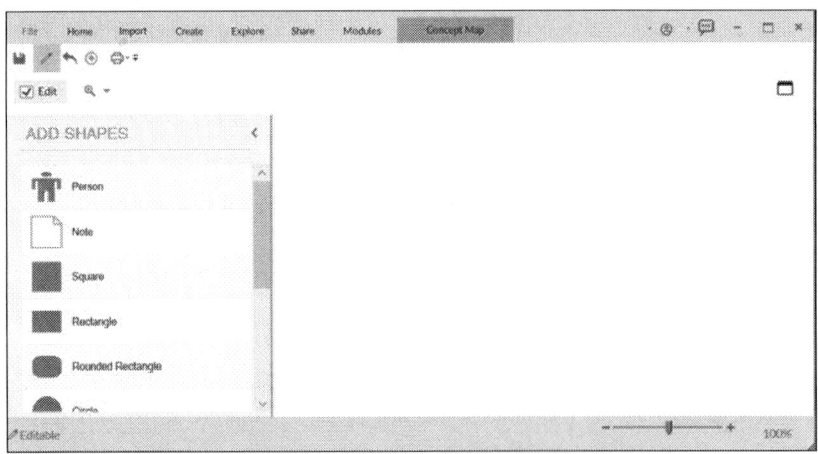

A new context dependent Ribbon menu, **Concept Map**, has now opened.

To insert shapes you drag them from the **Add Shapes** panel to the Concept Map or you right-click and select **Add Shapes**.

You can also insert project items by:

5 Go to **Concept Map | Add Project Items**
or right-click and select **Add Project Items...**

The **Select Project Items** dialog box appears:

Select item or items to be inserted in your Concept Map. Finish with **[OK]**.

Connectors

First you need to select the proper type of pointer by going to **Concept Maps | Connector** and the pointer type is changed. Then you select *the from* item and drag the pointer to *the to* item. Then the map can look like this:

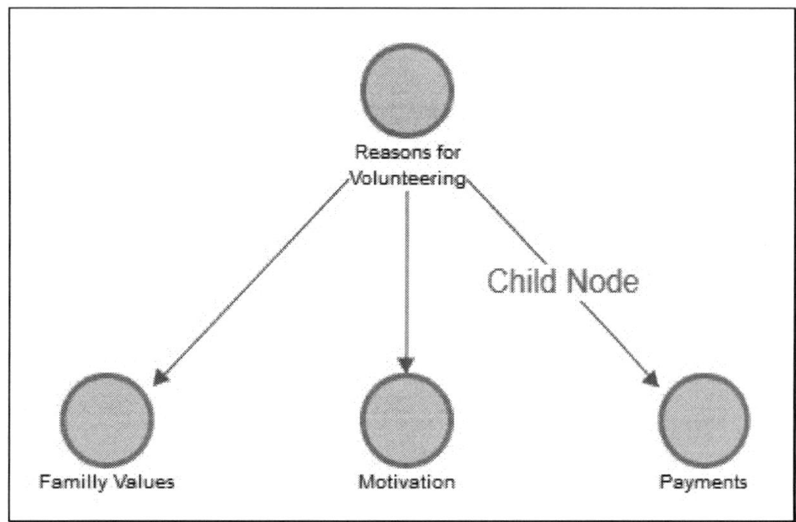

Concept Maps are unique as you may select a region with the pointer and create a rectangular area and all items within this area are thus selected.

The default type of connector is an arrow. This can be modified by selecting a connector and go to **Concept Map | Change Connector** and you will find the following options: *One Way*, *Symmetrical* and *Associative*.

You can insert text in Shapes and Connectors by selecting, right-click and select **Edit Label** or [**F2**]. Changing fonts, font attribute, color and size you need to select text and to go to **Concept Map | Format Text**.

Layout

You can modify the layout of a map manually by moving any item with the mouse or drag in a corner of a selection to change the size or the proportions between height and width. The connectors between items will adopt as were they elastic.

You can also align the items by going to **Concept Map | Align** offering the following options:

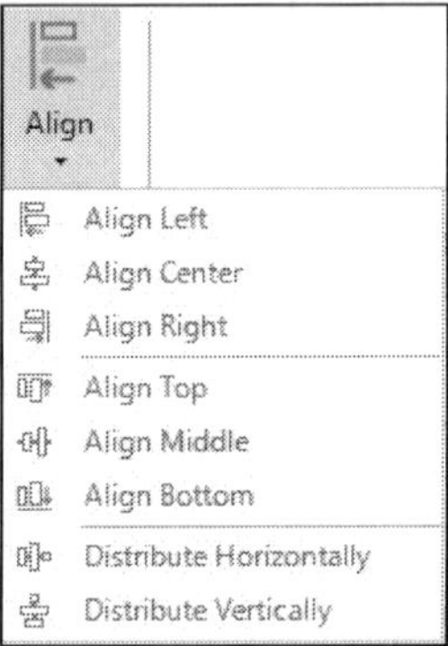

The first selected item will be reference for the items then selected.

You can also make items equally sized by going to **Concept Map | Resize** offering the following options:

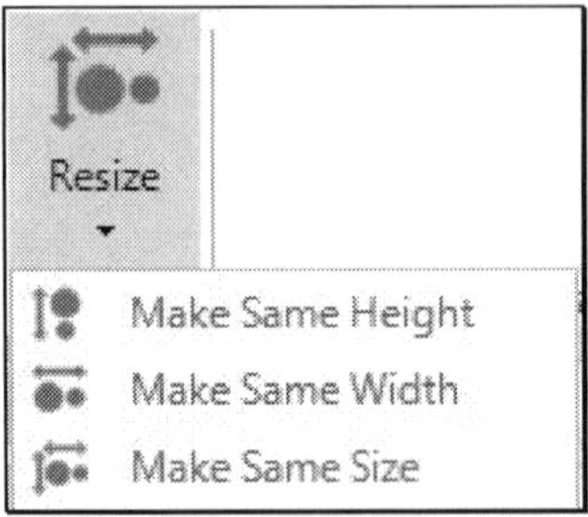

The item first selected is the size reference for the then selected items.

Deleting Graphical Items

1 Select one or more graphical items.
2 Right-click and select **Delete** or the [**Del**] key.

Exporting Concept Maps

Open a Map, go to **Share | Export → Export** or right-click and select **Export → Export Map...** or **[Ctrl]** + **[Shift]** + **[E]**.

Maps can be exported in the following file types: .JPG, .BMP, .GIF, TIF, or .PNG.

You can also copy the whole map or selected items and then go to **Home | Clipboard → Copy** or **[Ctrl]** + **[C]**.

26. CHARTS

Charts

Charts are graphics that easily and clearly can illustrate how sources have been coded. The generic way to create Charts is using the Chart Wizard.

1 Go to **Explore | Charts → Chart...**

The **Chart Wizard - Step 1** appears:

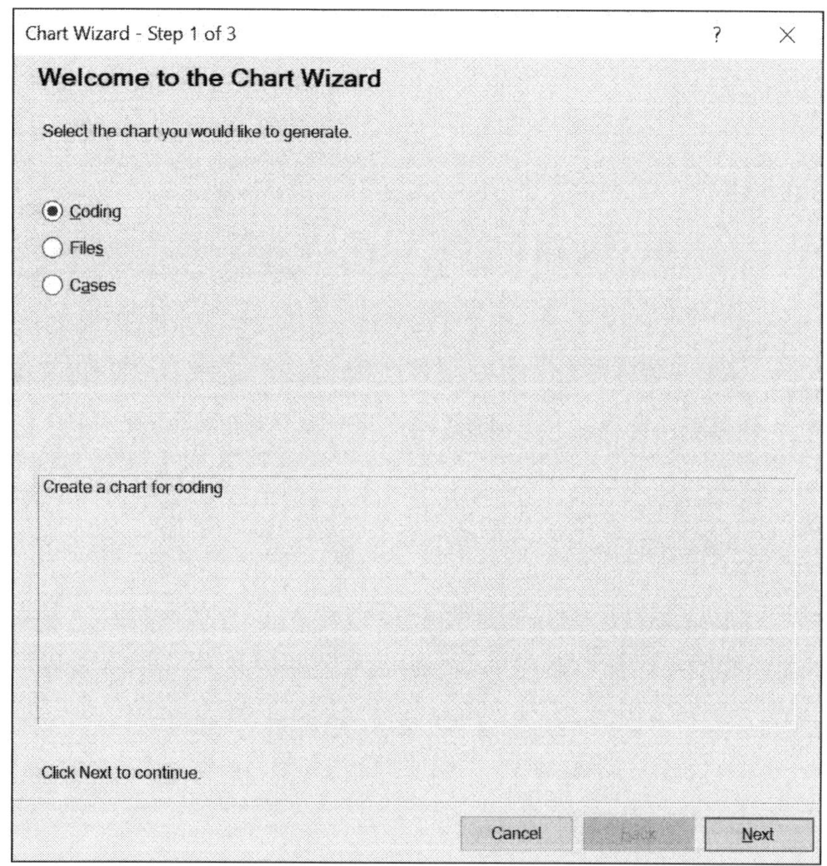

2 Click **[Next]**.

The **Chart Wizard - Step 2** is shown and the options are:

Coding (Create a chart for coding) and the alternatives are:

Coding for a File
Coding by Case attribute value for a File
Coding by Case attribute value for multiple Files
Coding for a Code
Coding by Case attribute value for a Code
Coding by Case attribute value for multiple Codes

Files (Create a chart for files, externals or memos) and the alternatives are:

Files by attribute value for an attribute
Files by attribute value for two attributes

Cases (Create a chart for Codes) and the alternatives are:

Cases by attribute value for an attribute
Cases by attribute value for two attributes

Option	Comments
Coding for a File	Show the Codes coding a selected file. This chart could show, for example, percentage of coverage or number of references.
Coding by Case attribute value for a File	Show coding by Case attribute value for a file. For example, chart a file to show coding by one or more Case attribute values.
Coding by Case attribute value for multiple Files	Show coding by Case attribute value for multiple files. For example, chart two or more files to show coding by one or more Case attribute values.
Coding for a Code	Show files coding to a selected Code or Case. The chart could show, for example, percentage of coverage.
Coding by Case attribute value for a Code	Show coding by Case attribute value for a Code or Case. For example, chart a Code to show coding by one or more Case attribute values.
Coding by Case attribute value for multiple Codes	Show coding by Case attribute value for multiple Codes or Cases. For example, chart two or more Codes to show coding by one or more Case attribute values.
Files by attribute value for an attribute	Display files by attribute value for an attribute. For example, chart an attribute to see how the files which have that attribute are distributed across the attribute values.
Files by attribute value for two attributes	Display files by attribute value for two attributes. For example, chart two attributes to see how the files which have those attributes are distributed across the attribute values.
Cases by attribute value for an attribute	Display Cases by attribute value for an attribute. For example, chart an attribute to see how the Cases which have that attribute are distributed across the attribute values.
Cases by attribute value for two attributes	Display Cases by attribute value for two attributes. For example, chart two attributes to see how the Cases which have those attributes are distributed across the attribute values.

We select the option **Coding** and **Coding for a file**.

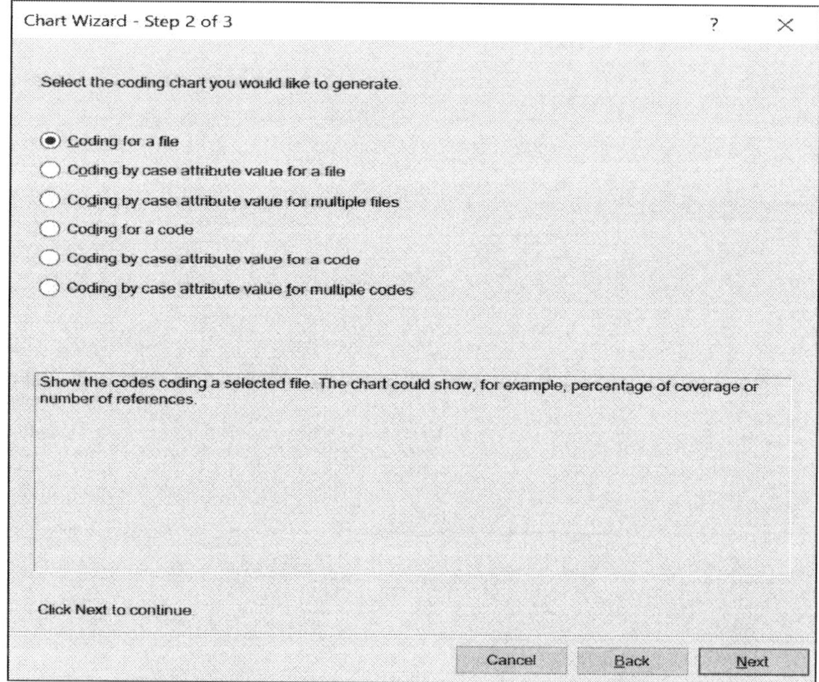

3 Click **[Next]**.

The **Chart Wizard – Step 3** appears:

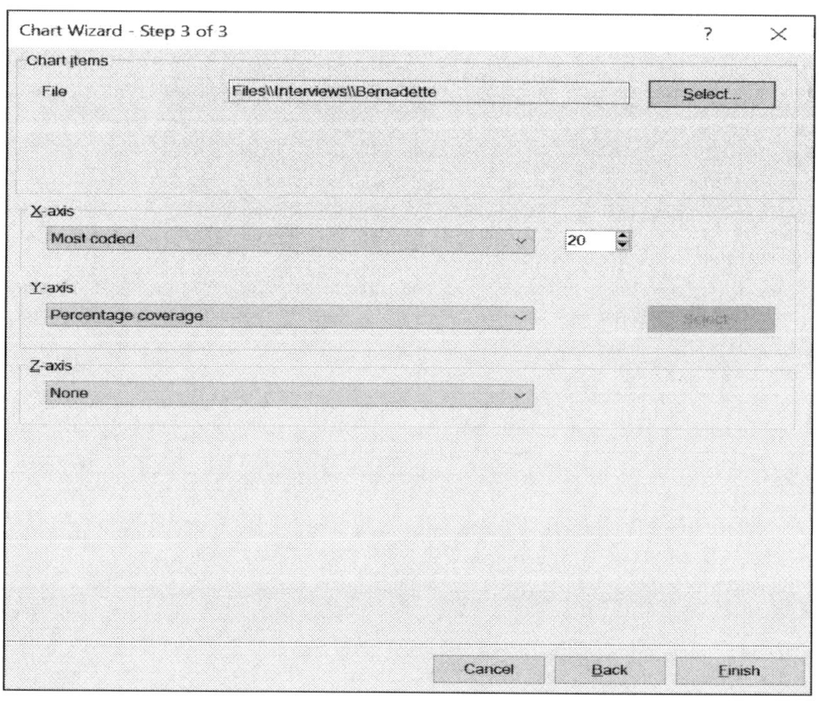

4 Use the **[Select]** button to choose the item that you will visualize, then **[Finish]**.

The result can be like this:

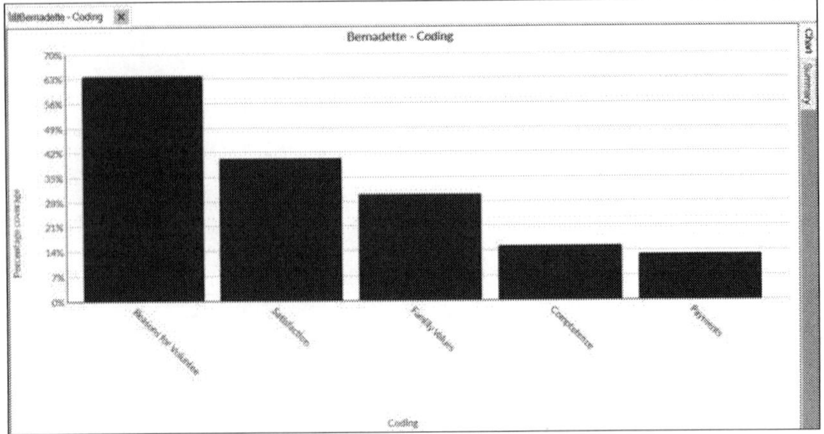

The context dependent ribbon menu **Chart** opens and makes it possible to modify the formatting, zooming and rotating. By going to **Chart | Type** the following drop-down menu shows:

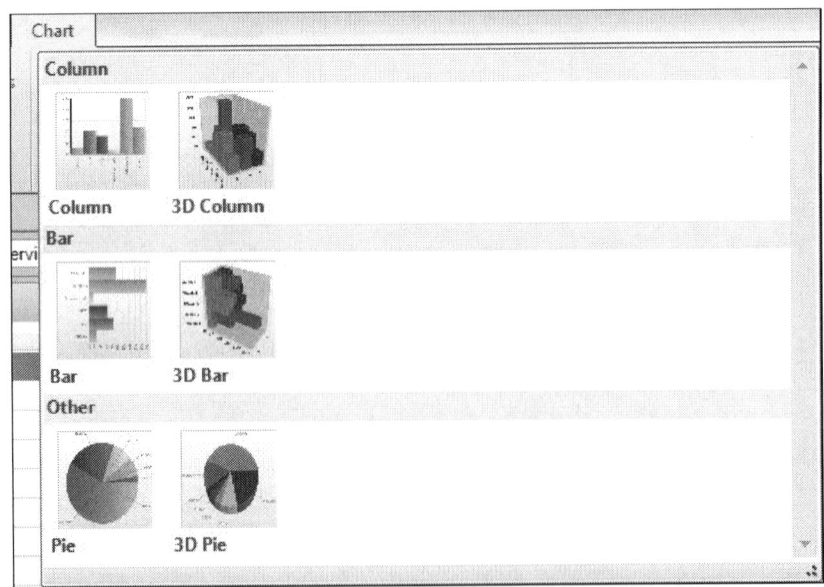

Here you can choose from creating a column, a bar or a pie diagram.

What else can you do with a Chart?

- Hover over the chart and you can read the exact coverage.
- **Chart <File> Coding**:
  Double-click on a bar and you will open the selected Code in a Highlight mode for the current File.
- **Chart Coding for a Code**:
  Double-click on a bar and you will open the selected source in a Highlight mode for the current Code.
- **Edit Labels**: Title and Axis.

The *Summary* tab displays a list with Codes and their coverage:

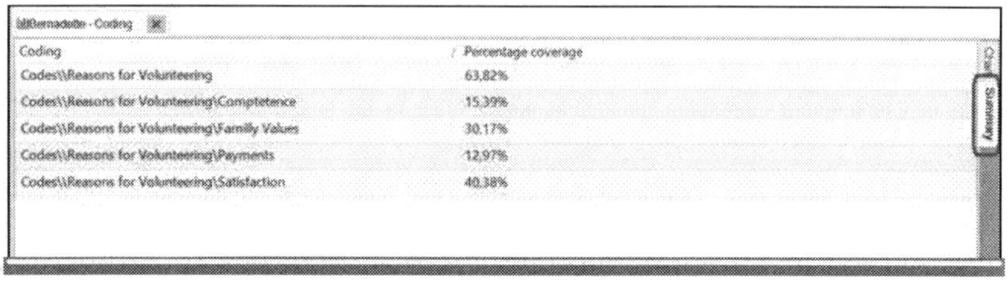

Bernadette - Coding

Coding	Percentage coverage
Codes\\Reasons for Volunteering	63,82%
Codes\\Reasons for Volunteering\Competence	15,39%
Codes\\Reasons for Volunteering\Family Values	30,17%
Codes\\Reasons for Volunteering\Payments	12,97%
Codes\\Reasons for Volunteering\Satisfaction	40,38%

- ♦ -

During a work session you can also start from the List View:

1 Select the item in the List View that you want to visualize.
2 Go to **Explore | Chart → Chart Document Coding**
  or go to **Explore | Chart → Chart Document Coding by Attribute Value**.

The graphic is then shown directly when you select **Chart Document Coding**. Selecting **Chart Document Coding by Attribute Value** the dialog box **Chart Options** appears (same box as the **Chart Wizard - Step 3**). From there you proceed as above. These charts cannot be saved as items in the project but can be exported, or copied, see below.

If you want to display more than 20 items in a chart then:

1 Open a chart.
2 Go to **Chart | Select Data**.

The **Chart Options** dialog box appears:

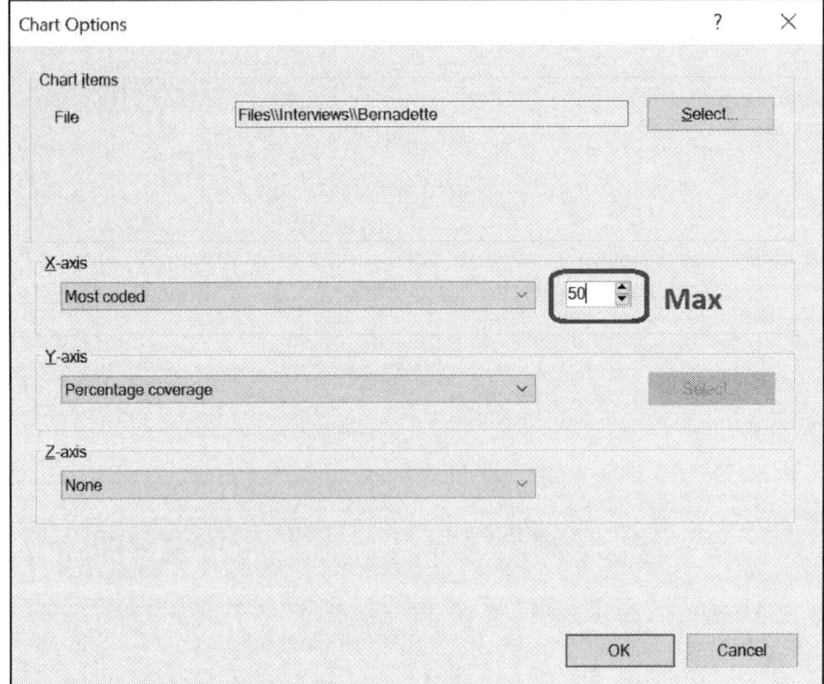

3 Modify your settings, then **[OK]**.

Exporting Charts

Create a Chart and go to **Share | Export | Export** or right-click and select **Export Chart...** or **[Ctrl]** + **[Shift]** + **[E]**. Decide file name, location, and file type: .JPG, .BMP, .GIF, .PNG, .PDF, or .SVG, then click **[Save]**.

You can also copy the whole Chart by going to **Home | Clipboard → Copy** or **[Ctrl]** + **[C]**.

Hierarchy Charts

Hierarchy Charts makes it possible to visualize how source items and Codes are coded and classified and hierarchically organized with qualitative comparisons. The general method to create Hierarchy Charts is using the Hierarchy Chart Wizard.

1 Go to **Explore | Hierarchy Chart → Hierarchy Charts...**

The **Hierarchy Chart Wizard** – **Step 1** appears:

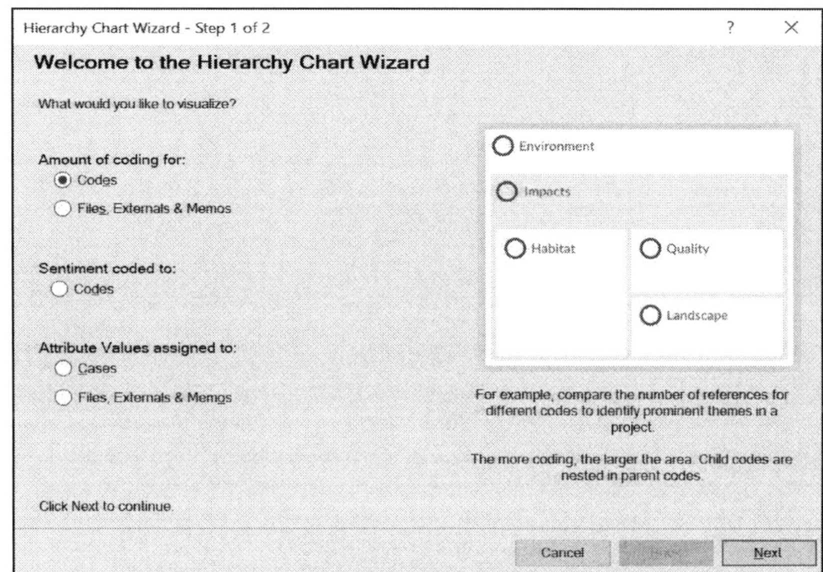

2 We accept to analyze Codes. Click **[Next...]**.

The **Hierarchy Chart Wizard** – **Step 2** appears:

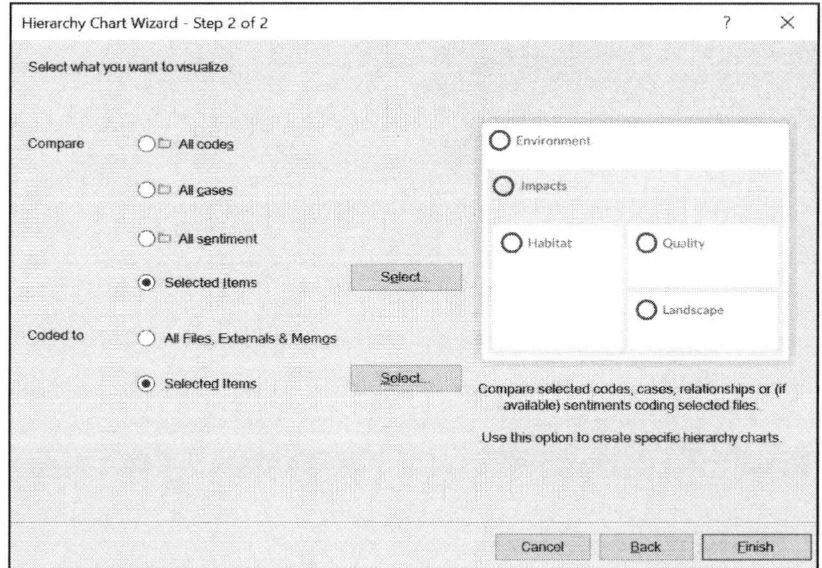

3 With the **[Select...]**-buttons we have selected Codes and Cases for analysis. Click **[Finish]**.

A new context dependent ribbon, **Hierarchy Chart,** appears. The result looks like this and the size of the different fields represent the number of references:

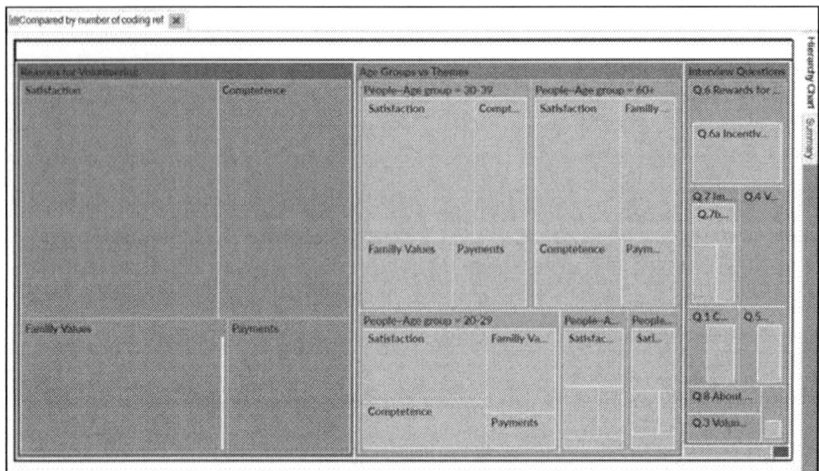

You can change the chart type by going to **Hierarchy Chart | Sunburst**:

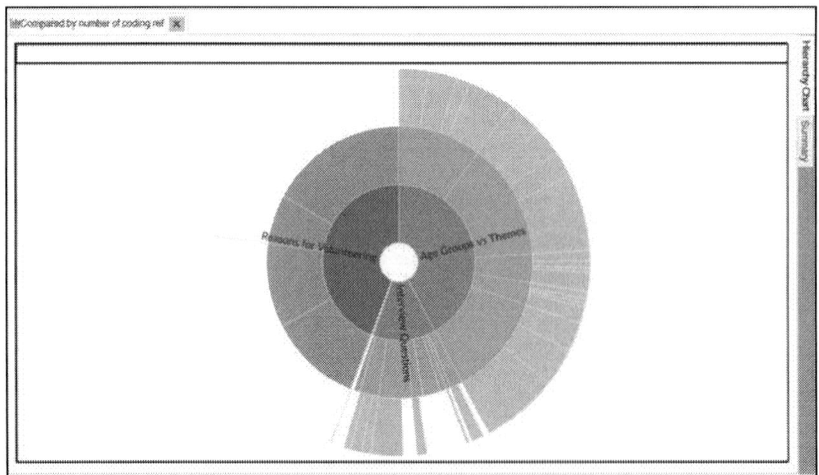

You can open a certain field by right-clicking and selecting **View References** or **[Ctrl]** + **[Shift]** + **[O]**. Then a new Coding Query with a Preview result will open. If you want to save this result as a new Code you will follow the instructions described earlier. These charts cannot be saved as items in the project but can be exported, or copied, see below.

Exporting Hierarchy Charts

Create a Chart and go to **Share | Export → Export** or right-click and select **Export Hierarchy Chart...** or [**Ctrl**] + [**Shift**] + [**E**]. Use the file-browser to decide file name, location, and file type: .JPG, .BMP, .GIF, .PNG, .PDF, or .SVG, then click [**Save**].

You can also copy the whole diagram or selected items by going to **Home | Clipboard → Copy** or [**Ctrl**] + [**C**].

27. DIAGRAMS

Explore Diagrams

This type of diagram is a dynamic preview offering a visual analysis of a selected project item and its connections to all other items. Dynamic means that the diagram is updated as soon as any item is modified and preview means that such diagram is created and not saved unless it is exported and saved in any external format.

1 Select an (one only) item in the List View that you want to analyze.
2 Go to **Explore | Diagrams → Explore Diagram**.

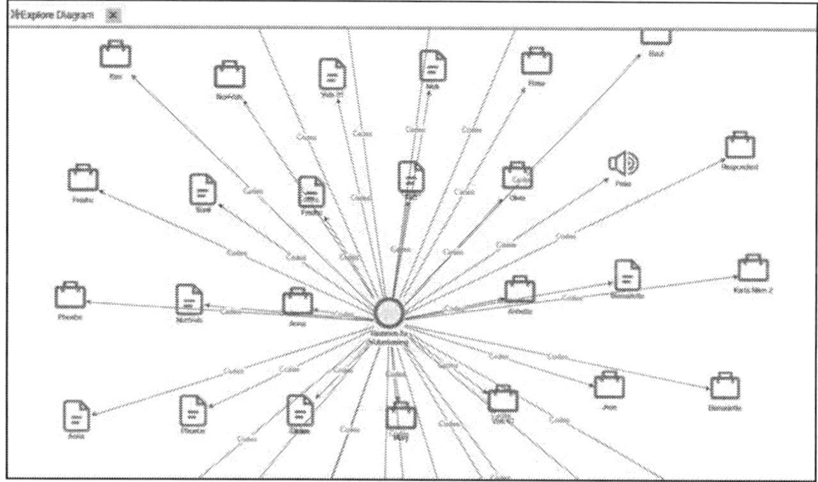

The context dependent **Explore Diagram** ribbon is opened.

You can select which type of connected items you want to display by going to **Explore Diagram | 'Display'** with the following options:

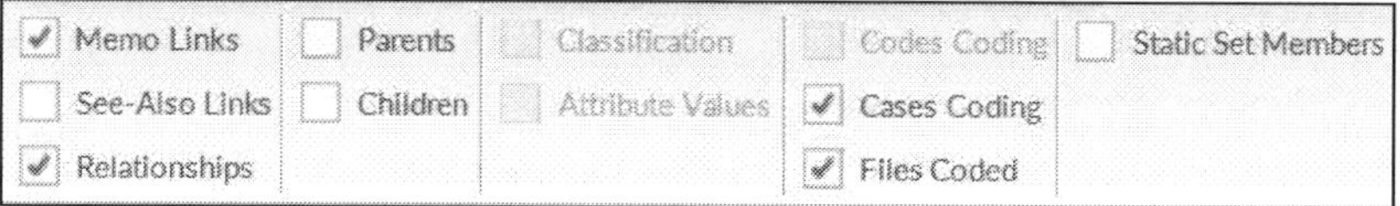

You can also proceed by selecting any item from the diagram and then go to **Explore Diagram | Change Focus** or right-click and select **Change Focus**. Then a new diagram is shown with the newly selected item in focus:

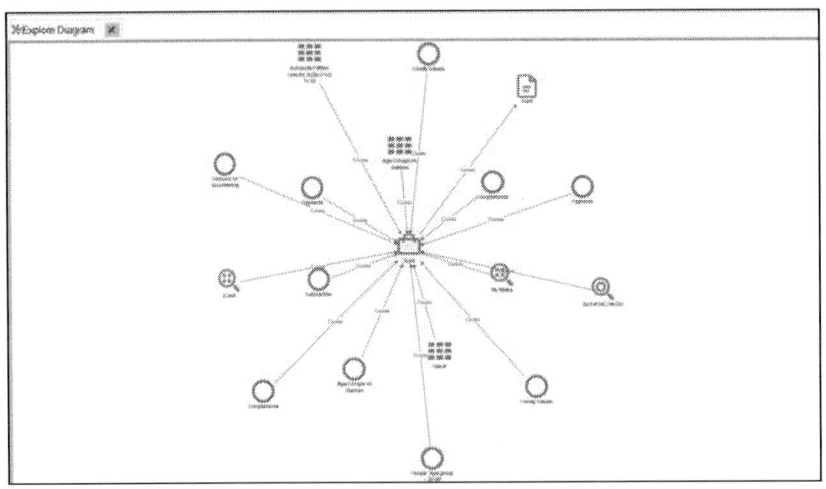

Now you can alternate between these two diagrams using **Explore Diagram | Back** or **Explore Diagram | Forward**. You can also right-click and alternately select **Back** or **Forward**.

From these diagrams you can open any item by going to **Home | Item → 'Open' → Open Item** or **[Ctrl]** + **[Shift]** + **[O]** or right-click and select **Open Item...** or double-click.

You can also go on in your analysis and select again a new item and **Change Focus**. With this option you can go backwards or forwards in many steps.

Optional Display Modes

Go to **Explore Diagram | 'Display'** and you will access several display options like Classification, Attribute Values, Codes, Cases, Sources, or Set Members. These diagrams cannot be saved as items in the project but can be exported, or copied, see below.

Exporting Explore Diagrams

Create an Explore Diagram and go to **Share | Export → Export** or right-click and select **Export Diagram...** or **[Ctrl]** + **[Shift]** + **[E]**. Use the file-browser to decide file name, location, and file type: .JPG, .BMP, .GIF, or .PNG, then click **[Save]**.

You can also copy the whole diagram or selected items by going to **Home | Clipboard → Copy** or **[Ctrl]** + **[C]**.

Comparison Diagrams

This type of diagram is a dynamic preview offering a visual analysis of two selected project items and how they are related to each other and their connections to all other items. Dynamic means that the diagram is updated as soon as any item is modified and preview means that such diagram is created and not saved unless it is exported and saved in any external format.

1 Select <u>two</u> items in the List View for this analysis.
2 Go to **Explore | Diagrams → Compare**.

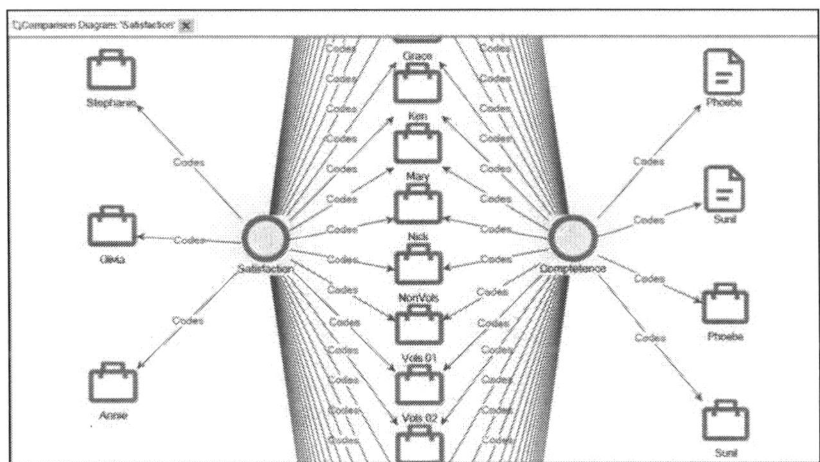

The context dependent **Comparison Diagram** ribbon is opened.

The two related items to be compared show the commonly connected items in between and the unique items to the left and to the right respectively.

From a Comparison Diagram you can open any item by going to **Home | Item → 'Open' → Open Item** or **[Ctrl]** + **[Shift]** + **[O]** or right-click and select **Open Item...**

If you prefer not to select comparison items first, you can go directly to **Explore | Diagrams → Compare Files, → Compoare Codes,** or **→ Compare Cases.** If you select *one* item first, the option **Explore | Diagrams → Compare With...** appears. In those cases you will have to select items before you create the Comparison Diagram.

Optional Display Modes

Go to **Comparison Diagram | 'Display'** and you will access several display options like Classification, Attribute Values, Codes, Cases, Sources or Static Set Members:

☑ Memo Links	☐ Parents	☐ Classification	☐ Codes Coding	☐ Static Set Members
☐ See-Also Links	☐ Children	☐ Attribute Values	☑ Cases Coding	
☑ Relationships			☑ Files Coded	

Exporting Comparison Diagrams

Create an Explore Diagram and go to **Share | Export → Export** or right-click and select **Export Diagram...** or **[Ctrl]** + **[Shift]** + **[E]**. Use the file-browser to decide file name, location, and file type: .JPG, .BMP, .GIF, or .PNG, then click **[Save]**.

You can also copy the whole diagram or selected items by going to **Home | Clipboard → Copy** or **[Ctrl]** + **[C]**.

Cluster Analysis

Cluster analysis is an exploratory technique that you can use to visualize patterns in your project by grouping sources or Codes that share similar words, similar attribute values, or are coded similarly by Codes. Cluster analysis diagrams provide a graphical representation of sources or Codes to make it easy to see similarities and differences. Sources or Codes in the cluster analysis diagram that appear close together are more similar than those that are far apart.

1 Go to **Explore | Diagrams → Cluster Analysis...**

The **Cluster Analysis Wizard – Step 1** appears:

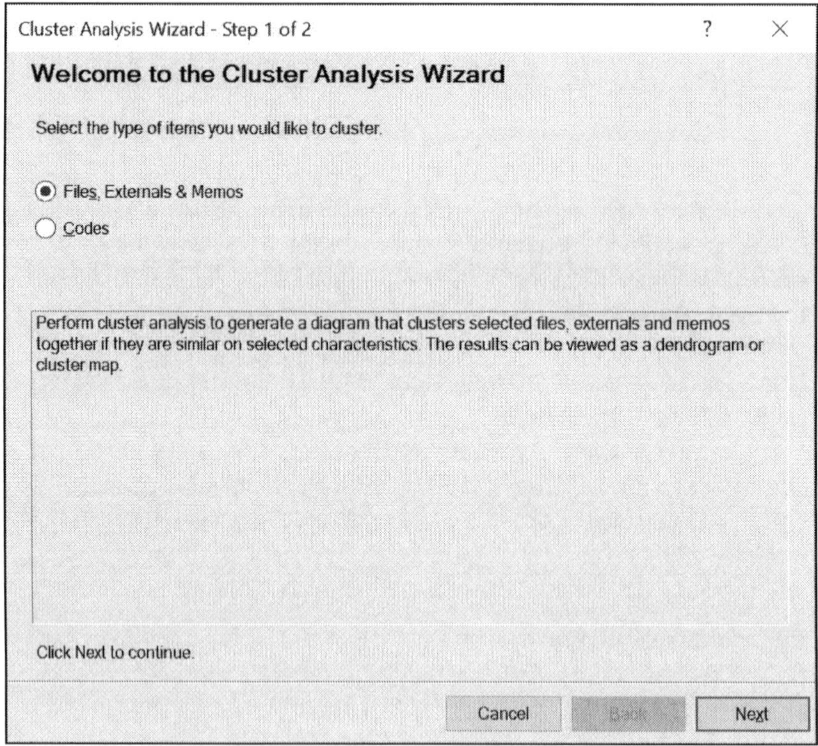

2 We want to analyze selected Source Items, like selected PDF articles. We select the *Files, Externals & Memos* option and click **[Next]**.

The **Cluster Analysis Wizard - Step 2** appears:

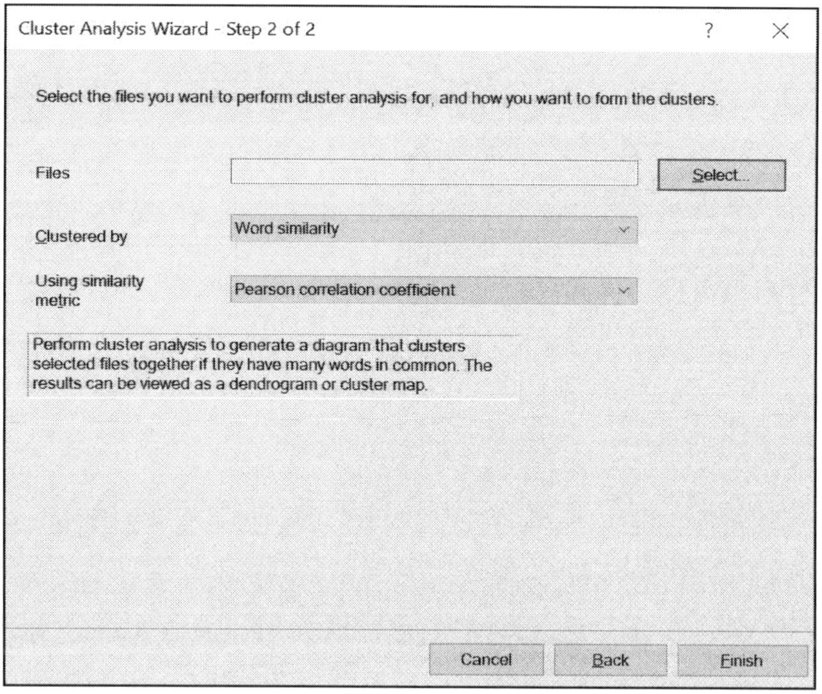

Cluster Analysis Wizard - Step 2 of 2

Select the files you want to perform cluster analysis for, and how you want to form the clusters.

Files [Select...]

Clustered by: Word similarity

Using similarity metric: Pearson correlation coefficient

Perform cluster analysis to generate a diagram that clusters selected files together if they have many words in common. The results can be viewed as a dendrogram or cluster map.

[Cancel] [Back] [Finish]

Under the **Clustered by** drop-down list you find the following options: *Word similarity, Coding similarity,* and *Attribute value similarity.*

Word similarity: The words contained in the selected sources or Codes are compared.

Sources or codes that have a higher degree of similarity based on the occurrence and frequency of words are shown clustered together. Sources or Codes that have a lower degree of similarity based on the occurrence and frequency of words are displayed further apart. Stop words are excluded when using this measure of similarity.

Coding similarity: The coding at the selected sources or Codes is compared.

Sources or Codes that have been coded similarly are clustered together on the cluster analysis diagram. Sources or Codes that have been coded differently are displayed further apart on the cluster analysis diagram.

Attribute value similarity: The attribute values of the selected sources or Codes are compared.

Sources or Codes that have similar attribute values are clustered together on the cluster analysis diagram. Sources or Codes that have different attribute values are displayed further apart on the cluster analysis diagram.

Under the **Using similarity metric** drop-down list you find the following options: *Jaccard's coefficient, Pearson correlation coefficient,* and *Sørensen coefficient.*

3 The **[Select]** button opens the **Select Project Items** dialog box and we select the PDF articles.
4 Click **[Finish]**.

The context dependent Ribbon menu **Cluster Analysis** opens and you can choose between 2D Cluster Map, 3D Cluster Map, Horizontal Dendrogram, Vertical Dendrogram or Circle Graph. The default diagram is the Horizontal Dendrogram:

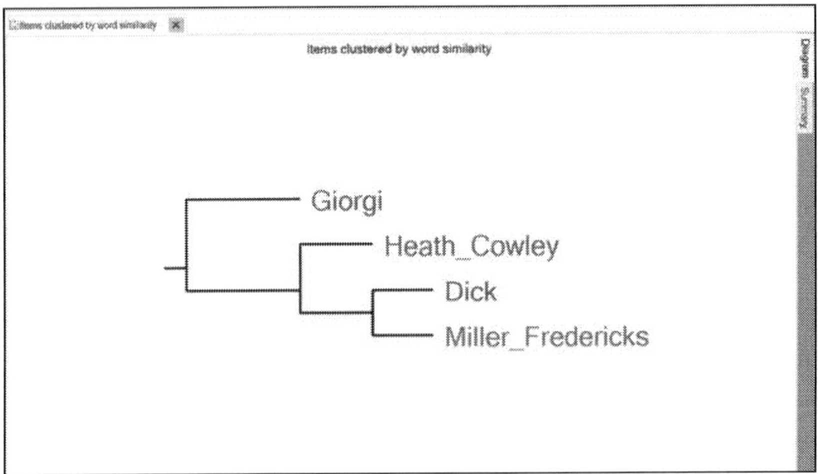

Go to **Cluster Analysis | 'Type' | Vertical Dendrogram** and the following diagram is shown:

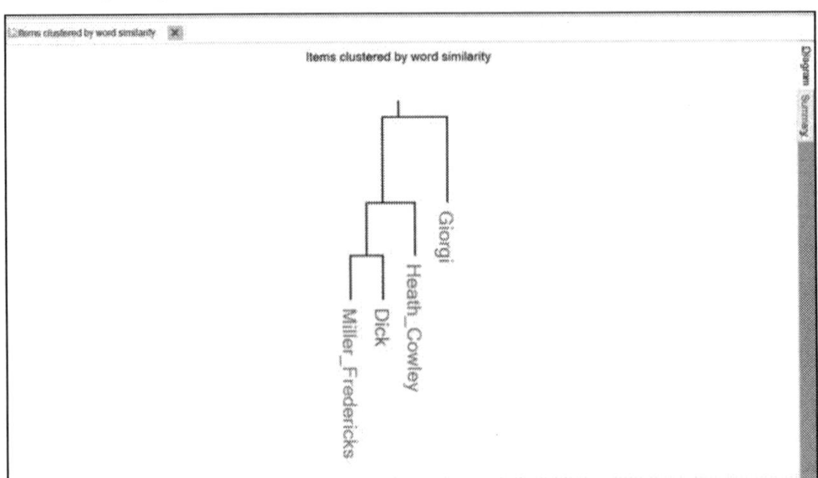

Go to **Cluster Analysis | 'Type' | 2D Cluster Map** and the following diagram is shown:

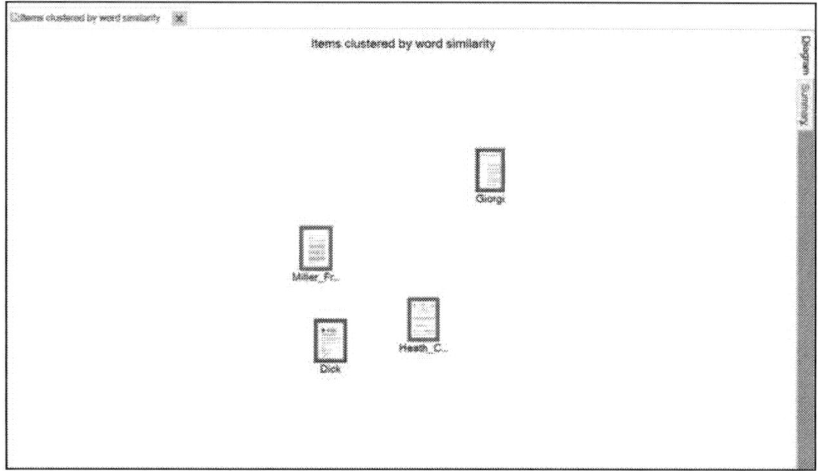

Go to **Cluster Analysis | 'Type' | 3D Cluster Map** and the following diagram is shown:

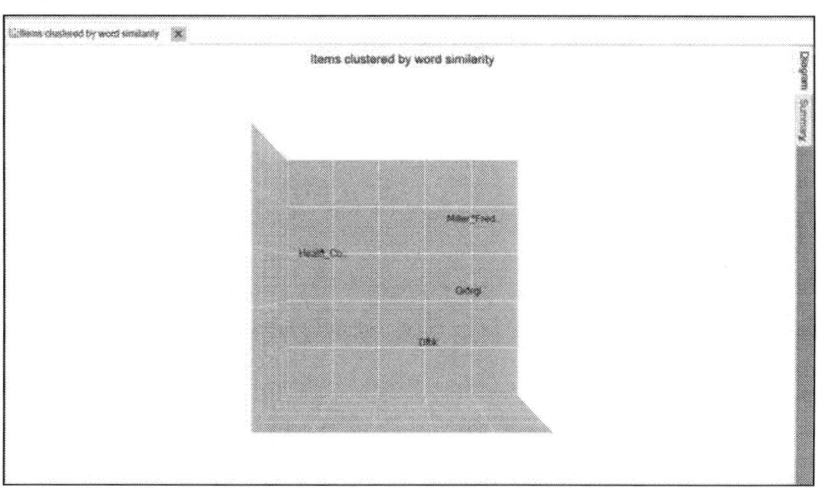

Go to **Cluster Analysis | 'Type' | Circle Graph** and the following diagram is shown:

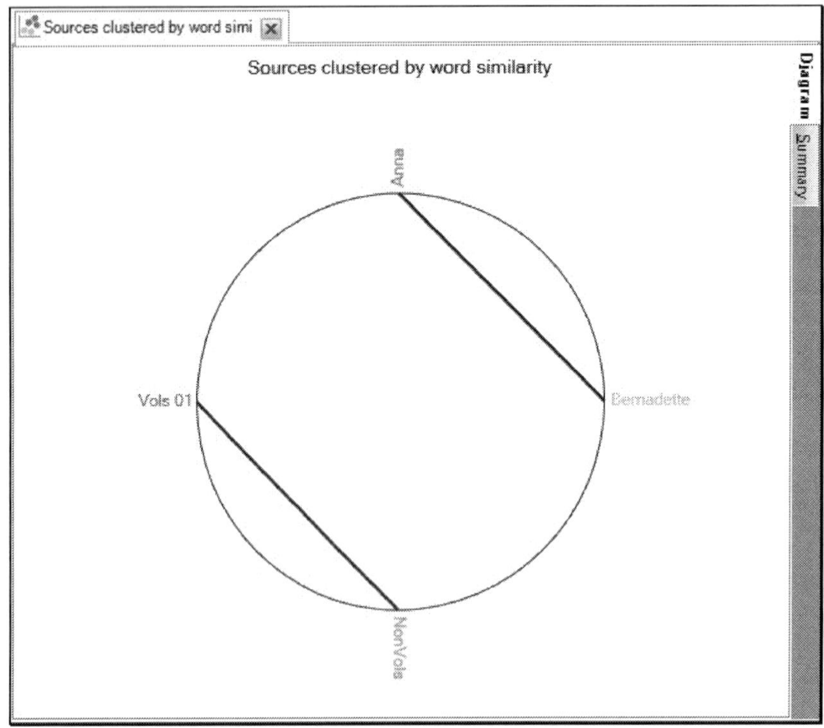

A circle where all the items are represented as points on the perimeter. Relations between items is indicated by connecting lines of varying thickness and color.

Similarity is indicated by blue lines–thicker lines indicate stronger similarity. Dissimilarity is indicated by red lines–thicker lines indicate stronger dissimilarity.

The **Summary** tab to the right shows the current metric coefficient for each pair of items in the cluster:

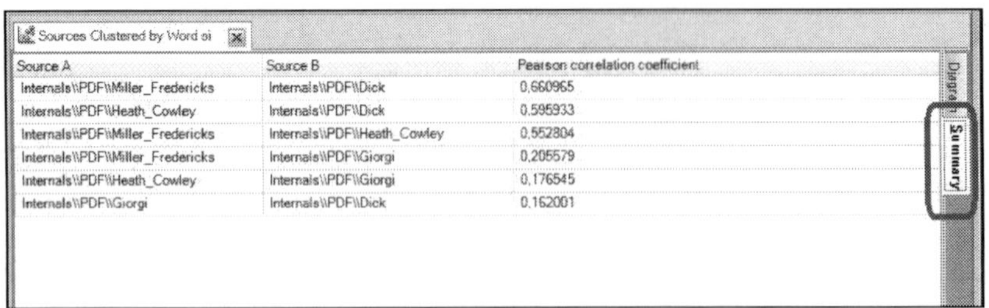

Sources Clustered by Word si

Source A	Source B	Pearson correlation coefficient
Internals\\PDF\\Miller_Fredericks	Internals\\PDF\\Dick	0,660965
Internals\\PDF\\Heath_Cowley	Internals\\PDF\\Dick	0,595933
Internals\\PDF\\Miller_Fredericks	Internals\\PDF\\Heath_Cowley	0,552804
Internals\\PDF\\Miller_Fredericks	Internals\\PDF\\Giorgi	0,205579
Internals\\PDF\\Heath_Cowley	Internals\\PDF\\Giorgi	0,176545
Internals\\PDF\\Giorgi	Internals\\PDF\\Dick	0,162001

With **Cluster Analysis | Select Data** you can choose the metric coefficient.

The Cluster map applies a certain color for each cluster in each type of cluster diagram. In order to study the clustering structure, you can vary the number of clusters as any number between 1 and

20 (10 is default) in each type of cluster diagram by going to **Cluster Analysis | Clusters**.

A Cluster map can also be used like this: Select an item in the cluster diagram, right-click and the menu alternatives are: **Open <File type>** (or double-click or key command **[Ctrl]** + **[Shift]** + **[O]**), **Export Diagram, Print, Copy** (the whole graph), **Run Word Frequency Query, Item Properties, Select Data**.

Exporting Cluster Analysis Diagrams

Create a Cluster Analysis Diagram and go to **Share | Export → Export** or point at the diagram, right-click and select **Export Diagram...** or **[Ctrl]** + **[Shift]** + **[E]**. Decide file name, location and file type: .JPG, .BMP, or .GIF, confirm with **[Save]**.

You can also copy the whole Cluster Analysis Diagram by going to **Home | Clipboard → Copy** or point at the diagram, right-click and select **Copy** or **[Ctrl]** + **[C]**.

28. REPORTS

The Folder Structure for Reports

The project folder structure for Reports are: Formatted Reports and Text Reports. The default folders as shown in the Navigator are:

These folders and the names are not possible to delete, move, or rename. The folder names are depending on the user interface language setting, see page 39. However, the user can create subfolders to the default folders **Reports\\Formatted Reports** and **Reports\\Text Reports**.

Formatted reports contain summary information about your project that you can view and print. You could check the progress of your coding and run a report that lists your files and codes that code them.

A text report lets you export a collection of data to a text, Excel or XML file. In some cases you can use this data for complementary analysis in other applications.

Understanding Views and Fields

In Formatted Reports and Text Reports, a view is a group of related data fields. There are five different views: Files, File Classification, Code, Case Classification, and Project Items. When you build a Formatted Report or a Text Report, select the View which contains the fields you want to include.

View	Comment
File	Report on files including which Codes code the files. This view also includes collections, which you could use to limit the scope of your reports.
File Classification	Report on the classifications that are used to describe your files. You can create reports that show the classifications in your project or how your files are classified. This view does not contain any coding information. To report on coding in files, choose the File view.
Code	Report on the Codes in your project including files they code, coding references, and any classifications assigned to them. This view includes 'intersecting' Codes which is useful for reporting on how coding at two Codes coincides—for example see which 'cases' intersect selected themes. This view also includes collections, which you could use to limit the scope of your reports.

Case Classification	Report on the classifications, attributes and attribute values used to describe the people, places and other cases in your project. You can use this view to show the classification structure, or the demographic spread of classified Cases. This view does not contain any coding information. If you want to report on coding at Codes, choose the Code view.
Project Items	Use this view to create reports about the structure of your project. Report on your project and the Project Items, including the types of Project Items and who created them.

Formatted Reports' and Text Reports' Templates

NVivo comes with 8 pre-defined Formatted Reports' templates and 8 pre-defined Text Reports' templates ready to be used for any NVivo project. These templates can be deleted or modified by the user. New Formatted Reports and Text Reports can be created by the user for the current project or be exported to other users working with any other NVivo projects.

The pre-defined Formatted Report templates are located in the **Reports\\Formatted Reports** folder:

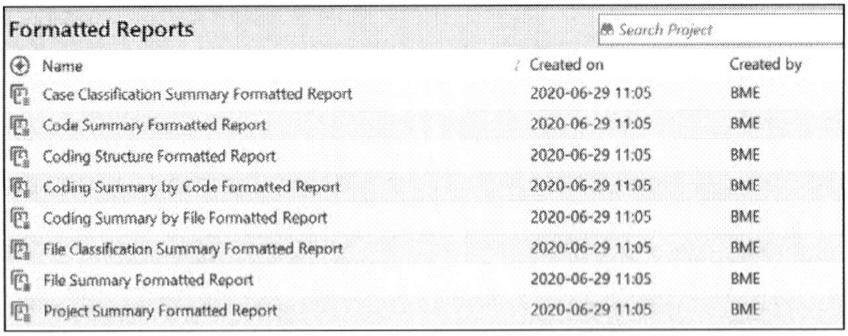

Formatted Reports | Search Project

Name	Created on	Created by
Case Classification Summary Formatted Report	2020-06-29 11:05	BME
Code Summary Formatted Report	2020-06-29 11:05	BME
Coding Structure Formatted Report	2020-06-29 11:05	BME
Coding Summary by Code Formatted Report	2020-06-29 11:05	BME
Coding Summary by File Formatted Report	2020-06-29 11:05	BME
File Classification Summary Formatted Report	2020-06-29 11:05	BME
File Summary Formatted Report	2020-06-29 11:05	BME
Project Summary Formatted Report	2020-06-29 11:05	BME

The Formatted Reports' templates that include *contents* are 'Coding Summary By Code Formatted Report' and 'Coding Summary By File Formatted Report'.

The pre-defined Text Reports' templates are located in the **Reports\\Text Reports** folder:

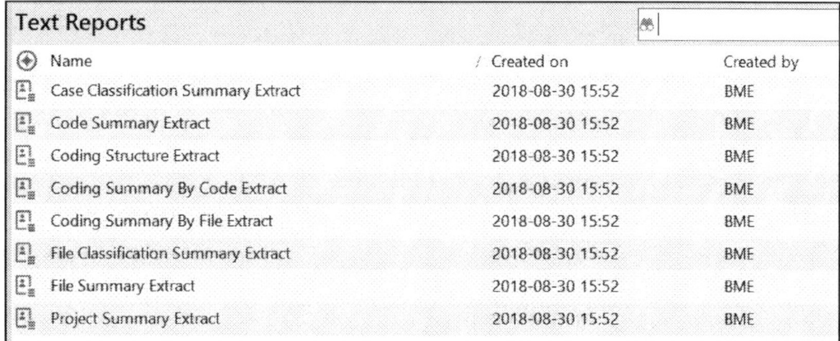

Name	Created on	Created by
Case Classification Summary Extract	2018-08-30 15:52	BME
Code Summary Extract	2018-08-30 15:52	BME
Coding Structure Extract	2018-08-30 15:52	BME
Coding Summary By Code Extract	2018-08-30 15:52	BME
Coding Summary By File Extract	2018-08-30 15:52	BME
File Classification Summary Extract	2018-08-30 15:52	BME
File Summary Extract	2018-08-30 15:52	BME
Project Summary Extract	2018-08-30 15:52	BME

The Extract templates that include contents are 'Coding Summary By Code Extract' and 'Coding Summary By File Extract'.

Formatted Reports

Creating a New Formatted Report via the Report Designer

1 Go to **Share | New Formatted Report → New Formatted Report via Designer...**

The **New Report** dialog box appears:

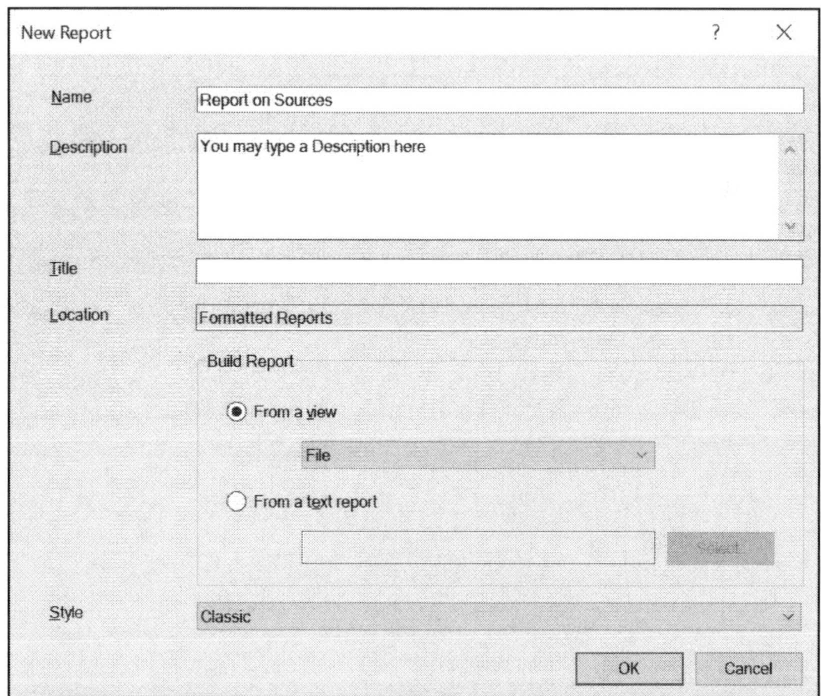

We have typed a name (title) of the Report and we have selected the View *File*.

2 Click **[OK]**.

A new context dependent Ribbon menu, **Designer**, is now opened and is opened each time a Formatted Report is created. If you prefer the option *From a text report* you will need to select an extract from the existing Text Reports' templates and you will inherit the view and fields from that template.

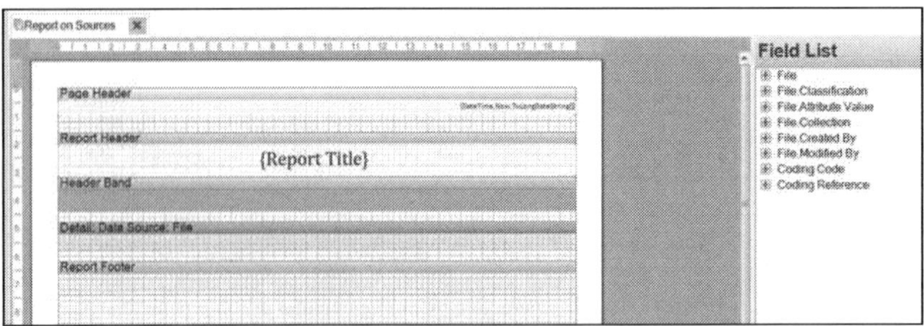

The key to understanding the **Report Designer** is the idea of controls. Controls are static fields with label data or dynamic fields with data. The following graph will explain. First you select a field from the list of field headings in the Field List panel to the right. Then go to **Designer | Add Field/Modify** or right-click and select **Add Field**. The result is two controls, Label Control and Field Control.

The text or Image controls are created when you click on an empty space immediately below one of the band headers, for example the Report Header. Then an empty control, which is rectangular, is created. From here you go to **Designer | 'Labels'** for insertion of Report Title, Report Location, User Name, Date and Time, Project Name or Page N of M.

You can also create your own text box or an image like a logo. Go to **Designer | Text** or **Designer | Image**. All such controls can easily be resized, moved, deleted etc. Editing text is made by double-clicking the text in question and then either go to **Designer | Text** or **Designer | Image** for modification.

In case you need to edit fonts, color or size then select the control and go to **Designer | 'Format'** and make the modifications you need.

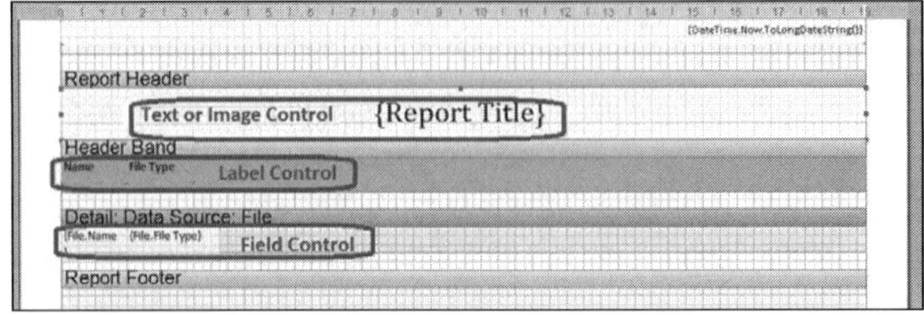

Designer | Layout can be used to go between Tabular or Columnar layout for a non-grouped report and Stepped, Blocked or Outlined layout for a grouped report.

A Grouped report is created by going to **Designer | Group** and then you select the field or fields that will create structural headings in the report.

Designer | Sort makes it possible to change the sorting principles and **Designer | Filter** offers an option to introduce a filter either with fixed or user-prompted settings.

Example of a Formatted Report based on File View

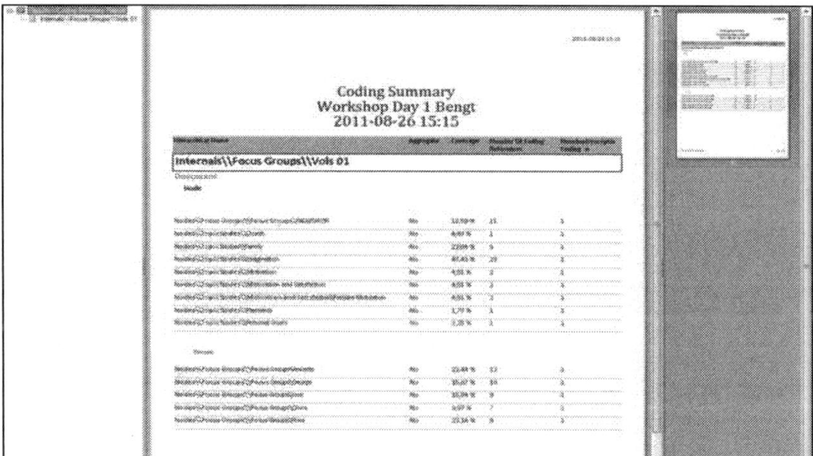

Creating a New Formatted Report via the Report Wizard

The Report Wizard provides a systematic method for creating a new, custom report for your project:

1 Go to **Share | New Formatted Report → New Formatted Report via Wizard...**

The **Formatted Report Wizard - Step 1** appears:

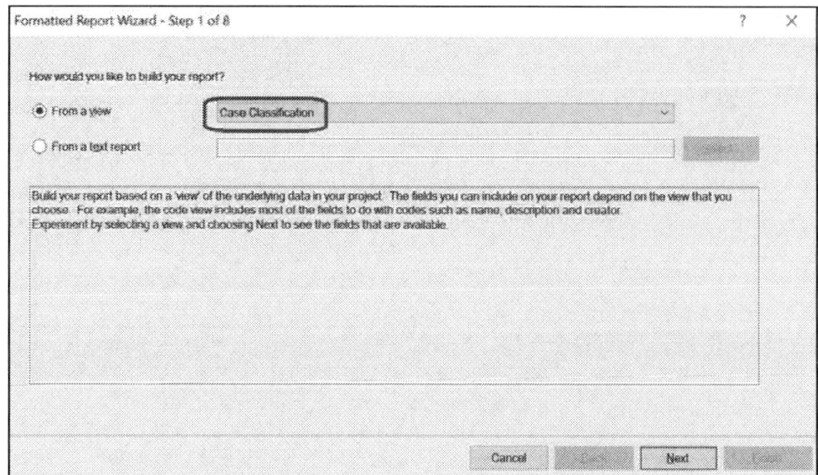

2 Select *Case Classification* from the **From a view** drop down list. If you prefer the option **From a text report** you will need to select an extract from the existing text report templates and you will inherit the view and fields from the chosen text report.

3 Click **[Next]**.

The **Formatted Report Wizard** - **Step 2** appears:

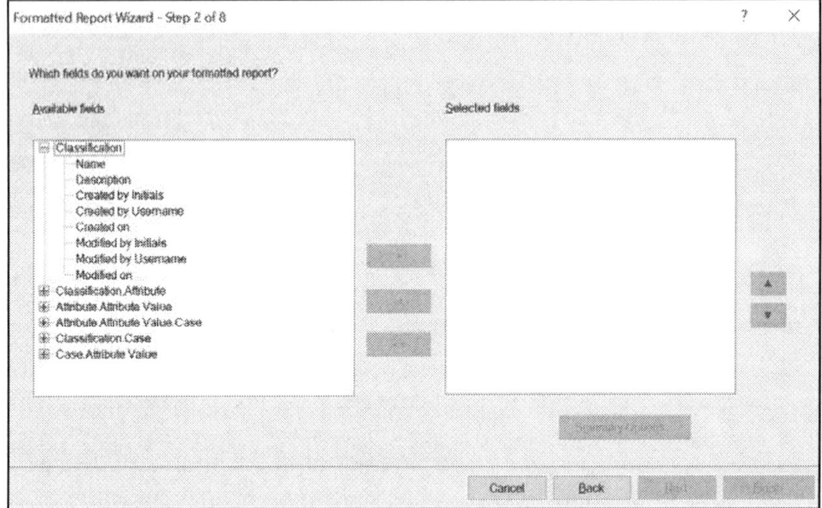

4 Expand the field headings and select the fields from the left box that will form the Report and click the [>] button which brings over the fields to the right box.

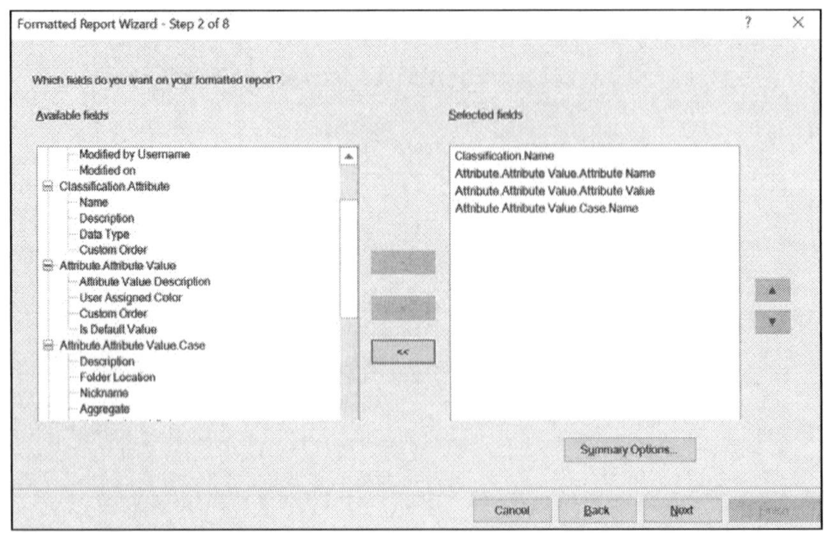

5 Click **[Next]**.

The **Formatted Report Wizard** – **Step 3** appears:

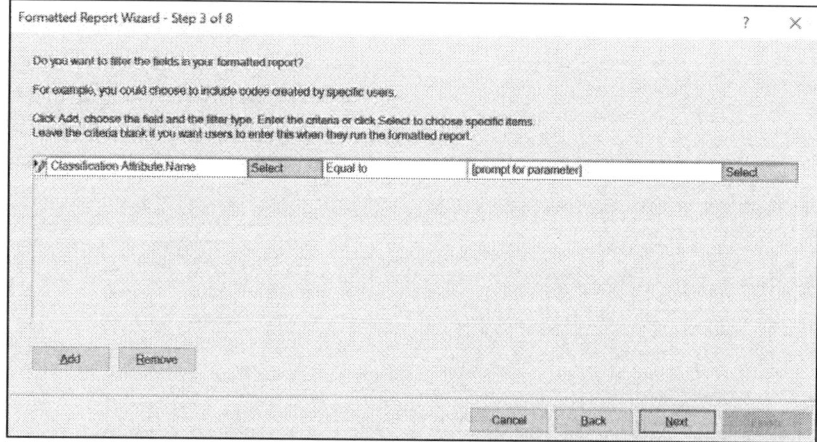

6 Use the **[Add]** button to create the first filter row and then the **[Select]** button to select the field that shall limit the report. If you leave the right textbox as *[prompt for parameter]* then the user will be prompted to select a parameter each time the report is run.

7 Click **[Next]**.

The **Formatted Report Wizard** – **Step 4** appears:

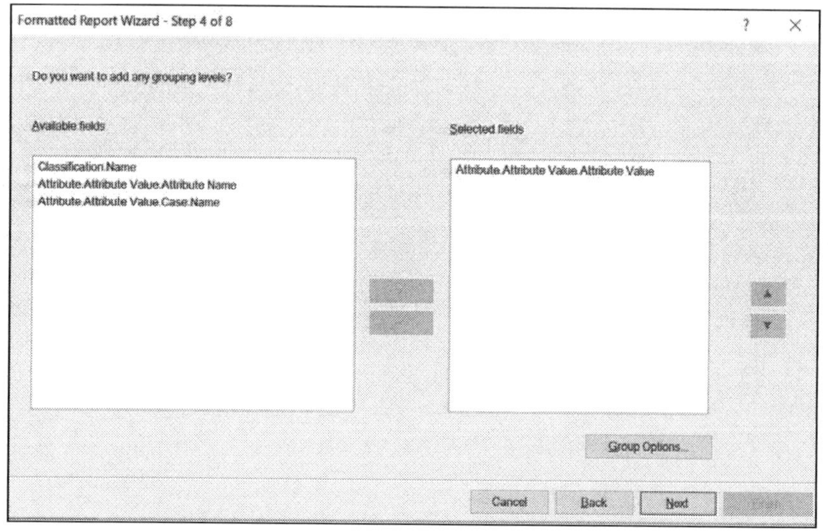

8 Grouping is a way to introduce headings in the Report thus making the report easier to read. We select *Attribute.Attribute Value.Attribute Value* and use the [>] button to bring it over to the right box.

9 Click **[Next]**.

The **Formatted Report Wizard – Step 5** appears:

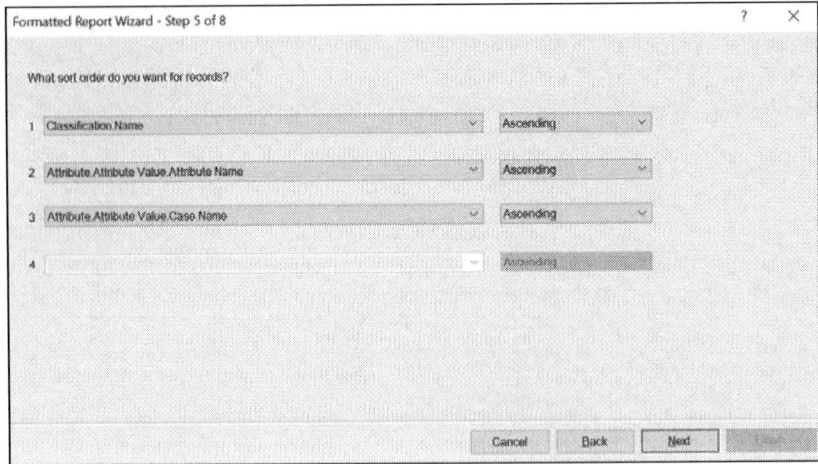

10 We decide the sort order by using the drop-down lists.

11 Click **[Next]**.

The **Formatted Report Wizard – Step 6** appears:

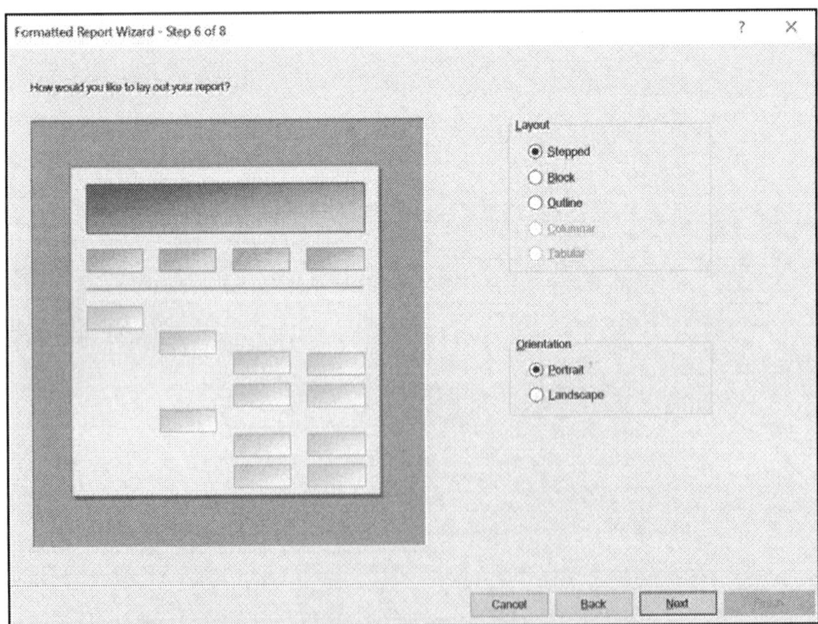

12 We accept the default settings which are *Stepped* layout and *Portrait* orientation.

13 Click **[Next]**.

The **Formatted Report Wizard** - **Step** 7 appears:

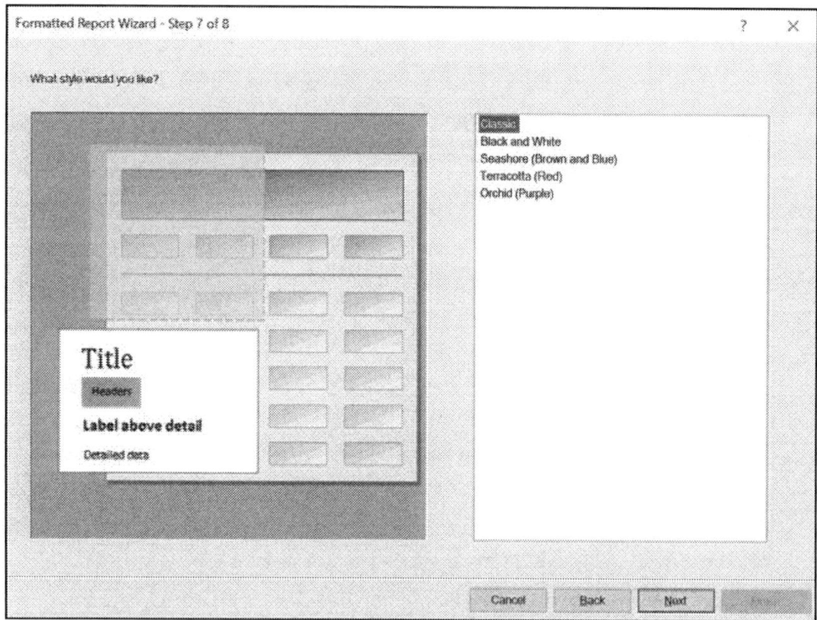

14 We accept the default setting which is the *Classic* style.

15 Click [**Next**].

The **Formatted Report Wizard** - **Step 8** appears:

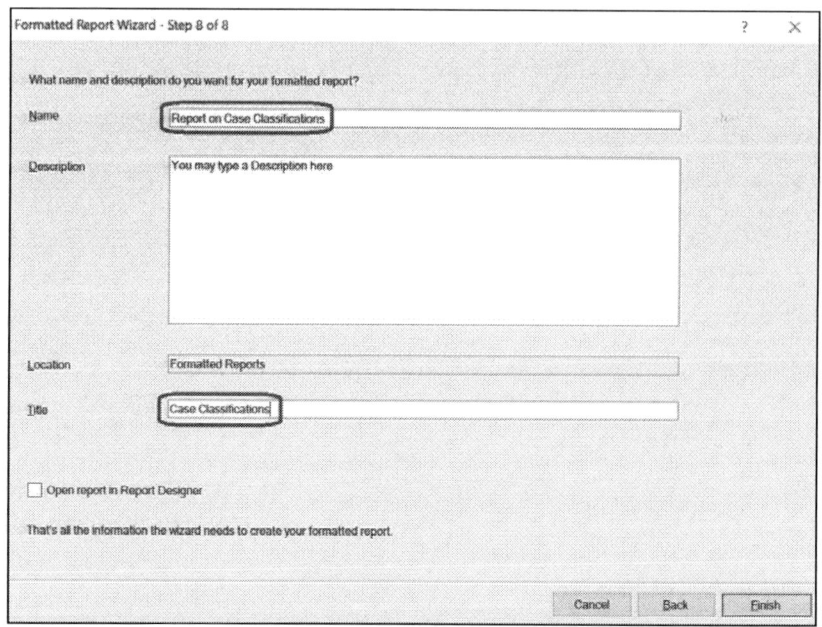

16 Finally, we type the Name and Title of the Formatted Report and optionally a Description.

17 Click [**Finish**].

The new **Formatted Report** opens:

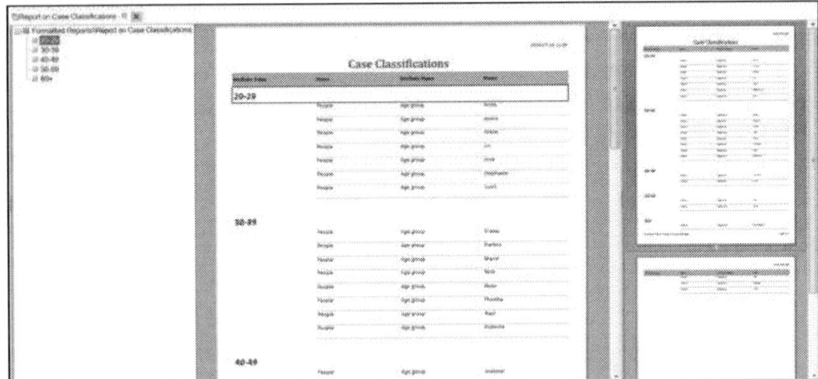

The left panel is called **Report Map** and can be used to easily find a certain headings in the Report. The right panel is called **Thumbnails** and can be used to find a certain page. Report Map and Thumbnails can be hidden/unhidden with **Formatted Report | Report Map** or **Formatted Report | Thumbnails**, two toggling functions.

From this view you can print the Formatted Report or export the Report as a Word document.

Exporting the Result of a Formatted Report

1 Select the **Reports\\Formatted Reports** folder or its subfolder.
2 Select a Formatted Report in the List View.
3 Open the Formatted Report.
4 Go to **Share | Export → Export**
or right-click and select **Export → Export Formatted Report...**
or **[Ctrl]** + **[Shift]** + **[E]**.
5 Decide file name, location, and file type: .DOC, .DOCX, .XLS, .XLSX, .PDF, .RTF, or Web formats. Click **[Save]**.

Exporting a Formatted Report Template

1 Select the **Reports\\Formatted Reports** folder or its subfolder.
2 Select a Report template in the List View.
3 Go to **Share | Export → Export**
or right-click and select **Export → Export Formatted Report...**
or **[Ctrl]** + **[Shift]** + **[E]**.
4 Decide file name and location. The file type is already determined as .NVR. Click **[Save]**.

The exported item is a Formatted Report template that can be imported and used by other projects.

Importing a Formatted Report Template

1 Go to **Import | Reports → Formatted Report**.
Default folder is **Reports\\Formatted Reports** or its currently open subfolder.
Go to 4.

alternatively

1 Select the **Reports\\Formatted Reports** folder or its subfolder.
2 Go to **Import | Reports → Formatted Report**.
Go to 4.

alternatively

2 Click on any empty space in the List View.
3 Right-click and select **Import Report...**
4 The **Formatted Report Properties** dialog box appears.
5 Select the Formatted Report template .NVR that you want to import. Click on **[Open]**.

The **Formatted Report Properties** dialog box appears:

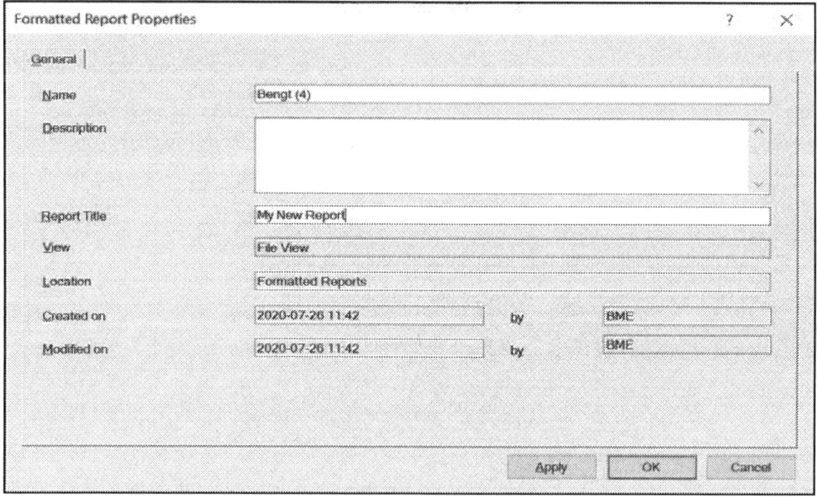

6 If you need you can change or modify the text in the dialog box. Click on **[OK]**.

Editing a Formatted Report Template

By opening a Report in Report Designer you can modify any parameter except the selected View and Style:

1 Select a report template in the List View.
2 Go to **Home | Item → 'Open' → Open Formatted Report in Designer...**
or right-click and select **Open Formatted Report in Designer...**
or **[Ctrl]** + **[Shift]** + **[O]**.

The result may look like this:

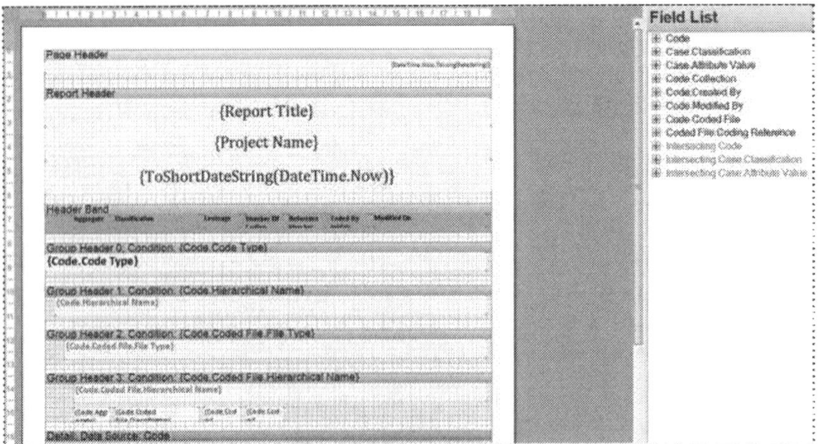

Here you can make any modification that Report Designer allows.

The new context-dependent ribbon tab **Designer** opens. Here you can change the layout, modify filters, modify headers and footers, change grouping and sorting. You can also add your own text and/or your own logo.

Creating a New Formatted Report based on an Existing Text Report

There is a possibility to create New Formatted Reports based on existing Text Report templates both by using Report Designer and Report Wizard.

Using Report Designer, dialog box New Report:

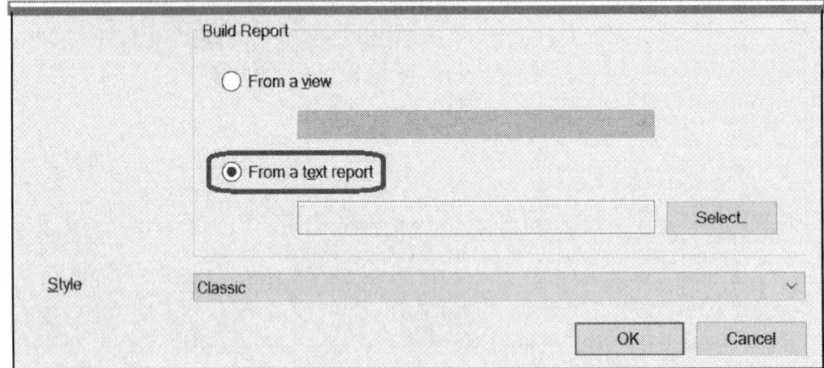

Select From a text report and with the [Select] button search for the text report template .NVR with your file browser.

Using **Formatted Report Wizard** - **Step 1**:

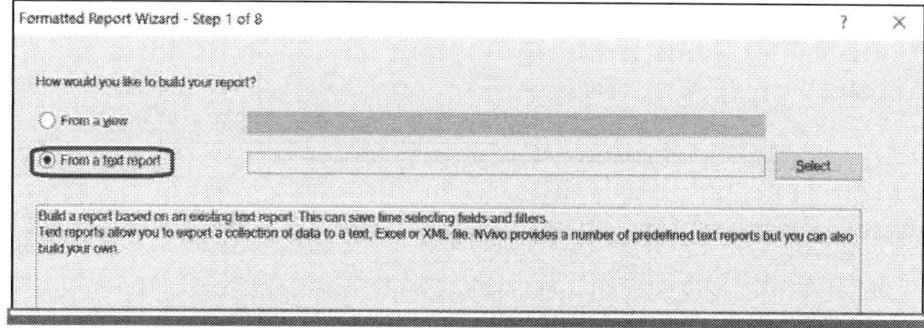

Select *From a text report* and with the **[Select]** button search for the text report template .NVR with your file browser.

Text Reports

Creating a New Text Report

An extract lets you export a portion of your data to a text file, an Excel spreadsheet, or an XML file.

1 Go to **Share | New Text Report**.

The **Text Report Wizard** – **Step 1** appears:

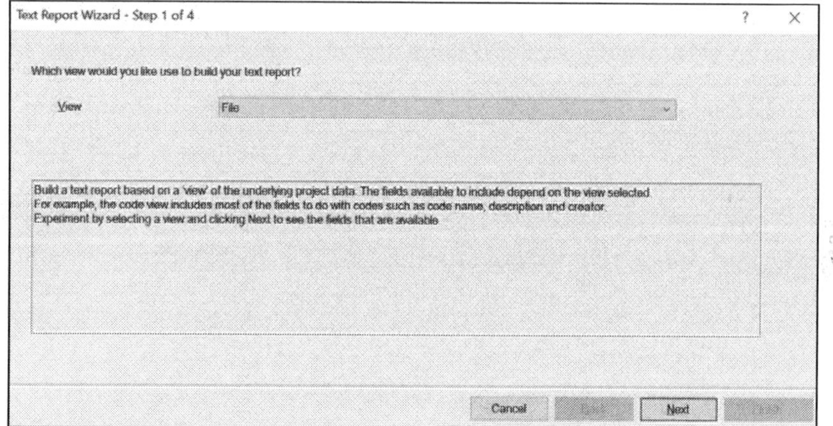

2 Select *Source* from the View drop down list.

3 Click **[Next]**.

The **Text Report Wizard – Step 2** appears:

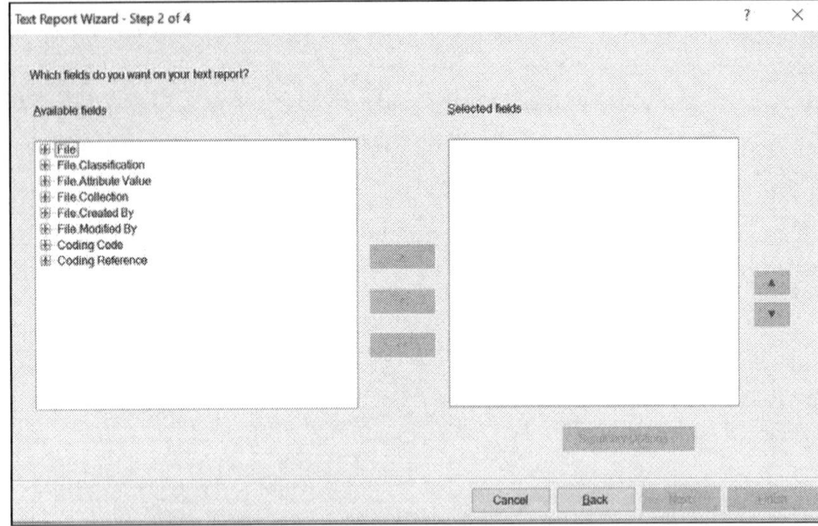

4 Expand the field headings and select the fields from the left box that will form the Text Report and click the [>] button which brings over the fields to the right box.

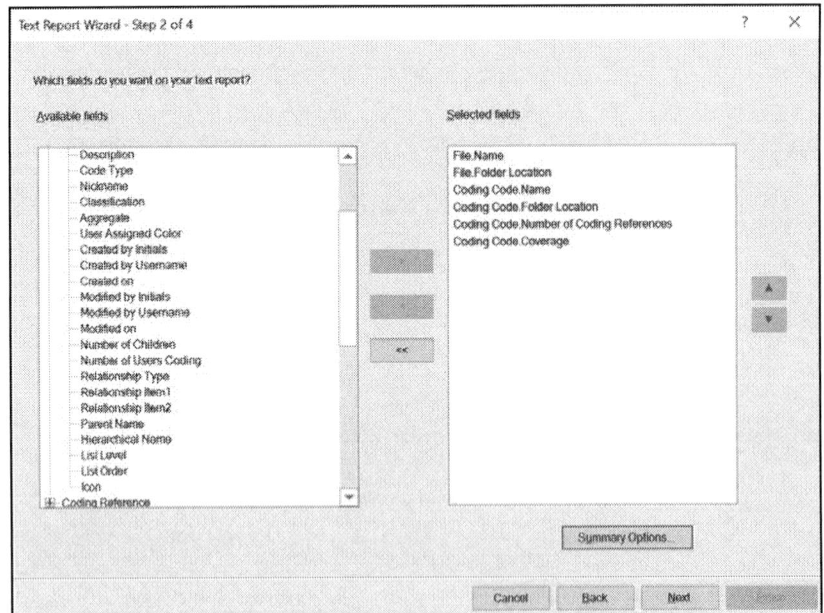

5 Click [**Next**].

The **Text Report Wizard** – **Step 3** appears:

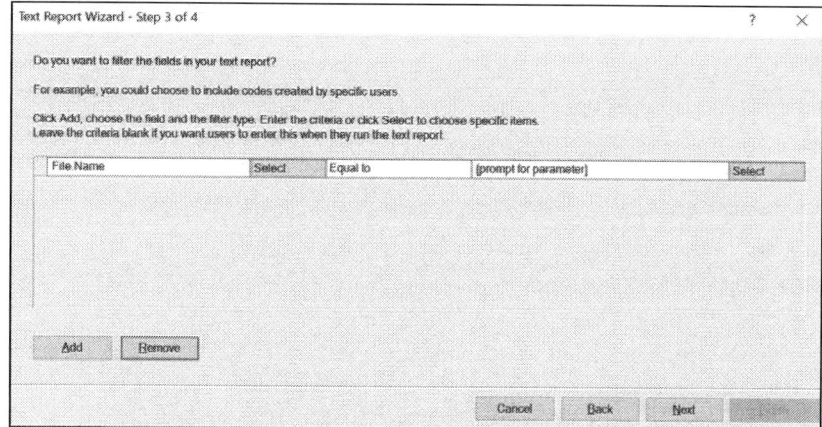

6 Use the [**Add**] button to create the first filter row and then the [**Select**] button to select the field that shall limit the report. Leave the right textbox as *[prompt for parameter]* and the user will be prompted to select a parameter each time the extract is run.

7 Click [**Next**].

The **Text Report Wizard – Step 4** appears:

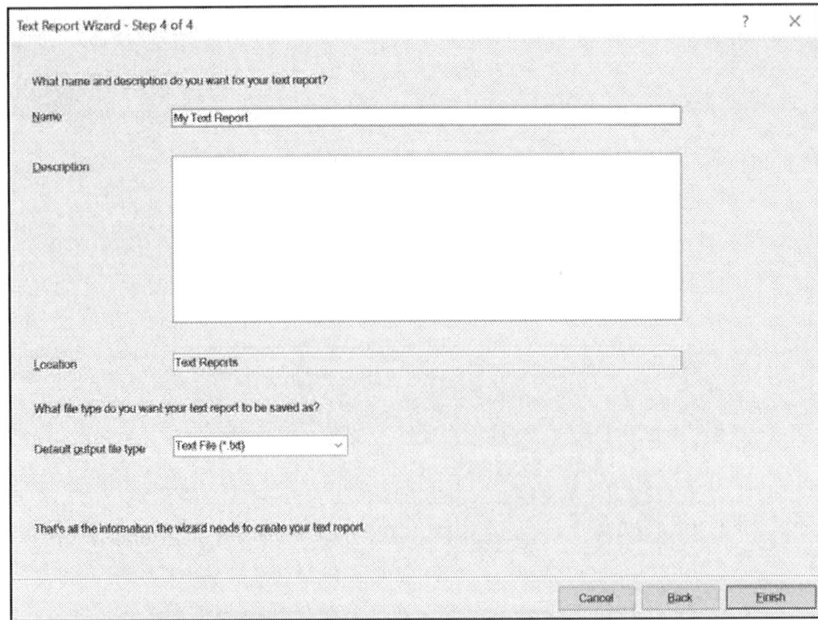

8 Type a name of the Extract (compulsory) and optionally a description. Default file type can also be set but can be changed before you run a Text Report. The file types that you can choose from are: .TXT, .XLS, .XLSX, and XML.

9 Confirm with [**Finish**].

Exporting (Running) a Text Report

1 Select the **Reports\\Text Reports** folder or its subfolder.

2 Select an Extract in the List View.

3 Double-click
or right-click and select **Run Extract**.

4 Decide file name, location, and file type. Click [**Save**].

Exporting a Text Report Template

1 Select the **Reports\\Text Reports** folder or its subfolder.

2 Select a Text Report in the List View.

3 Go to **Share | Export → Export**
or right-click and select **Export → Export Text Report...**
or [**Ctrl**] + [**Shift**] + [**E**].

Decide file name and location. The file type is already determined as .NVX. The result is an Extract template that can be imported and used by other NVivo projects.

Importing a Text Report Template

1 Go to **Import | Reports → Text Report**.
  Default folder is **Reports\\Text Reports** or its currently open subfolder.
  Go to 4.

alternatively

1 Select the **Reports\\Text Reports** folder or its subfolder.
2 Go to **Import | Reports → Text Report**.
  Go to 4.

alternatively

2 Click on any empty space in the List View.
3 Right-click and select **Import Extract...**
4 The **Import Text Report** dialog box appears.
5 Select the Text Report template .NVX that you want to import. Click on **[Open]**.

The **Text Report Properties** dialog box appears:

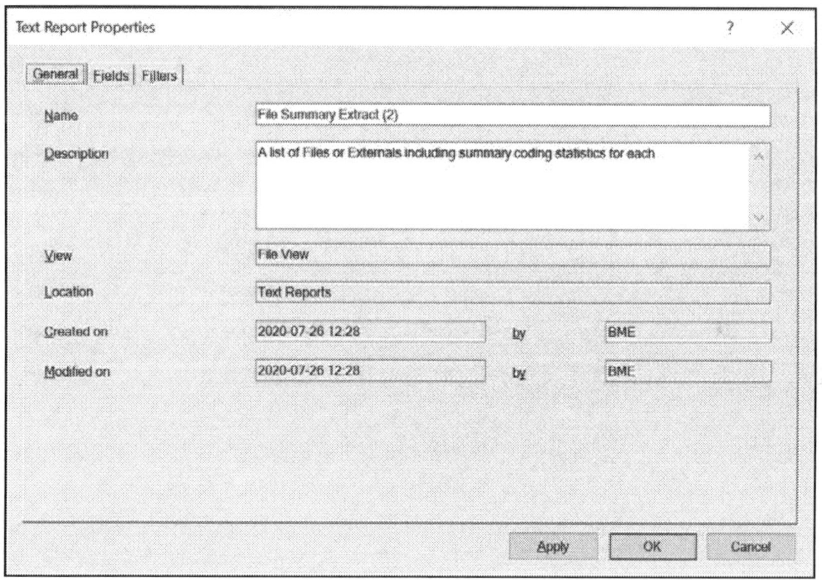

6 If you need you can change or modify the text in the dialog box. Click on **[OK]**.

Editing a Text Report

A Text Report can be modified by opening its Text Report Properties:

1 Select the **Reports\\Text Reports** folder or a subfolder.
2 Select a Text Report in the List View.
3 Go to **Home | Item → 'Properties' → Text Report Properties...**
  or right-click and select **Text Report Properties...**
  or **[Ctrl]** + **[Shift]** + **[P]**.

29. HELP FUNCTIONS IN NVIVO

An integral part of NVivo is the variety of help and support functionality for users.

Help Documents Online

1 Go to **File → Help → Help Resources → Help** or use the [?] symbol in the upper right corner of the screen or **[F1]**.

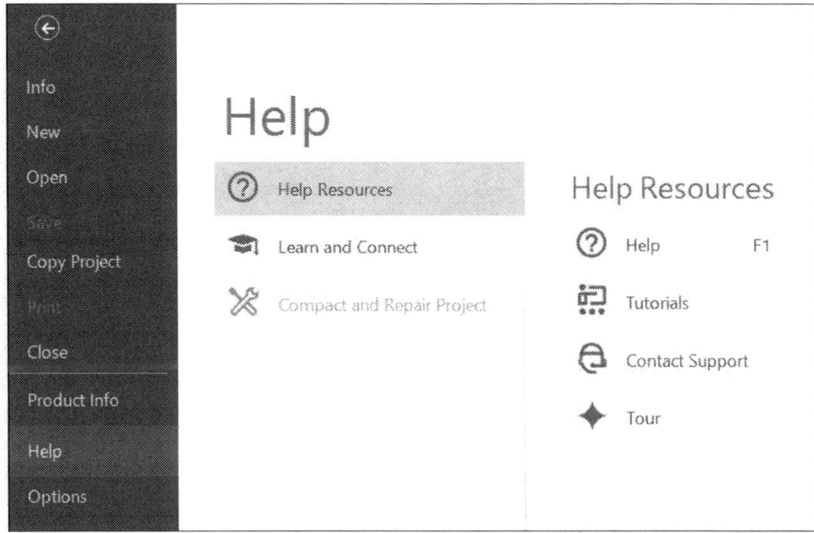

The initial view for **Online Help** is this:

Tutorials

NVivo has some tutorials in the form of video clips:

1 Go to **File → Help → Help Resources → NVivo Tutorials**.

Users can access QSR's online tutorials. Adobe Flash Player is required to play these tutorials.

Customer Hub

Users are offered a personal myNVivo account upon purchasing or extending an NVivo license. This account is used for license handling and during installation and activation of a license you will be asked to login with your personal account and NVivo will be remotely activated for you.

Direct URL to the portal is:

`https://portal.mynvivo.com`

1 Go to **File → Help → Learn and Connect → Customer Hub**.

NVivo Academy

QSR offers a whole program of online and onsite training for different skill levels in using NVivo for Windows and NVivo for Mac as well as solutions for collaboration.

1 Go to **File → Help → Learn and Connect → NVivo Academy**.

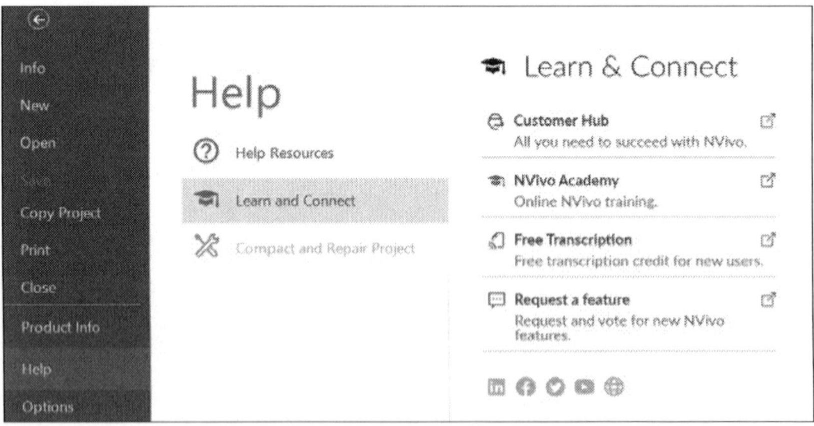

NVivo Integration with Office Products

NVivo - Integration allows you to send files directly from Microsoft Word, Excel and Outlook to NVivo (NVivo Mac accepts only Word and Excel files).

This function requires that you install Addins to your Office products. Read more about it here:

```
https://help-
nv.qsrinternational.com/20/win/Content/fi
les/office-add-in.htm
```

1 Go to **Modules | Collect Office Files**.

Support and Technical Issues

As a holder of this book you are welcome to contact **support@formkunskap.com** or Skype **bengt.edhlund** in any matter that has to do with installation problems or user procedures as described in this book.

In case of performance disturbances like NVivo unintentionally stops, an error log is created automatically. The log files are by default stored in My Documents folder of the current user. Such error log file has the following name structure **'err<date>T<time>.log'**. It is a text file and in case you need technical assistance you may be asked to forward such error log file to QSR Support or the local representative for analysis.

Software Versions and Service Packs

You should always be aware of the software version and Service Pack that you use. A Service Pack is an additional software patch that could carry bug fixes, improvements and new features. Service Packs are free for licensees of a certain software version. Provided that you are connected to the Internet and have enabled *Check for Update every 7 Days* (see page 40) you will automatically get a message on the screen when a new Service Pack has been launched. Always use the latest available Service Pack:

1 Go to **File → Product Info → About NVivo**.

The image shows the software version and installed Service Pack:

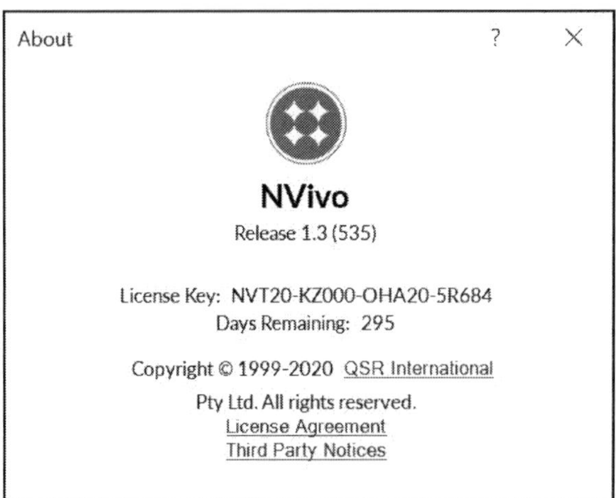

About
?
NVivo
Release 1.3 (535)
License Key: NVT20-KZ000-OHA20-5R684
Days Remaining: 295
Copyright © 1999-2020 QSR International
Pty Ltd. All rights reserved.
License Agreement
Third Party Notices

This message displays the first four groups of characters of your License Key number. This is good enough when you communicate with your support resources. But when you need to install or reinstall NVivo you will need all five character groups that form the complete License Key.

30. GLOSSARY

This is a list of the most common words, terms, and descriptions that are used in this book.

Advanced Find	Search names of Project items like Source items, Memos or Codes. Use **Find Bar - Advanced Find.**
Aggregate	Aggregate means that a certain Code in any hierarchical level accumulates the logical sum of all its nearest Child Codes.
Annotation	A note linked to an element of a Source item. Similar to a conventional footnote.
Attribute	A variable that is used to describe individual Source items and Codes. Example: age group, gender, education.
Autocoding	An automatic method to code documents using names of the paragraph styles.
Boolean Operator	The conventional operators AND, OR or NOT used to create logical search expressions applying Boolean algebra.
Case	A Case (earlier called Case Node) is a member of a group of Cases which are classified with Attributes and Values reflecting demographic or descriptive data. Cases can be people (Interviewees), places or any group of items with similar properties.
Classification	A collection of Attributes for Source items or Cases.
Classification Sheet	A matrix overview of the attributes and values of Source items or Cases.
Cluster Analysis	Cluster analysis or clustering is the assignment of a set of observations into subsets (called *clusters*) so that observations in the same cluster are similar in some sense. Clustering is a method of unsupervised learning, and a common technique for statistical data analysis used in many fields, including machine learning, data mining, pattern recognition, image analysis, information retrieval, and bioinformatics.

Code	A Code (earlier called Node or Theme Node) is often used in the context of a 'container' of selected topics or themes. A Code contains pointers to whole documents or selected elements of documents relevant to the specific Code. Codes can be organized hierarchically.
Codebook	A list of all Codes in any selected folder. Export formats include Word documents.
Coding	The work that associates a certain element of a Source item at a certain Code.
Coding Stripe	Graphical representation of coding in a Source item.
Coding Queries	A method to construct a query by using combinations of Codes or Attribute values.
Compound Queries	A method to construct a query by using combinations of various query types.
Concept Map	A Concept Map is a free-form visualization made up of different shapes and connectors. Shapes represent concepts (ideas, people, or data). The connectors between the shapes articulate links such as *this causes...*, *this requires...* or *this contributes to...*
Coverage	The fraction of a Source item that has been coded at a certain Code or Case.
Dataset	A structured matrix of data arranged in rows and columns. Datasets can be created from imported Excel spreadsheets or captures social media data.
Dendrogram	A tree-like plot where each step of hierarchical clustering is represented as a fusion of two branches of the tree into a single one. The branches represent clusters obtained at each step of hierarchical clustering.
Discourse Analysis	In semantics, discourses are linguistic units composed of several sentences – in other words, conversations, arguments or speeches. Discourse Analysis studies how texts can be structured and interrelated.
Document	An item in NVivo that is usually imported from a Source document.
Dropbox	A cloud-based software solution that allows file syncing across several computers.

EndNote	A powerful and convenient reference handling software tool.
Ethnography	The science that examines characteristics of different cultural groups.
Evernote	A popular cloud-based notetaking platform that creates text and voice memos.
Facebook	A social networking platform where users can become 'friends' and post content on one another's personal page ('walls'). Social groups are also available in Facebook (pages).
Filter	A function that limits a selection of values or items in order to facilitate the analysis of large amounts of data.
Find Bar	A toolbar immediately above the List View.
Focus Group	A selected, limited group of people that represents a larger population.
Folder	A folder that is created by NVivo is a virtual folder but has properties and functions largely like a normal Windows folder.
Framework	A data matrix that allows you to easily view and summarize areas of your data you wish to more closely explore.
Grounded Theory	Widely recognized method for qualitative studies where theories emerge from data rather than a pre-determined hypothesis.
Grouped Find	A function for finding items that have certain relations to each other.
Hashtag	A 'keywording' convention that places a number sign (#) before a term in order to allow text-based searches to distinguish searchable keywords from standard discourse.
Hyperlink	A link to an item outside the NVivo-project. The linked item can be a file or a web site.
In Vivo Coding	In Vivo coding is creating a new Code when selecting text and then using the *In Vivo* command. The Code name will become the selected text (max 256 characters) but the name (and location) can be changed later.
Items	All items that constitutes a project. Items are Sources, Codes, Cases, Classifications, Queries, Results, and Maps.

Jaccard's Coefficient	The **Jaccard index**, also known as the **Jaccard similarity coefficient** (originally coined *coefficient de communauté* by Paul Jaccard), is a statistic used for comparing the similarity and diversity of sample sets.
Kappa Coefficient	**Cohen's kappa coefficient, (K),** is a statistical measure of inter-rater agreement. It is generally thought to be a more robust measure than simple percent agreement calculation since **K** takes into account the agreement occurring by chance. Cohen's kappa coefficient measures the agreement between two raters who each classify ***N*** items into ***C*** mutually exclusive categories. If the raters are in complete agreement then **K** = 1. If there is no agreement among the raters (other than what would be expected by chance) then **K** ≤ 0.
LinkedIn	A professional social networking site where users become 'connections' and participate in group discussions in 'groups'.
Literature Review	A literature review is a type of review article. A literature review is a scholarly paper that presents the current knowledge including substantive findings as well as theoretical and methodological contributions to a particular topic. Literature reviews are secondary sources and do not report new or original experimental work. A complete literature review analyzes, synthesizes, and critically evaluates its sources in order to account for the current knowledge of the subject topic. Most often associated with academic-oriented literature, such reviews are found in academic journals and are not to be confused with book reviews, which may also appear in the same publication. Literature reviews are a basis for research in nearly every academic field.
Matrix Coding Query	The method to construct queries in a matrix form where contents in each cell are the result of a row and a column combined with a certain operator.

Medline	The world's most popular health research database.
Memo Link	Only *one* Memo Link can exist from an item to a memo.
Memo	A text document that could be linked from *one* Source item or from *one* Code or *one* Case.
MeSH	MeSH (Medical Subject Headings), the terminology or controlled vocabulary used in PubMed and associated information sources.
Mind Map	A Mind Map reflects what you think about a single topic and is usually created quickly or spontaneously. At the beginning of your project you might use a mind map to explore your expectations or initial theories.
Mixed Methods	My thoughts on mixed methods include two aspects. First is the integration of survey, test, rating, demographic data with qualitative media (and all interaction with those media in terms of excerpting and tagging). When done well, database queries can draw upon all data points in filtering, creating data visualizations to explore pattern, and basic retrieval. The second is the various ways of quantifying qualitative data in terms of creating new descriptor variables and the scaling or indexing of coded content across meaningful dimensions.
NFS	**Network File System (NFS)** is a distributed file system protocol originally developed by Sun Microsystems in 1984, allowing a user on a client computer to access files over a computer network much like local storage is accessed.
OCR	Optical Character Recognition, a method together with scanning making it possible to identify characters not only as an image.
OneNote	Microsoft's cloud-based notetaking platform that creates text and voice memos.
Pearson Correlation Coefficient	A type of correlation coefficient that represents the relationship between two variables that are measured on the same interval or ratio scale.

Phenomenology	A method which is descriptive, thoughtful, and innovative and from which you might verify your hypothesis.
Project	The collective denomination of all data and related work.
Project Map	Graphical representation of Project items and their relations.
PubMed	A popular health research database (cf. Medline).
Qualitative Research	Research with data originating from observations, interviews, and dialogs that focuses on the views, experiences, values, and interpretations of participants.
Qualtrics	Qualtrics is a private research software company, based in Provo, Utah, in the United States. The company was founded in 2002 by Scott M. Smith, Ryan Smith, Jared Smith and Stuart Orgill. Qualtrics software enables users to do many kinds of online data collection and analysis including market research, customer satisfaction and loyalty, product and concept testing, employee evaluations and website feedback. In 2012, the company received a $70 million investment from Sequoia Capital and Accel Partners, generally considered two of the top venture capital firms in the country. It was the largest joint investment to date by these two firms. In September 2014, Sequoia Capital and Accel Partners returned in Series B funding, led by Insight Venture Partners worth $150 million, a record for a Utah-based company. In May 2016 Qualtrics acquired statistical analysis startup Statwing for an undisclosed sum. Statwing is a San Francisco based company that created point-and-click software for advanced statistical analysis. Quantitative statistical analysis performed with Qualtrics is cited in a number of professional and academic journals.

Quantitative Research	Research that collects data through measurements and conclusions through calculations and statistics.
Ranking	The organization of results according to ascending or descending relevance.
References coded	*References coded* means a coded segment (text or image) of a source item.
RefWorks	A popular reference handling software tool.
Relationship	A Code that defines a relation between two Project items. A relationship is always characterized by a certain relationship type.
Relationship Type	A concept (often a descriptive verb) that defines a relationship or dependence between two Project items.
Relevance	Relevance in a result of a query is a measure of success or grade of matching. Relevance may be calculated as the number of hits in selected sections of the searched item.
Research Design	A plan for the collection and study of data so that the desired information is reached with sufficient reliability and a given theory can be verified or rejected in a recognized manner.
Result	A result is the answer to a query. A result may be shown as *Preview* or saved as a *Code*.
Saving Queries	The possibility to save queries in order to re-run or to modify them.
See Also Link	A link established between two items. A See Also Link is created from a certain area or text element of an item to a selected area or the whole of another item.
Service Pack	Software updates that normally carry bug fixes, performance enhancements, and new features.
Set	A subset or 'collection' of selected Project Items. A saved set can be displayed as a list of shortcuts to these Project Items.

Sociogram	A sociogram is a graphic representation of social links that a person has. It is a graph drawing that plots the structure of interpersonal relations in a group situation. Sociograms were developed by Jacob L. Moreno to analyze choices or preferences within a group. They can diagram the structure and patterns of group interactions. A sociogram can be drawn on the basis of many different criteria: Social relations, channels of influence, lines of communication etc.
Sørensen Coefficient	The **Sørensen index**, also known as **Sørensen's similarity coefficient**, is a statistic used for comparing the similarity of two samples. It was developed by the botanist Thorvald Sørensen and published in 1948.
Stop Words	Stop words are less significant words like conjunctions or prepositions that may not be meaningful to your analysis. Stop words are exempted from Text Search Queries or Word Frequency Queries.
SurveyMonkey	SurveyMonkey is an online survey development cloud-based company, founded in 1999 by Ryan Finley. SurveyMonkey provides free, customizable surveys, as well as a suite of paid back-end programs that include data analysis, sample selection, bias elimination, and data representation tools. In addition to providing free and paid plans for individual users, SurveyMonkey offers more large-scale enterprise options for companies interested in data analysis, brand management, and consumer-focused marketing. Since releasing its enterprise in 2013, business-focused services, SurveyMonkey has grown dramatically, opening a new headquarters in downtown Palo Alto.

Text Mining	Text mining or data mining is the procedure to identify meaningful patterns and relationships in unstructured data or information, typically text. Text mining is not a search engine, an information grabber or an interpreter. Text mining is an approach to analyze large amounts of text-based data that extracts meaningful semantic units from the text. Unlike traditional word analysis functions (i.e., word frequency queries), text mining extracts "noun phrases" that operate as whole linguistic units made of multiple words. For example, medical specialties are often more than one word, such as "ear, nose, and throat doctor". A text-mining tool would understand this to be a cohesive semantic unit, whereas word frequency queries would see this as 4 units: ear, nose, throat, and doctor.
Twitter	A social networking website where users post 'tweets' that contain a maximum of 140 characters.
Uncoding	The work that deletes a given coding of a document at a certain Code.
Validity	The validity of causal inferences within scientific studies, usually based on experiments.
Value	Value that a certain Attribute can have. Similar to 'Controlled Vocabulary'. Example: male, female.
Zotero	A reference handling software tool.

APPENDIX A – THE NVIVO SCREEN

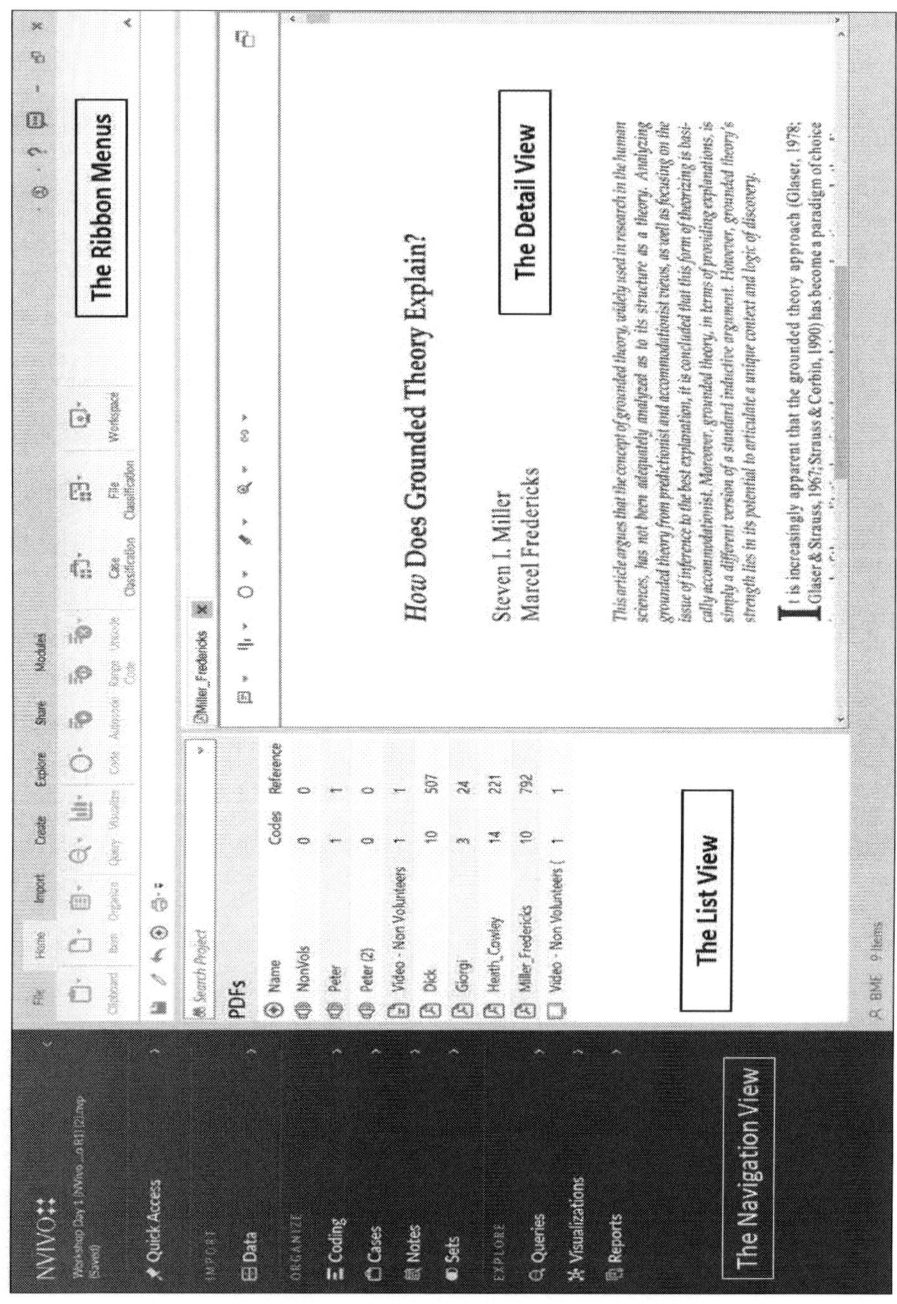

APPENDIX B – KEYBOARD COMMANDS

Listed below are some of the most useful keyboard commands. Many adhere to general Windows rules. Others are specific for each program.

Windows	Word	NVivo	Keyboard Command	Description
✔	✔	✔	**[Ctrl]** + **[C]**	Copy
✔	✔	✔	**[Ctrl]** + **[X]**	Cut
✔	✔	✔	**[Ctrl]** + **[V]**	Paste
✔	✔	✔	**[Ctrl]** + **[A]**	Select All
✔	✔	✔	**[Ctrl]** + **[O]**	Open Project
	✔[15]	✔	**[Ctrl]** + **[B]**	Bold
	✔[15]	✔	**[Ctrl]** + **[I]**	Italic
	✔[15]	✔	**[Ctrl]** + **[U]**	Underline
	✔[15]		**[Ctrl]** + **[K]**	Insert Hyperlink
		✔	**[Ctrl]** + **[E]**	Switch between Edit mode and Read Only
	✔	✔	**[Ctrl]** + **[Z]**	Undo
	✔		**[Ctrl]** + **[Y]**	Undo - Undo
	✔	✔	**[Ctrl]** + **wheel**	Zoom in and out
		✔	**[Ctrl]**+**[Shift]**+**[K]**	Link to New Memo
		✔	**[Ctrl]**+**[Shift]**+**[M]**	Open Linked Memo
		✔	**[Ctrl]**+**[Shift]**+**[N]**	New Folder/Item
		✔	**[Ctrl]**+**[Shift]**+**[P]**	Folder/Item Properties
		✔	**[Ctrl]**+**[Shift]**+**[O]**	Open Item
		✔	**[Ctrl]**+**[Shift]**+**[I]**	Import Item
		✔	**[Ctrl]**+**[Shift]**+**[E]**	Export Item
		✔	**[Ctrl]**+**[Shift]**+**[F]**	Advanced Find
		✔	**[Ctrl]**+**[Shift]**+**[G]**	Grouped Find
		✔	**[Ctrl]**+**[Shift]**+**[U]**	Move Up
		✔	**[Ctrl]**+**[Shift]**+**[D]**	Move Down
		✔	**[Ctrl]**+**[Shift]**+**[L]**	Move Left

[15] Only for English version of Word.

Windows	Word	NVivo	Keyboard Command	Description
		✓	[Ctrl]+[Shift]+[R]	Move Right
		✓	[Ctrl]+[Shift]+[T]	Insert Time/Date
	✓	✓	[Ctrl] + Click	Open a hyperlink
	✓	✓	[Enter]	New paragraph
	✓	✓	[Shift] + [Enter]	Line Break
	✓	✓	[Ctrl] + [Enter]	New Page
	✓	✓	[Ctrl] + [Home]	Go to beginning of document
	✓	✓	[Ctrl] + [End]	Go to end of document
	✓	✓	[Ctrl] + [G]	Go to
✓	✓	✓	[Ctrl] + [N]	New Project
✓	✓	✓	[Ctrl] + [P]	Print
✓	✓	✓	[Ctrl] + [S]	Save
		✓	[Ctrl] + [M]	Merge Into Selected Code
		✓	[Ctrl] + [1]	Go Files
		✓	[Ctrl] + [2]	Go Codes
		✓	[Ctrl] + [3]	Go Cases
		✓	[Ctrl] + [4]	Go Memos
		✓	[Ctrl] + [5]	Go Static Sets
	✓		[Ctrl] + [6]	Unlink
		✓	[Ctrl] + [6]	Go Maps
		✓	[Ctrl] + [7]	Go Formatted Reports
✓	✓		[Ctrl] + [W]	Close Window
✓	✓		[Ctrl]+[Shift]+[W]	Close all Windows of same Type
	✓	✓	[F1]	Open Online Help
		✓	[F4]	Play/Pause
		✓	[F5]	Refresh
	✓	✓	[F7]	Spell Check
		✓	[F8]	Stop
		✓	[F9]	Skip Back
		✓	[F10]	Skip Forward

Windows	Word	NVivo	Keyboard Command	Description
		✓	**[F11]**	Start Selection
		✓	**[F12]**	Finish Selection
	✓	✓	**[Ctrl]** + **[Z]**	Undo
	✓		**[Ctrl]** + **[Y]**	Redo
	✓	✓	**[Ctrl]** + **[F]**	Find
	✓	✓	**[Ctrl]** + **[H]**	Replace (Detail View)
		✓	**[Ctrl]** + **[H]**	Handtool (Print Preview)
		✓	**[Ctrl]** + **[Q]**	Go to Quick Coding Bar
		✓	**[Ctrl]**+**[Shift]**+**[F2]**	Uncode
		✓	**[Ctrl]**+**[Shift]**+**[F3]**	Uncode from This Code
		✓	**[Ctrl]**+**[Shift]**+**[F9]**	Uncode from current Codes
		✓	**[Ctrl]** + **[F2]**	Code
	✓	✓	**[Ctrl]** + **[F4]**	Close Current Window
		✓	**[Ctrl]** + **[F8]**	Code In Vivo
		✓	**[Ctrl]** + **[F9]**	Code to current Codes
		✓	**[Alt]** + **[F1]**	Hide/Show Navigation View
		✓	**[Ctrl]** + **[Ins]**	Insert Row
		✓	**[Ctrl]** + **[Del]**	Delete Selected Items in a Map
		✓	**[Ctrl]**+**[Shift]**+**[T]**	Insert Date/Time
		✓	**[Ctrl]**+**[Shift]**+**[Y]**	Insert Symbol
	✓		**[Ctrl]**+**[Alt]**+**[F]**	Insert Footnote
		✓	**[Ctrl]** + **[Enter]**	Carriage Return in certain text boxes

INDEX

E

F

O

P

Q

V,W

Y

Z

Printed in Great Britain
by Amazon